MIDCENTURY SUSPENSION

MODERNIST LATITUDES

MODERNIST LATITUDES

Jessica Berman and Paul Saint-Amour, Editors

Modernist Latitudes aims to capture the energy and ferment of modernist studies by continuing to open up the range of forms, locations, temporalities, and theoretical approaches encompassed by the field. The series celebrates the growing latitude ("scope for freedom of action or thought") that this broadening affords scholars of modernism, whether they are investigating little-known works or revisiting canonical ones. Modernist Latitudes will pay particular attention to the texts and contexts of those latitudes (Africa, Latin America, Australia, Asia, Southern Europe, and even the rural United States) that have long been misrecognized as ancillary to the canonical modernisms of the global North.

Barry McCrea, *In the Company of Strangers: Family and Narrative in Dickens, Conan Doyle, Joyce, and Proust*, 2011

Jessica Berman, *Modernist Commitments: Ethics, Politics, and Transnational Modernism*, 2011

Jennifer Scappettone, *Killing the Moonlight: Modernism in Venice*, 2014

Nico Israel, *Spirals: The Whirled Image in Twentieth-Century Literature and Art*, 2015

Carrie Noland, *Voices of Negritude in Modernist Print: Aesthetic Subjectivity, Diaspora, and the Lyric Regime*, 2015

Susan Stanford Friedman, *Planetary Modernisms: Provocations on Modernity Across Time*, 2015

Steven S. Lee, *The Ethnic Avant-Garde: Minority Cultures and World Revolution*, 2015

Thomas S. Davis, *The Extinct Scene: Late Modernism and Everyday Life*, 2016

Carrie J. Preston, *Learning to Kneel: Noh, Modernism, and Journeys in Teaching*, 2016

Gayle Rogers, *Incomparable Empires: Modernism and the Translation of Spanish and American Literature*, 2016

Donal Harris, *On Company Time: American Modernism in the Big Magazines*, 2016

Celia Marshik, *At the Mercy of Their Clothes: Modernism, the Middlebrow, and British Garment Culture*, 2016

Christopher Reed, *Bachelor Japanists: Japanese Aesthetics and Western Masculinities*, 2016

Eric Hayot and Rebecca L. Walkowitz, eds., *A New Vocabulary for Global Modernism*, 2016

Eric Bulson, *Little Magazine, World Form*, 2016

Aarthi Vadde, *Chimeras of Form: Modernist Internationalism Beyond Europe, 1914–2014*, 2016

Ben Conisbee Baer, *Indigenous Vanguards: Education, National Liberation, and the Limits of Modernism*, 2019

Midcentury Suspension

LITERATURE AND FEELING IN
THE WAKE OF WORLD WAR II

Claire Seiler

Columbia University Press
New York

COLUMBIA
UNIVERSITY
PRESS

Columbia University Press gratefully acknowledges the generous support for this book provided by Publisher's Circle members Paul LeClerc and Judith Ginsberg.

Columbia University Press
Publishers Since 1893
New York   Chichester, West Sussex
cup.columbia.edu
Copyright © 2020 Columbia University Press

Library of Congress Cataloging-in-Publication Data
Names: Seiler, Claire, author.
Title: Midcentury suspension : literature and feeling in the wake of
World War II / Claire Seiler.
Description: New York : Columbia University Press, 2020. |
Series: Modernist latitudes | Includes bibliographical references and index.
Identifiers: LCCN 2019054334 (print) | LCCN 2019054335 (ebook) |
ISBN 9780231194686 (cloth) | ISBN 9780231194693 (paperback) |
ISBN 9780231550949 (ebook)
Subjects: LCSH: American literature—20th century—History and criticism. |
English literature—20th century—History and criticism. |
Literature and society—United States—History—20th century. | Literature
and society—Great Britain—History—20th century. | Nineteen fifties.
Classification: LCC PS225 .S45 2020 (print) | LCC PS225 (ebook) |
DDC 810.9/005—dc23
LC record available at https://lccn.loc.gov/2019054334
LC ebook record available at https://lccn.loc.gov/2019054335

Columbia University Press books are printed on permanent and durable acid-free paper.
Printed in the United States of America

Cover design: Julia Kushnirsky
Cover photograph: Alamy

CONTENTS

CONTENTS

ACKNOWLEDGMENTS

As readers of *Midcentury Suspension* will discover, I love a good catalog. So it is a double delight to begin by acknowledging the support this book and I have received from many people and institutions.

A glimmer of *Midcentury Suspension* began to emerge at the very end of my doctoral work at Stanford University. Roland Greene saw and supported that glimmer, just as he had encouraged my fullest thinking throughout my graduate training. His model intellectual mentorship and warm friendship are anchors in my life. Nick Jenkins paid careful attention to my ideas and prose; he also freely shared his stunning poetic insight and some archival treasures—including the Gotham Book Mart photograph—that cracked open my thinking. Also at Stanford, I benefited from Terry Castle's energy and candor; the wisdom and kindness of my late friend George Dekker; and from the collaborative spirit of the Stanford Humanities Center Poetics Workshop. During and since our charmed interval in San Francisco, I've marveled at the luck of making such brilliant friends there as Allison Carruth, Harris Feinsod, Heather Houser, Michael Hoyer, Hanna Janiszewska, Ruth Kaplan, Ju Yon Kim, and Lee Konstantinou. I thank in particular Allison, who has read and reread this project and who believed in its value when I could not.

Dickinson College has afforded intellectual inspiration and institutional support. For the former, I thank especially my departmental colleagues

ACKNOWLEDGMENTS

Carol Ann Johnston, Wendy Moffat, Siobhan Phillips, and Greg Steirer, who got my vision for this book and supported the time it took me to try to realize it; and Sarah Kersh and Sheela Jane Menon, who cheered me on in the later stages. Amy Farrell and Sharon O'Brien shared their friendship and steadying mentorship. My completion of the project was enabled by the professional savvy of Kelly Winters-Fazio and Denise McCauley, the coordinators of the academic departments I chaired while on the home stretch. I am grateful for support from Dickinson's Faculty Personnel Committee, which granted me an essential pretenure sabbatical, and from the College's Research and Development Committee, which funded necessary travel and the invaluable research assistantships of Julia Barone, Lisa Borsellino, Noah Fusco, and Emma Rodwin. Working with these four terrific students—and with so many others—made this book and my broader work infinitely more rewarding than it otherwise would have been. And more fun.

Teaching at a liberal arts college deepens my awareness of the debt I owe to the extraordinary faculty with whom I studied at Middlebury College. I happily acknowledge Stephen Donadio, John Hunisak, John McWilliams, William Nash (who gave me a much-needed nudge), Katy Smith Abbott, and two truly life-saving professors: Murray Dry, in whose legendary course on the American political regime I first read *Invisible Man*, and my dear friend Brett Millier. Brett taught me how to read poems before I knew one could do such a thing for a living and to "eat happiness like bread."

A junior faculty fellowship at the American Academy of Arts and Sciences provided time to work on this book and access to the libraries at Harvard University, which transformed it. Along with their camaraderie during a ridiculously snowy winter, my fellow AAAS Visiting Scholars—Alex Acs, Michael Brownstein, Brent Cebul, Maggie Gram, Emily Remus, Robin Scheffler, and Sunny Yang—as well as our program director, Larry Buell, shared their collective intellectual verve. A National Endowment for the Humanities Summer Seminar made it possible for me to complete archival research on Elizabeth Bishop. Back when, the following fellowships at Stanford enabled me to pursue a scholarly career at all: the Gerald J. Lieberman Fellowship in the Humanities, the Mabelle McLeod Lewis Memorial Fellowship, and the Carolyn Killefer Dissertation Fellowship.

The many archivists and librarians who enriched my work on this book include Ronald Patkus and Dean Rogers of the Vassar College Archives and Special Collections Library; Kathleen Dow and Kate Hutchens of the

University of Michigan Libraries Special Collections; and Molly Schwartz-burg, formerly of the Harry Ransom Center at the University of Texas at Austin. At Dickinson, the Waidner-Spahr Library staff gracefully managed my endless requests for interlibrary loans and deliveries from storage.

Midcentury Suspension benefited immeasurably from airings of some of its ideas before audiences at the AAAS, American Comparative Literature Association, American Literature Association, Modernist Studies Association, Modern Language Association, the Heyman Center for the Humanities at Columbia University, the Mahindra Humanities Center at Harvard University, McGill University, and the Stanford Humanities Center Poetics Workshop. At these and other venues, I've been buoyed by generative suggestions, great questions, and welcome encouragement from colleagues including Bob Antonio, Jason Baskin, Kristin Bluemel, Stephanie Burt, Marc Conner, Bonnie Costello, Thomas Davis, Marisa Galvez, Rachel Galvin, Melissa Girard, Brian Glavey, Bethany Hicok, Janice Ho, Emily Hyde, Peter Kalliney, Benjamin Kahan, Edward Mendelson, Melanie Micir, Justus Nieland, Brigitta Olubas, Paige Reynolds, John Paul Riquelme, Roy Scranton, and Johanna Winant. Among such inspiring colleagues, I am especially grateful to Marina MacKay, who gave this project a detailed reading in its zygote stage and has championed my work ever since; Allan Hepburn, who offered consistent moral and intellectual support and good humor, as well as opportunities to present my work; and Paul Saint-Amour, who kept faith with this project as it grew and offered unfailingly kind and patient perspective on my writing of it.

Jessica Berman's enthusiasm helped this book find its home in the Modernist Latitudes series. At Columbia University Press, Philip Leventhal believed in the manuscript, got its idiosyncracy, and provided the perfect editorial balance of big-picture guidance and helpful production deadlines. Monique Briones gave this book her skillful editorial attention, as did production editor Susan Pensak. Deak Nabers and the reader for CUP who remained anonymous gave the kinds of thorough and thoughtful reports of which writers dream.

An earlier version of part of chapter 3 and a sliver of the introduction were published as "At Midcentury: Elizabeth Bowen's *The Heat of the Day,*" *Modernism/modernity* 21, no. 1 (2014): 125–45; the germ of chapter 4 first appeared in "Francis O'Hara, War Poet," *Contemporary Literature* 54, no. 4 (2013): 810–33. I thank Lytle Shaw and the anonymous readers of these articles. Marjorie Perloff connected me with Maureen O'Hara Granville-Smith, Frank O'Hara's sister. Maureen generously talked with me with about her brother's life and legacy and allowed me to quote from his Hopwood materials. Michelle Niemann offered clear-eyed, whip-smart, and refreshingly practical advice as I prepared the manuscript for review.

Many friends enhanced my work on this book and my life as I worked on it, among them: Anne Baldwin, Maria Blackburn, Heather Champion, Vince Champion, Laura Crescimano, Alyssa DeBlasio, Bill Durden, Elke Durden, Stephanie Engelsen, Peggy Frohlich, Manu Kalia, Sarah McGaughey, Mike Monti, Susan Perabo, Robert Pound, Dave Richeson, Victoria Sams, Molly Schwartzburg, Casey Seiler, Rachael Seiler, Jamie Smith, Ed Snajdr, Adrienne Su, Shonna Trinch, Eric Vázquez, and Jeff Wood of local treasure Whistlestop Books.

It's my great fortune that many of the names already printed in this catalog of acknowledgment and gratitude could land in this last part of it, on family. Mine expanded while I figured out this project, and my happiness with it. I thank all the Seilers for their welcome and love. With her characteristic senses of perspective and humor, Cybele Maylone rolled with this project's presence in our essential lifelong friendship. My big-hearted big brother Dave Bowen and his family, Ellie Sato and Siena and Maia, are my number 1 champs. Colonel hung out with me for probably 80 percent of the writing of this book, and I thank him and Chauncey for making sure every day has a healthy balance of love, silliness, and impatient reminders that it's time to take a break or take a walk. This book honors the memory of my late grandparents, Gerald and Arlene Bowen and Arthur Sands Newcomer and Eleanor Cupler Newcomer, whose service in World War II and whose lives afterward first sparked my curiosity about the midcentury. It would have been unimaginable without the love and example of my parents, Stephen Bowen and Ellen Newcomer, who instilled in Dave and me their commitments to education—and to creating fair access to it—as democratic necessities.

Finally and always, this book is for Cotten, the water beneath the water, whom I love beyond measure.

MIDCENTURY SUSPENSION

INTRODUCTION

The Midcentury Problem

On November 9, 1948, the Gotham Book Mart and Vanguard Press cohosted a reception for Dame Edith and Sir Osbert Sitwell. Celebrated as writers and as patrons of modernism, the Sitwell siblings had recently arrived in Manhattan at the start of an American tour. Theirs was one of many such visits British writers made to the United States in the late 1940s, when the easing of wartime travel restrictions coincided with a wave of stateside Anglophilia. No obscure literary affair, the Sitwells' visit merited a seven-page spread in *Life* magazine on December 6, 1948.[1] There, amid an all but requisite set of photographs of Dame Edith in full aristocratic-eccentric splendor, appeared what has since become an iconic photograph of literary Manhattan at the middle of the twentieth century.

Already in 1948, *Life*'s punning title for this image, "A Collection of Poets," could not quite hold. The original caption strains by hyphenation to fit "Playwright-Poet" Tennessee Williams and "Novelist-Poet" Gore Vidal into the "collection." Readers of *Life* would know Williams, standing at left in the back row, as the author of *A Streetcar Named Desire* (1947), for which he had recently won the Pulitzer Prize for Drama, and might well know Vidal, third from left in the back row, as the author of one of the year's more notorious novels, *The City and the Pillar* (1948). In fact, in the late 1940s, the fourteen writers posed awkwardly around the Sitwells were so plainly

FIGURE 0.1 Writers gathered at the Gotham Book Mart to welcome the Sitwells, November 8, 1948. Getty Images. Creator: Lisa Larsen.

working across genres as to defy standard literary categorization or tidy journalistic pun. The photograph captures writers at different stages of their careers, affiliated with various national literatures, involved in several aesthetic movements, representative of disparate political commitments, and situated in a range of institutional contexts. Afforded a fuller identifying caption than *Life*'s, the Gotham Book Mart photograph records a midcentury literary variety—and, this book will argue, vitality—that reigning models for understanding transatlantic twentieth-century literature and culture tend to elide.

The Sitwells sit, dignified, at the center of the group. Behind them, from left to right, the young writers Williams, Richard Eberhart, Vidal, and José Garcia Villa lean against bookcases. In 1948, Eberhart was a busy poet and verse dramatist who still held a day job at the Butcher Polish Company in

Cambridge, Massachusetts. The Filipino poet Villa, a favorite of Dame Edith's, was at work on his book of experimental comma poems, *Volume II*, which New Directions would bring out the next year.[2] Perched on a stool to the Sitwells' right is the Englishman Stephen Spender. Best known then as a member of the Auden generation of the 1930s, Spender had recently published a memoir, *European Witness* (1946), about the devastation he saw on two visits to Germany in the summer and fall of 1945, and a new volume, *Poems of Dedication* (1947). The older American poets Marya Zaturenska and Horace Gregory, a married couple, sit on a bookshelf behind Spender. Russian-born Zaturenska had won the Pulitzer Prize for Poetry a decade earlier, for *Cold Morning Sky* (1937); Gregory was a well-regarded poet-critic and a professor at Sarah Lawrence College. The pair had recently collaborated on *A History of American Poetry, 1900–1940* (1946).[3]

At the foreground of the photograph are, from left to right, William Rose Benét, Charles Henri Ford, Randall Jarrell, and Delmore Schwartz. Though it must have been coincidental, the seating of Benét and Schwartz across from one another, heads to camera, makes a fitting image of a changing literary guard. Benét, a poet and editor who had just brought out a *Reader's Encyclopedia* of world literature (1948), had helped found the *Saturday Review of Literature* in 1924; Schwartz, a prominent poet more than twenty-five years Benét's junior, was in 1948 an editor of the little magazine *Partisan Review*, then at the height of its outsize influence on U.S. intellectual and literary culture. Within months of the Gotham Book Mart gathering, the *Saturday* and *Partisan* reviews would come to stand for the opposing sides of middlebrow reactionary conservatism and highbrow liberal tolerance, respectively if not entirely fairly, in the controversy surrounding Ezra Pound's receipt of the first Bollingen Prize for *The Pisan Cantos* (1948).[4] Seated cross-legged on the floor between Benét and Schwartz is Ford, a surrealist poet and another favorite of Dame Edith's. Not long after the Gotham gathering, she would write a laudatory preface to Ford's *Sleep in a Nest of Flames*, which, like Villa's *Volume II*, was published by New Directions in 1949. Behind Schwartz, Jarrell leans back against the bookshelves, his eyes cast down. His most recent book of poems, *Losses* (1948), confirmed his status as a "prominent high-brow soldier-poet of America's war."[5] That Jarrell never saw combat speaks to the larger redefining, at midcentury, of terms like *soldier-poet* and *war poet*.

Jarrell was also, by any definition, the preeminent young poet-critic of the day, and one peer whose work he especially admired was Elizabeth Bishop. In the Gotham Book Mart photograph, she stands with her hands folded, ladylike, on the back of the chair of her mentor, Marianne Moore. Bishop made her name with her first book, *North & South* (1946), and by November 1948 was two years into a first-reading agreement with the *New Yorker*. Moore, in striking black hat, was at work on her translation of La Fontaine's fables and was the lone woman among the group of senior American modernists achieving belated or renewed fame—or, in Pound's case, infamy—after the war.[6] Moore's *Collected Poems* would win the Pulitzer Prize and the National Book Award in 1951. Last but as far as possible from least, there is W. H. Auden. Taller on his feet than most of the writers in this "Collection," Auden nonetheless sits atop a library ladder, presiding and removed. A towering figure in American letters by 1948 and a U.S. citizen since May 20, 1946, Auden was the author most recently of *The Age of Anxiety: A Baroque Eclogue* (1947), which book-length poem gave "the age" its name.

Finally, at the foreground of the photograph, an empty chair. Who might have sat there? One can make predictable sense of the Gotham picture by imagining the empty chair taken by a writer who obviously "belongs" in one of the literary lineages, affinity groups, or rivalries that by now can be too readily legible in it. Conversely, since the Gotham Book Mart photograph depicts a refreshing literary variety but, unsurprisingly for the late 1940s, next to no racial diversity, another model for reading the image is to imagine seating an excluded writer in the empty chair, thus practicing in microcosm the expansion of the canon that has justly motivated a good deal of literary scholarship since at least the 1970s. In conversation with but in contrast to these and like models for molding the archival particularity of the Gotham Book Mart photograph into period-historical coherence, *Midcentury Suspension: Literature and Feeling in the Wake of World War II* proposes still a third approach. This book invokes the Book Mart picture not as evidence with which to correct or confirm established critical templates for reading in—or, too often, reading through—the midcentury period, but rather as an emblem of the problem that the midcentury still poses for twentieth-century literary studies. Iconic yet enigmatic, the Gotham Book Mart photograph depicts nothing so clearly as how *un*pictured, how partially seen and selectively analyzed, the literary middle of the twentieth century remains.

Midcentury Suspension asks: what would it mean to approach Anglo-American literature and culture of the middle of the twentieth century from a critical vantage other than those long afforded by *modernism* and *postmodernism* or, in more recent years, by the *new modernist studies* and *Post45*? What new insights emerge from approaching the midcentury synchronically, rather than seeking diachronic *late modernist* causes or *cold war* or *postwar* effects? What would twentieth-century literary and cultural study look like if it were to understand *midcentury* as something more than a dating modifier of such institutionalized fields and categories? What might we gain from reading the century not forward from the modernist heave, but outward from its historical middle? Or from broaching *midcentury* as a substantive alternative to periodization by ostensibly discrete *wartimes*?

This book takes the midcentury as problem—and possibility—for thought rather than as foregone conclusion of modernism or bland transition to our own contemporary age. Out of neglected archival, print culture, discursive, and literary records of what it will show was a self-consciously *midcentury* period, the book finds and asserts suspension—the sense of being between beginnings and endings, lapsed certainties and new potentialities, recent horrors and strange, often opaque futures—as a heuristic for reading transatlantic literature and culture of the late 1940s and early 1950s. Restoring suspension as a principal imaginative construct of the midcentury and developing suspension as a critical practice for reading it, the book reconfigures periodic logics of twentieth-century literary study that have long produced and still maintain the comparative obscurity of self-reflexively *midcentury* literary projects, structures of feeling, and habits of mind.

Midcentury Suspension advances four interlocking arguments, each at a deliberate pace and place. It begins by excavating the seemingly drab term *midcentury* from print, public, and literary culture of the Anglophone North Atlantic in the wake of the Second World War. It thereby traces the emergence of the rhetorical and discursive conditions for a distinctly midcentury literature that cohered around the 1950 mark. Next, over four chapters, the book discerns how various registers of suspension—including the tropological, affective, behavioral, and sensory—shaped the midcentury works of a group of major writers. More accurately, the book attends to the suspensions that structure the midcentury works of a deliberately wide-ranging collection of writers who have not been studied together before—a *non*group composed of Auden, Samuel Beckett, Bishop, Elizabeth Bowen, Ralph Ellison, and Frank O'Hara. If this "collection" seems at least as eclectic as the one squished into the Gotham Book Mart photograph, then this apparent eclecticism bespeaks the third line of argument running through *Midcentury Suspension*. As it recovers material and conceptual connections among its six core writers and the irreducibly historical atmosphere of the midcentury, the book demonstrates that the apparent idiosyncrasy of its core archive is extrinsic to middle of the century itself. As distinct from the progressive, prepositional grammar of *from . . . to* that underpins much twentieth- and twenty-first-century literary scholarship across national and linguistic traditions, *Midcentury Suspension* hovers *at* midcentury. What it finds there, or *then*, is a critically rich but unmined set of experiences, feelings, and ideas of suspension in the century's fraught middle. Much more than a shared theme among writers, suspension constitutes, in this book's final line of argument, a historically rooted and conceptually expansive new model for reading transatlantic literature of the midcentury.

EPOCHAL KEYWORDS

Each term of this book's title names a site of inquiry. To the extent that *suspension* harmonizes with concepts that, despite generally negative connotations, have helped to drive the discipline of literary studies since at least the New Critical turn (e.g., ambiguity, indeterminacy, deferral), it invites scholarly attention. But it is hardly self-evident that *midcentury* merits critical inquiry. For one thing, only in the histories of art and industrial design and in the market for antiques and replicas does *midcentury* currently do any reliably descriptive work. In those fields and spaces, *midcentury modern* denotes the sleek, streamlined aesthetic meticulously recreated in the television series *Mad Men* (2007–15), set in the late 1950s and early 1960s.[7] For another, *midcentury* lacks the aesthetic potency or geopolitical referentiality of the terms or phrases—such as *postwar* or *late modern, cold war* or *after 1945*—for which it is often used as a rough synonym. It scans as neutral or arbitrary. For still another, although *midcentury* applies now mostly as a time stamp, the time stamp it provides is imprecise. In twentieth-century historiography, literary and otherwise, *midcentury* is an accordion term: it expands and contracts to designate any span of years from the 1930s through the 1970s.

Nor does persistent underestimation of midcentury literature help. Maybe counterintuitively, one finds ample evidence of routine minimization of midcentury writing in the expanding body of scholarship aiming to reanimate interest in the midcentury, in its assorted spans, or to revalue specific writers and works of the 1940s and 1950s.[8] In this burgeoning field, it has become common practice to proceed from, so as to correct, an inherited assumption that midcentury writing was somehow lacking and resigned to being so. Scholars of British fiction of the period are prone to cite as their provocation Malcolm Bradbury's essay " 'Closing Time in the Gardens': Or, What Happened to Writing in the 1940s" (1987), in which the novelist, who came of age in 1950, describes the "relative artistic silence of the period from 1939 till toward the end of the late 1940s."[9] Not that anyone had to wait until the 1980s to receive this wisdom. In August 1948, Bishop and Robert Lowell, for example, had fun with a "wonderful" letter she received from *Poetry* magazine: "It requests a contribution & congratulates me on my poetry's having 'perceptivity' & 'sureness,' etc., that 'seem often to be lacking in the output of the *run-down sensibility of the forties.*' I think we should make a modest fortune by working out a prescription for run-down sensibilities," Bishop wrote.[10]

The apparent vacancy of *midcentury* finally points to two larger, mutually inflected habits of mind that shape familiar perceptions of the chronological progress and ethical-historical regress of the twentieth century. The first habit, to which I will return, is academic and disciplinary: especially but not exclusively in the British and U.S. contexts, modernist and twentieth-century literary and cultural studies still tend to describe the midcentury in terms of cultural or historical forces that were either spent or incipient, or as a period remarkable primarily for witnessing the dusk of modernism or the dawn of "the period formerly known as the contemporary."[11] The second habit is a popular one: it has long been commonplace to think of oneself or one's times as located within a century, and to attach some meaning, however vague, to the unit of the century itself. One might consider in this vein the powerful career of Henry Luce's phrase "the American century." First articulated in *Life* in February 1941, the phrase yoked a call for the international exercise and expansion of U.S. power to the apparent neutrality of the chronological unit. Or one might think of the many early prognostications about the character of the twenty-first century, such as the "Google century," the "China century," and the "digital century" or its epochal cousin, the "digital age." These descriptors respectively accede to corporate branding of historical time, imply the threat posed to U.S. power by an implicitly racialized nation-state, or assert a tacitly optimistic technological paradigm in the face of the political, humanitarian, and environmental crises that characterize the twenty-first century thus far. In each formulation, the arbitrary unit of the *century* launders loaded assumptions about what the future must be and on whose terms it ought to be envisioned or protected.

At and in part motivated by the turn of the present century, the philosopher Alain Badiou began to concentrate on what thought might be contained in the unit of the century. His book *Le Siècle* (2005; English translation, 2007) describes the historical emergence of *the century* as a keyword only in the twentieth century and asks "if the phrase 'twentieth century' bears a certain pertinence for thinking, in a manner that goes beyond mere empirical calculation."[12] Rather than take "the century as an objective datum," Badiou begins his investigation by sketching out three historical narratives to which the phrase *twentieth century* can "plausibly" refer: the communist century (1914–89), the totalitarian century (1917–76), and the liberal century, which begins, "at the earliest, after the seventies (the final years of revolutionary fervor), [and] lasts only thirty years."[13] To facilitate "the passing of judgments" on what occurred in the twentieth century, Badiou argues, these and like distillations at once curtail the span of the century and summon *the century* as "some kind of objective or historical unity."[14] The century's chronological wholeness validates, at least rhetorically, historical narratives that are necessarily partial and ideologically suspect.

Checking habitual historiographical recourse to "the century" as a manifest whole, Badiou asks how the twentieth century "has come to be subjectivated."[15] The century needs philosophical inquiry, he argues, not only because the idea of the century itself prompted much of the most significant thought and art of the twentieth century but also because "the century" became a principal means by which that art and thought, especially avant-garde art and thought, understood or effected its own historicity. This reasoning might seem tautological. For Badiou that is part of the point—and the stakes of attempting to "think" the century could not be higher. By his logic, if we assume we cannot or need not "think" the century, then we risk ceding this key category of understanding to the "order of the unthinkable, or of the intractable" attributed to Nazism specifically or Evil in general.[16]

For *Midcentury Suspension*, the utility of Badiou's *Le Siècle* resides equally in its core project—the exertion of intellectual pressure on a category so accustomed as to seem inconsequential—and in its principle of selection. Badiou announces his intention to work inductively: "Our privileged documents will be the texts . . . which evoke the meaning that the century held for its own actors; documents which, while the century was still underway, or had only just begun, made 'century' into one of their keywords."[17] The canon that comes across in Badiou's lessons evinces, and extends, the history of imperialist chronologies: in his study, the twentieth century is "subjectivated" mostly by white European male artists. His privileged documents are also often documents of privilege. But it also noteworthy that Badiou's program implies that the substantive meanings of *the century* become perceptible or somehow important at either the beginning ("only just begun") or the end ("was still underway") of the twentieth century. If the century's "meanings" are tacitly assumed to coalesce at its chronological poles, or to be articulated only toward epochal turns, then even in the most thoroughgoing contemporary philosophical investigation of *the century* as a category, the midcentury drops out of view. In constructing the twentieth century as an ideational whole made up of the sum of its early and late parts, Badiou's method forecloses even the question of the particular "relation" the midcentury "entertained with the historicity of its own thought."[18]

At the historical middle of the twentieth century, however, *midcentury, 1950*, the *half-century*, and like terms achieved the status of keywords in Raymond Williams's sense. Though Badiou does not acknowledge Williams, it is difficult to think of his conceiving of *Le Siècle* without the model of *Keywords: A Vocabulary of Culture and Society* (1976). Or perhaps without William Empson's *The Structure of Complex Words* (1951), either. That both *Keywords* and *Complex Words* originated at midcentury is no coincidence.

Different as they are from one another, Empson's esoteric and Williams's demotic project are alike in step with a broad, intense scrutiny at midcentury of the deceitful, immoral, and ultimately murderous ends toward which various actors, including politicians and literary critics, had bent language and distorted plain vocabulary. (*Deceitful, immoral, murderous:* I adapt these damningly accurate adjectives from George Orwell's classic essay "Politics and the English Language" [1946], the pithiest distillation of the period scrutiny of usages so contorted and lexicons so euphemistic as to amount to criminality.)[19] Whereas Empson and Williams are now often taken as emblematic of, respectively, the academic ascendance of the New Criticism and the assertion of Marxist theory after the Second World War, *Complex Words* and especially *Keywords* also attest to disparate thinkers' need at midcentury for a conceptual and practical vocabulary to make sense of their historical moment. Inconspicuous in their ubiquity, *midcentury* and its cognates spoke to this need.

The association of Empson with the New Criticism is mistaken, but it does manage to keep the midcentury origin of *Complex Words* in view.[20] Meanwhile, the midcentury provenance of Williams's keywords project has perhaps been a victim of the enduring utility of keywords as method. The interdisciplinary and cross-field adaptability of *Keywords* pulls critical attention away from the felt historical conditions, shared affective experiences, and lived atmosphere within which Williams began his "record of an inquiry into a *vocabulary*" in the late 1940s.[21] The irony is plain: it is to Williams, more than to any other literary or cultural theorist, that we owe the expansion of literary and cultural analysis to include such inchoate things *as* felt conditions, shared affects, and lived atmospheres.[22]

The midcentury provenance of *Keywords* is crucial to *Midcentury Suspension*; so, we will come to see, are Williams's first inklings, at midcentury, of structures of feeling, which he began to sketch out in print in 1954. But to keep our gaze on *Keywords* for the moment: in part because the book was not published until 1976, Williams opened the introduction to the first edition with a brief intellectual-institutional memoir in which he traces the roots of his inquiry to the years 1945–48:

In 1945, after the ending of the wars with Germany and Japan, I was released from the Army to return to Cambridge. University term had already begun, and many relationships and groups had been formed. It was in any case strange to travel from an artillery regiment on the Kiel Canal to a Cambridge college. I had been away only four and a half years, but in the movements of war had lost touch with all my university friends. Then, after many strange days, I met a man I had worked with in the first year of the war, when the formations of the 1930s, though under pressure, were still active. He too had just come out of the Army. We talked eagerly, but not about the past. We were too much preoccupied with this new and strange world around us. Then we both said, in effect simultaneously: "the fact is, they just don't speak the same language."

It is a common phrase.[23]

The "common phrase" that sums up the first part of this midcentury origin story doubles as the opening exhibit of the need for *Keywords*. First, the "problems of [the] meanings" of the idiom *not speaking the same language* prove to be "inextricably bound up with the problems it was being used to discuss."[24] Second, the idiom is "common" in at least two senses: it is familiar or frequently spoken and it is demotic. As Williams explains, by 1945, *not speaking the same language* had long denoted differences "between successive generations, and even between parents and children" and between social classes "in a particular country" or, one might add, between racialized groups.[25] Third, the idiom meant "something more general," in that it provided a means of naming an otherwise inarticulable sense "that we have different immediate values or different kinds of valuation, or that we are aware, often intangibly, of different formations and distributions of energy and interest."[26]

This last meaning of *not speaking the same language* is vintage Williams. It lines up with his abiding interest in "intangibles," "energies," feelings, and like structures, and with his attention to "values" and experiences either before they harden into ideology or that never do achieve fixed form. In elaborating on his own jarring return from artillery regiment to elite university, Williams also recalls the idiomatic expression doing new and specific cultural work in late 1945. When he and his old acquaintance resorted to "they just don't speak the same language," they were getting at something more than how their prewar political commitments and Army service distanced them from the social world of Cambridge and drew them closer to one another. In late 1945, the idiom of *not speaking the same language* had to do both with the two men's experiences of the recent past and with their shared experience of a present that "too much preoccupied" them. Hence the subtle brilliance of Williams's temporal observation: it is not simply that he and his friend "don't speak the same language" as others in the idiomatic sense; it is also that they register idiomatically their sense of distance from their contemporaries "in effect simultaneously." That is, they recognize their shared feeling of "strange"-ness in the "world around us" at the same time, in a shared historical present at once created and characterized by their strange preoccupation with it.

As Williams narrates the origin of *Keywords*, he emphasizes that a sense of acceleration, of rapid changes occurring or occurred but not yet comprehended, effected "this new and strange world around us." That this acceleration made itself felt in language was much more than a matter of semantics, for, in Williams's now common view, "some important social and historical processes occur *within* language."[27] Typically, Williams explains, in a "critical encounter" in which one retreats to "the fact is, they just don't speak the same language," one is at some level registering "a process quite central in the development of a language when, in certain words, tones and rhythms, meanings are offered, felt for, tested, confirmed, asserted, qualified, changed. In some situations this is a very slow process indeed; it needs the passage of centuries to show itself actively, by results, at anything like its full weight."[28] At Cambridge in 1945, however, this process had sped up almost beyond belief. But it had not sped up beyond one's capacity to perceive the acceleration:

In other situations the process can be rapid, especially in certain key areas. In a large and active university, and in a period of change as important as a war, the process can seem unusually rapid and conscious.

Yet it had been, we both said, only four or five years. Could it really have changed that much?[29]

Williams found that "it" really had changed that much, with "it" meaning, in quick succession, "politics and religion" and then Williams's career-making inquiries first into "a single word, *culture*," and then also into "*literature*" and "society."[30]

In 1948, Williams recalls in *Keywords*, he read "but could not accept" T. S. Eliot's *Notes Towards the Definition of Culture* (1948), another midcentury work concerned with the problems of meaning contained in a single resonant word—though a work that, despite the hedging in its title, proves far more confident in its authority to delimit *culture* than Williams's connective, relational keywords model would be.[31] In pointed contrast to Eliot, Williams recalls "one day" in the late 1940s when, "in the basement of the Public Library at Seaford . . . I looked up *culture*, almost casually, in one of the thirteen volumes of what we now usually call the OED: the Oxford *New English Dictionary on Historical Principles*. It was like a shock of recognition."[32] Williams writes with a novelist's sense of drama of this moment, when he sat symbolically beneath a public repository of "culture" and in a coastal town rather than at the center of English academic prestige: "this was the moment at which an inquiry which had begun in trying to understand several urgent contemporary problems—problems quite literally of understanding my immediate world—achieved a particular shape in trying to understand a tradition."[33] *Culture and Society* was published in 1956; *Keywords* would take another twenty years to develop. Neither *century* nor *midcentury* appeared in the first edition. But the latter certainly qualified when Williams began his inquiry. As the neat round number of 1950 approached and lingered, *midcentury* and like terms routinely featured "in discussions and arguments which were rushing by to some other destination."[34]

AT MIDCENTURY

The middle of the twentieth century prompted a chorus of epochal stock-taking unlike anything seen in a previous era.[35] Two pairs of counterexamples begin to sketch out this point. One: where the imminent arrival of the chronological middle of the nineteenth century does not propel Karl Marx and Friedrich Engels in the *Manifesto of the Communist Party* (1848), Charles Olson's poetry manifesto "Projective Verse 1950" cites the midcentury year as its occasion. When reprinted in poetry anthologies today, the titular date of "Projective Verse" is often placed in editorial parentheses. Olson, however, foregrounded *1950* in his appeal for what "Verse now, 1950, if it is to go ahead, if it is to be of essential use, must" do, or stop doing.[36] Two: the half-century mark does not seem to have resonated particularly with that great chronicler of nineteenth-century social life in England, Charles Dickens, whose classic bildungsroman *David Copperfield* appeared serially between May 1849 and November 1850.[37] At the middle of the twentieth century, L. P. Hartley published a bildungsroman, *The Go-Between* (1950), that is best known today for the

Harold Pinter–Joseph Losey film adaptation (1971), as the source text for Ian McEwan's *Atonement* (2001), and for its opening line: "The past is a foreign country: they do things differently there."[38] In *The Go-Between*, a young boy named Leo gradually realizes the uses to which he is put by adults carrying on a clandestine affair across class lines in 1900. In the prologue and epilogue between which the novel suspends the childhood narrative, the adult Leo imagines a conversation with his twelve-year-old self, who, in his diary of the fateful summer of 1900, had imbued "the coming glory of the twentieth century" with supernatural wonder.[39] Young Leo would surely reproach his adult self for letting the events of his boyhood limit him to a "dull dog" life.[40] He would rebuke the adult Leo's self-rationalizing with exclamatory insistence on the half-century: "But you have had half a century to get over it! Half a century, half the twentieth century, that glorious epoch, that golden age that I bequeathed to you!" The adult Leo imagines responding with a rhetorical question to which the direct answer can only be *no*: "Has the twentieth century . . . done so much better than I have?"[41]

Olson's urgent "Verse now, 1950" and Hartley's repetition of "half a century, half the twentieth century" play on much broader yet unremarked discursive patterns of midcentury thinking—Hartley to lament, Olson to incite. Self-consciously *midcentury* works published around 1950 typically followed one of two templates, or combined them. In the first, the *half-century* model, the span from 1900 to 1950 justified a look back over the development of a field or phenomenon during the first half of the twentieth century. Hartley's depiction of Leo makes such retrospection into narrative scheme, as the child of 1900 reproaches the adult of 1950 in epochal terms—"Half a century, half the twentieth century"—rather than, say, ethical or moral ones. The second template for such stocktaking was the *at midcentury/1950* model, wherein the chronological moment necessitated a look around at the contemporary state, peril, or promise of a given field or issue. By hitching his call for a "composition by field" to the portentous year *1950*, Olson turns a convention of the time into an avant-garde spur.

In addition to such qualitative, canny registers of a self-reflexively *midcentury* idiolect in the period's literature in English, there is the sheer staggering quantity and range of it, long since lost to critical view. English-language contributions to the spate of *midcentury* stocktaking were commissioned by sources as disparate as the New Zealand Antarctic Society and the American Jewish Committee; *at midcentury* incitements and *half-century* surveys were published by prestigious university presses and commercial houses and imprints in the U.S. and the UK.[42] Representative titles of half-century retrospectives published in the first decade after the war include *The Growth of Major Steel Companies, 1900–1950* (1953); *The Big Business Executive: The Factors That Made Him, 1900–1950* (1955); and *Interpreting the New Testament, 1900–1950* (1951).[43] The "at midcentury" model prompted *Aeronautics at the Mid-Century* (1952) by the then-head of the Department of Aeronautical Engineering at MIT, Jerome Clarke Hunsaker; *Egypt at Mid-Century* (1954), the second of the economist and historian Charles Philip Issawi's three major books on Egypt; *The Architect at Mid-Century* (1954), a two-volume study commissioned by the American Institute of Architects; *The Arts at Mid-Century* (1954) edited by the artist, poet, and arts advocate Robert Richman; and French scholar André Siegfried's *America at Mid-Century* (1955).[44] Meanwhile, the Philosophical Library of New York put out an extensive Midcentury Reference Library, with dictionaries on topics including linguistics, psychoanalysis, atomic energy, tobacco, "last words," and "American maxims." The complete set ran to over fifty volumes.

Literary scholars, publishing houses, and anthologists on either side of the Atlantic were not going to miss the *midcentury* wave. Rolfe Arnold Scott-James published *Fifty Years of English Literature, 1900–1950* in 1951, and Leon Edel *The Psychological Novel, 1900–1950* in 1955.[45] The right-wing U.S. publishing house Henry Regnery, founded in 1947, announced its market presence by bringing out a six-monograph series celebrating the development of literary genres in the U.S. over the first half of the twentieth century. The best-known titles in it are William Van O'Connor's *An Age of Criticism, 1900–1950* and Louise Bogan's *Achievement in American Poetry, 1900–1950*.[46] Midcentury anthologies included Wallace Fowlie's *Mid-Century French Poets: Selections, Translations, and Critical Notices* (1955), Phyllis Maud Jones's *Modern Verse, 1900–1950* (1955), Louis Untermeyer's combined "Mid-Century Edition" of *Modern British Poets* and *Modern American Poets* (1950), and John Ciardi's *Mid-Century American Poets* (1950).[47]

Like the Regnery series, Gregory and Zaturenska's *History of American Poetry, 1900–1940*, F. O. Matthiessen's *Oxford Book of American Verse* (1950), and similar works, Ciardi's anthology shared in the period project of consolidating, so as to champion, a national literature befitting the new superpower. Singing in the key of the many stocktaking works published during the midcentury decade (1945–1955), the first sentence of Ciardi's foreword turns chronological non sequitur into *midcentury* herald: "As the mid-century comes upon us, it must be evident to all who care to look that America has achieved an important body of poetry."[48] In Ciardi's volume, the midcentury mark plays rhetorical host to his assertion of the finally achieved "maturity" of American verse, which at midcentury was no longer to be understood as apprenticed to the English tradition, and yet was still bound enough to English poetry to have to declare its independence. If scholars of postwar U.S. poetry remember *Mid-Century American Poets*, it is usually as an early antimodernist salvo in the "anthology wars" that raged across the 1950s and 1960s. Reading against this grain, Edward Brunner suggests that when Ciardi was working on the project, "the very idea of assembling a definitive anthology of *contemporary* poetry was already an aggressive action."[49] Positioned synchronically rather than disciplinarily, however, *Mid-Century American Poets* looks less "aggressive" than accustomed in its pronounced contemporaneity. In fact, Ciardi had originally conceived of the anthology as a retrospective 1940s book, but he and his publisher, Twayne, recognized that *Mid-Century* had more market traction.[50] At least for a while.

Around 1950, lyric poets, too, took up the *midcentury* occasion explicitly, as witness Roberta Margaret Grahame's *Last Bell at Midcentury* (1951) and the newspaper poet Frances Frost's *Mid-Century* (1946). Printed in both *Harper's* and the Poets' Column of the *New York Times Book Review*, the title poem of the latter apostrophizes the twentieth century from the vantage of its middle. The titular "Mid-Century" names a semiepochal persona who speaks entirely in tidy quatrains and rhetorical questions, voicing an apt if unconvincing despair at the twentieth century's horror. "O century of grief" and "O century of sorrow," the midcentury itself pleads:

Shall we in the steel-pocked terror of our earth
devise some alchemy, some starry magic
whereby a child gone mad may yet give birth
to a new child less murderous and tragic?[51]

So clunky is the conceit of the child as redeemer of the future in this usage that one might miss a chilling effect of Frost's vision: according to the

"Mid-Century" who speaks the poem, the future might, at best, be not peaceful but only somewhat "less murderous and tragic" than the half-century just endured.

Journalists joined in the accounting of the twentieth century to date and in the public discursive project of *at midcentury* self-assessment and projection. Monographs by well-regarded reporters included *Fire in the Ashes: Europe in Mid-Century* (1953) by Theodore H. White; *In One Ear: 107 Snapshots of Men and Events Which Make a Far-Reaching Panorama of the American Situation at Mid-Century* (1952), a collection of essays by Eric Sevareid; and *Midcentury Journey* (1952) by William L. Shirer. The editors of the *Christian Science Monitor* and *Harper's*, too, published books hooked to the chronological mark of the midcentury. Frederick Lewis Allen, of *Harper's*, wrote a social history, *The Big Change: America Transforms Itself, 1900–1950* (1952), and the *Monitor*'s Erwin D. Canham wrote *Awakening: The World at Mid-Century* (1951).[52]

As these titles suggest, popular history flourished around 1950, a point perhaps best illustrated by the launch of the British magazine *History Today* in January 1951. The magazine's very title attested to the deeply if opaquely "historical" feeling and tenor of the midcentury present; the foreword to its inaugural issue elaborated the point. It begins: "January 1951 seems a particularly appropriate moment to launch a new historical magazine. Every adult alive today—more especially those of us whose memories reach back to the period before 1914—can claim to have lived through one of the most astonishing phases of recorded history." Without once using the word *war*, the foreword goes on to summarize the "gigantic changes" of "the last fifty years," invoking "history in the widest meaning" to peddle late-imperial self-congratulation and national self-promotion. It announces, for example, that one of *History Today's* first projects would be a series on British towns and cities whose "historical treasure[s]" the magazine's writers would, "like open-cast miners, but more gently and beneficently," unearth and usher "into mid-twentieth-century daylight." This national-artifactual display meant to stand counter to the "bewilderingly swift" pace of change in the twentieth century to its midpoint. When the keyed-up foreword of *History Today* asserts that "each age has an individual mood," the implication is that the midcentury, of all ages, would know.[53]

Art exhibitions, professional conferences, special issues, and advertisements also swam in the *midcentury* waters. The English-Speaking Union of the United Nations curated *British Art. The Last 50 Years. 1900–1950*, a loan exhibition in New York with a catalog by Kenneth Clark and Allan Nevins. The midcentury also appealed on the conference circuit, which saw meetings such as "Librarians, Scholars and Booksellers at Mid-Century," hosted by the Graduate Library School of the University of Chicago in 1951; "General Education at Mid-Century," a conference held at Florida State University, November 20–22, 1950; the "Mid-Century Congress on Christian Education," which convened representatives of African Methodist Episcopal Church congregations in Atlanta, August 1–4, 1950; "The Caribbean at Mid-Century," the University of Florida's first annual conference on Caribbean studies, December 7–9, 1951; and "The Social Sciences at Mid-Century," a conference of the University of Minnesota Social Sciences Research Center, April 19–21, 1951.[54]

The two highest-profile such conferences in the U.S. were the "Mid-Century Convocation of the Massachusetts Institute of Technology" (March 31–April 2, 1950) and the "Mid-Century White House Conference" (December 3–7, 1950). The former brought together an international roster of scientists, philanthropists, humanist scholars, and diplomats. Most notable among the speakers was Winston Churchill, whose quintessentially *midcentury* address, "The Twentieth Century—Its Promise and Its Realization," was printed in U.S. and British newspapers and broadcast in both nations.[55] (The next month, *Time* would name Churchill the "man-of-the-half-century" in its "Half-Century Supplement.")[56] The Mid-Century White House Conference, as the 1950 meeting of the decennial White House Conference on Children and Youth was broadly known, received significant national and local press coverage. When President Harry S. Truman addressed the conference on December 5, 1951, he alleged that international communism posed the greatest threat to youth welfare and national security. Not all journalists were buying Truman's line. In their analysis of findings presented about the effects of segregation on the well-being of minority children, the editors of the *Chicago Defender* wrote that the Mid-Century Conference had "given new impetus to the whole fight for civil rights and true freedom in the United States."[57]

The *Defender*'s conclusion chimes with broader coverage of the public occasion of the midcentury in African American newspapers. Reportage, editorials, and features in outlets such as the *New York Amsterdam News, Philadelphia Tribune,* and *Pittsburgh Courier* demonstrate the utility of the midcentury mark in the early postwar civil rights struggle in the U.S. and in international solidarity movements. In much of this coverage, *1950* stood, on the one hand, for the egregiousness of African Americans' thwarted progress toward full U.S. citizenship in the first half of the twentieth century and, on the other, for the promise that might be realized in the century's second half. Looking to that next chronological horizon, the National Council of Negro Women created a "Mid-Century Register" to be deposited at the Library of Congress. The group encouraged African American women involved in advocating for civil rights to sign the document as "an assurance that the world will know about you in the year 2000 A.D."[58] Insofar as the rhetorically resounding year *1950* underlined the continuing injustice of U.S. racial politics—a liability that, as Mary L. Dudziak has shown, both civil rights activists and cold war adversaries exploited—the midcentury mark offered a chronological reference point by which to underscore the extremity and indefensibility of state-sanctioned segregation and racialized violence in the U.S.[59] If at *1950* the U.S. could not reform to meet its own democratic ideals, then its hypocrisy was fast approaching, if not already past, the irredeemable.

Midcentury became a rallying point for solidarity among black American communities and oppressed groups throughout the world. In the view of the *Philadelphia Tribune* editorial staff on the eve of 1950, the "chief problem facing us Americans on this New Year's Day in this Mid-Century Year" was to "do our part to make sure that the next half of the twentieth century will see the growth of freedom throughout the world."[60] Some months later, the *New York Amsterdam News* reported on the organization of the Mid-Century Conference for Peace, held in Chicago on May 29–30, 1950. The conference followed from "a Call issued by AME Zion Bishop William J. Walls," who tied "the American people's insistent demand for peace in the world" to African Americans' domestic "battle for full freedom today."[61] In harnessing his Call to the midcentury occasion, Walls updated W. E. B. Du Bois's century-mindedness in *The Souls of Black Folk* (1903), wherein "the problem of the Twentieth Century is the problem of the color-line."[62]

Meanwhile, in political speeches and documents of the midcentury decade, the *half-century* lexicon served rhetorically in nearly all arguments, including and especially in the shoring up of British and the expansion of American imperial power. These documents and oratories often co-opt the portent of the *midcentury* mark to mask the duplicity of proffering high-toned democratic rhetoric while perpetuating racial injustice or resisting anticolonial struggle. In both Truman's "Four Points" second inaugural (1949) and Churchill's "Sinews of Peace" address (1946), *half-century* thinking toppled into euphemism, providing an idiomatic foothold from which to assert, respectively, the rightness of an American-made peace and the "abiding power of the British Empire and Commonwealth" in the second half of the twentieth century.[63]

For politicians, political scientists, and diplomats making their cases for Western or more specifically American-style democracy around 1950, it became customary to advocate domestic security policies or to qualify predictions about the future with a gesture toward the newly real possibility that the century might not reach its end. George F. Kennan modeled and exacerbated this sensibility in his book *American Diplomacy, 1900–1950* (1951). At its opening, he remarks, characteristically for the period, that "a half-century ago, Americans felt themselves secure in the world." At midcentury, however, "our national consciousness is dominated . . . by a sense of insecurity greater even than that of many of the peoples of western Europe who stand closer to, and in a position far more vulnerable to, those things that are the main source of our concern."[64] Kennan here dances around "those things" he considered of "concern" at the half-century, namely, Soviet communism's systemic threat to global capitalist order and the emerging nuclear arms race. He almost didn't have to name them, for as we will see in chapter 2, lists of "sources of concern" and their accompanying affects—in Kennan's case, "a sense of insecurity" and "vulnerability"—were in ample supply in the discursive world of the Anglophone North Atlantic at midcentury. In citing the half-century span rhetorically to contain new uncertainties, then, Kennan was no outlier. Even otherwise unconcerned feature stories of the period capitalized on the unit of the half-century to obfuscate, and in some cases to domesticate, new fears—as in, for example, Virginia A. Smith's blithe mention of the atomic bomb in her story about new furniture for TV-watching, published in the inevitable *midcentury* special issue of the *Home Magazine* of the *Los Angeles Times*: "If it were not for the A-bomb, we would probably be calling this next half century the Television Age."[65]

Finally, given the profusion of self-conscious, if not always self-aware, *midcentury* thinking, it will hardly be surprising that mainstream magazines like *Time, Life, Vogue,* and *Parade,* the Sunday newspaper magazine, as well as newspapers such as the *Boston Globe, Washington Post,* and *Times* of London also contributed to "at midcentury" discourse, many by publishing special issues to commemorate the midcentury mark.[66] What is surprising is that such coverage routinely acknowledged the arbitrariness of the unit of the half-century. The January 2, 1950, issue of *Life* announced a departure from its standard documentary procedure thus:

This week, instead of being concerned with the world around us, LIFE surveys an entire half century. In deciding to devote an issue to the spectacle of the U.S. when it was emerging as the most powerful of all nations, some rather arbitrary decisions had to be made.

The first one concerned the date of a mid-century issue. It is argued from a purely arithmetical point of view that this issue should be appearing at the beginning of 1951. But LIFE is stringing along with such authorities as the Library of Congress and Mark Sullivan, the most widely read historian of the early century, who said that Jan. 1, 1900 "seems to the eye and sounds to the ear more like the beginning of a century than Jan. 1, 1901."[67]

"It is argued," *Life* observes, that 1950 is not in fact the midcentury. And indeed, it was argued. An article titled "Time Experts in a Battle on Just What Time It Is," printed in the *New York Times* on December 29, 1949, begins by noting that "government experts split today on whether next Saturday night will be just another New Year's Eve or the end of the first half of the twentieth century."[68] The Library of Congress and the Astrophysical Department of the Smithsonian voted for January 1, 1950; the Naval Observatory and the Interstate Commerce Commission for December 31, 1950; and cranky letters to the editors of magazines and newspapers from the period alternately chided and defended the publications for their placement of the midcentury mark at January 1, 1950.[69]

In London, the *Times* exercised greater chronological circumspection than its New York counterpart. On January 1, 1951, a *Times* editorial titled "Mid-Century" rapped others' eager mid-epochal knuckles: "Sound chronologists, who have waited to celebrate the turn of the twentieth century until its actual mid-point, must needs do so in more chastened spirit than those who, their enthusiasm outrunning their computative powers, chose to light their bonfires a year ago." The editorial goes on to assert that the contested chronological mark signified, in any case, nothing so much as the staggering collapse of "optimism" in the twentieth century thus far. Hartley's mature Leo might have written it:

The world to-day looks out upon a dark and doubtful prospect, in a mood as remote as can well be conceived from that which prevailed on New Year's Day of 1901. The great Queen, who had given her name to so majestic and so prosperous an epoch, was fading out of life; but men felt that in her time the current of history had been finally directed into such broad and well-marked channels that now it must needs flow forward uninterrupted. Theirs was the last generation that could still found its thinking upon the belief in progress as the law of life.[70]

How could "the age of anxiety"—as the midcentury, care of Auden, dubbed itself—possibly compete with such nostalgic recollection of monarchical time?

Alternately pedantic and inspiring, despairing and rallying in their own time, these debates about the meaning and timing of the midcentury mark, like the range and ubiquity of the midcentury lexicon and discourses themselves, prove instructive today. Already in 1950, the pull of *midcentury, 1950*, and the like was understood to draw from little more than arbitrary chronology. Yet the pull and the occasion the midcentury provided were undeniably compelling. To excavate midcentury-speak across fields, venues, and registers is to come to realize that its prevalence owes in significant part to the comprehensibility of the midcentury mark or the half-century unit. In the *at midcentury/1950* pattern, the simple chronological measure counterbalanced the purported incomprehensibility of the political, existential, scientific, cultural, and technological realities signaled by the portentous date. In the *1900–1950/half-century* mold, the measure tempered the horrors and accelerations of the first half of the twentieth century, as well as the uncertainty that laced prognostications about what the remainder of the century would, should, or might well not see. Amid the habitually decried collapse of old systems of order and meaning across the first half of the twentieth century, and with renewed vigor around 1950, calendrical time itself proved durable, even strangely comforting. The mid-epochal lexicon exceeded mere chronological reference: it testified to an atmosphere pressurized by the known horrors of its recent past and the new terrors and promises of its unknown future, a time whose felt characteristics and lived or anticipated events *midcentury* enabled historical subjects alternately to itemize and euphemize, harness and hold at bay. In in its endless and varied usages, *midcentury* recorded in its currency an incredible sense of historical weight exerted on the present, a pressure often described as a feeling of historicity itself. (To this last point: throughout this book, I occasionally italicize *midcentury* to recall this specific historical usage or when context necessitates emphasis on the term as keyword rather than empty time stamp.)

From television-oriented home furnishings to fashion magazines, celebrations of U.S. poetry to last grasps at British world power, and civil rights activism to calendar-year sticklerism, this record of *at midcentury* thinking could be extended beyond all critical utility. For scholars of modernism, the *midcentury* discursive swell may well recall Michael North's remark, in *Reading 1922: A Return to the Scene of the Modern* (1999), about his array of the many achievements of that year: "The difficulty in making such connections is getting them to stop somewhere."[71] With respect to the self-reflexive idiolect of the midcentury, there are at least two additional difficulties. First, while the import of the year 1922 as modernist sign was never in doubt, but rather in need of expansion and renovation, *midcentury* has not seemed the kind of marker that shimmers with its own importance. In its time, however, and as it variously beckoned to a disastrous recent past, an unknowable future, and a fraught present, the *midcentury* lexicon registered a hyperawareness of that present as suspended, by definition temporarily, at the middle of the century—a moment when *midcentury* did, in fact, shimmer with import. The question was then and, since *midcentury* has continued to elude critical inquiry, the question remains now, in what that import consisted. Second, where *1922* long denoted high modernist pedigree and ratified the narrative of a radical break for the new, the *1950* vocabulary was always demotic, occasional, and arbitrary; it was felt and provisional. This book maintains that the occasional, felt, and provisional are antithetical neither to the historical nor to the culturally and critically salient. This claim is not new to this project, of course; something like it is at the heart of affect theory and studies. It bears emphasizing, however, that this idea—that the felt if not fully articulated dimensions of a period constitute grounds of inquiry into it—traces roots, once again, to Williams's midcentury thought.

Williams's first attempt to sketch out structures of feeling, in *Preface to Film* (1954), emerged out of his acknowledgment of a limit to any analysis of works of art taken to be characteristic of given historical periods. Put simply, the limit was and remains that the retrospective analyst cannot know what the period *felt like*; she can at best perceive that an artwork still registers some incipient feeling of its fleeting historical present. "All the products of a community in a given period are, we now commonly believe, essentially related, although in practice, and in detail, this is not always easy to see" within the period itself, Williams wrote in 1954. Thus "in the study of a period, we may be able to reconstruct, with more or less accuracy, the material life, the general social organization, and, to a large extent the dominant ideas."[72] But even the most robust of such historical-analytical inventories will impose on "the study of a period" a secondary clarity that, at odds with the felt experience of the time, will leave aside its "*structure of feeling*." How, then, could one seek out such experience? In this earliest account of the concept, *structures of feeling* names something expressed most effectively, which is not say directly or diagnostically, in works of art. Williams holds that there will always remain some "element" of a work of art that defies explanation by reference or reduction to an "external counterpart" of the work's historical period.[73] This elusive "element" itself is the structure of feeling, he explains, and "it is only realizable through experience of the work of art."[74] Works of art, then, were for Williams at midcentury not simply records of experience, but conduits of it.

As the word *element* hints, Williams first described the immeasurably influential and portable concept of structures of feeling by way of an extended chemistry metaphor, or as a kind of experiment in period-artistic solutions and retrospective-analytical precipitates: "While we may, in the study of a past period, separate out particular aspects of life, and treat them as if they were self-contained, it is obvious that this is only how they may be studied, not how they were experienced. We examine each element as a precipitate, but in the living experience of the time every element was in solution, an inseparable part of a complex whole."[75] Between the heterogenous, liquid quality of solution (a period itself) and the solidity of a precipitate (an element "separate[d] out"), there is suspension.

Some of the language of Williams's chemistry metaphor would survive into his later elaborations of structures of feeling, most notably in *The Long Revolution* (1961) and *Marxism and Literature* (1977).[76] But Williams's initial attempt at the concept merits attention for at least two reasons. First, it suggests that the emergence of the idea of structures of feeling relied in part on the midcentury's ineluctable if indefinite sense of its own historicity.

For Williams, it seems, there was something about the midcentury as it was demotically felt and experienced that would compel cultural analysts to concede the limits of their own retroactive analyses of past periods and to work to redress them. Second, *Preface to Film* restores to view how very provisional the concept of structures of feeling itself was. The idea was not yet, or maybe could not yet be, nailed down within midcentury experience generally as a "complex whole" or specifically as the moment preoccupied and fascinated Williams. In its 1954 articulation, *structures of feeling* reads, like *not speaking the same language* in *Keywords*, as a contemporaneous instance of what Williams tries to describe.

Twentieth-century literary scholarship, particularly modernist scholarship in an affective key, occasionally nods to *Preface to Film*. But rushing by the midcentury germ of structures of feeling means overlooking how deeply in keeping Williams's earliest gesture to the idea in fact was with the inchoate, unfixed "solution" of the period in which he began to think about it. It means missing, too, how fully his thinking—and the very vocabulary of his thinking—spoke with and to a range of contemporaneous expressions, literary and otherwise, of the midcentury's sense of its own historical suspension.

SUSPENSION

Midcentury discourse bespeaks the period's own attempt to grasp its historicity, apprehend its present, and describe its feeling. *Midcentury, 1950, half-century*: these keywords faced forward and backward alternately and at once, placing the period and its subjects in a present understood as an irreducible middle. To dismiss as empty the proliferation of *midcentury* thinking is to dismiss a key discursive, rhetorical, and idiomatic means by which people tried or were encouraged to conceive of their lived experience of an epochal time marked as such. For literary and cultural historians to presume the inconsequence of the general attachment at midcentury to being and feeling *midcentury* is, in the first place, to preclude analysis of how writers formalized, questioned, and otherwise made use of popular attachment to chronological self-positioning. It is also, we will see, to cede *midcentury*, like other outwardly neutral chronological markers, to more entrenched disciplinary configurations and ideological manipulations. If *midcentury* has functioned to date as a relatively inert term in twentieth-century literary studies, then that inertia owes not to its lacking demonstrable contours. The vacancy of the term owes rather to subsequent underestimation of midcentury thinking *as* one demonstrable contour, as a significant pattern of thought in the years around 1950. Suspension is another.

In contrast to literary periods or movements, which can be institutionalized into apparent sequential inevitability, *midcentury* discourse often articulated the period's profound sense of its own historical middleness, its feeling of suspension amid unclear onsets and outcomes. Contributors to the *midcentury* discursive swell frequently gestured toward suspension as an experiential, atmospheric, or felt historical condition of the period. Or, they turned midcentury historicity itself into something like what Williams was beginning to think of as a structure of feeling. In her "Pursuit of Democracy" column in the January 14, 1950, issue of the *Pittsburgh Courier*, for example, Marjorie McKenzie wrote of those endless journalistic responses to the 1950 mark. Or, as the *Courier* headlined the column, she "View[ed] Journalists Squeezing Last Vestige of Historicity from the Passing of Mid-Century." McKenzie found that the midcentury present had a just sense of its own historical significance even if—or maybe because—it could not quite name in what that significance consisted. *Midcentury* yielded for her, as for many others, an "intense" feeling if not yet a clear meaning. "I have been reading comments on the meaning of the midcentury in press and periodical[s] with extraordinary interest. I have discovered that my own intensity about 1950, whether interpreted by *Vogue* or *Time*, is a widely shared emotion. The world is engaged in a search, and its people act as if 1950 were a key and a sign," McKenzie wrote.[77] Never mind that everyone already understood that "to select any arbitrary moment for assessment and speculation may be to deal with pure illusion," she continued:

I have been observing the journalists trying to squeeze as much meaning out of the fact that 1950 is upon us [as they did out of the United States' atomic bombings of Japan]. Though they don't quite bring it off, they have got something. The formality of 1950 is not so special, but the era is. The sense of our era, explosive, unpredictable, full of wonder and potential good has enthralled us.

I feel in 1950 as if I were on the edge of my seat, standing on tiptoe, peering around the corner.[78]

To describe her feeling in and of 1950, McKenzie lists idioms for a felt expectancy, an embodied anticipation (seat, tiptoes, peering eyes). Like Williams's *not speaking the same language*, these phrases are clichés on purpose. Their commonness speaks to the ease with which McKenzie expected her readers to recognize her description of how, beyond the mere "formality of 1950," "the era" in fact felt. Other such forgotten gestures to the midcentury's self-conscious suspension are almost startlingly on the nose. In the historian Eric F. Goldman's hugely popular book *The Crucial Decade: America 1945–1955* (1956), for example, a chapter on the summer of 1950 is titled "Suspended Moment" and recalls a palpable feeling of suspension as a "weird" effect of that season.[79]

In the late 1940s and early 1950s, more prominent literary writers now associated with various categories of nation, identity, genre, movement, and period routinely evoked the strange suspension of their "immediate world," to borrow Williams's phrase. The midcentury present bore, in the American poet Wallace Stevens's phrase, "the weight of primary noon" (1947).[80] Suspended self-consciously at the chronological middle of a century already defined by two global wars and newly exposed to a nuclear future, writers, thinkers, and readers alike conceived of themselves as living through, as the Anglo-Irish novelist Elizabeth Bowen titled her great midcentury book, *The Heat of the Day* (1949). Whether chronological, as in the *midcentury* lexicon, or figurative, as in Bowen's, Stevens's, and countless other writers' evocations of midcentury contemporaneity, such terms attest to a sense of suspension in the middle that wound its way through the literary and cultural discourse of the Anglophone North Atlantic in the decade after the Second World War. Such terms, tropes, and images of suspension merit critical retrieval. They constitute an intrinsic conceptual vocabulary through which to read midcentury cultural artifacts, to discover how the period apprehended and felt its own historicity, and in turn to recalibrate the dominant periodic logics of twentieth-century literary studies.

Unlike *midcentury*, *suspension* has never lacked for interest from philosophers and aesthetic theorists or, in the nearer term, from literary critics, art and cultural historians, and psychologists. The transhistorical utility and transdisciplinary dexterity of suspension, as both term and concept, draw in the first place on the word's irresistible range of meanings and connotations. Suspension pertains to both space, as in hanging or hovering, and to time, as in a pause or rest. Suspension suggests a holding pattern, a freezing or delay of action or progress, a deferral of decision, or a temporary revocation of a normal state of affairs. Distinct from paralysis, suspension effects a charged stillness, wherein a subject's cognitive or somatic movement is temporarily excepted from the imperative to decision or action, but within which the subject can move and be moved. *Suspension*, from the Latin root *suspens-*, can in institutional contexts signify punishment or postponement and can more generally carry a hint of eager anticipation, anxiety, or suspense. (Chapter 3, on Bowen and Beckett, recovers a crucial distinction between suspension and suspense at midcentury.) Yet even as *suspension*'s juridical, political, affective, and biological connotations tend toward the negative, suspension can also connote space and time for deliberation and consideration, for an epistemologically sound uncertainty or a generative attentiveness. Suspension can forestall the rushed conclusion, the undue assumption, the precipitate action; it can signal a creative deferral, effect a stay (e.g., of execution), characterize an ecstatic concentration, or constitute a pleasurable protraction (e.g., of experience or of desire).

As Jonathan Crary writes in his important book on the conditions and character of modern attention (1999), *suspension* "implies the possibility of a fixation, of holding something in wonder or contemplation, in which the attentive subject is both immobile and ungrounded. But at the same time suspension is also a cancellation or an interruption . . . even a negation of perception itself."[81] The varied and sometimes contradictory meanings of suspension serve Crary's effort to counter an entrenched critical emphasis on distraction—as in Walter Benjamin's account of "reception in a state of distraction"—as the fundamental condition of postindustrial subjectivity.[82] In Crary's account, modern subjectivity relies on a precariously two-fold dispensation of human perception. The subject's necessarily provisional, approximate, and temporally bound perception lends itself to management by "institutional power" and in accordance with imperatives to productivity and consumption.[83] The partiality or contingency of one's perception does not matter, so long as it can be disciplined to afford the requisite attention to a given task. Thus the capacity to pay attention amounts to both "the means by which an individual observer can transcend . . . subjective limitations and make perception *its own*" and "a means by which a perceiver becomes open to control and annexation by external agencies" or principles—or, as scholars of long eighteenth-century and cognitive-scientific literary studies have shown, by literary conventions.[84]

For Crary's account of how "attentive norms and practices" were man-
ufactured to define and regulate modern subjectivity, the value of *suspension* resides "as much in evocation as description."[85] For the present book,
the value of *suspension* includes and exceeds its evocative range. If some
of the general meanings or connotations of *suspension* align intuitively
with even the most basic understanding of the geopolitical situation of
the late 1940s and early 1950s, then one way of describing the work of *Midcentury Suspension* is to say that it substantiates—which is also to say that
it complicates—the intuitive aptness of suspension for thinking with and
about cultural artifacts of the midcentury. And there is a blunter distinction to be made too: where Crary, like many theorists and critics drawn to
the term, chooses *suspension* as the most apt descriptor for the processes
he describes, this book did not so much choose suspension as *find* it at
midcentury.

It should be clear that to credit a distinctly midcentury suspension is not
to deny precedents for thinking about or in terms of suspension across aesthetic and philosophical traditions or academic disciplines and subfields. In
literary studies organized around genre, *suspension* in the twinned senses of
anticipation and exception was integral to the epistolary development of the
novel, remains central to debates about lyric, and characterizes the pastoral
from Virgil's *Eclogues* through Auden's *The Age of Anxiety: A Baroque
Eclogue* (1947).[86] Suspension resonates with Aristotelian unity and with
foundational theorizations of *ataraxia*, the equilibrium or freedom from
worry as variously conceived by ancient Stoics, Epicureans, and Skeptics
("those who suspend"). Enlightenment and Romantic accounts of the beautiful and the sublime draw on suspensions of various kinds. Edmund Burke
(1757) defines the "passion caused by the great and sublime in *nature*" as
"astonishment," or "that state of the soul, in which all its motions are suspended, with some degree of horror" and "the mind is so entirely filled
with its object, that it cannot entertain any other, nor by consequence reason on that object which employs it."[87] Immanuel Kant, too, posits the
sublime as an experience of the observing subject rather than as a quality
of the phenomenon observed and, in the third *Critique* (1790), describes
the suspensions of faculties—understanding or imagination, singly or in
relation to one another—necessary to produce certain kinds of aesthetic
judgments.[88] And in a letter to his brothers (1817), John Keats coined the
phrase "negative capability" to venerate that quality of a man "capable of

being in uncertainties, mysteries, doubts, without any irritable reaching after fact and reason."[89]

Keats thought Coleridge lacked negative capability. His argument with the elder Romantic notwithstanding, it was Coleridge who alit on what is unquestionably the most famed articulation of suspension as aesthetic principle: "that willing suspension of disbelief for the moment." Writing in *Biographia Literaria* (1817) of the composition of *Lyrical Ballads* (1798), Coleridge explains that Wordsworth was to concentrate on "subjects . . . chosen from ordinary life." His own "endeavors" were to be "directed to persons and characters supernatural, or at least romantic; yet so as to transfer from our inward nature a human interest and a semblance of truth sufficient to procure for these shadows of imagination that willing suspension of disbelief for the moment, which constitutes poetic faith."[90] Without the cooperation of savvy poet and "willing" reader, the poem will fall flat. Thus condensed, Coleridge's idea clearly owes much to Aristotle's preference for probable impossibilities over impossible probabilities.[91] This debt is well known. More striking is how thoroughly Coleridge's conceptualization of "shadows of imagination" and "poetic faith" relies on mechanisms of suspension. The poem that engenders this special quality of belief is at once result, emblem, and engine of experiences occurring outside of, or in a suspension of, typical spatial, temporal, and rational orders.

Coleridge's diction of mobility conveys the spatial quality of the poetic suspension he describes, as the *willing suspension of disbelief for the moment* takes the metaphorical form of movements in, occupations of, and projections across space. There is the "transfer from our inward nature" into the text of a poem and, implicitly, onward to the "willing," not willful, reader; and there is the likening of the poem to those flickering "shadows of imagination." Figured as "shadows" rather than, to use a related word in the Romantic vocabulary, as "intimations," the poet's imaginative projections have spatial implications: they occupy space by shading it, creating and holding "a human interest" there.

These spatial implications complement the temporal dimension, or the privileged temporariness, of the "willing suspension." The prepositional phrase "for the moment" is not strictly necessary to Coleridge's formulation, since *suspension* already implies impermanence; casual citation of "willing suspension of disbelief" usually omits it. But "for the moment" articulates the temporal limit of the suspension of one's rational critical faculty. It also glances at the special temporality of this suspension itself, as the poem aims to usher the reader into *the* (transcendent, continuous) rather than *a* (idiosyncratic, serial) privileged "moment" of poetic faith. Finally, at the level of prose syntax, "for the moment" enacts the temporal suspension characteristic of that "which constitutes poetic faith," deferring ever so briefly the longer its theoretical enunciation.

One can also follow along with suspension on a tour of twentieth-century literary history and aesthetic theory. At one of the epoch's ends, suspension characterizes phenomenological "bracketing" (Edmund Husserl's adaptation of *epoché* [1906]), obtains in T. S. Eliot's account of the "historical sense" that animates the poet's relation to tradition and "his own contemporaneity" at once (1920), and harmonizes with Freud's description, in *Civilization and Its Discontents* (1930) and elsewhere, of the intoxicating, ego-obliterating capacities of art. At the other, the many and sometimes contradictory meanings of *suspension* line up with ideas associated with the academic institutionalization of, and serial upheavals in, social and literary theory since the 1930s and 1940s—ambiguity, indeterminacy, *différance*, and, more recently, states of impasse or exception.[92] Suspension chimes with hallmarks of modernist form, as in the nonpurposiveness of stream-of-consciousness narration, the sudden yet lasting "apparitions" of imagism, and the fascination with and terror induced by aerial perspective and mechanized flight.[93] Recurrent tropes and emblems of the airborne in modernist works find writers from F. T. Marinetti to Hart Crane to Virginia Woolf attending to the perspectival, symbolic, and psychological effects of age-old and modern suspension technologies, including suspension bridges and airplanes, both unto themselves and as weaponized in the century's wars.

This last point brings us to precedents for midcentury suspension to be found in the historical emergence and critical study of late modernism, especially in Britain. Perhaps in part because the Second World War was quicker and the postwar slower to arrive there than in the U.S., scholars have been especially attuned to the formal manifestations not only of the war but also of the anticipation of global violence that characterized British late modernism and that frustrates any tidy periodic divide between its interwar and wartime phases. This book's chapters return to and extend this discussion, teasing out how inchoate *midcentury* portents were subsumed into dominant postwar narratives. For now, though, one might call up as pre-echoes of a distinctly midcentury suspension even just the gerundive titles and interstitial premises of the many novels that depict "the climate of anxiety, suspense and speculation" that Steve Ellis, adapting E. M. Forster, calls "the 1939 state" and Leo Mellor conceptualizes as a "prolonged 1939."[94] Such works "written on the very periphery of war" include Henry Green's *Party Going* (1939), Orwell's *Coming Up for Air* (1939), Woolf's *Between the Acts* (1941), and the novel Evelyn Waugh left unfinished when the war broke out, *Work Suspended*.[95]

Or consider the arrival at suspension in Eliot's *Four Quartets* (1943), perhaps the supremely canonical poem of late modernism, and a work that scholars have accordingly situated within British wartime politics, imperial declension, and transatlantic exchnage.[96] The last quartet, "Little Gidding," begins:

> Midwinter spring is its own season
> Sempiternal though sodden towards sundown,
> Suspended in time, between pole and tropic.[97]

Sibilance presides over these opening three lines. The complete declarative sentence of the first line lacks a period, allowing a quiet hiss—of "spring," "season," "sempiternal," "sodden," "towards," "sundown," and, finally, "Suspended"—to carry over the first line break into the atmospheric elaboration of the second and third lines. At the close of the sentence, a pivot is both audible and punctuated: the beat at ", between" moves this "suspended" moment from the register of "time" to the register of space; it shifts the poem sonically, too, from its air of sibilance to a plosive zone "between pole and tropic." Written in the middle of the Second World War, Eliot's meditation on the fleeting and the eternal, the sudden (so close to "sodden") and the "sempiternal," has been taken to culminate English high modernism. It also begins to sound out what would become a key imaginative construct of the midcentury: suspension.

MODIFIED MODERNISMS

It lies outside the scope of this introduction to flesh out the rich history of suspension and related concepts as they range widely and deeply across aesthetic, critical, and literary theory from classical antiquity to disciplinary present. One might well thicken my necessarily partial catalog of suspensions synonymous with or proximate to familiar theoretical concepts, turning suspension into an aperture through which to pursue that thinking through, across, and outside fixed literary periods for which scholars increasingly call. In his *On Literary Worlds* (2012), for example, Eric Hayot argues that, to counteract the "ideologization of periods," scholars "ought to ... develop *and to seek to institutionalize* a variety of competing concepts, including transperiodizing ones, for the study of literary history."[98] Suspension could rank as an omnibus concept in this sense, although the heuristic value of suspension, which always already resists the logic of the totalizing claim, the grandiose proclamation, or the clear boundary, would, I think, be imperiled by the imperative to institutionalize it. A more pressing question in the present context, however, is what it means to invoke such an ambitious, far-reaching call for transperiodizing models at the start of a book that deliberately adopts the scope of a single decade. Isn't *Midcentury Suspension* another book in which periods "get shorter as we get closer to the present?"[99]

Yes and no. This book does not stake out rigid period boundaries for the midcentury and then defend them to the death. It rather proceeds from the observation that not all periods have been constructed equal. Nor do they exert equal sway as institutionalized categories within the broader system of periodization. "Period," Hayot writes, "is the untheorized ground of the possibility of literary scholarship. And so we live with its limitations and blind spots."[100] Yes, and yet the relatively brief timespans that fall between canonical periods also comprise some of those "blind spots" and thus can serve in the vital project of dispelling the larger, stronger period clouds that overshadow them. It might seem counterintuitive to state as much, but there may be no better evidence *than* the midcentury of blind spots created by canonical periods and sustained by the disciplinary logic of periodization. For the *midcentury* imaginary both falls between the tectonic plates of modernism and its many afters and frustrates the alternate model of periodizing the literary twentieth century by reference to putatively discrete wartimes. Even as the new modernist studies, cold war cultural studies, Post45, postwar literary studies, postmodernist studies, and more subfields dispute their periodizing terms for twentieth-century literature, the internal self-concepts of the "crucial decade"—principally, suspension—go unremarked, their larger utility for literary study and cultural history untapped.[101] This book, therefore, credits and conceptualizes the terms, tropes, and ideas with which, in and beyond its literature, the middle decade of the twentieth century expressed the feeling of its own historicity.

There is no need here to rehearse the rewards and limitations of dia-chronic versus synchronic studies. Each has its merits as each has its moment. But recall once more North's synchronic work in *Reading 1922*, wherein concentration on the watershed year of the publication of *Ulysses* and *The Waste Land* recast literary modernism in relation to cultural pro-ductions and ephemera from well outside the sphere of high culture. The key difference with respect to reading the midcentury now is that scholars have not historically assumed that *1950* or *midcentury* marks any kind of *annus mirabilis*. All of which finally brings us back around to the interlock-ing set of disciplinary habits and period configurations that, like the pop-ular habit of century thinking, license critical inattention to the literary midcentury as it articulated itself.

Some of the basic premises of twentieth-century literary studies deflect attention from what the *midcentury* meant or effected in literary works and cultural productions of the years around 1950. With a standard periodic logic that still tacitly or expressly adheres to the century's halves or poles, twentieth-century literary studies all but inevitably construes the midcen-tury as a pivot between wars or kinds of war, a foregone conclusion to mod-ernism, a transition to a proliferating array of later modernisms, or some combination of these. In other words, we still split the century in half at or around its middle, whether by 1. reference to the Second World War and its global aftermath, including the postcolonial turn; 2. citation of bland but plainly not neutral chronological cognates for postwar events or develop-ments, as in the boldface years 1945, 1950, or 1960; or 3. depiction of a central organizing movement, modernism, which was once laced tightly into the shopworn corset of "modernism and postmodernism" and has now loosened to spread across the twentieth century and into our contemporary.[102]

The extraordinary resilience of the progressive line that runs, albeit under changing signs, *from* modernism *to* the contemporary is nowhere more evident today than in the vibrant field of the new modernist studies. Over the past two decades, scholars of modernism have rightly reassessed what modernism was, when it happened, and how it worked—what insti-tutions, practices, technologies, and networks facilitated and extended the modernist turn.[103] The new modernist studies has reenvisioned modern-ism as prismatic and plural rather than monolithic and static, as transna-tional and cosmopolitan rather than restrictively European-American and metropolitan.[104] One paradox of the new modernist studies, however, is that even as one of its central projects has been to create an inclusive and expansive account of what modernism was, that project has extended the heuristic and historical reach of modernism, as a dominant category, across twentieth-century and into twenty-first-century literature and culture. The effort to overhaul once standard accounts of singular Modernism now underwrites a critical discourse of *modified modernisms*, wherein modifiers that are variously metacritical or qualitative (*new* itself, *bad*, *meta-*, *weak*), spatial (*planetary, global, transnational*), or, most germane to this book, temporal (*late, inter-, midcentury*) or geopolitical (*interwar, World War II, postwar, cold war*) attach to the institutionally legible rubric of *modernism*, and thereby draw modernism into ever more spaces and ever later historical times.[105] In the cases of transnational, postcolonial, global Anglophone, and non-Anglophone texts and writers, scholars have confronted the exclusions and persistent biases of the new modernisms, if not yet entirely corrected for them.[106] The critical practice of identifying sequentially later modernisms is less obviously deleterious. But it is no less restrictive.

The new modernist creep forward across the twentieth century allows the assumptions and priorities of historical or institutional modernisms to preclude inquiry into the midcentury and its literary and cultural productions through other, less deterministic period optics. The relevant critical vocabulary and heuristic method for the midcentury are supplied by disciplinary standards, rather than sought in the record of the period; that critical vocabulary in turn reinscribes the norms of an elongated modernist studies rather than reanimating the midcentury's cultural imaginary and seeking the vocabularies (in the fullest sense) writers developed to evoke the historicity of the midcentury and what it felt like. If more and more imaginative literature of the midcentury—and, for that matter, since the midcentury—garners attention primarily for its elegiac, revisionary, or revivifying relation to modernism, then even the newest, most contested modernism sets a perimeter. It imposes a limit on how one can understand not just the writing of the midcentury but the cultural forms of the past century-plus. Thus the discourse of modified modernisms risks consolidating a chronologically progressive but functionally conservative disciplinary practice. To the extent that the new modernist studies maps onto the logic of century thinking, the field has gradually but forcefully assembled an account of the twentieth century as *the modernist century*.

The aim of this book is not to join modernist scholars in either calling out the "intense self-scrutiny" of modernist studies or endorsing its "weak" self-theorizing.[107] Nor is it to discount those critical revaluations of the field. This book, instead, argues the need for, and aims to demonstrate the efficacy of, pausing midway along the long modernist line that subtends a great deal of twentieth-century literary scholarship, especially in the U.S. and British contexts in the wake of the Second World War. This book looks elsewhere than modernism for purchase on *midcentury*. It looks to the midcentury itself. Reading in a neglected range of archives, it recovers from within the period a self-reflexive attachment to being and feeling *midcentury* and a concomitant sense of suspension. The book seeks out how and to what ends midcentury writers channeled a deep and broad awareness of being pitched at the middle of the twentieth century. It teases out representative and revelatory suspensions that took shape in and gave shape to transatlantic literary culture at the moment when the aftereffects of the Second World War were materially and psychologically present, but when disciplinary and popular narratives of the *postwar*, much less of a long *modernism*, had not yet crystallized.

ARC, ARCHIVE

To reiterate: *midcentury* became a keyword in Williams's sense at the middle of the twentieth century, but its import as more than a moot chronological marker has long since been lost to literary and cultural history; *suspension*, long of critical use in and beyond literary and aesthetic theory, achieved specific conceptual currency at midcentury. *Midcentury Suspension* works across genres and other accustomed literary categories—including period categories—to consider how, before *midcentury* settled into critical inertia, major writers conceived of their lived, felt, discursive, and historical experience of the midcentury itself. The chapters to follow draw out various registers of suspension in and across six key writers' works that were composed and published around 1950. Rather than pulling suspension out of the critical ether, so to speak, the chapters gradually build it up and out in several directions from the midcentury's archival ground. Each chapter thus contributes to an approach to the midcentury problem—or possibility—that is more prismatic than linear, more atmospheric than taxonomic. The book's narrative procedure, then, is not to provide a baseline account of suspension as an imaginative construct in 1945, and then to measure changes to that construct as the midcentury wore on through 1955, by which latter point the currency of *midcentury* had largely expired and the murky middle began to be viewed through other, sturdier frames. Instead, the chapters to follow trace a narrative circuit through and across texts like Bishop's *A Cold Spring* (1955), which tropes the "historical" discourse of the midcentury; works like Auden's *The Age of Anxiety* and Ellison's *Invisible Man* (1952), which probe the equation, in that discourse, of history itself with *feeling*, and more particularly with *a* feeling, anxiety; and projects such as Elizabeth Bowen's *The Heat of the Day*, Samuel Beckett's *Waiting for Godot*, and Frank O'Hara's first book manuscript, which are all in various and surprising ways "about" the Second World War as it was remade in the service of the postwar.

Chapter 1 takes up Elizabeth Bishop's critically neglected second volume of poems, *A Cold Spring*. I begin with it because the book's composition history roughly spans the midcentury decade and because the book itself offers one of the richest explorations of suspension as trope and as ethos for perceiving the midcentury present. Chapter 1 describes, first, how suspensions of many kinds organize the forms of *A Cold Spring*, and thereby expands on the tropological capacities of suspension itself. Next, the chapter accounts for why and how the suspensions of *A Cold Spring*, yet unsought, trouble critical readings of Bishop and of other writers in the keys of late modernism, cold war obliquity, and lyric theory. Third, the chapter restores Bishop's key poems of the late 1940s to the patently "historical" discourse of the period. It discovers in Bishop's "timeless" descriptive poems—poems about looking at and trying to make sense of a world in which knowledge like "water seems suspended"—a deeply timely investigation of historical subjectivity and knowledge.[108] Braiding tropological coherence and situational contingency, and bracketing the biographical-geographical bent of Bishop scholarship, this chapter contends that the historicity of *A Cold Spring* inheres in the deferrals, pauses, and "days of suspension" its poems create and record.[109] The volume remakes the lyric subject as, or also as, a self-consciously historical subject at and of the midcentury.

Chapter 1 begins to get at how, in Anglophone North Atlantic public, literary, and intellectual discourse of the midcentury, the words *history* and *historical* themselves often connoted a feeling at least as powerfully as they denoted a series of past events. Chapter 2 recovers the powerful transformation of this diffuse historical feeling, or feeling of history, into acute and civically responsible anxiety in early postwar print culture. More specifically, the chapter moves from the multivalent trope of suspension in Bishop's midcentury poetics to the felt registers of suspension that shape the long poem that gave the midcentury an indelible name, W. H. Auden's *The Age of Anxiety*, and a novel that riveted it, Ralph Ellison's *Invisible Man*. Along with their unusual public stature around the half-century mark, *The Age of Anxiety* and *Invisible Man* share what chapter 2 describes as a critical affective historicity. These works achieved in their own time, and now afford, invaluable critical purchase on the rhetoric of anxiety that swept across midcentury discourse and continues to preponderate in literary and cultural historiographies of the cold war and postwar. Drawing on the composition histories, narrative designs, and organizing affects of *The Age of Anxiety* and *Invisible Man*, as well as on the surprising print proximity of Ellison and Auden at midcentury, this chapter finds Ellison and Auden challenging, rather than submitting to, the consensus anxiety of the midcentury.

The next chapter investigates the behavioral analogue of suspension— waiting, killing time—that defines the midcentury works of Elizabeth Bowen and Samuel Beckett. At midcentury, Bowen and Beckett wrote self-consciously midcentury works that map characters' quotidian experiences onto plotlines that get emphatically stuck, suspended in the middle of an unfolding series of events. Or rather, of nonevents. Both Bowen's novel *The Heat of the Day* and Beckett's first play *En Attendant Godot* (premiered 1953) foreground characters for whom there is "nothing to be done" but to wait, and to wait without any indication as to when, how, or whether their suspension will end.[110] Where the historicist turn in Beckett scholarship has located the Second World War within the apparent ahistoricism of *Godot*, this chapter finds a distinctly midcentury humor in Beckett's elaborate staging of suspension. Conversely, the more extensive project of chapter 3 is to reposition *The Heat of the Day*, long understood as a great novel of the war, as also and more pointedly a vital midcentury novel of the middle of the war, and thus as a novel that depicts an acclimation to a wartime feeling of suspension that outlasts the war itself. Bowen's unpublished manuscript drafts, correspondence, and nonfiction about midcentury contemporaneity reveal that her critically *midcentury* vantage motivated her imaginative recovery of the uncertain middle of the war. *The Heat of the Day* creates an imaginative record of a protracted middle duration that was, as Bowen worked on the novel in the late 1940s, fast being rewritten into the self-justifying clarity of the postwar.

Finally, "The Sonic Suspensions of Frank O'Hara" discovers a surprising sensory suspension—in the form of charged listening—in the early work of this quintessentially postwar–cold war poet. Dropping as its archival anchor the young "Francis" O'Hara's first and still unpublished book of poems (1951), chapter 4 attends to the conspicuous amount of listening that this famously breezy poet of New York chatter does in his early work. The poems of O'Hara's first book manuscript often hold still and listen or try to catch silences and subtle modulations between louder sounds and more consistent noise. Reading these motifs as connected to but not circumscribed by O'Hara's service as a U.S. Navy sonar operator during the Second World War, this chapter explores how experiences of auditory suspension reverberate across O'Hara's career. Put another way, the chapter harnesses the heuristic potential of midcentury suspension to argue that O'Hara's poetics sounds the war that remains, always, audible in the postwar.

O'Hara was younger than Auden, Beckett, Bishop, Bowen, and Ellison. That much hardly needs stating, except that O'Hara's young outlier status—what is he doing in this book?—points back to two important elements of the rationale for the literary archive and synchronic methodology of *Midcentury Suspension*. Any one of the six writers on whom I focus could stick out as the proverbial sore thumb, and for reasons—among them, sexuality, race, and nationality—that will seem far more consequential than lived age. The constellation of, to cite some familiar tags, New York School O'Hara, great African American Novelist Ellison, middle-generation poet Bishop, postcolonial genius Beckett, voice of the 1930s Auden, and late modernist Bowen might well seem strange on the face of it. Yet the representative works collected and analyzed in this book share a fascination with suspension as a condition of experience, perception, feeling, and creativity at a historical moment profoundly aware of its being in the middle of the century. The apparent idiosyncrasy of this collection of writers owes less to the substance of their midcentury work than it does to the elongated line of modernism and the attachment to discrete wartimes that still broadly govern the study of twentieth-century literature. Those familiar period frameworks too often determine the questions we pose about the century's entire literature and about the literature of its hazy, suspended middle.

Chapter One

THE TIMELY SUSPENSIONS OF ELIZABETH BISHOP'S *A COLD SPRING*

. . . my answer is *it all depends.*

—ELIZABETH BISHOP, FROM A STATEMENT ON HER POETICS FOR *MID-CENTURY AMERICAN POETS* (1950)

In the summer of 1951, Elizabeth Bishop was staring down a September 1 deadline for her second book. She had made her name five years earlier with her debut volume, *North & South*, published on August 20, 1946. *North & South* met with a warm reception in which poet-critics praised the "modesty" and "uninsistence" (Marianne Moore), "restraint" (Randall Jarrell), "accuracy" (Louise Bogan), and "splendor and minuteness of her descriptions" (Robert Lowell).[1] Success begot success. Between the summers of 1946 and 1951, Bishop won fellowships from the Guggenheim Foundation (1947–48), the American Academy of Arts and Letters (1951), and Bryn Mawr College (1951–52). The *New Yorker* signed Bishop to a first-read agreement; *Partisan Review*, the *Nation*, *Poetry*, *Quarterly Review of Literature*, and other big and little magazines sought her contributions; Bishop served as poetry consultant to the Library of Congress (1949–50); and John Ciardi included her work in his anthology of contemporary poetry, inevitably but not inconsequentially titled *Mid-Century American Poets* (1950) and distinguished by the poets' statements of their principles. (When pressed by Ciardi to write of her poetics at midcentury—or, in a sense, pressed *by* the swell of *midcentury* reckoning—Bishop wrote about everything depending on everything else. She wrote about suspension.)[2] Also on either side of 1950, and as she worked on her second book, Bishop spent two residencies at Yaddo (summer 1949, fall 1950); recorded readings of her poems for posterity at the Library of Congress and Harvard University; began her friendships with her two closest peers, Lowell and Jarrell; and attended numerous high-profile literary events, including the Gotham Book Mart reception for the Sitwells, to which Moore evidently had to drag her.[3]

Success also begot pressure, expectation. So it was that in the summer of 1951 Bishop wrote several times to colleagues and friends about pulling her second book together ahead of deadline. To her editor at the *New Yorker*, Katharine S. White, she wrote on June 21, 1951: "I've got about 2/3rds of my book at Houghton Mifflins and hope to have the rest of it there in a few weeks. So far it doesn't jell very well but I trust it will when I've finished the rest."[4] Those few weeks later, on July 11, Bishop wrote in the same vein but in a more jocular tone to Lowell of the book she was planning to call "Concordance": "My book is about 85% at Houghton Mifflin, but I must confess it doesn't jell at all yet. Maybe the other 15% will prove to be pure pectin."[5] It did. Within a week of writing to Lowell, Bishop finished what became the title poem of her second book.[6] "A Cold Spring" describes a season of suspension. It makes a keynote poem out of a trope Bishop had been developing in her work across the late 1940s. Suspension is the "pure pectin" of *A Cold Spring*.

Fittingly, however, for a book named for a poem about the belated arrival of spring in Maryland in 1950, Bishop would miss her September 1, 1951, deadline for her second book manuscript—by over three years. *A Cold Spring* was thus marked externally by suspension in the form of delay well before Bishop finished it. And although *A Cold Spring* includes several of her most lasting poems—"At the Fishhouses" (first published in 1947), "Over 2,000 Illustrations and a Complete Concordance" (1948), "Cape Breton" (1949), the title poem (1952), and "Arrival at Santos" (1952) chief among them—the suite has been marked by suspension of another kind, a sense of its incompletion, since Bishop was finally persuaded to append it to a republication of her first book in 1955.[7] The composite volume *Poems: North & South—A Cold Spring* won the Pulitzer Prize for Poetry in 1956, but *A Cold Spring* remains Bishop's most critically neglected collection.[8]

Delayed, neglected, but not incoherent. It would be difficult to overstate how thoroughly suspension suffuses *A Cold Spring*. As trope, suspension reverberates across both that core cluster of Bishop poems—all of which are about looking outward, inhabiting the present world as the poems perceive it—and across the volume's more personal, self-referential poems alike. Right from its title poem of seasonal deferral, *A Cold Spring* culti-vates suspensions of various kinds. The trope lodges in the grammatical, linear, and syntactic units of which the *Cold Spring* poems are built and in their occasions and themes, in the sensory worlds the poems create and the practices of observation, description, and perception with which they experiment. The core poems of the volume activate many of those dimensions of suspension that have historically made the concept so fruitful for theorists of aesthetics and attention: temporal pause and spatial hover, ethical deliberation and procedural deferral, affective ambivalence and cognitive fascination, epistemological uncertainty and investigative openness.

The readings that anchor this chapter will tease out the subtle means by which suspension came to "jell" *A Cold Spring* as Bishop worked on the volume roughly over the course of the midcentury decade, between 1946 and 1954. By way of introduction, however, the bluntest evidence for the tropological coherence of *A Cold Spring* is this: forms of the very word *suspension* recur three times in the eighteen poems of the original suite, and in three of Bishop's best known and loved poems at that.[9] In "At the Fish-houses," the observation "The water seems suspended / above the rounded gray and blue-gray stones" initiates a concluding conceit that yokes the water to "what we imagine knowledge to be" (*PPL* 53). As "Over 2,000 Illustrations and a Complete Concordance" weighs the respective epistemological claims of book learning and travel, the poem clocks the staged quality of stock illustrations in which birds and smoke seem "suspended on invisible threads," posed for the picture (*PPL* 44). And in the apostrophe that interrupts the shoreline approach of "Arrival at Santos," the phrase "eighteen days of suspension" checks, with perfect rhyme, an imperious Northern tourist's presumption of "complete comprehension" of the Bra-zilian port city (*PPL* 65). That each of these enunciations of *suspension* bears in some way on knowledge is no coincidence. The semantic tethering of the trope to "what we imagine knowledge to be" condenses the ethos of *A Cold Spring*, whose key poems are predicated on sustained looking rather than imposed order, on deliberate observation rather than prophetic declama-tion or lyric self-reflection. The poems envision even the possibility of knowledge in and of their historical present as resting on experiences of suspension.

I use the phrase *historical present* deliberately, and to refer to the strong, but often only vaguely signifying, "historical" tenor of both *midcentury* discourse and Bishop's midcentury book. For this chapter argues that the descriptive poems of *A Cold Spring* suspend themselves somewhere—or sometime—between the special timelessness of lyric and the everyday time that scholars have shown to sponsor the aesthetic innovations and geopolitical stakes of high and late modernism.[10] The *Cold Spring* poems variously draw on suspension to disperse and sometimes to dissolve the would-be lyric or late modernist subject into a present that the poems themselves—like the *midcentury* discursive culture in which they took shape and circulated—mark as "historical," if not otherwise clearly meaningful.

Yet if *suspension* has been hiding in almost too plain sight in *A Cold Spring*, then one reasonable question is why the trope has gone largely unexamined, much less understood historically. The answers point most directly to patterns in the Bishop scholarship, much of which relies on biographical explication of certain kinds, and so refers poems back to aspects of the poet's lived experience understood as "private" or "personal." The force of, in Gillian White's phrase, "the Bishop biographical paratext" remains such that even challenges to that paratext sometimes end up remodeling rather than retiring it.[11] Then there is the accumulated sway of what can be complementarily called "the Bishop tropological paratext," which conceives of Bishop's poetics in terms derived from the retroactive master trope she provided in 1976 for the whole of her work: geography.[12] Since the most studied aspects of Bishop's life align more or less neatly with geography, these paratexts prove mutually reinforcing, and Bishop's midcentury book and its key trope at best hover somewhere near the periphery of the Bishop "map."

A crucial and farther-reaching argument of the present chapter, however, is this: though it has been licensed in part by the customary emphases on biography and geography in the Bishop scholarship, the elision of the historicity—and even of the question of the historicity—of Bishop's second book and its organizing trope replays in author-specific miniature what *Midcentury Suspension* describes as a persistent critical disinterest in thinking about the midcentury in terms other than those supplied by established period and disciplinary frames. Bracketing both familiar associations with the signifier "Bishop" and habitual construal of *midcentury* as a synonym for ostensibly more important—and certainly more firmly fixed—things, this chapter restores the timeliness and historical resonance of the suspensions of *A Cold Spring*. Timeliness in the literal sense that Bishop developed the suspension trope uniquely and, by her standards, emphatically as she worked on her second book at midcentury. And timeliness in a more atmospheric sense, too, in that it is through suspension that *A Cold Spring* both relates and relates to the feeling of its historical present without trading in topicality in the narrower, more accustomed sense. While the suspensions of *A Cold Spring* opened a set of important developments in Bishop's own poetics, to be sure, the volume also participated in and, we will see, achieved a distinct critical purchase on the broader creative and discursive production of a conceptual vocabulary at, of, and for the self-reflexively historical middle of the twentieth century. *A Cold Spring* is a *midcentury* book by more than default. It is a vital document of the historical feeling of the middle of the twentieth century, a volume whose manifold suspensions disclose a historicity as yet unlooked for.

A MIDCENTURY "SPRING"

I begin where Bishop's midcentury book does, with the title poem. Placed first in the volume it names, "A Cold Spring" initiates several patterns and practices of suspension that recur across the suite. Taken up first in this chapter, "A Cold Spring" will also serve in it to index the current illegibility of suspension as an epochal trope at and for the midcentury. Bishop began work on "A Cold Spring" in the spring of 1950, during her miserable year as poetry consultant to the Library of Congress. Under "The Year 1950" printed on the title page of an imposing business-managerial datebook in which Bishop sporadically tried to keep a journal that year, she wrote, "Just about my worst, so far—."[13] From Washington, D.C., she would often escape to the Havre de Grace, Maryland, farm of the physicist Jane Dewey, the "friend in Maryland" to whom the poem was originally dedicated when it was published in the *New Yorker* on May 31, 1952. Bishop's earliest notes toward "A Cold Spring" evince a self-canceling ambivalence about broaching a spring poem at all. An early fragment tries four lines, only to interrupt the poem with two variations on a demurral: "(Oh do not ask me / to say anything profound about it!)" and "(Please do not ask me / to [*two illegible canceled words*] try my ingenuity / Right <u>now</u>, do not ask me to be profound. about it.").[14] Neither the apostrophic imperative nor the resistance to profundity nor even the trace of the poet ("me") would make it into "A Cold Spring." By the final version of the poem, the draft condition of ambivalence characterizes the late season itself.

Like the volume it names, "A Cold Spring" is marked by suspension even before it properly begins, in its title and epigraph. Hovering between the "cold" of winter still lingering in its title and the benedictory promise of its final word, "summer," "A Cold Spring" evokes a period of protracted in-betweenness (*PPL* 43–44). As the landscape poem unfurls in fits and starts over two stanzas, it mines the interstitial character of the interim season, forestalling the triumphant arrival—*spring is here!*—conventionally associated with the spring poem. The atmosphere of "A Cold Spring" is more in keeping with that of other roughly contemporaneous spring poems— Wallace Stevens's "Motive for Metaphor" (1947), wherein spring and autumn are realms of "half" and not "quite," or Philip Larkin's sly "Coming" (1950), with its central reassurance that "It will be spring soon, / It will be spring soon"—than it is with Gerard Manley Hopkins's classic sonnet "Spring" (1877, 1918), from which Bishop takes her epigraph: "Nothing is so beautiful as spring."[15]

Where the season rushes forth in the exuberant octet of Hopkins's sonnet, the opening of "A Cold Spring" barely moves. The first line, a sentence fragment, only restates the poem's title and punctuates it with a colon, so that the poem opens into a doubly marked pause:

> A cold spring:
> the violet was flawed on the lawn.
> For two weeks or more the trees hesitated;
> the little leaves waited,
> carefully indicating their characteristics.
> (*PPL* 43)

Hesitation, waiting, care: attributed to signs of spring—"flawed" violet, trees and leaves personified only to wait—these qualities of suspension apply equally to the shape of the whole first stanza of "A Cold Spring." Though it runs to fourteen lines, the stanza declines to flesh out the sonnet form it implies, much less to emulate Hopkins's aptly sprung rhythm or enhanced Petrarchan rhyme. Short lines and marked end-stops create a halting rhythm suited to the delayed spring, while the lone rhyme of the first stanza—"hesitated"/"waited"—pronounces the not-quite-sonnet's evocation of suspension rather than vernal renewal. Since "hesitated" concludes a pentameter line and "waited" a trimeter one, the couplet effects a paradoxical abruptness: the sound of the rhyme completes quickly, even as its semantic content emphasizes the poem's suspensions of season and sonnet form.[16]

To its deceleration of the spring poem and noncompletion of the sonnet, "A Cold Spring" goes on to add other suspensions that recur across the volume. Among these are three patterns of suspension—self-inscriptive, spatiotemporal, and imagistic—that will establish the centrality of this trope to *A Cold Spring*. The first, self-inscription, names a poem's mechanism for describing or commenting on itself even as it describes some other thing, as in the "trees" or "little" leaves whose waiting and hesitation also characterize the motion, such as it is, of the first stanza of "A Cold Spring." Self-inscription relies on a kind of suspension in which the poem both does its work—in this case, its descriptive work—and at the same time seems to float outside itself to perceive how it is working. This effect is not unique to Bishop.[17] But what is distinct about the self-inscriptions of *A Cold Spring* is how often the poems describe their own forms by reference to other instances or kinds of suspension. For a few examples: when "The Bight," a poem saturated with simile and metaphor, envisions water "Absorbing, rather than being absorbed," it also sees how the structure of metaphor sustains both tenor and vehicle, rather than subsuming the one into the other (*PPL* 46). When "At the Fishhouses" observes "All is silver: the heavy surface of the sea, / swelling slowly as if considering spilling over," the lines register the poem's own slow, sibilant "swelling," its suspension at water's edge, not quite ready to plunge (*PPL* 50). After a long middle stanza that links places and memories on an anaphoric, hypotactic string of *and*s, the final stanza of "Over 2,000 Illustrations and a Complete Concordance" begins with a sentence fragment: "Everything only connected by 'and' and 'and'" (*PPL* 46). As the line makes a self-inscriptive wink at the disorderliness of travel and memory alike, it also describes the additive, though not conclusive, syntax of the preceding stanza. Equally striking: the *Cold Spring* poems often make these self-inscriptive gestures in poems that, like "Cape Breton" and "A Cold Spring," eschew entirely the convention of the lyric *I* and in poems that, like "At the Fishhouses" and "Over 2,000 Illustrations," almost do. These poems conceive of their own poetics while avoiding or making a point of suspending the grammatical sign of the lyric speaker or its oft-presumed referent, the biographical-psychological self. Intertwined and mutually sustaining, these self-inscriptive and subjective suspensions ultimately participate in the *Cold Spring* poems' construction of a specifically historical subjectivity.

Self-inscriptive suspensions inflect and sometimes sponsor the second register of suspension that "A Cold Spring" models: the spatiotemporal. The *Cold Spring* poems often note things—objects, birds, insects, vehicles—moving in space and time, in various directions and at various paces, but typically without ascribing to those things progress or momentum toward an end. In "A Cold Spring," things observed in suspension are also often emblematic of the poems' own suspension in time and space. Consider once more the poem's opening lines, which cite two temporal scales (seasonal and calendrical) and move in space first from "lawn" to "trees" and then, zooming in, to their "little leaves." There is movement of focus, but not progress, within the poem's opening pause. In its long second stanza, the poem relies on prosy indicator words—"The next day," "then one day," "Now"—to chronicle movement forward in time, if in relative and uneven temporal measures. But even as these throwaway markers indicate temporal advance, the poem's descriptive pace and procedure resist the forward march.[18] The poem slows down as markers of calendrical, quotidian time appear and try to assert themselves—a trace, perhaps, of the heavy business calendar book in which Bishop jotted down her earliest ideas for this poem. Instead of speeding up as the season warms and the calendar pages turn, "A Cold Spring" begins to spin similes and metaphors whose increasingly protracted elaboration slows the hustle that those quotidian indicators try to impose.

A roaming spatial quality complements the temporal suspension of "A Cold Spring." As the poem notices various spaces and details, it names them: "the wood," "hills," "a white front door," and "shadowy pastures" come into and fall out of the view of the second stanza, but are not organized under a single, stable vantage. In another self-inscriptive passage, the poem offers a figure for its own evocation of spatial mobility without a manifest point of orientation or destination. When "A Cold Spring" notices "Greenish-white dogwood" and "blurred redbud," diction, rhyme, enjambment, and image all contribute to the poem's depiction of suspension in space:

> Greenish-white dogwood infiltrated the wood,
> each petal burned, apparently, by a cigarette-butt;
> and the blurred redbud stood
> beside it, motionless, but almost more
> like movement than any placeable color.
>
> (*PPL* 43)

"Blurred" as if seen in motion, the "redbud" is also fixed in place twice over: the verb "stood" reads and sounds, ever so briefly at the line break, like an end-stopped rhyme with "wood." Next, the adjective "motionless," inserted between commas, at once briefly pauses the line and keeps the sentence in audible "motion" over another line break. Catching all this simultaneity of movement and stillness, the wonder of the image is that it expands not on the most obvious characteristic of the "redbud," its eponymous color, but rather on its kinetic quality: even when "stood" still, the redbud's very color appears "unplaceable."

The spatiotemporal mobility—neither paralysis nor progress, but suspension—that runs through "A Cold Spring" repeats across *A Cold Spring*. "Faustina, or Rock Roses" ties spatial confinement (to a sickbed) to telescopic time, a single precipitate moment that is either "freedom at last, a lifelong / dream of time and silence" or "the unimaginable nightmare / that never before dared last / more than a second" (*PPL* 56–57). "The Argument," a lovers' quarrel poem, meditates on the "Days" and "Distance" separating the lovers (*PPL* 60–61); and the tender love poem "The Shampoo" describes "lichens" as "still explosions on the rocks," which "grow / by spreading" (*PPL* 66). The pun on "still" records the lichens' twinned mobility and stillness, their creeping variation on suspension in time and space: the lichens grow imperceptibly over time and "still" exist in the present; they also spread in space across the rocks, and thus move even as they remain "still," in place.

Such spatiotemporal suspensions work in concert with the most obvious register of the trope that organizes *A Cold Spring*: its imagery. The final image of the title poem doubles as the keynote image of the suite:

> Now, from the thick grass, the fireflies
> begin to rise:
> up, then down, then up again:
> lit on the ascending flight,
> drifting simultaneously to the same height,
> —exactly like the bubbles in a glass of champagne.
> —Later on they rise much higher.
> (*PPL* 44)

Fireflies that look "exactly like" champagne bubbles make for a simile so charming that it is easy to overlook the poem's riffing, once again, not on the most distinctive feature of fireflies—their brief flashes of light—but rather on their suspension, their floating in air. In fact, this image of "fireflies" on the "rise" figures suspension in about every conceivable way. As the fireflies float "up" and "down," "ascending" and "drifting," prepositional and gerundive grammar underscores the insects' movement in space ("rise," "flight," "height") and time ("Now," "then," "simultaneously"), while the rhyme of "flight" and "height" reproduces in sound the insects' synchronized suspension in air. The syntax that conveys most of this final image is itself suspended: the sentence drifts over two colons in as many lines; ranges over two comma-marked, end-stopped lines; and finally, with a dash, extends beyond a line break into the champagne likeness for the fireflies' suspension. And there is more yet: another dash extends the image still further, beyond the hard-won period and a hard line break to the fireflies' "Later" "rise." Lastly, the image of the fireflies' suspension culminates "A Cold Spring" even as it defers the poem's conclusion. For this final image doubles as the poem's most dilated one: just at the end of the poem, the suspended fireflies delay its final projection of "summer."[19]

Once more, the image of fireflies floating in air inaugurates a pattern in which nearly every poem in *A Cold Spring* notes or implies something suspended in air. Among many examples: "Black-and-white man-of-war birds soar / on impalpable drafts" and "blue-gray shark tails are hung up to dry" in "The Bight" (*PPL* 46–47); bats take "uncertain staggering flight" in "The Prodigal" (*PPL* 54); there are "Rags or ragged garments / hung on the chairs and hooks" in "Faustina, or Rock Roses" (*PPL* 56); "The Argument" remembers "all that land / beneath the plane" (*PPL* 60); and "little flags / feed their limp stripes into the air" in "View of the Capitol from the Library of

Congress" (*PPL* 53). The first line of "Rain Towards Morning" reads "The great light cage has broken up in the air," and "O Breath" interrupts itself to "See the thin flying" of hairs around a woman's nipples (*PPL* 59). "The Mountain" resignedly bids "the moon go hang" and "the stars go fly their kites" (*PPL* 63); and the whimsical refrain of "Invitation to Miss Marianne Moore" wishes the senior poet will "please come flying" (*PPL* 63–64). The sensory and symbolic worlds of *A Cold Spring* are replete with emblems of suspension.

At once a poem about the delayed arrival of spring and a poem in which spring never exactly arrives, "A Cold Spring" coalesces the poetics of suspension that gradually, over the late 1940s and early 1950s, came to organize Bishop's midcentury book. Beyond the tropological cohesion of a discrete suite of poems, however, what do the representative suspensions of "A Cold Spring" finally signify? Self-inscriptive, spatiotemporal, and imagistic suspensions—and also, for that matter, the subjective, syntactical, grammatical, and attentive ways of suspending we have begun to see: what does the pattern of suspension in *A Cold Spring* really mean? Such questions are predictable, given that critical readers are long accustomed to treating gaps and silences in texts—suspensions, whether marked as such or not—as sites of repressed psychic content or unconscious ideology.[20] Even bearing in mind important challenges to suspicious critique and strong theory, the question of what the suspensions of "A Cold Spring" finally signify would seem to border on the imperative, if only because suspension is written all over, rather than hidden beneath, the surface of *A Cold Spring*.[21]

There are three interpretive models one can most readily adopt to make sense of Bishop's poetics of suspension. These models pertain to the histories of a movement-period (modernism), a geopolitical conflict (the cold war), and a genre (lyric). They may be called, respectively, 1. the *late modernist allegory*, an exponent of the discourse of modified modernisms that seeks signs of modernism's declension, self-elegy, or self-willed extension in works of and after the Second World War; 2. the *cold war referential index*, which decrypts writers' engagements, complicit or subversive, with the rhetorical and political obliquities of the cold war—obliquities instantiated in the very phrase *cold war*; and 3. the *lyric circumference*, wherein a poem's or poet's or poetics' consent to or contestation of "lyric as poetic norm" (M. H. Abrams, 1953) certifies its or her significance.

It could go without saying that *late modernist allegory, cold war referential index*, and *lyric circumference* all have value. What certainly needs stating, however, is that when it comes to the suspensions that characterize Bishop's midcentury suite, each model would run into the limits perhaps not of critique per se, but of critical prescription. "Applied" to "A Cold Spring" and the volume it names, these models by now function more like templates for confirming movement, geopolitical, or genre historiographies and meanings already in place than they do as heuristic tools for discovering the historicity folded into the tropological coherence and formal dexterity of the poems themselves; they provide definitive molds into which to pour Bishop's poems of the diffuse midcentury present. By way of demonstration, and to prepare the ground for a historically synchronic, discursively situated account of the suspensions of *A Cold Spring*, let me offer brief schematic renderings of how *late modernist allegory, cold war referential index*, and *lyric circumference* would handle the suspensions of Bishop's midcentury keynote poem.

- *Late modernist allegory.* "A Cold Spring" depicts modernist subsidence: after self-theorizing revolutionary "heave," self-reflective deferral. The poem takes belated modernist Hopkins as its stated antecedent and high modernist Eliot of "The Waste Land" as its implied one, recasting the superlative cruelty of April as a hesitant but ultimately benevolent spring, replacing devastated urban space with increasingly verdant farm, answering alienated continental subject of the first postwar with complacent American scene of the second, and so forth, right down to the Whitmanian lilacs that bloom in both poems. Bishop's season of suspension finally amounts to a belated, lower-key, and knowingly "flawed" flowering of the modernism it must elegize and elongate. The theorization of sequentially later modernisms provides a new means of confirming a point argued by several Bishop critics since well before the new modernist turn, namely, that Bishop was a "post"-modernist poet by virtue of more than her lived age.[22]

- *Cold war referential index.* Given even the general association of the early cold war with anxiety and suspense, this index might be more likely than *late modernist allegory* to pick up on the held-still air of "A Cold Spring." To read the poem as a coded undermining of U.S. cold war rhetoric might be to emphasize the titular adjective (why not "late?") and would certainly be to emphasize the otherwise off-key, ominous diction—suggestive of a nuclear bomb ("One day, in a *chill white blast* of sunshine") and military-intelligence spy work ("Greenish-white dogwood *infiltrated* the wood")—that intrudes on the peaceful if in this light eerily unpeopled landscape of "A Cold Spring" (*PPL* 43, my emphases).[23] According to this index, the absence of the lyric *I* suggests the eye of the surveillance state looming over one woman writing to another, the barely coded "friend in Maryland." If, like the calf born in the first stanza, these women seem "inclined to feel gay," then the outward quietism of "A Cold Spring" masks the poem's subversive counterobservation of the incursions of U.S. cold war policy, foreign and domestic, on sexualities deemed treacherous.[24]

- *Lyric circumference.* My examples of *late modernist allegory* and *cold war referential index* readings demonstrate how those interpretive machines would likely run on "A Cold Spring." But an exemplary reading of the poem according to the *lyric circumference* exists in the scholarship. In an extended *ut pictura poesis* analysis of Bishop's engagement with modern art, Peggy Samuels ranks suspension, which she construes in mostly perspectival terms, among several "seemingly quirky pictorial strategies" Bishop began to adapt for lyric in the late 1930s and the 1940s from the work of modern visual artists.[25] Samuels posits "A Cold Spring" as a poetic analogue of Alexander Calder's hanging mobiles, which create their observer's "place in the 'field' without the observer's having given rise to the motions" of the mobile.[26] In Samuels's *lyric circumference* reading, the poem naturally turns the art "observer" into its own "speaker" and "orients the lyric speaker as a heavier and more stable element within the curving, ascending, . . . descending, and shifting relations of shapes and motions of the landscape."[27]

What Samuels's inventive reading neglects—even must, by its own terms, neglect—is that "A Cold Spring" neither clearly projects a lyric "speaker" nor ever "speaks" an *I*. Instead, addresses to a second person frame the poem: the opening dedication to "a friend" and the closing lines in which "your shadowy pastures will be able to offer / these particular glowing tributes," the suspended fireflies, "every evening now throughout the summer" (*PPL* 44). These addresses install someone other than the presumed "speaker" as the owner, so to speak, first of the gift of the poem and later of the real property the poem describes. The second-person frame defies the subjective coherence a *lyric circumference* reading imputes to the lyric *I*, even in the absence of that *I*. The "speaker" of "A Cold Spring" is not a "heavier or more stable" center of subjective gravity in it. Rather, the poem itself is suspended, multiply, in the present it inhabits.

None of this is to deny the validity of claims about Bishop's work, or about other midcentury texts, that these established programs of interpretation underwrite. It is more simply to observe that even if readings under the banners of *late modernist allegory, cold war referentiality index*, or *lyric circumference* were to address the manifold suspensions that organize *A Cold Spring*, these interpretive models may not be equipped to accommodate the very characteristics of suspension—among them, uncertainty, inconclusiveness, irresolution, fascination, absorption—that contribute to its conceptual-theoretical value generally and constitute its specific aptness for a period that routinely articulated itself in terms of its own epochal and historical middleness. The templates I've outlined would or do already measure the import of Bishop's season of suspension in relation to modernism, as refraction of cold war obfuscation, or in deference to lyric. Prereconciled to these imperatives, the sense of suspension manifest in "A Cold Spring" and the volume it names slips out of view—as, on a larger scale, does the critical capacity of suspension, at midcentury and now, to pause progressive period logics and to loosen the grip that historical, political, or genre teleologies have on midcentury literatures. Consider, to this last point, the ease with which Samuels finds that to the extent they speak to "broader trajectories in literary history, [Bishop's] interart relations unveil a particularly illuminating strand in the multiple transitions between modernism and postmodernism."[28] Or, for another counterexample, consider that despite their historically fraught geography and registers of British imperial decline, Bishop's two great atmospheric North Atlantic poems of the late 1940s, "At the Fishhouses" and "Cape Breton," like "A Cold Spring," still evade the *cold war referential index*.[29]

Contra both the generative irresolution of suspension itself and the specific utility and dexterity of suspension as a periodic self-concept at midcentury, our critical tendency is to resolve the trope through which Bishop figured her midcentury contemporaneity into the disciplinary logics of our own posterity. So let me rephrase the inevitable question. Rather than "what do the suspensions of *A Cold Spring* finally signify?" I ask instead and in keeping with the unfixity of suspension itself: what did the suspensions of *A Cold Spring* provisionally signify as Bishop worked on the volume between 1946 and 1954? How did her poetics of suspension emerge, develop, and structure her imagination of a midcentury present constantly marked in contemporaneous literary, intellectual, and public discourse as "historical?"

How might attending to some of the discursive conditions, aesthetic categories, and professional contingencies that bore on Bishop's midcentury work in turn help to loosen the interpretive hold that a relatively static set of period, genre, movement, and affinity categories exerts not only over her work in particular but over the literary midcentury?

To take up these questions, I turn next to the trio of historically inflected and thus, by Bishop's own standards and those of midcentury discourse alike, more "serious" poems she wrote and first published in the *New Yorker* and *Partisan Review* in the late 1940s. As "At the Fishhouses" finds the suspension trope, it also moves Bishop's poetics into new epistemological and historical territory. "Over 2,000 Illustrations and a Complete Concordance" and "Cape Breton" in turn tie suspensions of various kinds to the midcentury historical present as it was consolidated in the discursive culture in which these poems were imbricated and by which they were informed. To resituate this trio of poems in their *midcentury* discursive habitat is to discover how they remake the lyric subject speaking in a timeless present as a historical subject suspended at midcentury—even to the point where, in the deep time and encroaching historical present of "Cape Breton," there is barely a grammatical trace of a subject at all. There are only presence and perception, a dispersed subjectivity enabled and characterized by suspension and marked as historical. This trio of classic Bishop poems makes a timely meditation on the discursive historicity of the midcentury present.

HISTORICAL MIRROR

The composition and initial publication of "At the Fishhouses," the first entirely new poem Bishop wrote after the publication of *North & South*, synchronized precisely with her arrival as a professional poet. Bishop began making notes toward the poem, which she envisioned titling "Geographical Mirror," in July 1946, right when Houghton Mifflin was distributing advance copies of *North & South* for review in the United States.[30] She worked on "At the Fishhouses" for the next seven months and sent the completed poem to the *New Yorker* on February 13, 1947. A watershed poem in Bishop's career, "At the Fishhouses" recapitulates the "modest" descriptive poetics for which Bishop was being roundly celebrated while she worked on it, before gradually moving to an abstract meditation on "what we imagine knowledge to be." Suspension facilitates this shift: it first enables the poem's redirection and recalibration of its attention, then character-izes the form and substance of its concluding, though hardly conclusive, epistemological-historical vision.

"At the Fishhouses" begins in an anecdotal key and an interstitial time: "Although it is a cold evening, / down by one of the fishhouses / an old man sits netting" (*PPL* 50). Throughout its long first stanza, this poem about diur-nal and industrial ebb at a dilapidated Nova Scotia harbor treads ground familiar from *North & South*. The methodical description of place recalls the scenic evocation of "Florida"; the anecdotal occasion recalls "The Fish"—so much so that Robert Lowell more or less equated "At the Fishhouses" with the latter.[31] As the opening movement of "At the Fishhouses" logs details of messiness and wear, it acknowledges its own worn-in quality. Irregular tetrameter and pentameter lines make up most of the first stanza, and create a jagged—or, for a shoreline stanza, a fittingly wavy—edge running down the page. Toward the end of the first stanza, however, lines begin to hover closer and closer to iambic pentameter. As it returns to the old man, kin to Words-worth's leech-gatherer, the stanza draws itself to a comparatively neat close:[32]

> He has scraped the scales, the principal beauty,
> from unnumbered fish with that black old knife,
> the blade of which is almost worn away.
> (*PPL* 51)

The first stanza concludes with the poem's single line of perfect iambic pen-tameter, the rhythmic drift to a kind of metrical perfection audibly echo-ing the line's pat semantic summary of the theme of dilapidation and long use.[33]

If "At the Fishhouses" ended with the "almost worn away" blade, it would be a prototypical early Bishop poem. That is no mean thing. But "At the Fishhouses" resolves in its middle stanza to exceed the tidy conclusion of its first. Wedged between two stanzas each over twice its length, the mid-dle stanza, a sestet, looks on the page like a hinge and works in the poem as one.[34] Coterminous with one long sentence, the short middle stanza reads:

> Down at the water's edge, at the place
> where they haul up the boats, up the long ramp
> descending into the water, thin silver

tree trunks are laid horizontally
across the gray stones, down and down
at intervals of four or five feet.
(*PPL* 51)

The sestet's dilation of description and syntax holds the attention of the poem in suspension, pausing it just at "the water's edge." The grammatical subject ("tree trunks") appears only at the beginning of the stanza's fourth line, and takes no action when it does. Neither the poem nor the sentence nor the grammatical subject makes clear progress toward an end in the middle stanza. But neither poem nor sentence nor subject is precisely static either: though fixed in place themselves, the "tree trunks" enable movement between elements; and the sentence's vertiginous assemblage of positioning words—"down," "at," "haul up," "up the long ramp," "horizontally," "across," "down and down," "intervals," "four or five feet"—both matches its syntactical suspension and amplifies its sense of movement.[35] In its middle stanza "At the Fishhouses" hovers between air and water, land and sea, surface and depth; somewhere in its middle stanza, the poem also resolves, without quite stating its resolution, to push past its internal "edge."

It takes a few tries. The third stanza opens by trying to describe the water: "Cold dark deep and absolutely clear, / element bearable to no mortal, / to fish and to seals . . ." But it gets distracted by a seal, totemic and funny: "One seal particularly / I have seen here evening after evening. / He was curious about me. He was interested in music; / like me a believer in total immersion" (*PPL* 51). Implied but unpronounced until this point in the poem, the *I* enunciates itself here. Yet this is a self-canceling self-announcement: the *I* emerges not to speak in its own lyric voice, but rather to see the seal and sing received words to "him:" "I used to sing him Baptist hymns. / I also sang 'A Mighty Fortress Is Our God.'" (Homonymic play on another pronoun, "him"/"hymn," further undoes the would-be coherence of this *I*, as does a quick joke: the *I* is "a believer in total immersion," but neither *I* nor the seal is immersed in the water, as the "Baptist" note of their exchange would hint.) After ten lines about the seal, the stanza resets itself by reiterating the alliterative, adjectival description of the water. A corollary to the seal who "would disappear, then suddenly emerge / almost in the same spot, with a sort of shrug," this second attempt to conjure the water repeats the first one, only to cede again to the shrug of ellipses: "Cold dark deep and absolutely clear, / the clear gray icy water . . ." From its second attempt to look at the water, the stanza again retreats, this time to a space "Back, behind us" where "the dignified tall firs begin" (*PPL* 52).

It takes a line that begins with the word *waiting* and ends with the word *suspended*—a line framed on either side by suspension and paused with a period and sentence break at its middle—finally to impel the poem to start looking intently at the water. The framing of this line was hard-fought in the composition of the poem. A description of fir trees as Christmas trees in waiting was among the earliest images Bishop jotted down in her note-book in the summer of 1946. ("I know how they feel," she wrote there—an empathetic relation that would not make its way into the poem.) The "wait-ing" firs did not appear in "At the Fishhouses" until what appears to be the penultimate typescript draft, where "waiting," held over a line break, coun-terpoints "suspended" at the far edge of the line.[36] The ensuing passage is the crux of the poem; it begins with the fir trees

> waiting for Christmas. The water seems suspended
> above the rounded gray and blue-gray stones.
> I have seen it over and over, the same sea, the same,
> slightly, indifferently swinging above the stones,
> icily free above the stones,
> above the stones and then the world.
>
> (*PPL* 52)

The sibilance of the stressed phrase "seems suspended" sounds across the next five lines and over a sentence stop, as the stanza's rhythm speeds up and its view scales up. Repeated incantatory prepositions ("above," "above," "above") and sequential, almost causal syntax ("and then") move the poem from "sea" to "stones" to "world," creating a metonymic chain that turns the seeming suspension of the water—"slightly, indifferently swinging"—into both a figure for and a way of looking at "the world." The poem was looking at "water" that "seems suspended" "and then," as if of a sudden, is looking at "the world." The amplitude of this moment almost obscures its refusal of the paradigmatic instance of narcissism, lyric or otherwise. Looking at the sea, the *I* does not see its own face reflected, as the original title of the poem promised and its Romantic allusions might portend. The *I* rather sees the stones, the sea itself, and "the world." As the poem revises the self-reflective paradigm, it reconfigures the conceit of the lyric subject speaking as, or at least also as, a historical subject in "the world." From this point on, the poem suspends entirely the pronominal signature of lyric.

But this *I* was already more citational than original, more recitative than self-expressive. It is on this ground—as an extension of the poem's citational practice—that one can hear a timely trace of Bishop's initial critical reception in the poem's timeless moment of looking. Recall that Bishop's work on "At the Fishhouses" between July 1946 and February 1947 coincided with the appearance of the first reviews of *North & South*. Of these, the most important was Randall Jarrell's. In a group review, Jarrell hinted that he had saved the best for last: "The best poems in Elizabeth Bishop's *North and South* are so good that it takes a geological event like [William Carlos Williams's] *Paterson [I]* to overshadow them." Later:

In her best work restraint, calm, and proportion are implicit in every detail of metre or organization and workmanship; instead of crying, with justice, "This is a world in which you can't get along," Miss Bishop's poems show that it is barely but perfectly possible—has been, that is, for her. Her work is unusually personal and honest in its wit, perception, and sensitivity—and in its restrictions too; all her poems have written underneath, *I have seen it.*[37]

At Bishop's suggestion to Houghton Mifflin, Jarrell's distillation of her poems' claim would come to grace the dust jacket of the first edition of *Poems: North & South—A Cold Spring*; it has since become one the most quoted remarks in the Bishop criticism.[38]

Bishop herself was the first to quote it, in "At the Fishhouses." If the first stanza of the poem repeats the "calm" and "proportionate" poetics for which critics praised *North & South*, then this would-be *North & South* poem also has "I have seen it" written visually "underneath" it on the page. "I have seen it, over and over, the same sea, the same": the poet here acknowledges the pattern of her work, even as she tries to remake it and thus to surpass the very "restrictions" Jarrell values.[39] "At the Fishhouses" nods to the reception of *North & South*—and at precisely the moment when the poem cedes even its tenuous inscription of a discrete lyric subject, starts looking intently at the water, and begins a final movement toward history and knowledge that was, at this early point in her career, uncharacteristically heightened for "restrained" Bishop.

Suspension enables and suffuses this turn. In the poem's final movement, the examination of the water proceeds methodically through various ways of looking at, or seeking knowledge of, the water and water-as-world. Inhabiting a fascinated concentration, the poem moves in its ending from empirical observation of how the water "seems" to second-person warnings about a sensory experience of it: the pain that touching ("If you should dip your hand in") or tasting ("If you tasted it") the icy water would cause. As if heeding its own warnings, the poem moves next to analogical extrapolation, turning the water into a liquid approximation of knowledge. One of the most discussed passages in Bishop's work, the concluding sentence of "At the Fishhouses" reads:

> It is like what we imagine knowledge to be:
> dark, salt, clear, moving, utterly free,
> drawn from the cold hard mouth
> of the world, derived from the rocky breasts
> forever, flowing and drawn, and since
> our knowledge is historical, flowing, and flown.
> (*PPL* 52)

Like the end of the first stanza, these lines achieve an audible conclusion. Here, however, the aura of conclusion arises not from the surfacing of iambic pentameter, but rather from the sudden adoption of an authoritative, collective "we"/"our" and a profusion of aural effects sounded over several subordinate clauses and distributed over five lines. The triple rhyme of "we," "be," and "free"; hard-stress adjectival phrases ("dark, salt, clear," "cold hard"); causal and additive syntax ("and," "and since"); and the quick repetition and reconfiguration of words ("flowing," "flown") and of sounds (*f, w, d/dr*): these combine to resounding effect.

Resounding, but difficult to parse. The resplendency of this concluding sentence invites philosophical-epistemological gloss (of the poem's grasp of the historical contingency of all knowledge, for example) or psychoanalytic-biographical reading (of the poet's lost mother, conjured in the broken blazon of "cold hard mouth" and "rocky breasts").[40] Making sense of the sentence itself is another matter. Suspensions organize it. First, the sentence broaches "knowledge" through a simile that, as James Longenbach notes, already cautions that it is "provisional—doubly so": the water is "*like* what we *imagine* knowledge to be."[41] Next, the sentence revises the poem's intermittent refrain of descriptive adjectives and, roughly replicating the poem's own effort to forge a liquid description and an epistemological emblem, links water as approximate figure for knowledge to effort ("drawn") and extraction ("derived") from a geological-maternal source. Next, a conjunctive phrase, "and since," at once extends the rhetorical and imagistic energies of the last sentence of "At the Fishhouses" and belies a cluster of irresolvable elisions in the poem's final two lines. At the level of grammar, "flowing" is the gerundive form of the verb *to flow*; "flown" is the past participle of the verb *to fly*.[42] Flagged if not audibly paused by an Oxford comma ("flowing, and flown"), this quick pair of *flow*s reflects the fluid movement between material description and figurative likeness, empirical observation and imagination, that "At the Fishhouses" effects at its close. For this grammatical slide chimes with the suspension that characterizes the poem's concluding, not conclusive, claim about knowledge: "what we imagine knowledge to be" is neither static nor fixed but rather "flowing" (fluid, earthbound) and "flown" (aloft, airborne); it is "forever" (timeless) and "historical" (temporal). "What we imagine knowledge to be" amounts to a redoubled suspension.

There still remains the strange epistemological pivot at the end of "At the Fishhouses," where the poem suddenly invokes as given the "historical" condition of "our knowledge." Even as the comparatively inconspicuous conjunctive phrase "and since" pushes the poem's lofty final sentence over one last line break, it also, ever so briefly, promises a temporal measure that will chime with "forever" at the start of the line. Instead, the enjambment of "and since / our knowledge" shifts "since" from its temporal to its causal usage, allows for interpolation of a deductive premise, and asserts the "historical" condition of knowledge. Just at the end of a basically inductive poem, a received principle asserts itself. Yet the rhetorical swell of the conclusion all but washes over the oddity of the poem's late shift in register and its reach for a prefabricated idea.

Attention to Bishop's drafts helps to slow the "hypnotically eloquent" end of the poem enough to discern what is at stake in its late turn to the pronouncedly "historical."[43] The turn itself was a late discovery. Early drafts have in place the "rocky breasts" and, in various forms, the final reverberations of "flowing," "drawn," and "flown." But it took Bishop quite a while to figure out how to get from the geological-maternal image to the internal

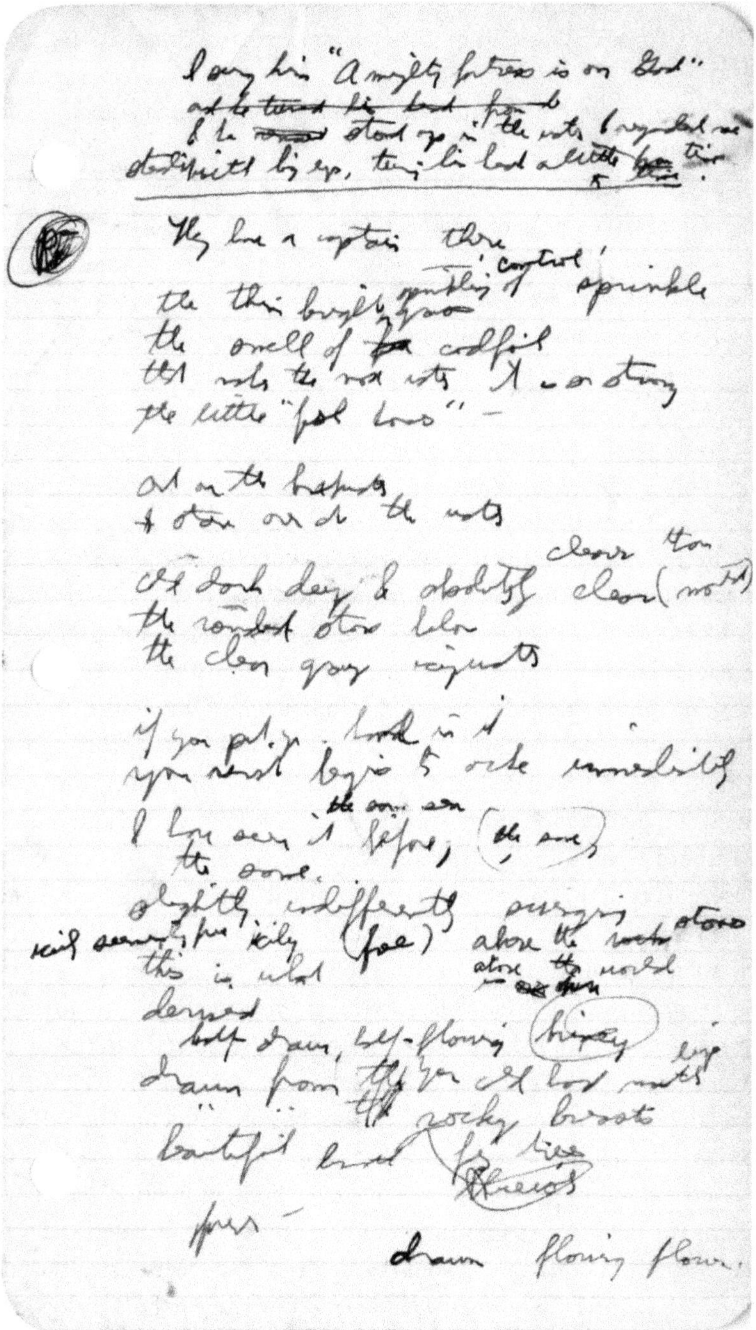

FIGURE 1.1 Elizabeth Bihop's first full autograph draft of "At the Fishhouses." The word *beautiful* modifies "fir trees" here and "knowledge" in subsequent autograph drafts. In Bishop's first typescript of "At the Fishhouses," *historical* replaces *beautiful*. Elizabeth Bishop Papers, Archives and Special Collections Library, Vassar College Libraries.

echoing pattern with which the poem concludes. In the first autograph draft
of the poem, Bishop tried:

drawn from the cold hard mouth [^*lips*] /
"   " the rocky breasts
beautiful [*illegible word*] fir trees
        [*illegible word, with arrow to insert*
        before "rocky"]
forever—

            drawn   flowing   flown.[44]

The "fir trees" would move to wait for Christmas. The word *beautiful*, which
records something more like a Romantic, aesthetic response to this scene,
would drop out of the poem entirely. As late as the last autograph draft,
there is still no bridge from "rocky breasts" to, as the final line reads in this
iteration, "forever flowing, drawn, flowing, flown." Only in the first typescript does the word *historical* finally arrive, replacing *beautiful* and supplying the poem's sole deductive premise. Put schematically, the poem's
conclusion evolved in composition and revision (always one and the same
for Bishop) away from aesthetic and toward historical experience.

The effects of this late shift to the "historical" are many. Two are crucial
in the present context. First, the turn caps the poem's recalibration of the
lyric subject, or its dispersal of that subject into the historical present the
poem evokes; second, Bishop's late arrival at "historical" gestures to the discursive historicity of the late 1940s. As for the first effect: from the vantage
of the end of "At the Fishhouses," it becomes clear that the lyric *I*, never
especially robust in the poem in any case, has retreated in stages. Having
announced itself in the poem only in relation to others (the old man who
"was a friend of *my* grandfather's," the seal who likes hymns), the *I* effaces
itself as the poem looks into the would-be mirror of the water and warns
"you" about the bodily pain it would cause. The *I* disappears just as the poem
claims for a simile ("like what we imagine knowledge to be") the detached
authority of the first-person plural pronouns that frame only the final sentence and bolster the invocation of the "historical" condition of "our knowledge." A poem Bishop originally envisioned as "Geographical Mirror" has
gradually revealed itself as a historical reflection. The poem's watery figure

for "what we imagine knowledge to be" reflects not simply a timeless lyric subject or the poet herself. It reveals a historical subject aware of her own suspension in the present, paying rapt attention to a sea that does not reflect her alone, and looking outward to describe "the world."

Second, as distinct from more general accounts of Bishop's career-long "meditating on the lability of historical understanding" or of "the vital role of history" in her poetics, the late turn to the "historical" in "At the Fishhouses" resonates with the self-consciously "historical" feeling of midcentury contemporaneity and inflection on midcentury discourse.[45] That is, suspensions within the poem engender a premise that, while tonally and epistemologically out of step with the rest of "At the Fishhouses" and with most of Bishop's work to 1947, lines up with the self-reflexively historical tenor of a range of intellectual, literary, and public discourse of the midcentury. My point is not that no one had ever observed that "our knowledge is historical" before 1947, of course. It is rather that *everyone* seemed to be observing as much in the late 1940s, even as the utility and promise of historical knowledge was up for constant debate. Indeed, the *New Yorker's* quick acceptance of "At the Fishhouses" can be taken as a local instance of just how accustomed such appeals to history and the "historical" present had become. It may be doubly telling in this vein that the famously sticklerish magazine had "scores of punctuation queries on the Fish Houses poem," but none about its grammatically dubious, epistemologically timely, and enduringly incoherent (in the best sense) conclusion. The *New Yorker* simply accepted the poem with its concluding suspension, its refusal to resolve itself.[46]

SERIOUS POEMS OF THE HISTORICAL PRESENT

Like Bishop herself, the *New Yorker* was striving for "more serious" writing in the late 1940s, a moment at which "serious"—always a slippery aesthetic category—often meant explicitly historical or historically-minded. For her part, Bishop's routine pursuit of "more serious," somehow heftier work would become a career-long pattern, albeit with shifting measures of seriousness. Around the publication of *North & South* specifically, her doubts about her work and how it would be perceived centered on her book's apparent detachment from the Second World War—from history—and prompted her to request that Houghton Mifflin add an equivocal note to the copyright page: "Most of these poems were written, or partly written, before 1942."[47] Signing a first-reading agreement with the *New Yorker* after the publication of *North & South* did not allay Bishop's concern about the seriousness of her work. The agreement looked more like a step away from seriousness and its accompanying prestige, especially because to that early point in her career, Bishop had published more work in the avowedly modernist, inarguably more prestigious, and, certainly by its own lights, "more serious" *Partisan Review* than anywhere else.[48]

Critics on the left, and especially in the New York intellectual orbit of *Partisan Review,* had for years maintained that the *New Yorker*'s aesthetic had served its upper-middle-class, consumer-capitalist complacency from the start. After the war, the *New Yorker*'s conspicuous effort to print more serious and historically minded work—an effort for which John Hersey's "Hiroshima" (August 31, 1946) stood as prose metonym—provoked only more, and more pointed, scorn in the pages of *Partisan* and from critics associated with it. Most famously, in a November 1946 letter to Dwight Macdonald's *politics,* Mary McCarthy rebuked "the Hiroshima 'New Yorker'" not simply for turning the U.S.'s atomic bombing into a human interest story, but for taking what "appeared to us all as a kind of hole in human history" and "fill[ing it] with busy little Japanese Methodists; [Hersey] has made it familiar and safe, and so, in the final sense, boring."[49] Far lesser outrages merited frequent comment: in the late 1940s and early 1950s, editors of and contributors to *Partisan Review* routinely picked the low-hanging fruit of the *New Yorker,* implicitly championing the modernist, "serious" *Partisan* intellectual against the mainstream Eustace Tilly, mascot of the *New Yorker,* whom they designated "amusing," and dangerously so. Tilly's upturned nose and gaze through a monocle symbolized to the *Partisan* circle nothing so much as the *New Yorker*'s historical and political myopia. *Partisan* was not exactly wrong, but its routine excoriation of the postwar *New Yorker* also provided it with something against which to define its own politics, which by the late 1940s had begun their drift toward (and ultimately far to the right of) the "vital center."[50]

Bishop and her *New Yorker* editor Katharine White knew the middling reputation of the magazine and its poetry all too well, and not simply as the consensus opinion of the intellectual left. In the September-October 1946 number of *Partisan Review,* for example, Jarrell's review of *North & South* followed directly on *Partisan* editor William Barrett's review of an academic study of little magazines. Barrett took the review as an opportunity to enumerate "poisons" developed in the 1920s. On his ignominious list, only the *New Yorker* merited elaboration: "Hollywood, the Luce publications, the radio, Stalinism, [and] *The New Yorker* (which exploits the new and rapidly growing audience of the sophisticated middlebrow zombie)."[51] Two issues later, Robert Warshow made a scathing assessment of the crosstown rival in his review of *Wild Flag*, a collection of *New Yorker* writings by E. B. White, Katharine White's husband: "The *New Yorker* has always dealt with experience not by trying to understand it but by prescribing the attitude to be adopted toward it. This makes it possible to feel intelligent without thinking."[52] Warshow noted that although the "strong shock" of "the Second World War and the atomic bomb have forced the *New Yorker* to become 'serious,'" that new seriousness "is only a substitute for humor." In his view, the magazine remained bent on assuring its readers that "history may kill you . . . but [if] you have taken the right attitude, you will have been intelligent and humane and suitably melancholy to the end."[53] Note how *history*—as word and force, as Second World War and lived "experience"— already courses through these examples of midcentury writers' customary opposition of "serious" *Partisan Review* to "amusing" *New Yorker*. This is no quirk of my own selections from the print record. Rather, the terms of this opposition match the historical pitch of midcentury public, intellectual, and literary culture in the Anglophone North Atlantic.

The discursive texture of the late 1940s was as inescapably "historical" as that of the 1930s was urgently "political." Evidence of the midcentury's sense of its own historical freight emerges everywhere from the period's idiolect and intellectual discourse, creating a record in the print culture of a discursively generated sense of historicity. As art critic Harold Rosenberg summarized the point, unhappily, in *Commentary* in 1948, "The area which intellectuals have most recently staked out for themselves as belonging to culture *par excellence* is the common *historical* experience. . . . To be accepted by the intellectual mass, experience must come wrapped in a time package."[54] *Midcentury* was one. Yet even as writers noted, rued, and capitalized on what we might think of as the discursive historical surround of the midcentury, both the fleeting trendiness of glimpses at history and the validity of historical knowledge itself came under renewed scrutiny. Reminiscent of the earlier "postwar" of the twentieth century, the late 1940s saw a flood of reflections on the world-historical destruction wrought in what was commonly, if resignedly, called "the recent war" and on the state of peril into which the twentieth century's unremitting violence—and escalation of methods of violence—had thrown both general ideas of history and any lingering belief in history as inherently progressive. In a moment understood and frequently figured as suspended not just after but between world-historical cataclysms, the once "redemptive" promise of historical progress and the "faith" one could place in "history" were attenuated past repair. These latter terms are Reinhold Niebuhr's, from *Faith and History: A Comparison of Christian and Modern Views of History* (1949), a book found in Bishop's library, now housed at Vassar College. Niebuhr was far from alone in finding "the time ripe ... to survey both the modern and the Christian and classical ideas of man's relation to history." For "most of the explanations of contemporary catastrophe are derived from principles of interpretation which were responsible for modern man's inability to anticipate the experiences he now seeks to comprehend."[55]

It was a given that the midcentury constituted a "crisis in human history," as John Dewey (Jane's father) put it in his 1946 contribution to a high-profile *Commentary* symposium.[56] That history or historical thinking would help resolve the "crisis" was not. Sidney Hook was well on his way to anticommunist cold warriordom when, in February 1948, he offered this representative lament about the suspicion of history swirling through public discourse: "In a period when so many large predictions have proved false, it is natural that the generous hopes based upon them should also decline. . . . Sometimes, this is accompanied by a profound distrust of any historical generalizations, even of any historical knowledge sufficiently reliable to guide intelligent action."[57] While, in Britain and the U.S., popular history enjoyed something of a heyday at midcentury, intellectual debate about the coherence, utility, and shape of historical knowledge raged—notably in *Partisan Review*, which, as any number of contemporaneous and subsequent commentators attest, served in the late 1940s as a byword for "serious" literature and thought.[58]

Given the reputations for "amusement" and "seriousness" that preceded the midcentury *New Yorker* and *Partisan Review*, respectively, "At the Fishhouses," with its final symbolic quarry producing the historical suspension of "our knowledge," would have seemed better suited to the latter; Bishop's next "more serious" poem would land there. Published in *Partisan Review* in June 1948, "Over 2,000 Illustrations and a Complete Concordance" turns a vestigial anecdote about reading an old family Bible into a period-typical assessment of traditional-authoritative versus modern-experiential forms of historical knowledge production and subject formation. This timeless poem was occasioned at least as much by contemporaneous reflection on history and the question of the historical as it was by the biographical antecedents or lyric precedents more commonly emphasized in Bishop scholarship.

Aptly for a poem that perceives the historical contingency of knowledge and subjectivity, the appearance of "Over 2,000 Illustrations and a Complete Concordance" in *Partisan Review* owes in part to a contingency. Katharine White, Bishop's champion at the *New Yorker*, was out of the office for health reasons when, per the terms of her first-read contract, Bishop sent "Over 2,000 Illustrations" and "The Bight" to the *New Yorker* on April 8, 1948.[59] True to form, Bishop professed to doubt whether either poem would be "usable." She seems to have hoped "Over 2,000 Illustrations" would not.[60] The *New Yorker* took nearly a month to reject "Over 2,000 Illustrations" on the not unusual grounds that the poem was "too difficult for a general magazine." Per Bishop's request, on May 3, 1948 William Maxwell sent "Over 2,000 Illustrations" on to Philip Rahv, coeditor of *Partisan Review*.[61] Rahv accepted it quickly. The *Partisan* editors positioned "Over 2,000 Illustrations and a Complete Concordance" first in their July 1948 number, where it directly preceded Jean-Paul Sartre's "Literature in Our Time." (Sartre subsequently revised the essay and gave it the title by which it is better known: "The Situation of the Writer in 1947.")

The first part of "Literature in Our Time" compares prewar novelists' sense of historical order with "the pressure of history" as Sartre and his "committed" contemporaries were "forced by circumstances to discover" it. Sartre writes of the novelist in 1947 in existentialist terms: "Perhaps a day will come when a happy age, looking back at the past, will see in this suffering and shame one of the paths which led to peace. But we were not on the side of history already made. We were ... *situated* in such a way that every lived minute seemed to us like something irreducible."[62] Sartre's essay ranks with Adorno and Horkheimer's *Dialectic of Enlightenment*—their "declaration of enlightenment, rationality, even history itself to be mythologies"—among oft-cited distillations of the historical mood of the early postwar.[63] If Adorno, Horkheimer, and Sartre are not the intellectual company in which one typically finds Bishop, the print record of the midcentury tells a different story. It shows "Over 2,000 Illustrations" opening onto "Literature in Our Time" and Bishop investigating the insistently historical predicament of the late 1940s.

In any case, the *New Yorker* was wrong about the poem. "Over 2,000 Illustrations and a Complete Concordance" is not more "difficult" than "At the Fishhouses." It is, however, more pronounced from the start and more systematic throughout about its intention to be "serious." The first sentence of the poem borrows the aspirational adjective Bishop used constantly with respect to her own work at midcentury: "Thus should have been our travels: / serious, engravable." As if answering the call to "serious"-ness, the three stanzas of "Over 2,000 Illustrations and a Complete Concordance" roughly overlay the *strophe/antistrophe/epode* procedure of Pindaric ode with the *thesis/antithesis/synthesis* process of dialectical reasoning. This structure houses a systematic comparison of two kinds of historical knowledge and the subjectivities they require or engender.[64] More specifically, the poem counterpoints the claims of formal, disciplined, authoritative knowledge, as figured by an implied Bible and received only by "The eye" in the long first stanza (thirty-one lines), to the claims of informal, unordered, experiential knowledge, as figured by embodied, sensorially rich, and affecting memories of travel in the long second stanza (thirty-three lines). Or, to borrow Niebuhr's terms, the first two stanzas compare "Christian and Modern Views of History."

A comparatively short (ten-line) third stanza achieves something like, but not exactly, a synthesis of both in the present of the poem.

> Everything only connected by "and" and "and."
> Open the book. (The gilt rubs off the edges
> of the pages and pollinates the fingertips.)
> Open the heavy book. Why couldn't we have seen
> this old Nativity while we were at it?
> —the dark ajar, the rocks breaking with light,
> an undisturbed, unbreathing flame,
> colorless, sparkless, freely fed on straw,
> and, lulled within, a family with pets,
> —and looked and looked our infant sight away.
> (*PPL* 46)

Initiated with a self-inscriptive line, the conclusion of "Over 2,000 Illustrations" disperses any coherent, singular subject (lyric, biographical, or
otherwise) at which the poem might have arrived into its fascination with
the finally named "book." The last stanza fuses the illustrations of stanza 1
and the embodiment of stanza 2, as in the aside where gilt "pollinates the"
(not "your" or "my") "fingertips"; it directs someone to "Open the book"
(twice) and it asks two questions. Or rather, it almost asks two questions:
as the stanza animates a foundational image of Christian tradition, "this
Old Nativity," it also suspends itself syntactically somewhere between the
extension of a question already moot ("Why couldn't we . . . ?") and the
period that closes the final line of the poem. Even as the poem draws to a
close, it unlocks an imaginative aperture—"Open" and "Open" and
"—the dark ajar"; and it envisions a temporary beholding ("our infant
sight" will age) and a wished-for state of attention, in and outside of time,
in which fascinated, plural subject ("we") is indistinguishable from fascinating object of attention.[65] "I am unable to exhaust the meaning of its
concluding line," John Ashbery wrote, at once glossing and replicating the
quality of absorption that the final line and stanza effect and toward which
poem aspires.[66]

The wonder of the third stanza notwithstanding, my paraphrase could
make "Over 2,000 Illustrations and Complete Concordance" sound like a
bland exercise. It isn't. Much of the poem's enduring appeal derives from
the strategies of ambivalence and deferral by which it unsettles its basic
argumentative architecture to create, in Bonnie Costello's gloss, an "opposition between the [first] two stanzas [that] is not absolute."[67] It is not simply that the disaffected list of illustrations in the first stanza gives way to
the somewhat baffled, wandering itinerary of the second. It is also that
nearly every element of the first stanza—words, syntactical structures, stereotypical or schematic "illustrations"—gets repurposed in the second. Thus
the two stanzas effect an internal "concordance" that already records the
incompleteness of either Bible or travel, illustrative archetype or immer-
sive experience, as epistemological grounds or as grounds for the world
order ("our Christian Empire") that the implied Bible has been made to
justify and the implicitly white travelers of the second stanza to inherit.

For just one fresh example of this ambivalent-concordant procedure,
the end of the second stanza answers the adjectives in the poem's

self-admonishing first sentence: "serious, engravable." As many readers have observed, the final tourist site on stanza 2's itinerary literalizes the deadening quality audible in "engravable": "It was somewhere near" Marrakesh that "I saw what frightened me most of all: / A holy grave, not looking particularly holy" (*PPL* 45). But "serious" also meets its midcentury match in the second stanza, with an adjective that picks up on Bishop's internalized aesthetic-historical vocabulary of the late 1940s: "In a smart burnoose, Khadour looked on *amused*" (my emphasis). This line renders rather silly both the "frightened" *I* and the poem's opening injunction to "serious"-ness. It also envisions "Khadour," apparently a local Moroccan tour guide and the only person named in the poem, as a tacitly raced inversion of the *New Yorker* and its readers in caricature.

Rahv and *Partisan Review* readers might well have heard resonances between Sartre's existential account of the writer "not on the side of history already made" and Bishop's depiction, especially in the first stanza of "Over 2,000 Illustrations and a Complete Concordance," of a failed return to the Bible as authoritative source of knowledge or faith. The poem's deflation of academic norms and disciplines tasked with explaining the historical past would also have delighted the *Partisan* circle, which in 1948 still "saw its role as preserving" an intellectual and cultural sphere outside of academe.[68] Hence the historical joke of the poem's title, which cites not the "Family Bible" revisited "after 20 yrs"/"20 yrs. later," as the first draft of the poem had it, but rather a pseudo-scholarly apparatus rendered in commercial ad-speak.[69] Ironically elevating secondary organization over primary source, scholarly "concordance" over divine Word, Bishop's titular revision elevates the poem's discursive occasion at the expense of its material-textual or biographical-familial ones. In a similar spirit, toward the end of its catalog of ekphrastic captions for schematic and stereotypical illustrations— "The Seven Wonders of the world are tired / and a touch familiar"; "Often the squatting Arab, / or group of Arabs, plotting, probably, against our Christian Empire"—the first stanza names those academic fields whose "vast and obvious" schema obscure the small and idiosyncratic scale of "the human figure / far gone in *history* or *theology*, / gone with its camel or its faithful horse" (*PPL* 44, my emphases).

Thus to reposition "Over 2,000 Illustrations and a Complete Concordance" in *Partisan Review* and, more broadly, amid the midcentury's emphatically historical discourse is not to suggest that the poem can be reduced to fashionable existentialist premise or emergent liberal consensus. It is rather, in the first place, to foreground the discursively *midcentury* character of the poem's basic comparative-historical project and, in the second, to discern how a pattern of suspension affords the poem its critical vantage on the historical discourse that occasioned and informed it. I have alluded to some of the strategies of deferral and ambivalence, of incomplete concordance, that shape "Over 2,000 Illustrations." It would risk cuteness to gather these under the heading of "suspension," except that the poem already does.

Suspension facilitates and, in one key turn of phrase, names the poem's timely critical perception of dominant forms of historical knowledge production. Organized around the perception of things "suspended," a sentence fragment caps the first stanza's list of captions for generic illustrations:

> Always the silence, the gesture, the specks of birds
> suspended on invisible threads above the Site,
> or the smoke rising solemnly, pulled by threads.
> (*PPL* 44)

Wrapping the illustrations enumerated thus far in a whispery sibilance, the fragment summarizes the first stanza and turns the poem toward the second. It reiterates the formulaic quality of the illustrations glimpsed thus far, a quality visible equally in background details prefaced by the definite article ("the silence, the gesture, the specks of birds" and "the smoke") and, supremely generic, in "the Site." (Bishop wrote in the capital "S" above "site" in the first autograph draft of the poem.)[70] Perfectly ambivalent, "Always" both records the repetitive visual schema of these images and undermines their claim to timeless truth. This fragment in which everything is seen to be "suspended," not as if suspended, shifts the first stanza away from its catalog of "illustrations" and toward grasping the limits of such archetypal images as bases for knowledge, much less for the self-justifying power of "our Christian Empire." The perception of a certain puppeteer staginess ("pulled by threads") suspends any lingering belief in the knowledge regime that, the poem perceives, consolidates itself in and by these "Over 2,000 Illustrations." In whatever print configuration, the first stanza realizes of the prefab images that "when dwelt upon, they all resolve themselves" (*PPL* 45).

Therein lies the problem. Preresolved into a self-justifying formula in which everything seen must confirm the authority of "God's spreading fingerprint," these illustrations neither invite nor reward a subject's dwelling on them at all. Nor do these illustrations necessitate *reading*, exactly, as the first stanza's action is usually glossed, or even looking in the rapt, out-of-time sense modeled at the ending of "At the Fishhouses" and later in "Over 2,000 Illustrations and a Complete Concordance." Instead, several details of the first stanza conspire to suggest that the subject as it would be constructed—which is to say, instructed—by the implied book and its scholarly apparatus needs only to see passively the tidy meanings prescribed by the images and in turn to submit to the authority they consolidate. The heavily punctuated paratactic syntax of the first stanza's catalog of illustrations, for example, simulates the effect of paging through a book, glancing at pictures. Synesthetic references to other senses prove self-canceling, since they all point back to the primacy of receptive sight: the poem hears only the "silence" of the images; the word *touch* indicates only the "touch familiar" quality of the illustrations. Most ingenious in this vein is a homonymic pair that articulates the reduction of subjectivity to sight alone: first, the capitalized "Site"; second, after the "suspended" fragment and the self-resolving images, "The eye drops, weighted, though the lines / the burin made" (*PPL* 45). In the latter example, the grammatical subject, "The eye," supplants the would-be *I*, lyric or otherwise, before it can even name itself in the poem. This easiest of puns captures the inertness of the model of subjectivity that the illustrations—schematic representations proffered in service of a lapsed authority—seek to engender.

Gillian White argues that "Over 2,000 Illustrations" exhibits "Bishop's understanding of the power of discourse" in general, "a power that greatly complicates and exceeds our pedagogic paradigms for 'tone' and 'speaker'" in lyric. The string of captions in the poem's first stanza helps anchor White's illuminating reading—in particular the lines "Often the squatting Arab, / or group of Arabs, plotting, probably / against our Christian Empire." For White, these lines are "difficult to interpret as voice," as is customary with lyric. "The chief difficulty is in the word 'probably,' which may belong to the ostensible speaker's personal response to the pictures before her (she may be racist) and, at the same time, register an impersonal awareness of how often such scenes would depict Arabs as plotters."[71] Absent from White's array of possibilities for the position of "the ostensible speaker" is the midcentury historical one by which the poem was informed and in which it was, in 1948, imbricated. The poem works beyond the lyric circumference to engage the explicitly historical mood of its own discursive time. Its critical perception of dominant modes of historical knowledge production and subject formation points not only to discourse as opposed to lyric writ large, but to a midcentury historical discourse rife with comparisons of a past once thought to be comprehensible to a present manifestly and yet incomprehensibly "historical"—a present Bishop accesses in *A Cold Spring* by way of suspension and characterizes as suspended. "Over 2,000 Illustrations and a Complete Concordance" is not simply discursive. It achieved at midcentury a critical discursive historicity.

Masquerading as a *New Yorker* tourist poem, "Cape Breton" fuses the suspension trope of *A Cold Spring* with the historical surround of the late 1940s that we have seen irrupt into the conclusion of "At the Fishhouses" and inform "Over 2,000 Illustrations and a Complete Concordance." Without citing the "historical" or enunciating "suspension" as the earlier poems do, "Cape Breton" enacts the mutual implication of the trope and *midcentury* historicity. Entirely eschewing a single, stable vantage from which or lyric subject through whom to articulate itself, this North Atlantic seascape poem inhabits a free-floating perceptivity of a present laden with history and historical trace. As it ranges across and among the receding coastlines of Cape Breton, the large island off the northeast coast of Nova Scotia, and the small "high 'bird islands,' Ciboux and Hertford," off Cape Breton, the poem beholds a landscape characterized by suspensions and visibly inscribed by almost the entire known history of the titular island (*PPL* 48). Suspending itself in a midcentury present marked as irreducibly if ineffably historical and inhabiting suspension as a condition of its own historical perceptivity, "Cape Breton" ultimately reimagines negative capability in epochal terms. It culminates Bishop's trio of poems about and of the self-conscious historicity of the late 1940s.[72]

"Cape Breton" ranks with "A Cold Spring" as an exemplary repository of the suspension trope that organizes Bishop's midcentury book. Most germane to the poem's fusion of organizing trope and historical present are its temporal and atmospheric suspensions. Echoing gerunds and unassuming calendrical notes serve the poem's temporal suspension in an ongoing present. Triplicate gerunds gently wave in the first stanza, as "The silken water is weaving and weaving, / disappearing"; in the third, another pair arises in a synesthetic image that first hears and then quickly envisions "thousands of song-sparrow songs floating upward / freely, dispassionately, through the mist, and meshing / in brown-white, fine, torn fish-nets" (*PPL* 49). And, in the final line, a deep historical duration becomes audible in the poem's continuous—and, reaching beyond its conclusion, its continuing—gerundive present: "an *ancient* chill *is rippling* the dark brooks" (*PPL* 50, my emphasis).[73] "Cape Breton" takes place on a specific day, the day of rest. The third stanza begins with an observation and an explication: "The wild road clambers along the brink of the coast. / On it stand occasional small yellow bulldozers, / but without their drivers, because today is Sunday." The next stanza elaborates on the pause in weekday routine, and relays details the *New Yorker* fact-checked, including "the closed roadside stand, the closed schoolhouse, / where today no flag is flying" (*PPL* 50).

At two points, "Cape Breton" inserts parenthetical asides about the habitual time of the island and the incursion of modern transport technologies. The first, only five lines into the poem, interrupts the scenic view with a bathetic variation on the classical sublime encounter with cliffs. This one scares "the few sheep pastured" on the "high" bird islands: "(Sometimes, frightened by aeroplanes, they stampede / and fall over into the sea or onto the rocks.)" Later, when "A small bus comes along, in up-and-down rushes, / packed with people" at the start of the fourth stanza, the poem pauses to observe that the bus usually transports supplies and industrial parts: "(On weekdays with groceries, spare automobile parts, and pump parts, / but today only two preachers extra, one carrying his frock coat on a hanger.)" (*PPL* 50). Bracketed by parentheses, these asides at once lift the poem briefly out of its observing-descriptive present and emphasize its subjective and spatiotemporal suspension in that present. Referring to habitual time in a poem composed almost entirely of observation in the present tense, these asides thwart habitual projection of a single—or singular—lyric speaker in an exclusively lyric present.

The atmospheric emblem of the suspension of "Cape Breton" is the "mist" that hovers in four of the poem's five stanzas. Itself a manifestation of elemental suspension, airy-water or watery-air, the mist "hangs in thin layers" across the entire poem. "Cape Breton" recasts this Romantic-climatic hallmark as a geological effect. In the second stanza, the mist is "like rotting snow-ice sucked away / almost to spirit; the ghosts of glaciers drift / among those folds and folds of fir: spruce and hackmatack—" (*PPL* 49). The simile condenses the inextricability of suspension and historical duration in "Cape Breton," rendering the deep time of the island manifest in the very atmosphere of its present. Extending the mist's suspension in and of historical time, the first two stanzas both conclude with still more intrusions of modern technologies, of transport and optics, into the island's sound- and landscape as heard and evoked metaphorically through the pervasive mist. The first stanza concludes, "and somewhere the mist incorporates the pulse, / rapid but unurgent, of a motorboat." The "fir" trees seen through the mist in the second stanza appear as if arranged in rows, "each riser distinguished from the next / by an irregular nervous saw-tooth edge, / alike, but certain as a stereoscopic view" (*PPL* 49).

Throughout, "Cape Breton" interleaves traces of the long history of the island into its ongoing present.[74] The first three stanzas record the Ice Age formation of the island seascape in those "ghosts of glaciers" and the subsequent natural, pretextual history of the island in its evergreens, "deep lakes," and "miles of burnt forests standing in gray scratches / like the admirable scriptures made on stones by stones." European colonization and Christian settlement ("our Christian Empire" of "Over 2,000 Illustrations" in another form) displace indigenous people in the space of a single simile that renders churches conspicuously white and reduces Native presence to the metonym of souvenir weaponry: "The little white churches have been dropped into the matted hills / like lost quartz arrowheads" (*PPL* 49). Industrialization and modernization bring the "motorboat," the "wild road" under construction, the bus, and the "aeroplanes."

But to list the historical deposits in the present of "Cape Breton" chronologically, as I have done, runs counter to how the poem in fact works. The poem is not so orderly: it rather holds these deposits of the past equally present and perceptible in its misty view. Still, the list illuminates two key aspects of the discursive historicity of "Cape Breton." First, many of the details I've adduced point to the most obvious—which is not to say unimportant—"meaning" of "Cape Breton," namely, that it is a poem of environmental conscience in which late modern capital and industry imperil a beautiful and sublime landscape. This reading can be tied to historical discourse of the midcentury, a potent strand of which asked, after the atomic bombings, whether "civilization" could "survive technics?"[75] Second, my rough chronological ordering of historical inscriptions points up the poem's relative silence with respect to the then-recent and contemporary history of Cape Breton, that is, of the island in the 1940s.

To this latter point, the autograph drafts of "Cape Breton" document Bishop removing any direct reference to the Second World War. A single notebook page from the summer of 1947 shows Bishop beginning to work out two poems: one, charmingly titled in childlike block capitals "WHERE I SPENT THE SUMMER," would gradually become "Summer's Dream"; the other, titled "BRITON COVE," appears to be the earliest fragment of "Cape Breton." Across the bottom of the page, Bishop has drawn a line and written a note under it, in prose: "'Bird Islands'—Ciboux & Hertford. About six miles out. During the war the planes practiced dropping bombs on a rock between the two. The sheep pastured there would get frightened and often stampede in a panic & fall over the cliffs into the sea."[76] Bishop worked over the aside about the poor sheep in the many subsequent drafts of "Cape Breton." Aerial bombing practice never made it into the poem. Instead the war and "the planes [that] practiced dropping bombs," as if of their own accord, become the quaint, dated "aeroplanes" that frighten the sheep pastured on the Bird Islands.

One might propose any number of sound reasons for this erasure. But the fact of it alone only heightens the poem's comparatively pronounced performance of its own incapacity to articulate the "meaning" of the present it inhabits. At the very center, the self-inscribed "interior," of the poem, the idea of suspension—this time, in the form of an abandoned end—leaps by association, identical rhyme, and syntactical dilation from the road under construction to the landscape itself as the poem describes it. First comes a sentence coterminous with a line: "The road appears to have been abandoned." The next sentence sprawls across eleven lines, seeking a "meaning" the poem already knows it cannot find. The sentence begins:

Whatever the landscape had of meaning appears to have been abandoned,
unless the road is holding it back, in the interior
where we cannot see,
where deep lakes are reputed to be
(*PPL* 49)

In this passage, the poem's only enunciation of a first-person subject ("we") also incapacitates that subject in multiple ways: sensorially, "we cannot see";

grammatically, "we" is not the primary subject of the long sentence in syntactical pursuit of the "interior"; and aurally, the sound patterning of the lines subsumes the would-be focalizing power of "we" into the reverberation of the pronoun's long *e* across "meaning," "appears," "interior," "see," "deep," "be," and, in the local pronunciation, "been." Unlike the "our" at the end of "At the Fishhouses," "we" emerges here not to invoke some general authority. The pronoun rather expresses a shared sense that "Whatever the landscape had of meaning appears to have been abandoned."

The eschewal of obvious and recent world-historical reference in the composition of "Cape Breton" and the perceived abandonment of "meaning" meet with ready glosses in Bishop scholarship. The compositional retreat from bombing practice to "aeroplanes" is perhaps all too explicable in terms of the myth, dated but tenacious, of the poet's general reticence on specific matters of geopolitical and personal history. Similarly, the language of the impenetrable "interior" and the aura of irrevocable abandonment lend themselves to the biographical paratext.[77] In the context of Bishop's *midcentury* work, however, the orbit of "Cape Breton" around a central "meaning" intuited but inarticulable, or that once obtained but now eludes, reads as itself deeply historical and of its time. In the studious absence of a discrete lyric subject, in the lingering presence of the historical past, and amidst a reimagined Romantic atmosphere, "Cape Breton" recasts negative capability as a midcentury condition. John Keats's "Man of Achievement especially in Literature" has the heroic capacity "of being in uncertainties, mysteries, doubts, without any irritable reaching after fact and reason"; his "sense of Beauty overcomes every other consideration" or confusion.[78] "Cape Breton" beholds a beautiful and even symptomatically sublime islandscape whose "meaning" it can express only as a figure of redoubled suspension: a song the poem can hear and, through a quick sensory morphing, almost see in the air, but that it cannot decipher or sing. A passage whose "meaning trouble[d]" the *New Yorker* amounts also the last possible gasp of the landscape's "meaning" in the historical "now" of the poem:

and these regions now have little to say for themselves
except in thousands of light song-sparrow songs floating upward
freely, dispassionately, through the mist, and meshing
in brown-wet, fine, torn fish-nets.

(*PPL* 49)

Confronted with the abandonment of meanings, "Cape Breton" simultaneously floats in and perceives its own suspension. The poem effects and inhabits suspension as a felt condition of historical experience at midcentury.

I have traced an arc from "At the Fishhouses" through "Over 2,000 Illustrations and a Complete Concordance" and on to "Cape Breton," drawing all the while on choices in composition, circumstances of publication, and contours of midcentury historical discourse and print culture that help to recoup the timeliness of these enduring Bishop poems. The manifold suspensions of Bishop's midcentury book served her effort to write "more serious" poetry in the late 1940s, a moment when, in and well beyond poetry, "serious" often meant in some way "historical." Perhaps the most celebrated and certainly the most controversial works of American poetry of the late 1940s, Robert Lowell's *Lord Weary's Castle* (1946) and Ezra Pound's *Pisan Cantos* (1948), respectively, mine New England *qua* American history and purport to synthesize global history and world historical thought. But Bishop's outward-looking descriptive poems of the late 1940s go historical by other means. The poems suspend themselves in presents in which the palpable weight or "meaning" of "history" defies explication by source or system. The historicity lodged in Bishop's midcentury suspension trope remains closed to critical view, however, if we lift the poems out of the discourse of the present they navigated or assume that historicity is synonymous with topicality—recorded only in explicit objects and express statements rather than also in experiences of suspension.

Even as Bishop arrived at the trope of suspension in "At the Fishhouses," suspension itself began to characterize not only *what* her midcentury poems describe (e.g., water that "seems suspended," smoke and birds "suspended on invisible threads," lingering mist) but *how* the poems, in the near or complete absence of a discrete subject, describe and inhabit a present fraught with history. Bishop's ostensibly hesitant, modest descriptive practices have long been valued in biographical and psychological accounts of her poetics. But the suspensions perceived and created in her poems of the late 1940s are also self-consciously and critically *historical*. They foster reflections of and on a midcentury present whose historicity was of constant concern, even as, if not because, it defied "complete comprehension."

SUSPENDING GEOGRAPHY

The phrase "complete comprehension" comes from "Arrival at Santos" (*PPL* 65–66). The penultimate poem of the original *Cold Spring* suite, "Arrival at Santos" was first published in the *New Yorker* on June 21, 1952, less than a month after "A Cold Spring" appeared in the magazine. The two poems are also conceptually proximate: a poem about the perhaps inevitable letdown of getting to where one is going, "Arrival at Santos" reads as a geographically marked analogue to the seasonal-temporal delay of "A Cold Spring." Where the interstitial season never precisely arrives in Bishop's midcentury keynote poem, "Arrival at Santos" never exactly disembarks at the Brazilian port city its title names. Spoken almost entirely in the persona of an imperious Northern tourist, "Arrival at Santos" moves briskly through spaces and stages of modern arrival: from an Atlantic steamer off the coast of Brazil to a "tender" that shuttles passengers to shore, through "customs," and, in the final sentence of the poem, quickly through the titular port city without ever quite landing in it. The poem ends with another elusive "interior": "We leave Santos at once; / we are driving to the interior" (*PPL* 66). This final projection of, not arrival at, "the interior" makes a fitting conclusion to a poem organized, as Linda Anderson writes, around "the idea of something delayed or unfulfilled."[79]

Only six lines and change in, "Arrival at Santos" delays its own narrative and spatial progress: it pauses suddenly to pose a dilated apostrophic question to the "tourist" persona who otherwise speaks or thinks the poem. Already before this early interruption, the tourist's sense of superiority to her new surroundings could not be plainer. Descriptors like "impractically shaped," "self-pitying," "frivolous," "feeble," and "uncertain" pile into her opening view of Santos; and as if in self-congratulatory contrast to the scene she finds "sad" and generally wanting, the "tourist" shapes her own description of that scene into quatrains so neatly rhymed as to tip into rigidity: "scenery"/"greenery" in the first quatrain, "blue"/"you" in the second. (Later, the rhyme scheme dictates that the second *s* of the place name "Glens Falls" must itself fall over a line and stanza break so as to protect the perfect alignment of the end words *fall* and *tall* [*PPL* 65–66].)

Having quickly established the tourist's patter and pattern, "Arrival at Santos" lifts itself away from her perspective to ask her a question that will hang, unanswered and perhaps unanswerable, over the seven quatrains to follow. Begun midline and midstanza, the question reads:

> Oh, tourist,
> is this how this country is going to answer you
>
> and your immodest demands for a different world,
> and a better life, and complete comprehension
> of both at last, and immediately,
> after eighteen days of suspension?
> (*PPL* 65)

As the apostrophe moves over the second stanza break, it moves, too, from spatial-geographic (scaling up from "country" to "world") to temporal-calendrical registers ("life," "at last, and immediately," "eighteen days"). The question makes this poem about nonarrival in space into a poem that is also about time in various measures all at once, and all held in the "suspension" named and effected in this beguiling instance of lyric apostrophe.

Read within *A Cold Spring*, the neat rhyme of "comprehension" and "suspension" articulates the organizing trope and ethos of Bishop's midcentury suite. Though the words accord sonically, "suspension" otherwise undoes "comprehension," much less "complete comprehension." Where the tourist makes "immodest" and impossible "demands," the poem itself makes an inquiry; while the tourist seeks self-advancement, the poem resides in a pronounced "suspension." Unsurprisingly, then, within the progression of "Arrival at Santos," the tourist's accidental answer to the question she cannot hear is to order someone to "Finish your breakfast"—not just to eat the meal, but to complete it. But the direct answer to the rhetorical question is *yes* regardless. "This" *is* "how this country is going to answer you"—not because of a failing of "this country," but because the tourist can only see the country as a failing.

If the tourist's sense of her superiority determines her view of the inferiority of the place she beholds, and thus restricts her apprehension of that place, then "Arrival at Santos" reverses a trajectory followed several times in *A Cold Spring*. Rather than fascination with something—water, a Nativity scene, a "meaning" in the mist—subsuming or even replacing a lyric subject, in this case the tourist fascinates the poem itself.

Subsequently repositioned as the opening poem of *Questions of Travel* (1965), and thus as a geography poem that marks Bishop's fateful arrival in Brazil, "Arrival at Santos" figured in Bishop's midcentury book as a poem that holds open the promise of an experience of suspension, an experience its own rushing, overly self-certain tourist persona cannot tolerate.

Suspension, in the form of delay, marked *A Cold Spring* as Bishop worked on the suite; suspension, in the form of a perceived dependency, has marked *A Cold Spring* since it was appended to *North & South* for book publication in 1955. Bishop herself compounded the latter impression late in her career, when she titled her final book *Geography III* (1976). As John Hollander remarked in his review of it, *Geography III* retroactively subtitled Bishop's previous volumes: *North & South* and *Questions of Travel* became *Geography I* and *Geography II*, respectively.[80] Like Jarrell's claim that "all her poems have written underneath, *I have seen it*," Hollander's observation has become something of a truism for Bishop's critics and readers. The trouble with the truism is that Bishop's summary *III* elides *A Cold Spring*, whose title alone marks the suite as a misfit in the geographic sequence of her career. Bishop's retrospective tally implies a qualitative assessment of her midcentury book, counting *A Cold Spring* as *Geography 1.5*, at best. It subsumes a volume deeply engaged with, imbricated in, and critically perceptive of the self-conscious historicity of the midcentury into the much tidier retrospective history of the consummate "poet's poet's poet" (Ashbery again), now revered.

But it merits recalling that over the course of the midcentury, the younger Bishop did labor to get *A Cold Spring* to "jell" and to persuade Houghton Mifflin that it did. In an increasingly agonized correspondence with her editors there, in 1953 and 1954, Bishop lobbied for stand-alone publication of the book. Her case rested on three standards. First, *A Cold Spring* was enough, in quantitative terms: in one letter, there are "enough" poems; in others, she has "*measured* the poems" for page length. Second, Bishop had attained sufficient professional stature to warrant publication of the new suite alone. She strains to mention, as if off-handedly, some of the signs of her professional achievement, such as the inclusion of "The Prodigal" in "*Best Magazine Poems of 1952* (or was it '51), etc." Third, the book was coherent: "I think the poems form a fairly unified book as they are now."[81] Houghton Mifflin was not persuaded. To the contrary, the house grew increasingly frustrated with Bishop.[82] In finally persuading her to accede to the composite volume, Houghton Mifflin won the book and lost the poet *Poems: North & South—A Cold Spring* was awarded the Pulitzer Prize, but Bishop would move to Farrar, Straus and Giroux with *Questions of Travel* and remain there for the rest of her career.

To reconstruct the timely coherence of Bishop's midcentury book around the multivalent, historically resonant trope of suspension is not to advocate for the replacement of one career-governing trope (geography) with another (suspension). Even in a single-author study, there would be little value in such a project; there is still less in the context of the present effort to restore suspension as a principal imaginative construct by which diverse writers conceived of, reckoned with, and in some cases muddled through the manifestly "historical" midcentury present. The point, then, is that Bishop's own organizing geography obscures *A Cold Spring* not only within her singular career but also as a meditation on, and expressly suspended in, its discursively historical time. Bishop's late geographic self-curation reads as an instance of the larger pattern of midcentury erasure wherein the inchoate meanings and significances afforded to the historical middle of the century *at midcentury* got lost in or revised to meet the guiding assumptions, certainties, and orthodoxies of other, much stronger, but not-quite-synonymous historical, period, and disciplinary structures. Where this chapter has attended to Bishop's troping of the emphatically historical texture of the midcentury present in *A Cold Spring*, the next chapter asks more explicitly how midcentury suspension felt. More to the point, it digs into how very and specifically anxious midcentury historical subjects were encouraged to feel as the postwar overtook the war—and how W. H. Auden and Ralph Ellison pushed back.

Chapter Two

W. H. AUDEN, RALPH ELLISON, AND THE MIDCENTURY ANXIETY CONSENSUS

Every alert citizen of our society realizes, on the basis of his own experience as well as his observation of his fellow-men, that anxiety is a pervasive and profound phenomenon in the middle of the twentieth century. The alert citizen, we may assume, would be aware not only of the more obvious anxiety-creating situations in our day, such as the threats of war, of the uncontrolled atom bomb, and of radical political and economic upheaval; but also of the less obvious, deeper, and more personal sources of anxiety in himself as well as in his fellow-men—namely the inner confusion, psychological disorientation, and uncertainty with respect to values and acceptable standards of conduct. Hence to endeavor to "prove" the pervasiveness of anxiety in our day is as unnecessary as the proverbial carrying of coals to Newcastle.

—ROLLO MAY, *THE MEANING OF ANXIETY* (1950)

It was as though he had not died at all, his words caused so much anxiety.

—RALPH ELLISON, *INVISIBLE MAN* (1952)

If there is an affect most readily associated with suspension, it is anxiety. Anxiety names a vague unease, a diffuse fear or state of anticipation engendered by threats known or unknown. As defined as an object of study within the fields that have historically offered the most thorough accounts of it—theology, philosophy, medicine, psychology—anxiety is often contrasted to its starker cousin, fear.[1] In this schema, anxiety is a subjective state whose object can be abstract, or even absent or imaginary, but fear knows its object. Fear compels a subject's action or decision; anxiety turns the subject inward on herself, deferring her action or forestalling her decision. Fear attaches to exigencies of survival, anxiety to questions of existence. While fear determines one's present, anxiety is always anachronistic in the root sense: it works outside of and across linear time. For the principal modern theorists of anxiety—Søren Kierkegaard in the nineteenth century, Sigmund Freud and Martin Heidegger in the twentieth—anxiety experienced in one's present is future-oriented. Yet the occasions for anxiety emerge from one's past, whether that past is construed in terms of the formation of the ego or as the fundamental condition of human existence.[2] Where fear arises from and can cease with the removal of a discrete or immediate threat, anxiety presents and can persist without a clear object and across spatial bounds. It is shape-shifting, migratory, and projective.

The characteristic temporal suspension of anxiety thus works in concert with its spatial dimensions—hence Sianne Ngai's observation of the "spatial grammar and vocabulary" on which disparate accounts of anxiety tend to rely.[3] The first *Diagnostic and Statistical Manual [of] Mental Disorders* (1952), for example, identified anxiety as the "chief characteristic" of all "psychoneurotic disorders" and supplied a set of spatial metaphors— among them, depression, displacement, deflection, and avoidance—to make discrete manifestations of anxiety available for diagnosis.[4] Lacking a singular point of origin or termination, anxiety can extend itself into proximate spaces or proxy objects, suspending its subject among them. Thus the effort to locate or treat the root causes or manifest symptoms of anxiety can compound its psychic and somatic effects on the anxious person or community of persons. Anxiety can become self-referential, perpetuated by the experience of being anxious.

If there was an affect most readily associated with the midcentury *at midcentury*, it too was anxiety. To claim as much is not precisely to ratify the premise of Rollo May's best-selling book of 1950, *The Meaning of Anxiety*, namely, that anxiety was everywhere and inevitable "in our society" and "in our day." It is more precisely to observe that assertions like May's of the historic pervasiveness of anxiety certainly did pervade the midcentury, when the capacity of anxiety to self-replicate found a discursive analogue across print and public culture of the Anglophone North Atlantic. (Forms of the very word *pervade* in fact pervaded midcentury anxiety discourse.) One might describe the broad elevation of anxiety at midcentury in terms of the selective tradition—never far, in Raymond Williams's thought, from structures of feeling. As Williams first described it in *The Long Revolution* (1961), and with more than default reference to 1950s novels, the selective tradition begins to operate within a given period, when "from the whole body of activities, certain things are selected for value and emphasis." This contemporaneous selection will generally "reflect the organization of the period as a whole." But, Williams cautions, "this does not mean that the [same] values and emphases will later be confirmed."[5]

The midcentury's selection of anxiety has been amply "confirmed." The period's internal selection of anxiety for its affective self-apprehension did not lapse with the self-consciously *midcentury* discourse that, this chapter will argue, helped to foster it. Since the late 1940s and early 1950s, anxiety has remained fixed as a reference point for understanding the immediate or long postwar periods, especially but not exclusively in a U.S. frame. Whether proffered as a diagnostic or explicated as a dexterous thematic, conceived of as historical *Stimmung* or mentioned in passing as a fact of the time, anxiety operates as something like an affective baseline in study of the cold war and postwar periods.[6]

Anxiety is a given, too, in recent and more probing inquiries into the distortions of temporality and unequal distribution of security, violence, and justice sanctioned in part by such constructs as *cold war, wartime,* and *interwar*—a list on which *postwar* clearly belongs. The U.S. legal historian Mary L. Dudziak, for example, argues that the putative exceptionality of *wartime* at once belies the porousness of war's chronological, legal, military and other operational bounds and helps to authorize the indefinite suspensions of civil liberties, due process, and the rule of law characteristic of wars without end. As an "intentionally contradictory" idea and an ambiguous constellation of "small wars, surveillance, and stalemate," the cold war is a case in point for Dudziak.[7] Yet for all the cold war's compounding ambiguities, its affective dimension stays fixed as premise in her account: "The Cold War era was a time of anxiety in America."[8]

Paul K. Saint-Amour reconceives of the related marker *interwar* in phenomenological terms. One line of argument in his generative book *Tense Future: Modernism, Total War, Encyclopedic Form* (2015) concerns how, by neglecting the "traumatizing power of anticipation," the interwar framework elides the felt texture of the period it names and the literary works it dates.[9] Saint-Amour proposes instead a "perpetual interwar analysis," which "offers a general portrait of late modernity as harboring, always, three simultaneous relations to the time of armed conflict. For at every moment in the world system of late-modern injury production, conflict is recollected, ongoing, and future-conditional all at once."[10] One important effect of Saint-Amour's model is to reframe the Second World War as interruption, rather than end, of an interwar condition. Another is to reveal continuities across artworks and experiences of the periods on either side of the war thus reconceived, or to "make more visible a range of phenomena shared by the interwar and Cold War periods: the logic of deterrence, the deranging effects of geopolitical suspense, the underwriting of peace in spaces conceived as central by the persistence of war in spaces conceived as peripheral."[11] Nestled between the logical and ethical grounds for Saint-Amour's call to "transperiodize the interwar condition forward," those "deranging effects of geopolitical suspense" seem to broach an affective claim. Traumatizing anticipation or anxiety engendered by "geopolitical suspense" would seem to be a key continuity between the interwar and cold war periods.

Neither the heuristic of midcentury suspension nor the midcentury's historical attachment to its own professed anxiety quite squares with such crucial efforts to rethink war-bound twentieth-century historiography and literary periodization. For even as critical war temporalities seek to discover analogical phenomena linking the interwar and the cold war, for example, these models also risk flattening out distinctions between the affective conditioning and vocabularies of the very periods they enable us to bridge. Among these distinctions are the immediate public remaking of anxiety as a normative feeling in "the West" in the early wake of the Second World War and, as this chapter documents, the concurrent promotion of anxiety as the requisite affective condition of democratic citizenship—as opposed to the construction of anxiety as, say, a subversive or pacifist feeling. The next chapter will return to the question of postwar or cold war suspense, and find Elizabeth Bowen and Samuel Beckett giving literary shape and expression to a certain acclimation to suspense, to something more like suspension, at midcentury. For now, suffice it say that while scholars across fields bring welcome scrutiny to the conventional practice of conceiving of cultural periods by reference to ostensibly discrete wars and wartimes, anxiety remains what one can fairly call the canonical affect of the post-1945 period.

This chapter has a different story to tell about midcentury anxiety, and about the discursive and literary conditions that fostered anxiety's promotion *at midcentury* as an all-but-compulsory affect of the much longer postwar. It is an origin story of sorts. To the extent that its selections and analyses are rooted in Anglo-American literary, print, and affective-discursive culture around 1950, this story proves consequential for the more general cultural-historical narrative of postwar anxiety. At the chapter's center are two works whose composition histories not only span the imaginary line that still separates *wartime* from *postwar* (or, in narrower disciplinary terms, *modernism* from *Post45*) but which also perceived and critiqued both the initial drawing of that line and the marshaling of public anxiety to fix it in place. Not at all coincidentally, both works also rank among the signal literary events of the decade after the Second World War: W. H. Auden's final long poem, *The Age of Anxiety: A Baroque Eclogue* (1947), and Ralph Ellison's first novel, *Invisible Man* (1952).

The former, for which Auden won the Pulitzer Prize in 1948, achieved extraordinary cultural salience. Upon the poem's publication, the title phrase "the age of anxiety," popularly attributed to Auden, was swiftly and, it has since proved, indelibly taken to give a name to "an age" in sore need of one. The latter, for which Ellison won the National Book Award in 1953, was broadly hailed as one of the greatest American novels since the war and has maintained like status even as the historical span and critical capacities of *postwar* and its functional synonyms have expanded.[12] Yet despite their unusual stature in Anglo-American literary and public culture at midcentury, *The Age of Anxiety* and *Invisible Man*, Auden and Ellison, are not likely to seem, now, to have much to do with one another. In keeping with the genre traditions, categories of identity and affinity, and period frames that typically organize the study of twentieth-century literature, the preeminent English leftist poet of the 1930s still appears most often in critical conversation with interlocutors like T. S. Eliot, Christopher Isherwood, Stephen Spender, or the many younger poets he influenced or mentored, the celebrated African American novelist of the postwar with Richard Wright, James Baldwin, Kenneth Burke, or Saul Bellow.[13] And although Auden and Ellison have both ranked as patently major writers in a long modernist line since well before the new modernist turn, they remain even after that turn central figures in effectively separate modernisms.

The "affective turn" in literary studies has demonstrated the viability of such apparently disparate groupings of texts and writers. But I want to stress at the outset that my own collocation of Ellison and Auden on the question of anxiety and other felt suspensions at midcentury grew in the first place out of the print record of transatlantic periodical culture of the late 1940s and early 1950s, where excerpts from and reviews of *The Age of Anxiety* and *Invisible Man* first appeared and where Auden and Ellison were often in close proximity, if not in direct conversation.[14] The two pieces of *Invisible Man* to see print in advance of the novel, for example, saw it in periodicals that also featured writing by Auden.[15] Most significantly, in October 1947, Ellison published the first chapter of *Invisible Man* as a short story in "Art on the American *Horizon*," a special double issue of Cyril Connolly's highbrow English little magazine. The issue advanced a dim if period-typical assessment of the prospects for "serious"—as opposed to popular or mass—literature, art, and culture in the new democratic superpower. It not only carried Auden's poem "Music Is International" but was also in very real sense brought to the U.S. *by* Auden, who was by then an American citizen and who had since 1939 been Britain's most infamous literary expatriate. The issue hooked its fashionable anxiety about serious art in the U.S. to the figure of Auden and filtered its concern through the vexed question of Auden's citizenship.[16]

Anxiety and citizenship also rank as central concerns of both *The Age of Anxiety* and *Invisible Man*. Both works counterpoint a persistent and, in Auden's case, a sometimes overstated thematic anxiety—a vague fear that something bad will happen—to other equally persistent affective registers of suspension: in *The Age of Anxiety*, boredom or the creeping sense that nothing interesting will ever happen; in *Invisible Man*, the unnamed narrator's confusion about what is happening to or around him, as well as about how he should feel about it. "*I too have become acquainted with ambivalence*," the narrator remarks of his own feelings in a hallucinatory dream in the prologue (*IM* 10). While anxiety is the feeling most readily associated with suspension per se, then, these works remind us that it is not the only or inevitable one; and while anxiety was the feeling newly and powerfully associated with democratic citizenship in *midcentury* discourse, *The Age of Anxiety* and *Invisible Man* variously trouble that association. Both texts were bound up with the meaning and feeling of liberal-democratic citizenship from the earliest wartime stages of their compositions through their postwar receptions. They were also, of course, authored by writers whose sexuality, nation of origin, and celebrity qualified

(Auden) and whose race restricted (Ellison) their access to full U.S. citizenship.

The expatriate war poem that named "the age" and the African American bildungsroman of the interwar that galvanized it: taken together and read within and against the rampant anxiety discourse of their time, this unfamiliar pairing recalibrates the perhaps overfamiliar explanatory power of anxiety for literary and cultural artifacts of the midcentury and, indeed, of the longer postwar. Along with remarkable public stature at midcentury, *The Age of Anxiety* and *Invisible Man* share a *critical* affective historicity. By that I mean: these works found at midcentury, and offer now, instructive critical vantage on the narrative of "pervasive and profound" anxiety that affixed to *midcentury* discourse and continues to preponderate in accounts of the period under other names. Situating *The Age of Anxiety* and *Invisible Man* in the affective-discursive culture within which they were written, circulated, reviewed, and "selected for emphasis" around 1950, then, also means revaluing the discourse of default *midcentury* anxiety that contributed to their selection.

For Auden's long poem and Ellison's novel diverge and even dissent from what this chapter terms "the midcentury anxiety consensus." The echo of the "liberal consensus" is deliberate. As it coalesced within proliferative anxiety discourse in the wake of the Second World War, the midcentury anxiety consensus braided a temporal-chronological reconfiguration of anxiety with a political redirection of the affect. Frequent assertion of anxiety as the dominant psychic experience "in the middle of the twentieth century" remade the basic "human" and anachronistic feeling of anxiety into, also, a specifically historical feeling and rendered anxiety as uniquely punctual to the midcentury. The narrative of anxiety's special attendance on *midcentury* entailed remaking *wartime* experiences of anxiety into *postwar* affective standards; construed anxiety not as "neurotic," but rather as reasonable and "responsible" around 1950; and, crucially, addressed itself less to the alleviation of anxious psychological selves or existential souls than to the production of "alert citizens" of liberal democracies. Auden's *Age of Anxiety* and Ellison's *Invisible Man* worked amid but against this growing consensus. These works check the overdetermined ascription of anxiety to both the *midcentury* present and the model of citizenship it required.

ANXIETY EVERYWHERE

The midcentury anxiety consensus consolidated within a broader discourse about anxiety at midcentury, one that went from emergent to dominant between the late 1940s and early 1950s. I begin at this broader discursive horizon for two reasons. First, in much the same spirit in which this book excavates *midcentury,* I seek to restore a sense of the range and variety of midcentury anxiety thinking. Often hitched to the midcentury occasion, anxiety ranged across multiple areas of knowledge and cultural production around 1950. Yet standard shorthand indicators of the collective anxiety of the late 1940s and early 1950s prioritize novels about and sociological studies of the alienating effects of the organizational state, nuclear anxiety, or "the human condition" primarily on one kind of subject: the white-collar or middle-class white man in a gray flannel suit.[17] Even the midcentury's best-known psychiatric and philosophical accounts of anxiety—the one formalized in the first *DSM* and the one exported with existentialism out of continental Europe—were parts of a much larger affective discourse for which neither is a perfect synecdoche. The *DSM* and Jean-Paul Sartre lent institutional-medical authority and intellectual sheen, respectively, to the burgeoning popularity of anxiety thinking. Second, the profusion of midcentury anxiety discourse did not simply exceed the scope of any single specialized vocabulary or field. The discursive prevalence of anxiety at midcentury also propped up the idea that anxiety necessarily inhered in postwar citizenship. Documenting the sprawl of writing about anxiety across midcentury print and public culture means restoring a sense of how commonplace and mainstream, diverse and popular—in a word, how *democratic*—anxiety was made to seem at midcentury. As Lyndsey Stonebridge notes in her important study *The Writing of Anxiety: Imagining Wartime in Mid-Century British Culture* (2007), "anxiety went cultural and existentially transcendent" in the U.S. by the 1950s.[18] But it is also and more specifically the case that anxiety, historically the "emotional province of white male intellectuals," went democratic, at least rhetorically, at midcentury.[19]

Central to this project was Rollo May's hugely influential book *The Meaning of Anxiety* (1950). May begins not by setting out "to 'prove' the pervasiveness of anxiety in our day," but rather by deflecting the burden of proof. (Note the scare quotes around the verb *prove*.) For May in 1950, the best if, in his view, unnecessary evidence for the "pervasive and profound phenomenon of anxiety in our day" was the proliferation of discussion, investigation, and invocation of anxiety. *The Meaning of Anxiety* opens with a catalog of works that had recently converted anxiety from a "covert" into an "overt," "*explicit*" concern. It seemed to May "as though in the present decade the explorations and investigations in such diverse fields as poetry and science, or religion and politics, were converging on this central problem, anxiety."[20] They were. To May's inventory of "overt" anxiety books published around 1950, one can add innumerable examples ranging from the published findings of research psychologists to scholarly monographs in theology and history, from empowerment guides by self-improvement gurus to quirky stories by feature writers, and from marketing materials circulated by pharmaceutical companies to reports and recommendations made by government officials and academic-professional organizations, among them the Commission on Liberal Education of the American Association of Colleges, the John Dewey Society, and the American Psychopathological Association.

In 1950, the last of these groups published the proceedings of its annual meeting in a volume titled *Anxiety*.[21] The volume's foreword voices a standard midcentury lament: "although it is widely recognized that anxiety is the most pervasive psychological phenomenon of our time and that it is the chief symptom in the neuroses and functional psychoses, there has been little or no agreement on its definition, and very little, if any, progress in its measurement."[22] Everyone was studying anxiety; no one quite knew what it was. Five years later, *Anxiety and Stress: An Interdisciplinary Study of a Life Situation* (1955), a book-length report on a longitudinal study of former paratroopers' mental health, cited sixty-four "pertinent" social scientific and medical studies of anxiety published in the late 1940s and early 1950s alone.[23] Similarly, the *DSM-I* arose out of military psychiatrists' experience treating combatants during the Second World War to become the founding document of postwar institutional psychology and psychiatry. Precisely because the codifying effort of the *DSM* was, as Allan V. Horwitz writes, precipitated by "the experiences of military psychiatrists during World War II" who found that their field's extant "categories were not appropriate for most of the psychic problems that soldiers developed," the first *DSM* is a quintessentially midcentury project: it turned extremities of war into postwar diagnostic norms, and anxiety into a master diagnosis.[24]

In theology, the Protestant thinkers Reinhold Niebuhr and Paul Tillich took up the historical and spiritual contours of anxiety in their respective monographs *The Irony of American History* (1952) and *The Courage to Be* (1952) and elsewhere in their writings of this period.[25] For Tillich in *Courage*, the "history of Western civilization" divides into three phases, each corresponding with a distinct kind of anxiety (ontic, moral, and spiritual).[26] In 1951, the Anglo-American Zen Buddhist thinker Alan Watts brought out *The Wisdom of Insecurity*—first chapter, "The Age of Anxiety"; in a 1946 issue of *Commentary*, Louis Finkelstein, then chancellor of the Jewish Theological Seminary of America, described prophetic and Rabbinic Judaism as the "remedy" to "modern man's anxiety." In his view, as in that of many others, the crisis of anxiety was "epitomized in the individual citizen of the Western countries who hungers for the self-esteem and freedom associated with democracy but will not assume the self-discipline and obligations his citizenship involves."[27]

Just adjacent to theological reflection, Wayne E. Oates's pastoral guide *Anxiety in Christian Experience* (1955) advised ministers on how to counsel congregants struggling with nine manifestations of anxiety, including "legalistic anxiety," "finitude anxiety," and the "anxiety reactions of the morally indifferent." Oates's exegetical premise is that the "end intention of the gospel is . . . to release man *from* the egocentric anxieties of life."[28] And Norman Vincent Peale's Christian self-help regime took off at midcentury in large part by seizing on the era's apparently—and certainly discursively—"pervasive" anxiety as a spur to personal growth. Peale's *The Art of Real Happiness* (1950), coauthored with the aptly named Smiley Blanton, includes a chapter on "How to Treat Depression and Anxiety." His wildly popular follow-up, *The Power of Positive Thinking: Ten Traits for Maximum Results* (1952), assures its readers that "you do not need to be a victim of worry," which is not quite the same thing as assuring you that you don't have to worry.[29]

If one was worried, however, and if neither religious faith nor psychotherapy nor self-help helped, one might try one of the new antianxiety medications that came to market in the late 1940s.[30] To advertise afresh a drug called Neurosine, which had been on the market for years, the Dios Chemical Company of Saint Louis, Missouri, circulated a pamphlet called "Anxiety: Modern Man's Chief Enemy." The pamphlet copy unwittingly exemplifies the fine line midcentury anxiety discourse had to walk: it describes anxiety as both pathological and typical, that is, as something that can and should be medicated and as something a patient should not be embarrassed to have medicated. Authored by an unnamed physician, the pamphlet hyperbolizes anxiety so as to normalize it: "in the world today . . . the sense of insecurity is greater than ever before and the pervading emotional tone is one of anxiety rather than hope." The whole "human race" is "well on its way to a collective anxiety neurosis"—and pharmaceutical companies to enormous profit.[31] By the later 1950s, this would become the cultural air wafting through Robert Lowell's pun on "the tranquilized *Fifties*" in "Memories of West Street and Lepke."[32]

Or education might help ease one's anxiety. In a report released in January 1948, the Commission on Liberal Education of the American Association of Colleges remade in timely terms an age-old argument for the centrality of classic works of literature to liberal education. The committee—which included literary scholars and poets (Lionel Trilling, Donald A. Stauffer, Robert Hillyer), the dean of Yale College, and the presidents of Kenyon College, Hunter College, and Wesleyan University—found that "modern youth are moved, not by ambition, but by anxiety." These anxious young people needed not Neurosine or Norman Vincent Peale, but the Great Books, whose stories "recreate powerful examples of human thought and conduct—show principles in action" without neglecting the liberal values of complexity and difficulty.[33] By sad contrast, in the committee's not at all controversial view, contemporary literature would likely just compound one's anxiety. For as often as the literature of the late 1940s was deemed lacking, it was said to be anxiety-ridden. To wit: in September-October 1950, the BBC aired J. Isaacs's six-lecture series on twentieth-century literature. In his second lecture, Issacs remarked that the buzzwords of the 1940s were "frustration, bewilderment, maladjustment," all summed up in the phrase he borrowed for the lecture's title: "The Age of Anxiety." Isaacs was at pains to explain that "anxiety" was "not confined to a number of unhappy and disturbed individuals such as we find in all epochs, but a collective malady. It is not confined to England alone; it is a world sickness." Joining in the chorus of the time, Isaacs observed that the "all-pervading sense of anxiety" around 1950 could make it seem as though "the whole civilized word is having a nervous breakdown."[34] In Isaacs's estimation, contemporary literature at best only reflected this regrettable condition.

Such pronouncements were so common that it can be refreshing, when following anxiety discourse on its trek across midcentury print culture, to find that some of it was funny. Or at least tried to be. On October 18, 1954, *Time* published a fluff piece about a Duke University researcher who ran a study testing the literal antecedent of the idiom "playing possum." The study suggested that possums were "even more beset than the average psychiatric patient by such traits as 'severe anxiety, neurosis, depression, and lack of initiative and recession into himself.'"[35] The humor, such as it is, of the piece depended equally on the idea of experimenting on neurotic possums (at one point, the lab animals are given "standard electric shock treatments") and on the *Time* reader's perception of how "average" anxiety had evidently—and how prevalent the discourse of anxiety had undeniably—become. Similarly, when in December 1956 *Mad* magazine finally put Alfred E. Neuman on its cover as a write-in-candidate for president, his slogan was "What—Me Worry?" The motto pushed metahumor about anxiety toward absurdism and made *not* worrying into a countercultural posture.[36]

Fittingly for an affect that maintains "a quality of *indefiniteness and lack of object*," as Freud writes in *Inhibitions, Symptoms, and Anxiety* (1926), the bibliographic record of midcentury anxiety could be extended indefinitely.[37] (The Hogarth Press reissued Alix Strachey's English translation of *Inhibitions, Symptoms, and Anxiety* [1936] in 1948, with another printing following in 1949.) Paradoxically for such an affect, however, the "objects" of midcentury anxiety were understood at midcentury, and have been understood since, to be anything but lacking. To the inevitable question—whence all this interest in anxiety at midcentury?—accounts of the period published around 1950 and more recently alike tend to agree that the "pervasiveness" of anxiety owed to a number of mutually implicated events and phenomena in the world system: the threat of nuclear annihilation, initiated by the United States' use of atomic bombs against Japan and symbolized by the image of the mushroom cloud; the dismantling of the British Empire and the accelerating shift from the political economies of colonialism to those of globalization; the early foment of postwar racial and, to some extent, gender equality movements; the tense standoff of the early cold war, encompassing juridical and social practices installed in the U.S. under the foreign policy directive of containment;

and the accumulated material, psychic, and political legacies of the First and Second World Wars and of the unremitting violence of the twentieth century to its midpoint.

Such a summary list of midcentury causes for anxiety has an admittedly leveling effect. Yet such ready lists—as in May's enumeration of "obvious anxiety-creating situations in our day"—became a fixture of midcentury thinkers' characterization of their historical present. Already in the early 1940s, "American intellectuals who identified themselves with world politics could recite a continuous list of crises leading up to World War II," as Mark Greif has written.[38] By midcentury, the list was in place, almost unfailingly laced with anxious affect, and thus eerily primed for extension. Here, for a well-known example, is Hannah Arendt in the mood-establishing overture to *Origins of Totalitarianism* (1951): "Two world wars in one generation, separated by an uninterrupted chain of local wars and revolutions, followed by no peace treaty for the vanquished and no respite for the victor, have ended in the anticipation of a third World War between the two remaining world powers. This moment of anticipation is like the calm that settles after all hopes have died."[39] Or, as Arthur M. Schlesinger Jr. remarked before reciting his version of the list at the opening of *The Vital Center: The Politics of Freedom* (1949), a touchstone of postwar liberal thought: "Western man in the middle of the twentieth century is tense, uncertain, adrift. We look upon our epoch as a time of troubles, an age of anxiety."[40]

Such lists and prognoses were so frequently reiterated at midcentury, and have been repeated so often since, that one important project in the last decade of cold war literary studies has been not so much to question the baseline anxiety of the period as to tease out, to adapt May's language, the non-"obvious" strategies writers developed to represent those "situations" and the anxieties they stoked.[41] Nonetheless, the grand affective-historical sweep of such period lists and prognoses can be difficult to see around. For the lists evince a sense of world-historical change not simply by calling on a suitable anxiety but by conjuring it forth. Schlesinger's and like liberal intellectual accounts invoke anxiety in part to oppose democracy to totalitarianism. By this familiar reckoning, totalitarianism preys upon people's anxiety in order to impose a criminally repressive regime as salve to it. But the comparatively neglected converse also holds: if human anxiety was vulnerable to totalitarianism, it also became necessary to recoup anxiety as useful, even "vital," to liberal democracy at midcentury.

My intention in documenting the sprawl of midcentury anxiety discourse is not to deny that the midcentury was an anxious time. (*That* would be as useless as, to borrow from May, "the proverbial carrying of coals to Newcastle.") It is rather to observe that the contours of anxiety itself— indefiniteness, mobility, malleability, self-replication, anachronism—make it at least reasonable, and at this point more illuminating, to tilt the inevitable question *whence all this interest in anxiety at midcentury?* away from the empirical and toward the discursive, away from anxiety as an assumed ground of the early postwar period and toward its rhetorical and discursive promotion as the affect most suited to the self-conscious *midcentury*. In documenting the sprawl of anxiety discourse at midcentury, then, I mean to shift focus away from the enumeration of objects of anxiety and toward the production of anxious subjects. Or, more precisely, toward the production of anxious *citizens* in the emergent postwar era.

Put another way: proliferating anxiety discourse is one thing; the patterns into which that discourse settled are another. What I term the midcentury anxiety consensus cohered around two mutually inflected rhetorical signatures: 1. the stipulation of anxiety as punctual to the midcentury, that is, as a historical feeling that necessarily accompanied the period's sense of suspension; and 2. the depiction of anxiety not just as an inescapably human condition but also as the legitimate affective condition of postwar democratic citizenship. May's *Meaning of Anxiety* stands as rule rather than exception in its articulation of both. May invokes the "citizen"—as distinct from the patient or person or self—as his audience throughout *The Meaning of Anxiety*. The preface to the first edition (1950) pitches the book "to the concerns of any intelligent citizen who feels on his own pulse the tensions and anxiety-creating conflicts of our day and who has asked himself what the meaning and causes of this anxiety may be and how the anxiety may be dealt with."[42] May was not an especially artful writer. Nonetheless, the syntax of this prefatory note reflects how thoroughly buffeted, even constituted, he found the "citizen" to be by anxiety: "concerns" precede and "tensions and anxiety-creating conflicts" follow the citizen; the citizen is both the object of May's address and an embodied male subject who "feels" anxiety "on his own pulse." Across the opening section of *Meaning of Anxiety*, May's syntax consistently forecloses on the possibility of envisioning citizenship at midcentury as free of anxiety. For May as for many others around 1950, good democratic citizens had to be "alert" citizens, and anxiety drove not simply one's psychological development toward adulthood but a man's exercise of democratic freedoms.[43]

Although anxiety was frequently said at midcentury to defy definition, its elusiveness hardly precluded prescriptions as to "how anxiety may be dealt with." In May's work, the answer is neither treatment nor analysis nor introspection, as one might expect from a psychologist, but civics and the practice of "responsible" citizenship. Only when he turns to "the political situation" in his opening chapter does May pause in his documentation of the emergence of anxiety as an "overt" concern to broach the question of how one should handle it. At the risk of contradicting his premise that midcentury anxiety has many causes, May writes that "the emergence of the atom bomb brought the previously inchoate and 'free-floating' anxiety of many people into sharp focus."[44] The baldness of the American vantage here is as startling now as it was typical then: by May's reckoning, what is important about the atomic bomb is not that the U.S. developed and deployed it but that it "emerged," not who died immediately in or as a result of the atomic bombings of Hiroshima and Nagasaki, but whose anxiety the bombings brought into focus.

For May, the question after "the atom bomb" is what "the West" is to do with its newly focused anxiety. To answer, he paraphrases Alfred Toynbee's prediction, made in *Women's Home Companion* in August 1949 and with the "cold" in cold war still in quotation marks, that "overt warfare on a world scale is not probable in our lifetime, [but] we shall remain in a 'cold' war for a generation."[45] May gasps at this "horrendous prospect!" and agrees with Toynbee that the "tension in the persistent cold war" can motivate the "bettering our own socioeconomic standards in the West." Going further, May asserts that "our political and social survival depends both on our capacity for tolerating the anxiety inherent in the threatening world situation (and thus not irrationally precipitating war as a way out of the painful uncertainty) and also on our capacity for turning this anxiety to constructive uses."[46] Not dwelling in anxiety but turning it to "constructive uses," not flailing in one's anxiety but using it as "motivation" for advancing "the West": May's is classic American cold war logic.

Yet his uncontroversial definition of citizenship as anchored in the capacity to "tolerate" and make productive use of "anxiety" also accepts an overhaul of the aspirational grounds of classic liberal democratic citizenship.
Citizenship at midcentury no longer rested on reason or Enlightenment
virtues, but rather on an affective state that would seem to suspend citizens' rational agency.

So accustomed now is the association of anxiety with imperatives of
democratic citizenship—"security" lying always on the other side of
anxiety—that one might not flinch at May's and others' forging of the association at midcentury. Still less conspicuous in our own present is the second rhetorical pattern that underwrote the midcentury anxiety consensus:
countless commentators leveraged being *at midcentury*, and the habits of
mind midcentury discourse nurtured, to normalize anxiety as a blunt historical fact of the early postwar. Around 1950, the surfeit of self-reflexive
midcentury thinking offered a perfect discursive host for a collective anxiety diagnosis. Recall that *midcentury* and like terms relied on a set of ambiv-
alences, if not outright contradictions: these terms were ubiquitous as
epochal markers of the present yet substantively indefinite; they were chronologically accurate enough, yet manifestly arbitrary; and they denoted a
sense of suspension between disastrous past and "threatening" future—
even as they provided a means of euphemizing those "disasters." In its
very vagueness and ubiquity, midcentury discourse aligns intuitively with
anxiety. The midcentury present and the feeling of anxiety: like two nega-
tives constituting a grammatical positive, these two inchoate diagnostics,
constantly paired, rhetorically constituted an epochal certainty.

For the frequency and ease with which he yokes midcentury thinking
and the period's sense of its "historical" present to anxiety, May is again
exemplary. Nearly every sentence in the opening section of *The Meaning of
Anxiety* binds a chronological marker of the midcentury present—"the
middle of the twentieth century," "in our day," "In 1950," "the present
decade"—to "pervasive" anxiety; the opening section is titled "Centrality
of the Problem of Anxiety in Our Day." This is no minor detail. For May,
the sheer existence and spread of anxiety discourse at midcentury suffice
to establish the "centrality" of the affect by 1950; by a similar logic of insistence, May's serial reiterating of chronological markers of the present
asserts anxiety's specific contemporaneity. Frequent repetition of chronological formula simply made anxiety punctual to "the present phase of our

century." But while the punctuality narrative itself was necessarily temporary (limited to "the present phase"), it proved instrumental in elevating
anxiety as affective custom of the longer postwar and cold war periods.

To this last point, the afterlife of May's work accords with a much larger
pattern we've begun to see, whereby inchoate *midcentury* occasions once
fostered arguments that hardened into fixed referents for the postwar period
or arguments that came no longer to require their *midcentury* tethers. By
the time May updated *The Meaning of Anxiety* for the better-known edition of 1977, anxiety had outlasted its one-time chronological host. In the
opening paragraph of the revised edition, anxiety is "a pervasive and profound phenomenon" not "in the middle of the twentieth century," but "in
the twentieth century." Where in the first edition May emphasized *1950* and
"our day" provided a temporal anchor for a range of more and less obvious
anxiety-provoking situations, by 1977 the ratio had flipped. May extended
the temporal span over which anxiety loomed, but narrowed the cause for
anxiety definitively to "the birth of the atom bomb."[47]

NAMING THE AGE

Both the rapid spread of midcentury anxiety discourse and the coalescence
of the midcentury anxiety consensus owe more to W. H. Auden's *The Age
of Anxiety* than to any other single text. More accurately, the selection of
anxiety at midcentury thrilled to the resonant title of *The Age of Anxiety*
and relied on a broad unwillingness to take seriously the presence of the
Second World War in the poem. Thanks largely to Auden's popularizing
force, "the age of anxiety" has long and widely applied as cliché catch-
phrase.[48] But its portability obscures both the timeliness and critical efficacy
of Auden's title phrase. Nor does it help that, immediately at midcentury,
the quotability of its title prompted some lasting misreadings—and, it
would seem, plain nonreading—of *The Age of Anxiety*. Understandably
then, some Auden scholars hold up the title phrase as something from
which the poem must be rescued.[49] Alan Jacobs, for example, intends his
invaluable critical edition of *The Age of Anxiety* (2011) "to aid those who
would like to read the poem rather than sagely cite its title."[50] Yes. And yet
Auden's ubiquitous title phrase also amounted to a principal means by
which midcentury writers and readers came to think of their time as a
uniquely, self-consciously anxious one.

The first half of Auden's title formula chimed with the broad effort to make sense of the historical present at midcentury by reference to an arbitrary chronological unit; the second half provides the strange comfort of even a negative diagnosis. In other words, *of Anxiety* is the flashier half of Auden's title, *The Age* is its timely base. Even setting aside for the moment habitual practices of chronological self-placement around 1950, the effect of any "age of" denomination arises from the portentousness of "the age," a phrase whose definite article and hortatory effect offset its indefiniteness as a chronological unit or temporal span. At whatever scale, "the age" summons the effect, rather than establishes the fact, of temporal limit, conferring an aura of comprehensibility on, rather than demonstrating the comprehensibility of, a span of time.[51] In Auden's midcentury title, "the age of" formula affords a fraught reassurance, since it ties not to a valorized process or achievement that defines a period, but to a negative affect commonly said at midcentury to defy temporal and spatial bounds, to "pervade" rather than to exalt the epoch.

The quick, double-stress alliteration of *a* surely helped sponsor the apparent self-evidence and in turn the broad adoption of "the age of anxiety" as a name for the self-conscious *midcentury*. As the first *a* gives way to the next, "age" and affect harmonize, as if naturally. It's catchy. And, as the several uses of the phrase already quoted in this chapter indicate, it caught on. Imagine the difference if Auden had titled the poem *The Era of Anxiety* or *The Age of Nervousness*. The American philosopher and educator Laurence Sears was more correct than he realized when he remarked in his contribution to *Educational Freedom in an Age of Anxiety* (1953), "It is not an accident that the title of Auden's poem . . . has become the theme of countless books and articles."[52] It was "not an accident" not simply in the sense that Auden's title seemed audibly to catch the affective tone of "the age" but also in the sense that Auden designed the title to stick.

Stick it did. Whether they loved or hated *The Age of Anxiety*, nearly every reviewer of the poem and borrower of its title agreed, expressly or tacitly, that Auden had crystallized the collective mood of the late 1940s and early 1950s. A tautology that, distilled, runs *"The Age of Anxiety* names our historical present because our present is an age of anxiety" quickly took shape in first reviews and press notices, spread across book reviews and little magazines, expanded into feature stories, inspired performing arts projects—including Leonard Bernstein's and Jerome Robbins's adaptations for symphony (1949) and ballet (1950)—and seeped irretrievably into period idiolect.[53] Auden's title provided both the specific phrase and an adaptable formula—*chronological unit to indicate the present + anxiety = apt description of the midcentury present*—that became commonplace gestures of affective epochal self-description in the late 1940s and early 1950s.

Constant quotation of the title of *The Age of Anxiety* took it as simply descriptive of the midcentury's affective self-concept. The poem itself, however, runs counter to the ready association of a vaguely bounded midcentury "age" with an affect that defies bounds. For one thing, the poem exhibits persistent uneasiness about precisely the kind of rhetorical grandiosity and summary tidiness its title imposes—indeed, right from its opening sentence, which undermines by bathos that period-intellectual tendency toward grand philosophical-historical pronouncement: "When the historical process breaks down and armies organize with their embossed debates the ensuing void which they can never consecrate, when necessity is associated with horror and freedom with boredom, then it looks good to the bar business" (*AA* 3). For another, the poem stands leery throughout of overly neat scenes. The five lyric "extracts" (Auden's word) the poet published in advance of *The Age of Anxiety* illustrate this point economically: each depicts a scene of suspect calm (a harbor at midday, an English country house, a regulated cityscape). These are poems set indeterminately before or after the proverbial storm, and in outwardly orderly scenes in which threats seem alternately and at once to loom and to have passed. For still one more, anachronism is everywhere in *The Age of Anxiety*. To read the poem is to be reminded, at just about every turn and contra the midcentury anxiety consensus, that anxiety is *not* punctual to any age, including and perhaps especially the age the poem was taken to christen. *The Age of Anxiety* depicts anxiety's past as always with it, even as the affect enacts itself in the present and projects itself into the future.

In contrast to anxiety as it structures Auden's poem, the many writers who promoted anxiety as punctual to the midcentury had to defy the characteristic anachronism of anxiety in the abstract. This effect emerges nowhere more clearly than in the rapidity and ease with which anxieties endured during the Second World War were woven into the professed affective atmosphere of the midcentury as it took discursive shape, subsumed into postwar institutions, or transformed into cold war default.[54] Specifically around 1950, understanding anxiety as uniquely contemporaneous with "the present phase of our century" entailed diminishing—or dismissing entirely—the then very recent war as both a persistent source of anxiety and a historical epoch during which people, even stateside Americans, became accustomed to pervasive anxiety and to understanding themselves and their time as anxious.

The transatlantic reception of *The Age of Anxiety* presents a local instance of this pattern. Auden's age-naming book foregrounds from its start a warbound acclimation to anxiety: already on the book's first page, the prose narrator remarks, "in war-time . . . everybody is reduced to the anxious status of a shady character or displaced person" (*AA* 3). Nonetheless, the critical and popular reception of *The Age of Anxiety* enacted a willful discounting of the war in the poem. Once more, consider Rollo May. May's chapter-long list of works that proved anxiety had "emerged into overt statement in contemporaneous literature" and other fields began, as all such lists did by 1950, with Auden's poem. May's priority in cataloging *The Age of Anxiety* is to assure his citizen-reader that the poem is not about the war during which it is set, in which two of its characters serve, news of which commences it, and to which the poem returns in its epilogue, as the sun rises on "a bright clear day for work and for war" (*AA* 106). Exemplary of the popular and literary reception of *The Age of Anxiety*, May credits the affective and thematic contemporaneity of the poem at the specific expense of the war it inhabits:

W. H. Auden has entitled his latest poem with the phrase which he believes most accurately characterizes our period, namely, *The Age of Anxiety*. Though Auden's profound interpretation of the inner experience of the four persons in this poem is set in the time of war . . . he makes it very clear that the underlying causes of the anxiety of his characters, as well as of others of this age, must be sought on deeper levels than merely the occasion of the war.[55]

In at least one sense, May is not wrong. If those "deeper levels" mean, say, philosophy or Christian theology, then it is true that Auden's depiction of anxiety draws on a range of thinkers, most especially on Kierkegaard. But the "underlying causes" of anxiety May goes on to list point not to philosophy, faith, or the human condition, but rather to indicators of historical contemporaneity, to an insistently *post*war account of the present. For May, *The Age of Anxiety* must be understood to capture the feeling of "our period" not that of "the time of war." An unstated corollary of this claim might be that to acknowledge the presence of the war in the poem is to risk reducing the poem's titular affect to a single, overpowering historical referent. The risk May takes instead—though it barely registered as a risk at all in 1950—is to reduce the recent war and "the time of war" to mere occasion.

Almost no reviewer of *The Age of Anxiety* in the late 1940s or critic since would dispute May's assertion that the poem is not solely about anxiety experienced during or otherwise attached to "the war." Nor do I mean to establish the Second World War as the singular antecedent for the affective atmosphere of *The Age of Anxiety*. Rather, I mean more modestly to note that May's representative proposition that *The Age of Anxiety* "characterizes our period" required neither ignoring the war as the poem imagines it nor treating the war as moot, as "mere" backdrop. Yet first reviewers in the late 1940s, May in 1950, and countless other midcentury borrowers of the title *The Age of Anxiety* breezily encouraged their readers not to be distracted by the persistence of the war in what they all agreed was the signature poem of the new postwar present.

Were it not for the prominence of *The Age of Anxiety* and its title phrase, the broad public elision of the war that permeates the poem might amount to nothing more than a minor quirk of reception history. But the stature of *The Age of Anxiety* allows for a fuller and perhaps more troubling understanding of the grounds for the poem's selection for emphasis. The midcentury elevation of *The Age of Anxiety* emblematizes the effort, undertaken in and well beyond transatlantic literary culture at midcentury, to leverage the stated pervasiveness of midcentury anxiety in service of the "alert" citizenship "our day" was said to require. If the two principal projects of the midcentury anxiety consensus—to depict anxiety as punctual to "the age" and to establish it as the affective condition of postwar democratic citizenship—structured the reception of *The Age of Anxiety*, then the hitches are many, but they come down to one: from its composition history and anachronistic formal design through its creeping boredom with anxiety, *The Age of Anxiety* unsettles the consensus that co-opted it. The poem maintains the continued presence of the war—and as the poem dilates, the psychic and material presence of continuous war—in an "age" that quickly determined to figure itself as *postwar* and used "pervasive" anxiety to do it.

"PERCENTAGE OF PERSONS EXPRESSING ANXIETY"

Auden began work on *The Age of Anxiety* in July 1944, completed the poem in early 1947, and saw it published in the U.S. on July 11, 1947. The English publication followed a year later, on September 17, 1948. Fleshing out this composition timeline proves difficult for reasons textual and biographical: there is limited draft material for *The Age of Anxiety*, and Auden's work on the poem was interrupted midway through by his service as a research analyst in the Morale Division of the United States Strategic Bombing Survey (USSBS), a military-civilian body created in November 1944 to determine, according to its summary report, "how air supremacy was achieved [over Germany] and the results which followed from its exploitation."[56] In plain speech, this means that Auden spent much of the spring and summer of 1945 in Germany, where he interviewed civilian survivors of Allied bombings on behalf of the U.S. War Department. Auden had no truck with the administrative euphemism. His friend Nicholas Nabokov, who also served in the USSBS, recalled his remarking of the Morale Division's name and work: "This *Morale* title still makes me squirm. . . . It is illiterate and absurd. How can one learn anything about morals, when one's actions are beyond any kind of morality? *Morale* with an 'e' at the end is psycho-sociological nonsense. What they mean to say, but don't say, is how many people we killed and how many buildings we destroyed by that wicked bombing."[57] Nabokov further remembered Auden asking if it was "justified to reply to *their* mass-murder by *our* mass-murder? . . . I cannot help but ask myself, 'Was there no other way?' "[58] The particular cruelty of the Morale Division's work—interviewing civilian survivors of aerial bombings with a view to improving bombing strategy and providing anticipatory justification of future air raids—was lost on neither Auden nor *The Age of Anxiety*.

The composition history of *The Age of Anxiety* is inextricable from the war and from the enormous American "postwar" research apparatus whose operations began in fact before the Allied victory. Auden himself left for Europe in late April 1945, before V-E Day, and arrived in Germany on May 5, 1945. He was back in the United States before V-J Day, by which point the USSBS was already initiating its gruesome reiteration in Japan. (Where Dudziak describes how the idea of wartime underwrites nation-states' prosecution of wars beyond their official ends, and of wars without end, the planning and operation of the USSBS makes a complementary point about when and how the anticipation of the *postwar* licenses the immediate or even premature remaking of *wartime* experiences to serve the aims of the state.) Before Auden's departure for Germany in late April 1945, he and his friend the novelist James Stern, another civilian who volunteered for the USSBS, planned to collaborate on a book about their experience. They signed a contract with Harcourt, Brace, the eventual American publisher of *The Age of Anxiety*, and took a $3,000 advance. Upon their return to the U.S., Auden showed little interest in writing the USSBS memoir. He resumed work on *The Age of Anxiety*, and Stern wrote his memoir of that wartime-postwar summer, *The Hidden Damage* (1947), alone. Auden's abandonment of the planned collaboration with Stern has been read as an act of principled reticence, as a demonstration of his belief that "the hitherto unimaginable should not be made into the subject matter of an aesthetic image."[59] However, available evidence—including Stern's memoir, the USSBS's *Summary Report for the European War* (1945), and the Morale Division's two-volume report *The Effects of Strategic Bombing on German Morale* (1946, 1947)—suggests that Auden's "morale" work in Germany did inform *The Age of Anxiety*, if in less topical or materially referential ways than a search for "aesthetic images" presumes. While images summoned from Auden's memory of his USSBS service might not have surfaced in his poetry until the later 1940s, the procedural work of interviewing civilian air raid survivors and the affective vocabulary of his USSBS work did.

The USSBS Morale Division aimed to "determine the direct and indirect effects of bombing upon the attitudes, behavior, and health of the civilian population, with particular reference to its effect upon the willingness and capacity of the bombed population to give effective and continued support to the German war effort."[60] To this end, between March and July 1945, the Morale Division interviewed 3,711 German civilians in 34 towns and cities. It piloted an experimental indirect interview study wherein Morale Division interviewers followed one of two schedules of questions designed to lead a respondent "by degree into the specific subjects about which information is desired."[61] But the set interview schedules did more than channel respondents away from yes or no answers and toward desired information: they also scripted interviewees' affective responses to the experiences they were to narrate. View-from-the-ground details of the effects of "raids" were the survey's "desired" subject; anxiety—whether unto itself or as a tangle of fear, weariness, uneasiness, tension, despair, and exhaustion—was its expected affect. All told, the word *anxiety* recurs some forty-seven times in the Morale Division's summary report.

The two interview schedules attest to two premises of the Morale Division study: first, that from anticipation through aftermath, air raids (euphemistically, "strategic bombing") caused widespread anxiety; second, that anxiety helped to erode German civilians' resolve to carry on with the war.[62] Schedule A, which concentrates almost entirely on air raids, alternates between asking respondents to describe their "feelings" and "state of mind" generally and supplying them with more specific emotional terminology. The schedule follows its requisite question about when the respondent first experienced an air raid with a series of questions about how raids, no longer in need of the modifier "air," made them feel during and after the bombing:

7. Did the first air raid surprise you, or had you expected it?
8. Did you believe at the time that there would be more raids on your town after this first raid, or did you think that your town would now be left alone?
9. (If further raids expected) What did you think *then that the future raids would be like*?[63]

Later, the schedule moves to questions about respondents' feelings as "raids" became routine:

16. Were you more and more afraid as the raids continued, or did you get used to them?
17. Did these repeated raids have any other effect on your state of mind?
18. Which of the following bombs did you find most terrible: Incendiaries, explosives, phosphorous, air mines?
19. Which were more terrible, day or night raids?[64]

The recollected anticipation of "*future raids*," the options to have become "more and more afraid" or grown accustomed to bombing, the relative terror of various kinds and timings of bombing: such queries compelled respondents to recollect and also to reexperience anxiety and fear, or what the Morale Division dubbed their "war weariness."

Sophisticated though the Morale Division research was for its time, in the long wake of the cultural turn in anthropology and of trauma theory, its report reads as tone-deaf at the very best, its interview schedules as if calculated to foster in interviewees the "almost perfectly functioning mechanism of repression" W. G. Sebald describes in *On the Natural History of Destruction* (2004).[65] Were its methods and aims not so inhumane, this social science interviewing project might once have seemed ripe for parody along the lines of "The Unknown Citizen" or other Auden anthology pieces of the late 1930s and early 1940s that satirize bureaucratic, positivist state regulation and surveillance. Instead, Morale Division interview procedure came directly to inform *The Age of Anxiety*, the Morale Division's affective quarry indirectly to suffuse it.

A key lyric passage at the center of the long poem offers the most telling instance of the former point. First published under the title "Metropolis" in *Commonweal* on December 20, 1946, the five-stanza poem surveys an orderly scene. Its title promises a cityscape poem, and the first two stanzas mostly oblige. With the confident air of a detective reading evidence or a tourist guide doling out useful tips, the first stanza observes a city already fixed as a "scene." In keeping with the whole of *The Age of Anxiety*, however, hints of foreboding quickly intrude on this metropolis, as when in the second stanza "the criminally inclined" run up against a punning inference that "The police must be large." In the middle stanza, these hints begin to chip away at the poem's observational certitude. Midway through, the poem makes a double turn: from detached third-person observation of the metropolis to inquiry about itself, and from cool enumeration to increasingly urgent interrogatives.

If "Metropolis" gives way in its final two stanzas to a series of questions so anxious as to collapse the illusion of distance between observer and observed, then the word that initiates this turn is *raids*. The hinge stanza reads in full:

> A married tribe commutes, mild from suburbia,
> Whom ritual rules protect against raids by the nomad
> Misfortunes they fear; for they flinch in their dreams at the scratch
> Of coarse pecuniary claws, at crying images,
> Petulant, thin, reproachful,
> Destitute shades of dear ones.
>
> (*AA* 60)

Suburbia and its denizens, commuters, were easy targets at midcentury, ready emblems of conformity and complacency. (Recall the commuters, "dense" in two senses, in Auden's "September 1, 1939.")[66] But by the end of the middle stanza of "Metropolis," the observer's empathy for the "fear" and desperation that compel the commuters' complacency impinges on his condescension to them. The observer depicts this damnably "mild," "married tribe" as grasping for a security figured in financial terms (the pun on "Misfortunes," "pecuniary claws," "destitute"). These anticipated "misfortunes" both make the line they initiate overrun the metrical pattern of the poem and far outstrip material or monetary fears, taking the terrifying shape of "crying images / Petulant, thin, reproachful," ghosts of "dear ones." The alliterative patterning of "ritual rules protect against raids" conveys an awareness that "rules" offer only illusory protection: "ritual rules" precede and, at least at the level of sound, produce the anticipated, feared "raids." The very word *raids* distills what we will presently see is the governing anachronism of *The Age of Anxiety*. At midcentury, and certainly for USSBS Major Auden, the word *air* inevitably attached to the word *raids*. But in "Metropolis," *raids* also connects, via *tribe* and *nomad*, to a past that long predates the metropolis coming under threat from the sky, a threat reinscribed in the aerial vantage of the poem.

The poem does not recover from the anticipation of "raids" and the "crying images" that follow from them. In the fourth stanza, the poem makes a stark turn from observation to interrogation. The turn coincides with the introduction of a "visitor" who asks questions without answer and whose urgency reveals more about his own anxiety than the observed "scene." The appearance of the proxy "visitor" remakes Auden's 1930s "stranger" gazing upon England into an outsider who is morally implicated in the increasingly troubling and unbounded "scene" of the metropolis.[67] As he asks questions, the visitor becomes conduit of and caught in the city's anxiety. He stutters his first question ("how, how"):

Well, here I am but how, how, asks the visitor,
Strolling through the strange streets, can I start to discover
The fashionable feminine fret, or the form of insult
Minded most by the men? In what myth do their sages
          Locate the cause of evil?
          How are these people punished?

(*AA* 60–61)

Once methodical in his observation, the "visitor"-speaker is "here" undone by his own interrogatives. His queries quickly ramp up from the trivial matter of a trendy hair clip—which, appropriately for both alliterative pattern and mood, is called a "fret"—to matters of belief and punishment. The escalating questions crescendo in the final stanza. Again like all the lyric extracts published in advance of *The Age of Anxiety*, and like the long poem itself, "Metropolis" worries at its end about the ultimate end. In its final stanza, "Metropolis" speculates by way of rhetorical questions and familiar tropes (climatological, biblical, technological) about death and the end of the world:

> How, above all, will they end? By any natural
> Fascination of frost or flood? Or from the artful
> Obliterating bang whereby God's rebellious image
> After thousands of thankless years spent in thinking about it,
> > Finally finds a solid
> > Proof of its independence?
>
> (*AA* 61)

In its final two stanzas, the poem dramatizes banal questions about local fashions giving way to existential ones. But the escalation dramatizes something more, and more specific, than timeless human anxiety. Its tangled syntax notwithstanding, the poem's final question broaches humankind's capacity for complete self-destruction, very much a new human achievement, if one must call it that, in the late 1940s. Both the "artful / Obliterating bang" and "God's rebellious image," as distinct from a believer's faith in God, are human fabrications. The inevitable midcentury association of "Obliterating bang" with the atomic bomb might seem too blunt, except that the poem deposits this rhetorical trace of the catastrophic weapon in a series of intensifying questions and on an ascending continuum with other forms of aerial surveillance (stanzas 1–2) and bombing ("raids" in stanza 3) that provoke anxiety and ensare citizens and surveyors of the metropolis alike in it.

The pace and phrasing of the poem's self-interrogation hold no space for response. The conclusion of "Metropolis" dispels any lingering notion of the observer-asker as immune to the city and citizens he encounters, much less as superior in his initial detachment from them. In light of Auden's work asking questions for the USSBS, this extract from *The Age of Anxiety* reads as an interview poem. "Metropolis" defies the affective assumptions that informed the Morale Division study and repels the quantifications of anxiety the study sought to produce. In its last two stanzas, the poem forestalls citizens of the "Metropolis" from having to answer its own desperate queries and the poet from making art out of their answers. The interviewer interrogates himself; it is only the observer-interviewer's own questions, anxiety, and despair that the poem has a right or duty to express. Such is the fate of Major Auden, the poet of *The Age of Anxiety*.

FORMS OF ANACHRONISM

Certified by endless repetition of its title and boosted by the celebrity of its author, the epochal-synoptic quality of *The Age of Anxiety* was at midcentury and remains a given, rather than an argument in need of making. It would be a difficult argument to make. As readers of *The Age of Anxiety* come to realize, the poem has "nothing specific to say about anxiety."[68] It rather induces a certain boredom with anxiety, which affect proves so unrelenting as to settle into predictability. Moreover, and as a brief description of the poem will confirm, *The Age of Anxiety* makes an unlikely candidate for spokespoem of the midcentury. Its principal formal and intellectual disqualifications are two: difficulty and anachronism. Auden's brazenly unfashionable subtitle, *A Baroque Eclogue*, already telegraphs both.

The Age of Anxiety comprises six parts, each designated by a rhetorical form whose conventions underpin the part. Between a prologue and an epilogue (parts 1 and 6), there are "The Seven Ages" and "The Seven Stages" of man (parts 2 and 3), a dirge (part 4), and a courtly masque (part 5). This structure is overlain by an omnivorous array of references to intellectual systems, spiritual traditions, popular forms, and literary styles and works. Among these: "The Seven Ages" borrows from Jacques's speech in act 2 of *As You Like It*; "The Seven Stages" stitches physiological symbolism drawn from *The Zohar*, the central text of Jewish mysticism, into the progressive structure of Kierkegaard's *Stages on Life's Way* (in Walter Lowrie's 1940 translation); the four main speaking figures in *The Age of Anxiety* correspond to C. G. Jung's four faculties of the psyche: thinking, feeling, sensation, and intuition; and then there are the countless allusions, of varying depth and duration, to *Moby-Dick*, *Finnegans Wake*, the *Purgatorio*, the *Carmina Burana*, *Peer Gynt*, Icelandic verse, English detective fiction, and broadcast news, among many other works and modes.[69]

While these allusions and intertexts reward scholarly explication unto themselves, many also open onto the timelier configuration of anxiety at midcentury. The Jungian symbolism of the four strangers, for example, does not preclude the narrator from introducing them by providing two then-requisite historical coordinates: their citizenship and military or civilian statuses. The group includes two servicemen on leave: Malin, a middle-aged medical intelligence officer in the Canadian Air Force, and Emble, a young Midwesterner who left college to enlist in the U.S. Navy. Its civilian members are Quant, an immigrant to the U.S. from Ireland, who works as a "clerk in a shipping office," and Rosetta, who seems to be an English expatriate (*AA* 4–5). If, as one critic argues, "the displacement of all four characters resonates with Auden's peripatetic movements" in the late 1920s and the 1930s, it is also the case that these strangers in a bar form a picture of North Atlantic whiteness derived from the British Empire.[70] Only Emble—the young man, "emblem" of the future—is a birthright citizen of the United States.

Historical anachronism should have further disqualified *The Age of Anxiety* from the status of midcentury spokespoem. The poem makes no direct comment on "the age" it was taken to name. Instead, *The Age of Anxiety* turns the characteristic out-of-timeness of its titular affect into a formal principle. Anachronisms configure the poem at several levels and in several ways. Among these are the poem's genre derivation, verse form, and historical setting. Auden's eclogue takes place in a modern, urban analog of the pastoral scene: a dingy Third Avenue bar in Manhattan, where the four strangers sit drinking, each alone. The war has brought them into the bar; war news on the radio, that technological hallmark of modernity, gets them talking to each other. Equal parts indispensable and intrusive throughout, the prose narrator describes how the war headlines interrupt the strangers' "separate senses of themselves, by compelling them to pay attention to a common world of great slaughter and much sorrow" (*AA* 9). Over the course of the night, and on the quotidian grounds on which allegory relies, the group charts a predictably boozy course from barstools to booth to one stranger's apartment and finally, at dawn, back to "the actual world where time is real and in which, therefore, poetry can take no interest"

(*AA* 108). When the strangers go their separate ways as the sun comes up, it is not even clear that they have learned one another's names. Their evening draws on the tradition of pastoral convening, yet is quintessentially modern in its apparent inconsequence.[71] In this sense, *The Age of Anxiety* is the Auden of the Yeats elegy, written on the eve of the Second World War— "For poetry makes nothing happen: it survives"—taken to a structural and thematic extreme.[72] It's not simply that nothing much happens in the long poem. *The Age of Anxiety* makes a point of making nothing happen.

The starkest anachronism of *The Age of Anxiety* is its verse form. The book-length poem sustains an idiosyncratic pastiche of Anglo-Saxon alliterative verse throughout, such that most lines sound three alliterated stresses punctuated by a hard caesura. Even the war news broadcast that convenes the four strangers participates in the alliterative pattern, albeit with abbreviated and exaggeratedly enjambed lines befitting headline news. The "official doctored message" fuses Second World War matter with archaic meter. Hence even the newsman's standard prefatory phrase, "Now the news," both marks its own contemporaneity and submits to the alliterative pattern:

> Now the news. Night raids on
> Five cities. Fires started.
> Pressure applied by pincer movement
> In threatening thrust. Third Division
> Enlarges beachhead. Lucky charm
> Saves sniper. Sabotage hinted
> In steel-mill stoppage. Strong point held
> By fanatical Nazis. Canal crossed
> By heroic marines. Rochester barber
> Fools foe. Finns ignore
> Peace feeler. Pope condemns
> Axis excesses.
> (*AA* 9–10)

The numbing staccato of the news report prompts each of the four strangers to think to themselves. Since what each thinks is a more or less topical war poem, *The Age of Anxiety* opens by participating in the expansion of the category of "war poetry" necessitated by the Second World

feature writers and reviews by established poet-critics and intellectuals linked the success of *The Age of Anxiety* to Auden's naturalization and ear for American speech, English reviewers and younger American poets attributed the failure of the poem in large part to Auden's "determination to be American."[75] A story in *Time* delighted in the American Auden and his new poem, but still gladly flashed the poet's English bona fides:

Though U.S. readers may still think of Poet Wystan Hugh Auden as an Englishman in exile, he has been a U.S. citizen since May 1946. As a U.S. man of letters, Auden at 40—old Oxonian, old leftist intellectual, Wandervogel, versifier extraordinary, theological lyricist—is a figure of great oddity, and of considerable importance. "The Age of Anxiety" glitters with evidence of both.... In U.S. letters, Auden's position is beginning to be as influential as that of his friend in England who also traded countries, St. Louis-born T. S. Eliot.[76]

In the mostly negative reviews by English and younger American writers, neither the default comparison to Eliot nor the fact of Auden's new citizenship worked to his or the poem's favor. In England, the publication of "Mr. Auden's first American production," as Patric Dickinson put it in *Horizon*, blew new air into the public fire over the poet's departure for the U.S. in 1939, a departure characterized as a treacherous abandonment of England on the eve of war.[77] The *Times Literary Supplement* gave fully three-quarters of its review to a eulogy for the Auden of the 1930s—the consummately English Auden of *Look, Stranger!* (1936) especially—at the expense of his American work: "it is impossible not to read into Mr. Auden's American dialogues his own *déraciné*, nostalgic predicament, the subconscious need for explanation which has developed into a neurosis."[78] In *Poetry Quarterly*, Wrey Gardiner turned the poem's wartime setting into an indictment of the poet for cowardice: "It is probable that some of the most lasting poetry of this war will have been found to have been written by non-combatants, conscientious objectors and those who fled, like Auden, beyond the seas."[79] In Gardner's estimation, *The Age of Anxiety* did not strengthen the probability.

That Auden's citizenship status became a node in the reception of *The Age of Anxiety* might be used to affirm the standard division of Auden's career into its early English and later American phases. Reading the reviews with the far broader midcentury anxiety consensus in mind, however, the accumulated weight of emphasis on Auden's citizenship points in a different direction. The national coordinates to which reviews of *The Age of Anxiety* were set testify to an emergent, if not yet at midcentury quite fixed, affiliation of democratic citizenship with Auden's titular affect. Reviewers were beginning to articulate the entanglement not just of Auden's citizenship with anxiety but of postwar citizenship generally with anxiety. This broader midcentury discursive context returns us to the special American number of *Horizon* (October 1947) in which Auden's "Music Is International," a kind of précis of *The Age of Anxiety*, and Ellison's "The Invisible Man" appeared. Published between the American and British editions of *The Age of Anxiety*, "Art on the American *Horizon*" epitomized the period preoccupation with and affective projection onto Auden's Americanness.[80]

"Art on the American *Horizon*" marked the high point of the little magazine after the war and also signaled its demise. Though the story of *Horizon*'s struggle to remain in print in the late 1940s exceeds the scope of this chapter, suffice it to say that the magazine's special-issue look to the U.S. reflected its own peril. The issue may lament the global redistribution of power, hard and soft, toward the U.S. after the Second World War, but it also reads as an instance of that shift.[81] Most of the issue's editorial content expresses the concomitant intellectual fixation on the dim outlook for serious literature, art, and culture in a U.S. driven by the excesses of capitalism and in thrall to mass culture. Part 1, "The Problem Defined," consisted entirely of contributions by *Partisan Review* stalwarts. Representative of their general view, William Phillips concluded his essay: "If America is to be looked to, as do some of our European friends, as a source of literary salvation, then all I can say is—God Save the King."[82] (A canny young Marshall McLuhan wrote that advertising had no problem; art, language, and design geared to sell products were flourishing in the U.S.) Little wonder that in his review of *Invisible Man* in 1952, the young American novelist Saul Bellow called the American number of *Horizon* "a louse-up of life in the United States."[83]

Its chief louse was Auden. For the American *Horizon*, editor Cyril Connolly's opening comment takes the form of a travelogue and makes Auden in America the aperture through which the issue focuses its dismal assessment of American cultural promise. In the first entry of the in-crowd travel diary, "Wystan" is there to greet his friend when he arrives in New York. As Auden pops back up across the introduction, Connolly laces his evocation of the poet's American incarnation with bafflement and disdain. Already in the first entry, the poet strikes Connolly not as an American per se, but as a character reminiscent of a quintessentially American cartoon-commercial product: Auden's "welcome is like that of the town mouse to the country mouse in the Disney film."[84] The arc of the entry bends toward mourning the artistic effects of Auden's transplantation, and arrives at the same comparison *Time* made, albeit to a different end. Walking through Manhattan on his first night in postwar New York, Connolly calls to mind not lines from the American or, for that matter, the English Auden, but from Eliot's "East Coker." "I found the skyscrapers depressing, a huge black ferro-concrete architecture of necessity shutting out the light from the treeless streets 'Whose constant care is not to please / But to remind of our, and Adam's curse / And that, to be restored, our sickness must grow worse.'"[85] Thus Connolly's first entry in his stateside travelogue rebukes Auden with a quotation from the expatriate poet who had moved in the proper direction across the Atlantic and written the great English poem of the war. By the time a reader encountered Auden's poem "Music Is International" (admittedly, not among his best) later in "Art on the American *Horizon*," and certainly by the time *The Age of Anxiety* was published in England, readers there were primed to read Auden's work as symptomatic not only of his American problem but also of *the* American "problem" as *Horizon* defined it.

This, of all things, is the transatlantic print artifact in which Ellison debuted the short story "The Invisible Man," later to become the first chapter of *Invisible Man*.[86] The story's appearance in "Art on the American *Horizon*" was something of a coup for Ellison. In the baldly segregated hierarchy of late 1940s Anglo-American periodical culture, it marked his move "up" from African American to white intellectual print spaces.[87] Better known by the unofficial titles of the smoker or the battle royal, "The Invisible Man" narrates the ritual humiliation of the unnamed narrator and several of his African American peers, who are made to fight one another, scour an electrified rug for counterfeit coins, and ogle a naked white woman, all for the self-affirming entertainment of a Southern U.S. town's white bosses.

As a contribution to the project of "Art on the American *Horizon*," Ellison's story served diagnostic and antidotal ends. On the one hand, "The Invisible Man" documents the systemic racist hypocrisy of a nation busily announcing itself as the democratic beacon of the postwar. If

Horizon's audience likely heard Ellison's story as "a plaintive cry for the amelioration of U.S. racial conditions," as Lawrence Jackson writes, then this was a cry Connolly's British readers were for many reasons more eager than his white American ones to hear.[88] On the other, Ellison's contribution was meant to stand as a daring artistic achievement that defied the racially compromised and, contributors to "Art on the American *Horizon*" agreed, aesthetically compromising American democracy.

Stand it has. But what can the print history of "The Invisible Man" reveal about the subtler, timelier work the story was doing in *Horizon*? "The Invisible Man" begins with the unnamed narrator witnessing the death of his grandfather and arrives, after the gruesome battle royal, at his receiving "a scholarship to the state college for Negroes" (*IM* 32). Just after this deeply qualified triumph, the story concludes with a nightmare vision in which the grandfather directs the narrator to open the briefcase the town's white bosses have given him. In the waking narrative the briefcase contains a letter informing the narrator of his scholarship; in the nightmare it holds an endless stack of letters that begin in a polite bureaucratic language used to mask racist institutional power and end up at slur: "Keep This Nigger-Boy Running" (*IM* 33). Of this outcome, the novel as published in 1952 would confirm what the narrative economy of the short story implies: the scholarship gives the narrator a ticket to further racist humiliation in a series of institutional contexts that rely on and sustain racial hierarchy in the U.S. As Timothy Parrish writes of the nightmare's replays across *Invisible Man*, "except for the last one, each chapter ends with some form of [its] message."[89]

As situated in *Horizon*, Ellison's story sharpened the withering assessment of U.S. higher education that preceded it, Jacques Barzun's "The Higher Learning in America." Elegizing a model of liberal education he saw as grievously imperiled by the G.I. Bill, Barzun held that if "by higher learning, we understand the play of the original mind upon matters of fact and within the bounds of the academy," then the U.S. had none. Higher learning had "been broken in to mass education" by the forces of democratization, credentialization, and commercialization. In Barzun's view, the "ideal" of "mass education" radiated "an aura of 'democracy,'" but reduced citizens to uniform mediocrity, incuriosity, and anxiety. The U.S. needed to educate its citizens, Barzun understood. By "mass education," he writes, he does not mean "the traditional demand for the intelligent voter." Instead, Barzun explains:

I am thinking rather of the need to classify, label, and 'process' the population. . . . The market decrees that a capable person whose education has been genuine but irregular shall be debarred from advancement, often from employment. Whereas— "You've a B.A. with two years of psychology? Then we can use you in our personnel department." A college degree, a whiff of psychology or accounting or child guidance, is becoming as indispensable to the common man as a birth certificate, a passport, a *carte d'identité*.

This commercial test spurs individual anxiety (in place of the former "ambition") and turns all education into vocational training.[90]

In Barzun's view, a college degree had become nothing more than another requisite piece of paper in the administration of documented citizenship and market employability, with "individual anxiety" as its first and inevitable outcome. In "Art on the American *Horizon*," Barzun's elitist indictment of an education he sees producing only anxious, credentialed citizens opens onto Ellison's short story. But the vision of education in "The Invisible Man" is clearer-eyed about the racial politics that configure even the inadequate system, as Barzun describes it, of higher education in the U.S. The narrator of Ellison's short story and novel has the kind of "original mind" the Columbia don might prize, but Jim Crow segregation restricts his access even to the false promise of the college degree as *"carte d'identité."* Far from developing his mind or preparing him for full citizenship, the narrator's "genuine" education in *Invisible Man* nurtures in him nothing so much as feelings of uncertainty, desperation, confusion. In a word: *anxiety*. Only at the end of the novel does the narrator voice—not entirely convincingly—his acceptance of the midcentury prescription for anxiety: social "responsibility" (*IM* 581).

INSERT: ANXIETY

As *Invisible Man* depicts it, the narrator's education begins with the death of his grandfather. With his last breath, the grandfather bequeaths to his grandson an account of black U.S. citizenship as vigilant subterfuge of the

American racial political regime or as ongoing, even perpetual, civil war.[91] The narrative and political import of the grandfather's speech cannot be overstated. Nor can these measures of the significance of the speech be extricated from one another. It was his grandfather, the narrator explains, who "caused all the trouble"—which is to say, in narrative terms, that his deathbed confession first occasions and then repeatedly punctuates the episodic plot of *Invisible Man* and, in political terms, that his dying words offer a model of democratic citizenship with which the narrator wrestles throughout the novel.

I use the verb *occasions* to take up a generative question Kenneth W. Warren poses about *Invisible Man*: "What might it mean . . . to think of Ellison's only completed novel as . . . an occasional piece?"[92] Warren asks this question in part so as to cut through an accumulated critical tendency to assess the politics of *Invisible Man*, or of Ellison in the long aftermath of the novel, according to stark political oppositions—e.g., neoconservatives versus black nationalists, radical leftists versus anticommunist cold warriors. In something of the same critical spirit, my reading centers on two occasions—internal to the novel, the grandfather's speech, and external to the novel, the midcentury and its anxiety consensus—to argue that *Invisible Man* makes a timelier critique of the affective life of democratic citizenship than either recrimination of Ellison as sellout to the postwar liberal consensus or recuperation of him as democratic visionary can accommodate.[93] Ellison assembled this critique at precisely the moment when anxiety became loudly and irrevocably associated not only with the self-consciously *midcentury* present but with "responsible" postwar citizenship. From the summer of 1945, when the voice of the unnamed narrator of *Invisible Man* famously interrupted Ellison's work on a topical Second World War novel, through October 1947, when chapter 1 of *Invisible Man* debuted in *Horizon*, and on through April 12, 1952, when the novel was published in the U.S., the twinned temporal and political assertions of the midcentury anxiety consensus became all but naturalized in mainstream American print culture and public discourse. To invoke an anxious citizenry, to reiterate the endemic anxiety of the *midcentury*: these and like gestures became around 1950 so familiar as almost to escape notice.

Invisible Man noticed. The critical affective historicity of the novel resides in its engagement with the midcentury embrace of an anxiety cast as democratic and punctual to it. Principally through the ghostly figure of the narrator's grandfather and the haunting occasion of his death, *Invisible Man* frustrates the terms of the midcentury's internal selection of anxiety, exposing the racialization—the implicit whiteness—of the anxiety attributed both to the early postwar present and to the citizenship it required.[94] At the very least, the narrator's grandfather upsets the punctuality claims of the anxiety consensus; a figure of out-of-timeness himself, he also stakes African Americans' prior claim to any model of American citizenship conditioned affectively by fear, insecurity, or anxiety. As the grandfather recurs across *Invisible Man*, the novel makes a timely counterargument against the perils of investing democratic citizenship with anxiety—that is, with an affect that by definition suspends citizens' agency. Read in the light of the midcentury anxiety consensus, the retrospective narrative of *Invisible Man* becomes something of a cautionary tale for the early postwar period its prologue and epilogue address.

First, the death scene that occasions the novel. Born into American slavery, the narrator's grandparents had, since the aftermath of the U.S. Civil War, "stayed in their place, worked hard, and brought up [the narrator's] father to do the same" (*IM* 16). Or had seemed to. As he lies dying, the grandfather reveals his deferential comportment as a politics of resistance. He has performed humility, not been humiliated; his performance has enacted and masked a systematic effort to undermine the U.S. racial political regime. In *Horizon* and in *Invisible Man*, the scene reads:

On his deathbed he called my father to him and said, "Son, after I'm gone I want you to keep up the good fight. I never told you, but our life is a war and I have been a traitor all my born days, a spy in the enemy's country ever since I give up my gun back in the Reconstruction. Live with your head in the lion's mouth. I want you to overcome 'em with yeses, undermine 'em with grins, agree 'em to death and destruction, let 'em swoller you till they vomit or bust wide open." They thought the old man had gone out of his mind. He had been the meekest of men. The younger children were rushed from the room, the shades drawn and the flame of the lamp turned so low that it sputtered on the wick like the old man's breathing. "Learn it to the younguns," he whispered fiercely; then he died.

(*IM* 16)

The grandfather's confession retroactively reframes his habitual deference as a lived immanent critique of the cruel paradox of African American citizenship—which is also to say, of citizenship itself—in a legally and socially segregated and thus only nominally democratic republic, a United States that, as *Invisible Man* goes on to dramatize, was built on and persists in institutionalized racial hierarchy and state-sanctioned racist violence.

Fittingly, paradox is the governing rhetorical figure of the grandfather's speech. How can one be a "traitor" to "the enemy's country?" How can "agree"-ability destroy? The grandfather inhabits, in order to undo, the restrictions of the citizenship he gained legally in "the Reconstruction" and lived out in its political failure.[95] As it is related gradually in gestures and recollections over the course of the novel, the grandfather's life forms a record of those restrictions and his defiance of them. At one point, the narrator recalls that white election officials tried to prevent his grandfather from exercising the right to vote extended to him in the last of the Reconstruction amendments, the fifteenth. The authorities "demanded that he quote the entire United States Constitution as a test of his fitness to vote. He had confounded them all by passing the test, although they still refused him the ballot" (*IM* 315). Neither deference nor subterfuge nor extraordinary civic preparedness endow the grandfather with the full rights of citizenship for which, as his deathbed speech suggests, he fought in the U.S. Civil War.

The grandfather's dying words "became a constant puzzle which lay unanswered in the back of my mind" (*IM* 16). The "deathbed advice" recurs to the narrator at nearly every moment of provisional triumph, revealed crisis, or would-be resolution in *Invisible Man*, from the nightmare vision with which the first chapter concludes through the final, famous crescendo of questions about his grandfather's meaning in the epilogue. That last, oft-quoted rereading of the grandfather's dying words marks the last in a long line of attempts in the novel to solve the "puzzle" of the grandfather and settle the "trouble" he started. It matters, however, that those earliest descriptors of the grandfather's speech, "trouble" and "puzzle," have affective as well as intellectual and political connotations. For it is primarily via feeling that the grandfather's speech initially rivets the young narrator's attention and subsequently holds it throughout his coming-of-age narrative. The novel marks the intensity of feeling in and created by the grandfather's death scene in countless ways, and from the beginning through the end of the novel. The death scene itself plays out in the heightened emotional key of melodrama, complete with the set of sentimental clichés (rushing the children out of earshot, dimming the lamp, drawing the blinds) by which the narrator's folks try and fail to contain the grandfather's dying words. The grandfather's own feeling persists all the way into the narrator's final attempt, in the epilogue, to understand him: "Perhaps he hid his meaning deeper than I thought, perhaps his anger threw me off—I can't decide," the narrator admits as the novel winds down (*IM* 574). Was the grandfather's negative affect a deflection ("threw me off")? Or is his "anger," as the language of feeling in this passage and throughout the novel suggests, constitutive of the grandfather's "meaning?"

What can get lost beneath the manifest import of the grandfather's death scene as narrative catalyst or political premise are its affective implications for *Invisible Man*. What of the feelings related in and sparked by the grandfather's speech, in its first utterance and its serial reiterations in the novel? Despite the prevailing New Critical injunction, in 1952, against considering readers' emotional responses to the texts they read, this is not a second-order question, for reasons both internal and external to the novel. Internally, the "puzzle" of the grandfather and his dying words does play out as a matter of thought, interpretation, and argument—in the close reading line of *what did he mean?* But the grandfather's "puzzle" also plays out, equally if not more persistently, as a matter of the narrator's feeling—in the line of *how do his words make me feel?* Or conversely, what is the narrator feeling when he recalls his grandfather's words? Externally to the novel, normative accounts of "alert," "responsible," democratic citizenship came increasingly in the late 1940s to hinge on a single if endlessly shape-shifting feeling: anxiety.

The print history of *Invisible Man* suggests that the affective-discursive atmosphere of professed anxiety *at midcentury* made its way into the generally tense narrative atmosphere of the novel and specifically into the novel's precipitating incident. This history begins where the unnamed narrator's life story does, with "The Invisible Man" as published in "Art on the American *Horizon*" in October 1947. In "The Invisible Man" and in *Invisible Man*, a paragraph break shifts the narrative from the event of the grandfather's death to a recounting of the narrator's and his folks' response to his deathbed speech. The paragraph break thus facilitates the first of the novel's many attempts to read the grandfather's dying words. Sometime between late 1947 and the novel's publication in 1952, Ellison added a single sentence to the interpretive paragraph. The sentence (unremarked in the criticism, italicized here) organizes the profusion of affects to follow in it:

But my folks were more alarmed over his last words than over his dying. *It was as though he had not died at all, his words caused so much anxiety.* I was warned emphatically to forget what he had said and, indeed, this is the first time it has been mentioned outside the family circle. It had a tremendous effect upon me, however. I could never be sure of what he meant.

(*IM* 16)

The added sentence foregrounds the affective dimension of the "trouble," or the novel, started by the old man's dying words. Anxiety and its cousins—fear, unease, bewilderment, despair, outrage, confusion, shame—go on to drive much of the episodic plot and characterization of *Invisible Man*. Yet already in its very grammar and syntax, the comma splice miniaturizes how anxiety works. The sentence replaces the grandfather's death with his "words" as the "cause" of "anxiety." As the second independent clause extends the sentence over its grammatical end, "so much anxiety," too, outruns its ultimate cause in the theoretical abstract and its local cause in this episode of the novel alike: death. Anxiety exceeds all ends, reaching from the grandfather to the narrator's folks and, finally and much more extensively, to the narrator himself.

As it describes the affective reverberations of the grandfather's words, the comma splice initiates an affective relay in which the last enslaved and the first two free generations of an African American family are compelled to embody different configurations of "anxiety," labeled as such. First, the grandfather owns a state of hypervigilance as the purposeful condition of his citizenship. To borrow from Ellison in the introduction (1981) to the thirtieth-anniversary edition of *Invisible Man*, the grandfather may have fought "for his self-affirmed right to fight" (*IM* xii). Having "give up [his] gun back in the Reconstruction," the grandfather understands himself to have carried on the war ("our life is a war") for the right to have rights, as per a common definition of citizenship. Second, the narrator's folks disavow the political substance of the grandfather's deathbed confession. They cannot, however, escape their affective inheritance. Made anxious themselves, they try to contain the threat the speech poses to their own sense of security ("this is the first time it has been mentioned outside the family circle"); yet their effort confirms nothing so much as the precariousness of that security. Third, from this opening scene through the novel's epilogue, the narrator lives in the "anxiety" that follows from his grandfather's words. For him, the grandfather's "deathbed advice" is made urgent in this first instance and kept present throughout the novel not only or even primarily by its elusive "meaning," but rather by feeling, the "so much anxiety" it incites. In this sense, the narrator's folks were not wrong to be "alarmed."

While the narrator remains troubled by his grandfather's speech for the rest of the novel, his parents all but disappear from it. The grandfather's death rewrites the Freudian primal scene as an experience of felt, if not yet understood, political revelation: the narrator's necessary separation from his parents occurs as a consequence of his perception of their effort to sweep his grandfather's dying articulation of his politics under the proverbial rug. The narrator will not, or cannot, comply with his folks' request that he "forget what [his grandfather] had said." Instead, the grandfather's deathbed revelation "had a tremendous effect upon me," the narrator recalls.

Much of that "effect" manifests as unsettled affect. The emotional tenor of the narrator's initial response to his grandfather's speech is so pronounced as to suggest that he understands his grandfather intuitively, if not yet substantively. He might not get it yet, but he feels it, so to speak: the narrator senses the inextricability of his grandfather's anger, urgency, and vigilance from his model of citizenship. Hence the narrator's first attempt to read the dying words amounts to a series of feelings. By the end of the first paragraph of reflection on the grandfather's death, "his words" have become "like a curse." They have made the narrator feel "guilty and uncomfortable," "puzzled," "a guilt," "afraid," and "more afraid" (*IM* 16–17). Varying levels of guilt and fear, discomfort and puzzlement: if the missing word for this tangle of emotions in "The Invisible Man" seems to be *anxiety,* then Ellison supplied it in *Invisible Man.* The novel gathers the narrator's bad feelings under the affective term selected, during the years Ellison spent writing it, for the midcentury's affective self-apprehension and model citizenship.

Timely emendation, however, does not equal endorsement. *Invisible Man* hardly affirms the political efficacy of anxiety for black citizens of the U.S., citizens whom the grandfather describes as conditioned to anxiety and vigilance over a much longer postwar.[96] Instead, the death of the narrator's grandfather both initiates and, as it echoes across *Invisible Man,* anchors the novel's refusal to align neatly with the consensus anxiety of the midcentury present. The novel's precipitating occasion posits a political anxiety that extends back at least to the legal expansion of U.S. citizenship in the aftermath of an earlier war. From that narrative opening through the midcentury present from which its prologue and epilogue issue, *Invisible Man* depicts anxiety as neither punctual to the postwar nor distributed equally or to equal effect among all citizens.

ANOTHER POSTWAR

The main narrative of *Invisible Man* proceeds from a speech that maps the anachronistic, mobile, and pliable qualities of anxiety in the abstract onto African American citizenship won during and lived out in the aftermath of the U.S. Civil War. Which is to say that anxiety in *Invisible Man* is not punctual at all, to the midcentury or otherwise. Anxiety rather forms an affective counterpart to the temporal dislocations that configure the novel and helps to sustain the narrative's evasion of precise historical dating. Those dislocations begin as early as the grandfather's demise—in fact, before it. Exemplifying the kind of chronological-historical arithmetic that *Invisible Man* baits but frustrates, chapter 1 broaches the deathbed scene by making a point of not exactly locating it in time: "It goes a long way back, some twenty years" (*IM* 15). Counting back from 1947, when "The Invisible Man" was published in *Horizon*, puts the narrator's high school graduation in about 1927. The next paragraph goes still farther back in historical time, to the narrator's grandparents' emancipation, "eighty-five" or "About eighty-five years go." Again, if one counts out from the Emancipation Proclamation, which "told [them] that they were free" on January 1, 1863 (preliminarily issued on September 22, 1862), then the narrator recounts his story in about 1947 or 1948:

I am no freak of nature, nor of history. I was in the cards, other things having been equal (or unequal) eighty-five years ago. I am not ashamed of my grandparents for having been slaves. I am only ashamed of myself for having at one time been ashamed. About eighty-five years ago they were told that they were free, united with others of our country in everything pertaining to the common good, and, in everything social, separate like the fingers of the hand.

(*IM* 15)

Along with the rhetorical hedging—"*some* twenty years," "*about* eighty-five years ago," "at *one time*"—the allusive texture of the novel's opening paragraphs confounds any effort to fix the narrative precisely in historical time. But if the gesture to Booker T. Washington's segregationist "fingers of the hand" image, from his "Atlanta Comprise" address of 1895, contributes to the difficulty of placing this passage historically, then negative affect compounds it. The narrator's admission of his one-time, misplaced shame thickens the historical murkiness of the opening passage. Not coincidentally, this admission of having "at one time been ashamed" of his grandparents' enslavement also doubles as the narrator's first clear disclosure of his race in the main narrative of *Invisible Man*.

As it prepares for the deathbed scene, the opening passage of chapter 1 sets two negative-affective coordinates—first shame, then anxiety—for several historical eras. The narrator reflects on his life from the vantage of the midcentury postwar; the grandfather's death and the subsequent events of the narrative happen in the interwar period; and the narrator, like and care of his grandfather, comes to understand himself as the result ("I was in the cards") of another war, the U.S. Civil War, and its aftermath. The language of the grandfather's "deathbed advice" goes on to layer in at least two more discursive temporalities. The grandfather refits the African American folk figure of the trickster as a "traitor" and "spy in the enemy's country," thereby describing his performance of meekness with diction inescapably resonant, in the late 1940s and early 1950s, with the early cold war.

This dense anachronism at the start of chapter 1 aligns with the temporal configuration of anxiety itself and with the narrative design of the novel, which suspends its retrospective interwar narrative between a prologue and epilogue voiced from the early postwar. Throughout, however, the Second World War itself—which was, even as Ellison worked on *Invisible Man*, discursively remade into the "postwar" or "cold war" and anxious either way—remains conspicuously absent from *Invisible Man*.[97] This absence amounts not to the kind of willful dismissal of the war that popular adoption of "the age of anxiety" required, but rather to resignification. The novel's referential, epoch-making, and affect-shaping conflict is not the Second World War but the U.S. Civil War. Its central conflict in the name of democracy is at home and ongoing, rather than abroad and won.

It was not always or inevitably so. Ellison's well-burnished story of how he began working on *Invisible Man* opens in the summer of 1945. Ellison, who had served in the Merchant Marine, was at work on a topical Second World War novel when a voice interrupted him with what would become the first sentence of *Invisible Man*: "I am an invisible man" (*IM* 3).[98] The war novel "upstaged" by the narrator of *Invisible Man* centered on an American pilot captured by the Nazis and held in a prisoner-of-war camp (*IM* xi). Recalling the abandoned book in the introduction to the thirtieth-anniversary edition of *Invisible Man*, Ellison explains that the protagonist-pilot "was the officer of highest rank and thus by a convention of war the designated spokesman for his fellow prisoners. Predictably, the dramatic conflict arose from the fact that he was the only Negro among the Americans" (*IM* xi–xii).[99] Lest this plot "sound a bit extreme," Ellison provides context for it: "historically most of this nation's conflicts of arms have been—at least for Afro-Americans—wars-within-wars. Such was true of the Civil War, the last of the Indian wars, of the Spanish American War, and of World Wars I and II. And in order for the Negro to fulfill his duty as a citizen it was often necessary that he fight for his self-affirmed right to fight" (*IM* xii). This was not an original point, to be sure.[100] But later in the introduction, as Ellison elaborates on the prehistory of *Invisible Man*, his list of discrete or exceptional U.S. wars begins to morph into something like the grandfather's account of his life as a citizen—that is, into a vision of continuous war. Ellison recalls that while he "was in the process of plotting a novel based on the war then in progress, the conflict which that voice was imposing upon my attention was one that had been ongoing since the Civil War" (*IM* xiv).

The grandfather says it better. But Ellison's composition tale helps to bring out the entwined historiographical and affective stakes of the grandfather's—and the novel's—resignification at midcentury of "the war" and "the postwar" as an earlier war and an ongoing postwar. The grandfather initiates both the novel's collapse of wartimes and interwars and its complementary depiction of anxiety as coterminous with, if not constitutive of, the legal provision of African American citizenship. "Whispered fiercely" only two paragraphs into the novel, the grandfather's "deathbed advice" pitches *Invisible Man* against the notion of discrete, unusual wartimes that interrupt durable, normal peacetimes, with corresponding affects attributed tidily, "age of anxiety"-like, to each. If, to recall Paul K. Saint-Amour, a perpetual interwar analysis discerns "the underwriting of peace in spaces conceived as central by the persistence of war in spaces conceived as peripheral," then the grandfather's understanding of his life as a war elaborates a crucial corollary.[101] The anxious and anachronistic texturing of his dying account of his citizenship insists upon how, even and perhaps especially within those spaces conceived as "central," some citizens enjoy a sense of peace that is underwritten by other citizens' and other people's ongoing struggle for their rights and protections—and, circling back to the normative democratic channel for midcentury anxiety, for their ability responsibly to exercise them.

FEELING LIKE A CITIZEN

The grandfather's deathbed revelation sticks with the narrator not because his model necessarily works, but because it makes him *feel* at all. This affective pull opposes a larger pattern in the novel, wherein the bad feelings attached to others' civic instruction, such as it is, of the narrator—the town's ruling class of white men in the battle royal episode, Dr. Bledsoe at the college campus, Mr. Emerson in a New York office, Brother Jack in the Brotherhood—tend to fall away once the symbolic energy of given episodes is exhausted. Ritual or institutional, formal or informal, most of the narrator's education trades in a pedagogy of humiliation. Again and again, authorities try not simply to dictate the narrator's thought, speech, and behavior but also to suppress any feeling that might not heed their dictation. Along with their outward exposure of racist injustice in the U.S., these trials work internally on the narrator. They exert an affective discipline on him, teaching him to feel abjectly anxious or, better still by their logic, not to feel at all. While many occasions instruct the narrator in self-abnegating feeling, I'll conclude with two that double as turning points in the novel: the Liberty Paint and Tod Clifton sequences. Distinct from the otherwise mostly headlong narrative pace of *Invisible Man*—the novel, too, is "kept running"—these two sequences turn on the most static, held-still moments of *Invisible Man*, passages marked in the prose as moments of suspension.[102]

First, the narrator lands in the Liberty Paint hospital after being injured in an explosion in the company's factory: "a wet blast of black emptiness that was somehow a bath of whiteness. It was a fall into space that seemed not a fall but a suspension" (*IM* 230). He wakes up in the factory hospital only to undergo electric shock treatment to which he does not consent. The episode dramatizes medicalized white authority operating on a black body and mind; it is also a scene of perverse pedagogy several times over: the doctors in the operating room are undergoing their medical training, the "voice" of one doctor instructs others about how the therapy will work, and the narrator is being educated, too, into his continued and forced submission to racialized power. When the narrator's body shakes in response to "more current" coursing through it, an "oily face" looks in and says, "They really do have a rhythm don't they? Get hot, boy! Get hot!" In response to the racist joke, the narrator recollects:

And suddenly my bewilderment suspended and I wanted to be angry, murderously angry. But somehow the pulse of current smashing through my body prevented me. Something had been disconnected. For though I had seldom used my capacities for anger and indignation, I had no doubt that I possessed them. . . . I tried to *imagine* myself angry—only to discover a deeper sense of remoteness. I was beyond anger. I was only bewildered.

(*IM* 237)

In his forced suspension, the narrator learns the intended lesson: he is made "remote" from negative emotions that would threaten the emphatically white powers operating on him in this scene.

To understand the second occasion of the narrator's affective disciplining—Tod Clifton's funeral and the Brotherhood fallout from it— necessitates backing up to recall the problem with the narrator's first speech on behalf of the Brotherhood: it dwelled in feeling. In his early oration, the narrator serially states his own feelings and appeals to those of his audience. The climactic conclusion of the speech rides an anaphoric refrain of "I feel" and rises in volume from a "husky whisper" to all-caps exclamation. The narrator confides in the audience, "I feel, I feel suddenly that I have become *more human*" and, on the basis of this feeling, envisions himself as "a new citizen in the country of your vision, a native of your fraternal land" and ultimately the whole gathered crowd as "THE CITIZENS OF TOMORROW'S WORLD!" (*IM* 346). The audience loves it. The Brotherhood does not. This oratorical embrace of feeling as grounds for a new citizenship turns out to be "the antithesis of [their] scientific approach" (*IM* 350). The narrator requires months of training with Brother Hambro to stop speaking the language of his feeling of citizenship and start speaking the language of their "ideology." When the narrator emerges from his four-month Brotherhood crash course, this word suddenly peppers the dialogue—"I've worked pretty hard trying to master the ideology," the narrator remarks—but it is never substantively specified (*IM* 359). Sometime during Hambro's instruction, "ideology" has extinguished the narrator's glimpse of a full, equal, and mutually recognized citizenship predicated on "feeling human."

Later, after police murder Tod Clifton, the narrator mimics journalistic brevity to describe how news of the killing spread through Harlem: "A photograph of Clifton was sent to the Negro papers and published. People were stirred and angry. Street meetings were organized." Amid these passive-voiced happenings, the narrator decides to hold a public funeral for Clifton and, "released (by the action) from my indecision, I threw everything I had into organizing the funeral, though moving in a kind of numb suspension" (*IM* 449). The funeral scene distributes the narrator's affectless suspension outward into the iconography of the memorial service: he sees "the cheap gray coffin moving high upon the shoulders" of the pallbearers, as if it "floated;" he hears "the steady rolling of the drums with muffled snares, and all other sounds were suspended in silence" (*IM* 451). That suspension carries into the narrator's funeral oration itself, too, as he replaces the life-story model of eulogy with a stunned repetitiveness befitting the suddenness of Tod Clifton's murder by police. Rather than narrate the young man's life, the narrator stays in an eddy of repetition, calling out and riffing on Tod Clifton's name, over and over.

In one of the many sets of symbolic bookends in *Invisible Man*—or, to adapt the narrator's language, "boomerangs" that ricochet across it (*IM* 6)—the narrator's final break with the Brotherhood owes to the same thing the party tried to drill out of him early on: feeling. When the narrator is hauled up to account for Clifton's funeral, the Brotherhood leaders rebuke him again for appealing to shared, public feeling in his eulogy. They dismiss any feeling of racial kinship or corresponding sense of racial politics as "racist nonsense." Of Clifton, the narrator explains, "If he'd been white, he'd be alive." Over objections, he continues:

"You don't really think that crowd turned out today because Clifton was a member of the Brotherhood?"

"And why *did* they turn out?" Jack said, getting set as if to pounce forward.

"Because we gave them the opportunity to express their feelings, to affirm themselves."

Brother Jack rubbed his eye. "Do you know that you have become quite a theoretician?" he said. "You astound me."

(*IM* 469)

Brother Jack digs further into his condescension as the exchange continues, reminding the narrator that he was "not hired to think" (*IM* 469). His theory dictates that the narrator "slander[s] the political consciousness of the people of Harlem" by speaking of and to their feelings (*IM* 470). But the narrator now understands—feels—differently: "Can't he see I'm trying to tell them what's real, I thought. Does my membership [in the Brotherhood] stop me from *feeling* Harlem?" (*IM* 471, my emphasis). The direct answer to this rhetorical question is *no*, and Jack cannot "see" in any case. The narrative soon literalizes Brother Jack's blindness when, in a bald caricature of willful ideological myopia, his glass eye pops out of its socket.

Within the suspension of Tod Clifton's funeral, however, uninstructed feelings reemerge as a means through which people might "affirm themselves" and the narrator might claim political agency outside of prescribed "ideology." *Might* because the remaining plot and the epilogue move away from this potential. Immediately after his break with the Brotherhood, the narrator dives temporarily into the cool affect that allows the mysterious figure of Rinehart to move across spaces and personae governed by neither the Brotherhood nor the state.[103] Within a day of his break with the Brotherhood, the narrator has plunged into the manhole from which, twenty years later, he speaks the prologue and epilogue. So a question remains open at the end of *Invisible Man*: what would a politics informed by "affirmed feelings" look like for the narrator? More to the point, what would it feel like?

To ask is to return to the fault line that runs through the entire reception of the novel, on the outer sides of which, again, *Invisible Man* prevails as postwar affirmation of American liberal-democratic principles or founders into self-betraying accession to colorblind anticommunist liberalism of the early cold war.[104] But it is to return by way of the less rigid affordances of feeling and occasion, anxiety and midcentury. The epilogue is the sticking point. When the narrator makes his famous last reckoning with his grandfather's advice, he still "can't decide" whether his grandfather's "anger" was a part of or a distraction from his meaning. But he presses on, part asking and part asserting:

Could he have meant—hell, he *must* have meant the principle, that we were to affirm the principle on which the country was built and not the men, or at least not the men who did the violence. Did he mean say "yes" because he knew that the principle was greater than the men, greater than the numbers and the vicious power and all the methods used to corrupt its name? Did he mean to affirm the principle, which they themselves had dreamed into being out of the chaos and darkness of the feudal past, and which they had violated and compromised to the point of absurdity even in their own corrupt minds? Or did he mean that we had to take the responsibility for all of it, for the men as well as the principle, because we were the heirs who must use the principle because no other fitted our needs? (*IM* 574)

As the culminating reading of the grandfather's dying words continues, it reproduces the tension built into the syntax of its first sentence, which wrenches away from a question mark and toward a period. A seeking uncertainty lingers in this prized passage, surfacing in its predominantly interrogative syntax, extrapolations away from the source text of the grandfather's speech, and reiterations of "the principle" without ever stating what "the principle" is. The novel expects its readers to know ("We hold these truths to be self-evident . . ."), but the substance of the "principle," like the Brotherhood "ideology" to which the narrator earlier submitted, remains unarticulated. The texture of the passage records the narrator not precisely concluding that his grandfather meant to teach him to "undermine" the United States' betrayal of its professed democratic ideals rather than those ideals themselves. He rather wills himself to conclude as much.

Later, at the end of the epilogue, the narrator tries to rouse himself to come up from underground: "Perhaps that's my greatest social crime, I've overstayed my hibernation, since there's a possibility that even an invisible man has a socially responsible role to play" (*IM* 581). The narrator's apparent resolution to seek, or to resign himself to, a "socially responsible role" frustrates many critics and readers. Little wonder, given the convenient vacancy of the ready-made phrase and the noncommittal grammar of "perhaps" and "possibility" in which it floats. The word *role* alone suggests a course still set for rather than by the narrator; the phrase deflates the narrator's glimpse, just a few pages earlier, of citizens' possibly grander, more probing, collective "responsibility for all of it" and, it would seem, for each other. And besides, the cruel debacle of the narrator's high school graduation speech long ago established that "social responsibility," far from fostering social "equality," enforces racial segregation (*IM* 30–32). Is this—this bland acceptance of status quo social responsibility—really what affirming "the principle" means?[105]

According to mainstream accounts of anxiety and citizenship around 1950: yes. The narrator's "socially responsible role" sounds eerily close to the contemporaneous prescription for anxiety proffered by Rollo May and the consensus his *Meaning of Anxiety* represented. "Responsibility" courses through May's work. Framed as individual and personal, "responsibility" offers both antidote to and prescription for one's requisite anxiety: it channels that anxiety toward "alert" citizenship. May concludes his survey of modern interpretations of anxiousness, for example, by waxing Kierkegaardian in a pop-psychological key: "To the extent that an individual seeks to avoid anxiety, responsibility, and guilt-feeling . . . he sacrifices his freedom and constricts his self-awareness. Availing oneself of possibilities, confronting the anxiety, and accepting the responsibility and guilt feeling involved result in increased self-awareness and freedom and enlarged spheres of creativity."[106] The blithe colorblindness on which May's counsel rests is only too obvious. He envisions expanding "freedom" following unfettered from an individual's choice to accept "responsibility." The whole of *Invisible Man* runs counter to the presumption.

Yet May's account of responsibility does read like a crude-terms version of the plot outcome the epilogue strains to impose on *Invisible Man*. The narrator's attempt to affirm "the principle" and to accept a "socially responsible role" could scan entirely as a disappointing internalization of the midcentury anxiety consensus—except that the affirmation is so audibly ambivalent and the projection so rhetorically unconvincing. The narrator's "socially responsible role" shuts down a would-be politics predicated on "feeling human" (as in the arena speech) or feeling *together* (as at Clifton's funeral). The epilogue thus dramatizes how, in its elevation of one suitable and often incapacitating feeling, the midcentury anxiety consensus foreclosed on the full range of "human" feelings on which a truly democratic politics might build. It does not undo the vital "affirmation" of democratic principle with which *Invisible Man* tries to conclude to observe that the linguistic texture of the novel's epilogue evinces an earned and timely skepticism about the affective premising of democratic citizenship on ineluctable anxiety and dutiful social responsibility at midcentury. Nor does it undo the novel's broader democratic aspirations to note that the narrator's vague intention to play a "role" leaves him right where his grandfather was long before the midcentury, when anxiety got remade and racialized into normative postwar democratic feeling, but denied even his grandfather's anger. It leaves him out.

Chapter Three

ELIZABETH BOWEN AND SAMUEL BECKETT
WAITING IN THE MIDDLE

A century halfway along its course may be considered due to declare maturity. . . . The twentieth century's development, however, has been in some directions so violently forced, in others so notably arrested as to seem hardly to be a development at all, or at least to be difficult to recognise if it is one.

—ELIZABETH BOWEN, "ENGLISH FICTION AT MID-CENTURY" (1950)

That's been going on now for half a century.

—SAMUEL BECKETT, *WAITING FOR GODOT* (1953)

Where do we find ourselves at about the middle of *Midcentury Suspension*? This book began with the observation that, in and well beyond the Anglophone North Atlantic literary sphere, a staggering range of writing of the midcentury evinced intense awareness of its position at the middle of the twentieth century. This much might have seemed moot. As we saw in the introduction, however, neither the tautology nor the arbitrariness of the midcentury mark precluded historical actors, readers, and writers from attaching historical significance to it or from conceptualizing themselves as *midcentury* subjects.

While *midcentury* obtained as a keyword around 1950, the half-century mark has left only a synonymic trace on the literary and cultural-historical vocabularies most often applied to transatlantic writing and culture of the decade or so after the Second World War. *Midcentury* provides, in critical usage, a variant term with which to date works and phenomena of the postwar or cold war or to locate them in relation to late, long, or otherwise modified modernisms. Herein lies a consequential irony: perhaps more intensively than our counterparts in any other subfields, we scholars of modernist and postwar literature have for some two decades interrogated our own periodizing gestures and field-building projects, doubling down on some and loosening up about others. Yet for all this self-scrutiny, the subfields that surround and often subsume self-consciously *midcentury* work, modes of expression, and habits of thought still tend to neglect the midcentury's vocabulary for apprehending, representing, or evoking its own historicity. The modernist and wartime period models that inform the study of twentieth-century literature have in this sense preluded *midcentury* excavation.

My contention has been that in keeping with many of the keywords Raymond Williams began to collect in the late 1940s and early 1950s, the very unassuming quality of *midcentury* ought to invite, not to discourage, inquiry into its potential substance. It merits recalling at this point that in conceptualizing keywords, Williams writes of the inextricability of "the problems of [the] meanings" of certain words from "the problems [they were] being used to discuss." He continues, "I have often got up from writing a particular note and heard the same word again, with the same sense of significance and difficulty: often, of course, in discussions and arguments which were rushing by to some other destination." From its commencement at midcentury, Williams's "record of an inquiry into a *vocabulary*" relied on effecting a pause in the "rushing by" to points known.[1]

As should be plain by its rough midpoint, the present book pauses an accustomed rush by the midcentury—a tendency to read expressions of the period according to modernist historiographical and war-bound temporal schemas and their incumbent interpretative agendas. It seeks out what cultural work *midcentury* once did or inspired, what range of historical feelings, forms, and experiences the midcentury vocabulary, in its wide range of usage and implication, once held open or might now reopen to critical view. Digging for the substance once lodged in *midcentury* and its lexical cohort thus also opens onto the more conceptual line of argument running through this book. Being at the middle of the twentieth century and feeling self-consciously midcentury, inhabiting an epochal middle at once freighted with historical significance and merely chronological, living at a midpoint made discursively ubiquitous and yet persistently vague of portent: such experiences attest to the period's sense of suspension. A surprising array of imaginative works of and about the midcentury present bear it out.

Suspension points in two directions: it emerges primarily out of a neglected *midcentury* consciousness and imaginary and it describes the heuristic practice this book has been developing. With the latter point in mind, I want to pause briefly to reiterate what suspension has thus far afforded beyond critical recognition of itself in the form of trope (chapter 1) and affect (chapter 2). In the case of Bishop's neglected *midcentury* book, the point is not simply that *A Cold Spring* coheres around the trope of suspension but also that this organizing trope remakes the lyric *I* as, also, a midcentury historical subject. Especially as it works in the poems that look outward, without an "I," at a present rendered "historical," Bishop's suspension trope achieves a timely historicity distinct from and irreducible to transhistorical lyric, modernist belatedness, or cold war topicality. The *Cold Spring* poems about looking at the world are suspended in their discursively "historical" present, one whose elusive "meaning" the poems decline to declaim—or, for that matter, to diagnose according to the pop-psychological fashion of the time. Chapter 2's account of the midcentury anxiety consensus makes Bishop's lyric suspension in the historical present only more striking. There, we saw Auden's and Ellison's major works of the late 1940s and early 1950s confront the midcentury's habitual profession of its own anxiety. Reiterated across and beyond cultural, academic, journalistic, literary, and political discourses, this consensus anxiety rendered the negative affect punctual to what was beginning to be called "*the* postwar" or "the 'cold' war," and as all but compulsory for responsible liberal-democratic citizenship under the sign of either. The wartime setting and pervasive anxiety of the text that, despite its endemic anachronism, gave an early name to the postwar, *The Age of Anxiety*; the absence of the Second World War from the plot of *Invisible Man* and the novel's resignification of "the war" as the U.S. Civil War: the temporal-historical configurations of these key midcentury works interrupted then—and now interrupt— the neat and still prevalent alignment of anxiety with the postwar.

Which is to say, more expansively, that the heuristic of midcentury suspension helps to restore the range of felt and experienced proximities to the Second World War, or of what was called at midcentury "the recent war," that were endemic to the *post*war period in its earliest emergence. Even as *The Age of Anxiety* and *Invisible Man,* and, for that matter, Bishop's *A Cold Spring,* forestall the establishment of anxiety as a master key for the self-consciously historical present around 1950, these works make possible a crucial distinction between diffuse midcentury suspension and the regimes of suspense and anxiety used to help underwrite the cold war. Suspended amid wars of various kinds and wartimes of various duration, these works challenge their accession to the sustaining logics—political or temporal, affective or historical—of any discrete conflict.

Midcentury suspension names, and affords a means of recovering, the timely efficacies of tropes, forms, affects—and, the present chapter argues, of a behavior and an idea—connected to but not synonymous with generalized postwar anxiety, keyed-up cold war suspense, and the programs of interpretation marshaled in service of either. The behavioral mode of suspension the present chapter takes up is waiting; the idea is the middle itself; and the midcentury text that offers the most revealing exploration of both, Elizabeth Bowen's *The Heat of the Day* (1949), brings the present book into still closer thematic proximity to "the recent war" and, more specifically, to the middle of the war as Bowen imaginatively recovered it at midcentury. A classic late modernist, postwar novel of the Second World War, *The Heat of the Day* also stands as a signal narrative of midcentury suspension.

Consider an indicative passage from midway through *The Heat of the Day*. In the fictional fall of 1942, the protagonist Stella Rodney accompanies Robert Kelway, her lover, on a day trip to his suburban family home. Stella is a Londoner and a sophisticated divorcée. Her response to the Kelway women has a tinge of cosmopolitan dismissal about it. Ready snobbery notwithstanding, however, the family confounds Stella.[2] Once she might have pegged them as middle-class English and been done with it. But now, perhaps for the first time, Stella perceives the inadequacy of class and nationality as explanatory categories for people she encounters:

The English, she could only tell herself, were extraordinary—for if this were not England she did not know what it was. You could not account for this family headed by Mrs. Kelway by simply saying that it was middle class, because that left you asking, middle of what? She saw the Kelways suspended in the middle of nothing. She could envisage them so suspended when there *was* nothing more.[3]

"Middle of what?" At once off-hand and piercing, Stella's question about the Kelway family articulates a driving inquiry of *The Heat of the Day*. Her answer—"suspended in the middle of nothing"—describes the predicament of the novel, one doubly pressing given the novel form's long cultivation of the thematic terrain of middle-class life. *The Heat of the Day* prompts at every turn the question of what it and its characters are suspended in the middle of. "The war" is the obvious but insufficient answer, implying a retrospective fixity to the war's temporal bounds and a progressive inevitability to its timeline, whereas *The Heat of the Day* holds such clarities in suspension almost entirely. The novel is set in what we will see was both the historical and the rhetorical middle of the war, and it arrays countless other middles around its potent setting. The evocative title of *The Heat of the Day* is thus only the first of many middles in which the novel dwells: there are middle times diurnal (the novel's opening at dusk, for example) as well as historical (its setting mid-war), and middle spaces (liminal places such as archways and windows). There are unmade decisions, in-between affects, uncertain loyalties; there are the trappings of middle-class life and, for the protagonist, of a midlife synchronous with the middle of the century.

Uncredited in the scholarship, the thoroughgoing middleness of *The Heat of the Day* is not lost on anyone in it: characters in the novel live and already understand themselves to live in, as the metafictional narrator expresses it, "the middle part of the story, so that none of the realisations along [its] course were what had been expected, quite whole, quite final" (*HOD* 146). The novel's would-be suspense plot unfolds slowly, even obliquely, in what the narrator refers to as "the lightless middle of the tunnel" (*HOD* 100), which quick revision of the old cliché underlines the invisibility, for almost the entirety of the novel, of the end of the war. Forestalling the promise of light at the end, the subverted cliché of "the lightless middle" participates in the larger project of the novel: its reimagination not simply of "the war" but of the felt experience of time in the emphatic *middle* of the war, at the point of greatest uncertainty about when, or whether, the war would end.

In these broad strokes, the resolute middleness of *The Heat of the Day* might seem a bit too tidy. But neither the novel's setting in the middle of the war nor its broader imaginative coherence around suspension in many middles was an obvious choice—or easily won. Bowen struggled to arrive at these temporal and conceptual dimensions of the narrative. Unpublished draft materials and correspondence reveal that her novelistic recovery of the middle of the war was unimaginable—and *The Heat of the Day* all but unfinishable—without the historical and conceptual vantage afforded by her writing from another middle that fascinated her: the midcentury. Or, to borrow from one of several nonfiction explorations Bowen made of "the very nature of the contemporary," the "character" of the "century halfway along its course," and the "sense of the 'now'" around 1950, the writer's critically midcentury "angle of vision" did more than enable the manifold

suspensions in the middle that constitute *The Heat of the Day*.[4] It motivated them.

This chapter teases out how Bowen's critical midcentury vantage came
to shape several formal qualities of *The Heat of the Day*, including its style,
genre play, central motif of waiting, characterization, and historical setting.
Moving among these narrative manifestations of suspension, Bowen's draft
materials, and her ancillary writings about the midcentury contemporary,
the chapter documents the novel's refusal to capitalize in any predictable
way on hindsight afforded and colored by victory in the Second World War
and quickly channeled toward new imperatives of the postwar and cold war,
most especially, perhaps, the imperative to English national self-reassertion.
The Heat of the Day requires a reading that brackets the tendency to think
of works of the late 1940s as emanating from either side of a clean, clear line
between war and postwar, hot war and cold war, much less as legible (or
laudable) primarily in the terms of a waning or a self-regenerating modernism. The novel rewards a reading that discerns its midcentury suspension amid, and in contrast to, retrospective narratives of the war that were,
even as Bowen wrote and rewrote *The Heat of the Day*, fast hardening into
apparent inevitability.

HISTORICAL WAITING

Before turning in earnest to Bowen at midcentury, let me pause to acknowledge that if waiting is the mode of behavior one would expect to find in a
book titled *Midcentury Suspension*, then this expectation owes more to
Samuel Beckett's *En Attendant Godot/Waiting for Godot* than to any other
work of the midcentury, *The Heat of the Day* included. The two works are
roughly contemporaneous: Bowen wrote or rewrote most of *The Heat of the
Day* after the war and saw the novel published in 1949; Beckett wrote his
first play between October 1948 and January 1949, during the period of
extraordinary productivity he famously referred to as "the siege in the
room."[5] After many delays, he saw *Godot* premiered on January 5, 1953, at
the Théâtre de Babylone in Paris. It is an understatement to observe that,
in addition to contemporaneity, *The Heat of the Day* and *Waiting for Godot*
share a fascination with waiting. The novel and the play depict what
characters do, think, feel, and say amid protracted uncertainty and without ends in view—in other words, what characters do in all but unrelieved

middles. Waiting and deferral characterize the narrative mode, plot, and stylistic texture of *The Heat of the Day* at least as thoroughly as they do the performance of *Waiting for Godot*.

Several scholars have brought Bowen into conversation with Beckett, typically on the grounds of the writers' shared Anglo-Irishness and occasionally, if unwittingly, with the effect of elevating Bowen's work by associating it with Beckett's.[6] In the late 1940s, however, both writers were thinking about conditions and experiences of suspension, and in conversation with the midcentury present. More to the point, both were in conversation with those inconspicuous terms by which the midcentury expressed its sense of portent: Bowen most powerfully but not exclusively in *The Heat of the Day*, Beckett with surprising and funny baldness in *Waiting for Godot*. Lest the ubiquitous keyword *midcentury* (*mi-siècle*) and its cognates seem too arbitrary a semantic quarry for a writer as rigorous as Beckett, one might consider that his work often walks precisely the line that *midcentury* once did, between arbitrariness and depth of meaning, between nonsense and significance.

The relevance of *Waiting for Godot* to any exploration of suspension per se is self-evident. From premise and plot to dialogue and stage directions, *Waiting for Godot* assumes and inhabits suspension. The play depicts neither the beginning nor the end of Estragon's and Vladimir's waiting. Gogo and Didi simply are suspended, waiting, in and through the present of the performance. And while the premise of *Waiting for Godot* could be one of anticipation—Gogo and Didi are not just waiting but, as they frequently remind one another and the audience, waiting for Godot—the play is absent suspense. From the start, there is next to no expectation that Godot will show. In fact, the play's first extended dialogue game makes a point of removing expectation straightaway. That game amounts to a recognizably methodical mathematical proof in which Vladimir, waxing scriptural, and Estragon, resigned to humoring him, weigh the probability of Godot's arrival by proxy reasoning about the likelihood of human salvation. The proof begins with Vladimir saying, mostly to himself, partly to Estragon, and apropos of nothing, "One of the thieves was saved." After a scripted pause, Didi remarks of his own theorem: "It's a reasonable percentage."[7] He is thinking about the two thieves who, according to the Gospels, were crucified along with Jesus. Only Luke records that Jesus saved one of the thieves. But where Didi seems at first to mean that a one-in-two chance of being saved is a "reasonable," as in a decent, percentage, the next several lines of dialogue calculate the reason-ability of the odds of salvation. The odds do not look good. Dragging poor Gogo along with him, Didi loosely does the math and finds that the chance of salvation is at best one in eight. But while the "percentage" chance of salvation might be dwindling, the dialogue is hilarious. It finally ends with the first iteration of the play's only certainty, itself made up of a suspension: "We're waiting for Godot." By that point, we the audience already know Godot is exceedingly unlikely to show.

Per Vivian Mercier's indelible synopsis of *Waiting for Godot*, "Nothing happens, twice."[8] Suspension is not strict paralysis or stasis, however, and things do happen within the play's waiting: Vladimir and Estragon fuss over their ragged clothing and bodily functions, bicker, eat root vegetables, encounter Pozzo and Lucky, greet the boy, and consider the likelihood of Godot's arrival. Mercier's quip nonetheless picks up on how routinely the tramps comment on "nothing" happening or conclude that there is "Nothing to be done" but wait. (*Nothing* is a keyword of the play, as it is of *The Heat of the Day*.) The sheer familiarity of *Waiting for Godot* makes it worth recalling that Beckett's stage directions routinely call for micro-reenactments, between and within lines of dialogue, of the play's chronic deferral. The sparse directions indicate *"Pause"* or *"Silence"* far more frequently than they do anything else, such that to experience a performance of *Waiting for Godot* is to be held in one long suspension built of a marked series of shorter ones.

Is there anything historical about this waiting, this suspension? Seán Kennedy notes that critics long accepted Beckett "at his word when he said that he had 'no sense of history.'"[9] No longer. By 2017, Emilie Morin could conclude thus of the historicist track widening through study of Beckett's work: "the idea that [his] writing remains inextricably bound to the aftermath of the Second World War and its traumas may well be the only line of interpretation around which his critics have rallied unanimously."[10] What is up for debate is not whether but how Beckett's work remains thus "bound" to the war and its wake. With respect to *Waiting for Godot*, important accounts of the play's historical salience tend to take for granted that they must look backward or project forward from the time of Beckett's writing, seeking out either the ghostly presence of the war in the play or, less convincingly, attributing to the play an uncanny projection of the total mood of the entire postwar.[11] In short, despite the marked historicist turn in Beckett scholarship in recent years, the *midcentury* timeliness of the play's performance of suspension remains elusive. It has become commonplace, for example, to read the *donnée* of *Waiting for Godot* as metabolizing Beckett's experience in the French Resistance, during which waiting was "the central activity." In advancing this now uncontroversial argument, Marjorie Perloff borrows from the logic of *Waiting for Godot* and reasons from absence: "The word 'war' itself appears nowhere in *Godot*" or in Beckett's fiction of 1945 and 1946, she writes. "But the very absence of the word has an odd way of insuring its prominence."[12]

Maybe. *Midcentury* discourse, by contrast, is not absent from *Waiting for Godot*. The characters speak in the period's vocabulary for its own historical-chronological present—at the middle of the play, no less. Early in act 2, Vladimir and Estragon register the ubiquity of *midcentury* thinking and poke fun at it, too, summarizing their waiting in contemporary idiom. The tramps have been trying to recall what they were talking about earlier in the evening—"I'm not a historian," an irked Estragon remarks (*Godot* 72). Characteristically undeterred by failure, they try next to recollect what they did the night before. Estragon finally stumbles on it:

VLADIMIR: (*sure of himself*). Good. We weren't here yesterday evening. Now what did we do yesterday evening?

ESTRAGON: Do?

VLADIMIR: Try and remember.

ESTRAGON: Do . . . I suppose we blathered.

VLADIMIR: (*controlling himself*). About what?

ESTRAGON: Oh . . . this and that I suppose, nothing in particular. (*With assurance.*) Yes, now I remember, yesterday evening we spent blathering about nothing in particular. That's been going on now for half a century.

(*GODOT* 73)

"That's been going on now for half a century" or, in the original French, "Il y a un demi-siècle que ça dure."[13] The jibe is self-aware twice over. Estragon's remark comments internally on the performance of the play and gestures outside the play to the "half a century" that everyone everywhere seemed "now" to be "blathering" about. Estragon may be no "historian," but his hyperbole for an unbearably long duration—"half a century"—winks in perfect contemporary idiom at what we have seen was a broad and oft-reiterated attachment to the century's midpoint. The play borrows the arbitrariness of *midcentury* idiolect, documents the organizing power of the unit of the *half-century* at midcentury, and renders the mid-epochal gesture both salient and silly. Plus, it's funny dialogue.

Kennedy argues of Beckett's works written just after the war that "the characters rarely express themselves historically, but this does not mean they have escaped history. More often, in fact, it is the manner in which they are ensnared by a history—the content of which they have forgotten (or have tried to forget)—that proves decisive."[14] Recalling Morin's observation, "history" seems here to mean the war and its traumatic aftermath—most obviously, in the case of Vladimir and Estragon, the trauma of displacement. Yet Gogo's dismissive line marks a moment when a character does express himself historically, if not in an accustomed sense. Historical expression in this instance surfaces not necessarily as repressed "content" or veiled hint of the war. It emerges in a timely idiom for the historical present of the late 1940s and early 1950s. Among its functions in the script, "half a century" dates *Waiting for Godot*, or dated the play for its midcentury audiences; and, much as the idiom operated in its currency, it allows Vladimir and Estragon to skirt the burden of recalling, much less of recounting, the "content" of what they may have endured or are still enduring in the onstage present, whether that recollection would point to the historically traumatic or the performatively mundane, or to both, or still elsewhere.

A similar timeliness laces the play's early dialogue on and subsequent enactments of probabilistic reasoning, too. *Waiting for Godot* can be described, without much cheekiness, as a series of dialogic probability tests, repeated with slight variation, as to whether there really is "nothing to be done." The performance of probabilistic reasoning in the abstract evinces the oblique midcentury historicity—the timeliness, again as distinct from the topicality—of *Waiting for Godot*. In the immediate aftermath of the Second World War, national and international defense organizations inexorably began calculating nuclear strike probabilities and likely civilian casualties. In addition to national bodies such as the French Ministry of Defense, formed in 1947, or the U.S. National Military Establishment, constituted in the National Security Act of 1947 and renamed the Department of Defense in 1949, one might consider the language and anticipation of "armed attack" that premised the North Atlantic Treaty as ratified on April 4, 1949.[15] By

1964, common knowledge of cool, cruel defense calculation scenarios would inform Stanley Kubrick's satire of them in his classic film *Dr. Strangelove or: How I Learned to Stop Worrying and Love the Bomb*. By the 1960s, probability tests had a kind of whistling past the graveyard effect, in that calculations of likelihood and fallout both kept nuclear dread at bay and drew it just close enough to foster citizens' acquiescence to burgeoning security and intelligence regimes. In the midcentury moment of *Waiting for Godot*, however, repeated probability reasoning makes Gogo and Estragon feel and seem only less secure in their situation.

Given its stature, *Waiting for Godot* might easily stand as metonym for the cultural salience of suspension generally, or of waiting in particular, at midcentury. That the play does not thus stand offers further evidence of the general tendency to elide the terms and concepts by which the midcentury expressed the feeling of its own historicity—or, in perfect Beckettian style, expressed its sense that it could not express its meaning. More specifically in the present context, the plain-sight obscurity of the play's "half a century" time stamp helps to frame what is at stake in crediting the midcentury "angle of vision" that drives the suspension of *The Heat of the Day*. In corrective contrast to a long tradition of readings for the human-universal or the existential abstract, scholars now understand *Waiting for Godot* to be at least as much about the war as it is about an existential middle. This chapter affords *The Heat of the Day* a reading that moves in the opposite direction to discover a novel at least as much about being suspended in a fraught historical middle as it is obviously about "the war" full stop. For *The Heat of the Day* shares with *Waiting for Godot* a distinctly midcentury historicity neither extricable from nor reducible to the war that both works are, in varying ways, "about" and whose temporal bounds they trouble.

SUSPENSION OF SUSPENSE

Plot summary of any good novel risks reducing it to a list of events. Summarizing a novel as hazy and atmospheric as *The Heat of the Day* hazards something of the reverse: it risks overstating the eventfulness of a would-be suspense novel "notable for its almost total lack of event."[16] *The Heat of the Day* is moreover a novel whose metafictional narrator never misses a chance to point out that nothing much is going on in the story. (The word *nothing* recurs some 170 times in *The Heat of the Day*, or on roughly every other page.) What a summary of Bowen's novel can best illustrate, then, is how systematically the novel invokes, only to defer, the trappings of suspense fiction—how thoroughly it suspends suspense.

When the novel opens in September 1942, Stella, the fortyish divorcée protagonist, works as a translator in a secretive organization connected to the British war effort. She has been in love with Robert Kelway for two years. Robert, wounded in the evacuation from Dunkirk in 1940, now serves as an agent in an equally clandestine intelligence operation in the War Office. For sixteen of its seventeen chapters, the novel remains in the fall of 1942. The last chapter zooms ahead, first to the Little Blitz in 1944 and then to a muted account of the end of the war in Europe. At two points, the narrative rewinds from its midwar present to describe the Blitz, when Stella and Robert met and fell in love. This romantic timing accords with the set of public narratives—"classless civilian solidarity" and sexual license among them—that quickly grew up around the Blitz.[17] The Blitz passages have achieved outsize prominence in the critical reception of the novel. For her part, in a BBC interview broadcast on May 2, 1950, Bowen referred to "the 1940-London pages in *The Heat of the Day*" in terms suggestive of an obligatory assignment. Such passages rank among "what I might cold-bloodedly call my 'descriptive pieces.'"[18]

When we meet Stella, on the first evening of the story but not until the second chapter of the novel—she arrives late to her own story—she is waiting for a shady acquaintance called Harrison, who has invited himself to her London flat. When he arrives, Harrison insinuates that he is a counterspy in a position to know that Stella's lover is a double agent working for the Nazis. If Stella ends her relationship with Robert Kelway and takes up with Harrison instead, then Harrison will see to it that Robert's inevitable arrest is deferred "for quite a time" (*HOD* 36). *The Heat of the Day* is thus, as Maud Ellman observes shrewdly, "driven by serial sexual harassment."[19] Harrison's attempt to extort Stella into prostitution stands as the most glaring instance, not the only one. Most of the rest of the plot revolves around Stella's equivocation and delay as she tries to decide whether to credit Harrison's accusation and accept his criminal bargain. Not that she tries very hard: by the end of the novel, she has deferred a decision about Robert long enough that she doesn't have to make up her mind. Toward the denouement of *The Heat of the Day*, he confesses his treachery and dies in a "fall or leap" from Stella's rooftop (*HOD* 327). As with just about every plot thread in this novel, the cause of Robert's death—accident or suicide?—remains uncertain.

Romance, love triangle, espionage, battle wounds, blackmail, and treachery during the Second World War: *The Heat of the Day* could be a gripping page-turner. It isn't. There is never much doubt about the espionage premise: Robert is a spy, Harrison a counterspy; as for the ready-made spy-suspense plot, it generates little of the narrative tension on which such plots conventionally rely. *The Heat of the Day* reads more as a counter-suspense novel, a cousin of the popular thrillers of which, Allan Hepburn explains, Bowen had a "circumstantial" knowledge "conditioned by the cultural currency of espionage plots in the 1930s and 1940s."[20] (Incidentally, suspense fiction coalesced as a literary subgenre during the aftermath of the Second World War. The first usage of "suspense fiction" recorded in the *Oxford English Dictionary* comes from the October 3, 1952, issue of *Spectator*.)[21]

The point is not simply that *The Heat of the Day* adopts a premise, plot, tropes, and character types familiar from suspense stories only to generate little feeling of suspense. The point is rather that the novel's invocation and subversion of the propulsive energy of suspense points up its sustained suspension in the middle. Bowen writes an intrigue novel whose suspense premise and plot become so dilated as to void suspense and turn it into suspension. As in *Waiting for Godot*, wherein marked pauses and silences undergird overt statements and enactments of the play's essential waiting, such heightened suspension of suspense does not magically create itself. Two formal features of *The Heat of the Day* prove integral to its maintenance of suspension at the levels of genre, plot, and pace: the central behavioral motif of waiting and the characterization of the spies.

First, the motif. What characters do most frequently in *The Heat of the Day* is wait. Rather than narrate, say, consequential discoveries, intriguing clues, or daring actions that would fantastically reassert the strength and coherence of British masculinity—à la James Bond, who appeared in 1953—Bowen returns again and again to depictions of characters and collectives waiting. Characters in *The Heat of the Day* wait for each other, for trains, for telephone calls; they wait to see what will happen in the next hour or year; and they wait to see what others will say or do in a series of meantimes. We first meet several characters in the act of waiting, as if they are waiting to be narrated as much as they are waiting for anything else. Introducing Harrison at an outdoor concert in the opening chapter, the narrator remarks, "Unmistakably he was waiting for something here." Louie Lewis, a young woman sitting near Harrison, tries to catch his eye: "That recurrent look of his . . . had begun to be noted, to be wondered at, then to be lain in wait for—it was at last to be trapped" (HOD 6). Louie thus enacts the predatory meaning of to wait: "to watch with hostile intent; to spy upon, to lie in wait for."[22] The young wife of a soldier, Louie is the central character of the novel's subplot. Late in The Heat of the Day, she becomes pregnant by a man who is not Mr. Lewis, a plot twist which reinforces her as a veritable figure of waiting and expectation, and of imagined futurity. The final chapter aligns her pregnancy and the birth of her son with the imminent, then achieved, Allied victory in the war. In keeping with its central motif, the novel depicts this arc toward V-E Day as a collective waiting: "Expectation came to its height, and stood: everybody waited" (HOD 367).

When Stella enters the novel, she, too, is waiting: for Harrison. She would rather not be. The narrator takes the occasion to generalize: "Nothing is more demoralising than waiting about for someone one does not want to see" (HOD 20). As, in her opening wait, Stella fusses idly with the cord on a window blind, her fidgeting subdues a material, domestic symbol of air war and blackout to the mundane posture of waiting. This dynamic remaking of war into waiting repeats across the novel, as when the narrator describes Stella's son Roderick's Army training as made up mostly of "long docile will-less waits for his turn for something further to happen, fatigues, inspections, or simply hanging about" (HOD 52). The waitings of various kinds pile up: Louie keeps "a look-out for Harrison in the park" (HOD 159); Robert waits for Stella at Euston Station (HOD 201); one evening, Stella signals the end of a muted argument over a restaurant dinner with a perfectly tautological observation straight out of Sartre on bad faith, though she gives more credit to the waiter's work: "We're keeping the waiter waiting" (HOD 223). And in one of countless instances wherein The Heat of the Day reads itself, the novel has a little fun with its serial reconfiguration of the waiting motif. In an inventive sequence late in the novel, Bowen writes one side, Stella's, of the inquest into Robert's death. Reading the protagonist's responses to questions about what she was doing the night Robert died, it becomes clear that the interviewer has quibbled her nonpurposive definition of waiting: "Before that? Simply waiting about.... No, not for anything in particular.... Very well, then I was not waiting. When he had gone I was simply there in the room" (*HOD* 341). Examples of waiting about—for events, arrivals, or information, for someone or something, for peace, or "not for anything in particular"—proliferate in *The Heat of the Day*. Every character waits repeatedly. As these waits accumulate, they perpetuate the temporality of suspension in which most of the novel unfolds.

Whether by atmospheric connection or direct statement, the narrator routinely ties discrete, private moments of waiting to public experience of "that 'time being' which war had made the very being of time" (*HOD* 109). In the novel's final glimpse of Stella's son Roderick, during the Little Blitz in 1944, he is visiting Mount Morris, an estate he has inherited in neutral Ireland. Thinking of Stella in London during the bombing, the estate's caretaker, Donovan, laments to Roderick:

> "All the same, it was a pity you couldn't prevail on her to wait here."
> "Wait here what for?"
> "The better times."
> "Oh."
> (*HOD* 355)

On leave from his wait-laden Army service, Roderick seems to have forgotten that one might wait for "better times" or for anything, rather than simply wait. In the temporal economy of the novel, his comical shrug of a response ("Oh.") attests to how acclimated its characters and narrator are—and by extension how accustomed its readers, too, become—to the multiply configured waiting that suspends suspense. In *The Heat of the Day*, Bowen depicts wartime not as a duration exclusively of perpetual suspense but as a duration in which characters become accustomed to the experience of functionally endless suspension and thus settle into an experience of duration possibly without end.

One of the achievements of Bowen's novel, then, is that it narrates wartime, a putatively temporary and exceptional kind of time, as it becomes inextricable from time itself—perhaps irretrievably so. The narrator's many interjections about waiting, time, and the feeling of waiting in time both contribute to this narrative achievement and become a principal means by which the novel keeps its readers in suspension, in wait. For the narrator's ruminative and authoritative asides frequently suspend the narrative in order to meditate on time, "their time," "our time," "history," and the experience of time as the war remakes it. The narrator emphasizes, for example, that Stella and Robert's romance owes not only to the material, professional, and psychic exigencies of the war but also, and more specifically, to what the war has been doing to the collective sense of time. "Wartime, with its makeshifts, shelvings, deferrings, could not have been kinder to romantic love," the narrator reflects. In this context, the novel's central couple "discussed any merging of their postal addresses not more seriously than they discussed marriage—happy to stay as they were, afloat on this tideless, hypnotic, futureless day-to-day" (*HOD* 109). Stella and Robert can indulge in this "futureless," nonreproductive relationship in part because of how their ages, genders, and life experiences line up with social expectations and their historical situation: Robert is a wounded hero; Stella has already fulfilled her social duty to bear children; and they are both about forty, in any case—outside the typical purview of the marriage plot.

In the oddly enchanted, gerundive ("shelvings, deferrings") wartime meanwhile in which they wait, the option of married blandness presents itself only in reaction to a crisis. Robert proposes to Stella after she confronts him with an allegation of his treachery. (A wonderfully sour comedic view of marriage punctuates this moment: the two have been talking vaguely of a picture of the *Titanic* when Robert proposes.) Stella suggests they go on waiting instead. Where "Roderick, at the beginning, had been the reason" for keeping the lovers' relationship as it was—separate rental flats, unmarried—now Stella calls on the historical situation to defer Robert's proposal: "There doesn't seem to be much to marry for, at the moment, does there? Why not wait till we see what's going to happen next? We always have" (*HOD* 109, 219). Stella figures their historical situation as an experience of temporal suspension, that is, as at once temporary ("for the moment") and enduring ("always"). Her deflection of Robert's proposal relies on the assumption that reasons to go on waiting will keep presenting themselves; it suggests that the lovers have forgotten that the suspended feeling of wartime might one day, perhaps, cease.

Robert's proposal follows on one of the most discussed passages in *The Heat of the Day*. In it, the narrator takes "Stella paused in the act" of pouring coffee as an occasion to meditate on the inextricable feeling of time, wartime, and history. As we readers are made to wait for the story to continue, the narrator explains that the lovers are not alone:

Their time sat in the third place at their table. They were the creatures of history, whose coming together was of a nature possible in no other day—the day was inherent in the nature. Which must have been always true of lovers, if it had taken till now to be seen. The relation of people to one another is subject to the relation of each to time, to what is happening. If this has not been always felt—and as to that who is to know?—it has begun to be felt, irrevocably. On from now, every moment, with more and more of what had been "now" behind it, would be going on adding itself to the larger story. Could these two have loved each other better at a better time? At no other would they have been themselves; what had carried their world to its hour was in their bloodstreams.

(*HOD* 217)

"Time," "history," "no other day," "the day," "moment," two uses of "always" and three of "now": the accumulation of temporal words holds open this abstract, lyrical rumination on "their time" in felt relation to "history" and "time" itself. As it negotiates the personal and the historical, "history" and "now," "their world" and "their bloodstreams," the passage distills such would-be distinctions into an understanding—described as a feeling, as *felt*—of the inextricability of people's lives from "time" or "what is happening." This may not be a new insight ("who is to know?"), the narrator concedes, but it is "now to be seen."

Easy to overlook as it modifies *felt*, the adverb *irrevocably* may be the essential word in this excursus. With it, the narrator captures a dawning sense that the feeling of "their time" is not temporary or limited to "what is happening." It will be "felt" after "what is happening" has happened and when the war is over, if it ends. The adverb quietly registers the collision of historical and narrative vantages in this passage: there is Stella, whose "pause" while pouring coffee in 1942 opens the narrative space for a meditation on time and history; there is the narrator, perceiving evidently from a later date the endurance—as opposed to the wartime exceptionality—of a new feeling of oneself in time and as a manifestly historical subject ("creatures of history"). Finally, there is the position of the passage in the narrative sequence of *The Heat of the Day*. This representative meditation on how the feeling of wartime had, by 1942, created a new feeling of time itself pauses the novel just at the moment of what would, in one kind of genre fiction, be a moment of riveting suspense (*Stella has confronted her traitor spy lover!*) and what would, in another kind of genre fiction, romance, be the climactic moment of tension and release (*will she accept her lover's proposal of marriage? She must!*). The narrator has readers, too, waiting at the table, not enjoying the gratification of romance or suspense, but rather witnessing the wartime feeling of suspension pervade a scene between lovers and begin to extend its duration "irrevocably" into the future.

The deferral of suspense in *The Heat of the Day* underlines the novel's narrative commitment to suspension; scenes of waiting repeatedly renew this suspension at the expense of suspense. Hence it is only fitting that the single most potent scene of waiting in the novel doubles as its most explicit exercise in the suspension of suspense. Stella walks home alone the evening after her visit to the Kelways' home. As she walks, she imagines occupied Europe and feels an encroaching threat: "Tonight, the safety-curtain between the here and the there had lifted; the breath of danger and sorrow travelled over freely from shore to shore" and the "very tension overhead of the clouds nervously connected London with Paris" (*HOD* 139). In this mood, Stella reaches the "less anonymous dark" of her street. Just as she begins to speed up toward home, however, the eerie sense that someone is watching her checks her determined pace:

That she should seem to perceive a figure posted, waiting, that she should instantaneously know herself to be on the return to a watched house, *could* be only another deception of the nerves. She had so dissolved herself, during the walk home, into the thousands of beings of oppressed people that the idea of the Someone was, at its first flash, no more than frightful fulfillment of expectation. Now her approaching footsteps were being numbered; no instinctive check or pause in them went unmarked. *Her* part—listening for the listener, watching for the watcher—must be the keeping on walking on, as though imperviously: the actual nerved-up briskness of her step, the tingle up from her heels as they struck the pavement, brought back what seemed to be common-sense. But her very decision that there could not be anyone synchronised with the evidence that there *was*—a match struck, sheltered, then thrown away. This—for how could it not be a watcher's object to stay obliterated up to the last moment?—was bravado, gratuitous. This was a sheer advertisement of impunity; this could not but be Harrison—for who else, by his prodigality with matches, in these days when there were to all intents and purposes none, gave such ostentatious proof of "inside" power?

Having come into inside range of the door and watcher, Stella shifted her bag to take out her key. Half-way up the steps she said over her shoulder, flatly: "Been waiting long?"

(*HOD* 140)

The style of Bowen's narration of Stella's walk is itself "nerved-up," the diction as charged as the syntax is circuitous, hesitant, and passive. Observations are reiterated or amplified: first Stella's steps are tallied, then no break in her stride goes "unmarked"; first the striking of the match is "bravado," then "sheer advertisement." The narrator tracks Stella's thoughts as she first tries to calm herself down and then begins to perform keeping her cool, acting her "part." Finally, just as Stella makes the "decision" that no one is hiding in the darkness waiting for her to return to her flat her "decision" meets its disproof. With the striking of a match, the passage begins to interject rhetorical questions that convey Stella's indignation with Harrison for presuming to call on her and trying to intimidate her. As Stella approaches her door, the passage settles itself down. It moves from "*could* be only" to "could not but be," or from Stella's italic-tenuous reassurance of herself to her acceptance of her initial hunch. Stella's recognition of Harrison's "ostentatious proof"—a single struck match—that he is unusually well-connected also stands as the novel's only piece of material evidence of either Harrison's or Robert's espionage activities. The match's brief flare replaces the ghostly human presence Stella has been sensing (all those "thousands of beings of oppressed people") with this one specific "Someone." Stella might be exasperated by Harrison's "figure posted, waiting," but she does not fear him; and a scene that had promised tension boils down to a question in no need of answer, "Been waiting long?"

This exemplary instance of waiting cancels a paradigmatic situation of suspense: a woman's walk home alone one night—during a war, no less, and under sustained threat from a man trying to extort her for sex—to find said shady man waiting for her. But Stella's walk home is exemplary of *The Heat of the Day* in another important way too: the style of this passage reenacts at the level of prose syntax the novel's suspensions of suspense. Here, as often in the novel, Bowen's prose already reads itself: the narrator and protagonist have already interpreted Stella's nervousness, as well as Harrison's reason for blowing his cover in the darkness. Even the pleasurable suspense of interpretation—the project, in this case, of tracking clues and figuring out whether someone is waiting and why—eludes.

PERIOD CHARACTERS

Like the spy premise, inert plot, and motif of waiting, much of the characterization in *The Heat of the Day* participates in the novel's suspension of suspense. Most notably in its figuring of the spy Kelway and the counterspy Harrison, *The Heat of the Day* cites characterological expectations of genre fictions only to subvert them. Once again, the novel announces this subversion. If it strains credulity, for example, to learn in the final chapter that Harrison and Kelway are both named Robert, rest assured that the characters and narrator already know it: *The Heat of the Day* acknowledges its central characters' incredibility, their sheer unlikeliness according to literary convention. Here is Stella on her exasperation with Harrison: "By the rules of fiction, with which life to be credible must comply, he was as a character 'impossible'—each time they met, for instance, he showed no shred or trace of having been continuous since they last met" (*HOD* 155). When Stella confronts Robert with Harrison's insinuation, he deflects her accusation by calling it "immaterial, crazy, brainspun, out of a thriller" (*HOD* 212). He accuses her of reading him like a genre novel and implicitly, given his loaded adjectives, as a hysterical woman reader would read a genre novel.

Bowen notes the extent to which Stella, too, frustrates other characters' attempts to read her according to a character type. If Stella's generally untroubled indecisiveness under the duress of Harrison's threat undoes the type of the damsel in distress, then she also disappoints an ex-cousin-by-marriage's expectation that she, an attractive divorcée, will be a femme fatale. The exchange makes a gendered inversion of the stereotypical genre-fiction-readers at whom Kelway seems to scoff. Not Stella but the cousin, one Colonel Pole, plays the novel's internal credulous reader: "Having never, at least so far as he knew, found himself eye to eye with a *femme fatale*, he had no means of knowing whether he now did so," the narrator remarks (*HOD* 90).

This cast of baldly unbelievable characters either did not sit well with or was lost on early reviewers of *The Heat of the Day*, who for the most part professed their respect for Bowen's earned stature as a novelist while regretting the incredibility of her spy story, and of its characters in particular. Subsequent critics have risen to Bowen's defense, justly celebrating, in Neil Corcoran's words, the novel's "wry exposure of its own fictionality" as manifest especially in its characterization. For Corcoran, "life's being not 'credible,' is the ethical and ontological chasm which yawns everywhere in the book."[23] Still, to pause on the terms by which first reviewers assessed the unbelievability of Bowen's characterization is to be reminded that such standards of assessment are historical as much as they are generic. In the case of *The Heat of the Day*, early reviewers snagged on the question of Robert Kelway's allegiance and motivation. The question was less "Is this character believable?" than "Is he believable in the late 1940s?" In *Partisan Review*, Elizabeth Hardwick called out Bowen for being "too cautious to mention the one thing that *might* have motivated Robert Kelway, anti-Semitism, since it is hard to see what else the Nazis had to export to England and America."[24] Orville Prescott's disbelief in Kelway stemmed from his belief in precisely the kind of worn cliché of cultural superiority that *The Heat of the Day* declines to peddle. Surely, Prescott wrote in the *New York Times*, "the treason of a British officer and a gentleman" needed more accounting for than Bowen provides.[25] (This American critic was even more invested in the mythos of upright upper-class English manliness than many of his English counterparts.) A still a more telling example of reviewers' dissatisfaction with Bowen's picture of Kelway comes from Diana Trilling, who proposed in the *Nation* that Bowen ought to have updated the character's treachery (perhaps to make it read more along the political lines of her husband Lionel Trilling's recent novel with the epochally apt title *The Middle of the Journey* [1947]). In her estimation, Bowen's choice to make Kelway a Nazi rather than a Communist "diminishes the stature of the story. And yet with striking ease Robert could be rewritten into a Soviet instead of a Nazi agent; Miss Bowen's insight into the psychological sources of his treachery is as pertinent to the one form of totalitarianism as to the other."[26] Privately, several of Bowen's literary friends shared Trilling's view.[27]

The untroubled anachronism of this suggestion recalls the ease with which reviewers and commentators proclaimed *The Age of Anxiety* to be not at all meaningfully about the war. If Trilling's comment betrays her postwar vantage, it also lays bare how thoroughly the anticommunist imperatives of the early cold war inflected the period's standards of characterological credibility and literary import. Trilling's and other readers' proposed change of Robert's allegiance could be made "with striking ease" only in the shallowest political sense. To retrofit Robert as "a Soviet" would have required wholesale resetting of the novel with respect to the Second World War and the shifting of international alliances during and after it. Trilling, of course, could not have known that the question of when and how to set *The Heat of the Day* in relation to the war was the single most difficult knot Bowen struggled to untangle as she worked on the novel. Regardless, she was unwilling, in 1949, to imagine that the relative opacity of Kelway's motivations resulted from a deliberate choice on Bowen's part.

Or perhaps even a subversive choice. Patrick Deer argues astutely on this point that the "seemingly perverse coding of the traitor [as a fascist agent] ironically undermines the certainties of burgeoning Cold War ideology."[28] Where the historical feeling evoked in Elizabeth Bishop's *Cold Spring* poems often escapes the *cold war referential index*, Bowen's characterization patently inverts it. Bowen opted not to parlay the putative fungibility of communism and fascism into an "easy" index of her spy characters' believability, adjust the rest of her novel-in-progress accordingly, and then bask in the book's newfound cold war relevance and "stature." And this despite the fact that the writing of the novel gave her more and more trouble.

Bowen's depiction of Kelway declines to subscribe to a cold war model of characterological credibility. Nor does her novel tell the anticommunist story that its readers were, by the late 1940s, being primed to believe. But there is more at stake in this defiance of emerging conventions of postwar and cold war fiction than blanket refusal of them. For it does not follow from Bowen's characterization of Kelway as fascist traitor and Harrison as Allied sexual predator that all gestures to what we might call "periodic characterization" in *The Heat of the Day* happen in the mode of refusal. Bowen's depictions of Kelway and Harrison disdain to gratify cold war spy and, for that matter, war hero tropes that were pressed into the service of rebuilding the English national self-image in the postwar, to be sure. Her more thorough characterization of Stella, however, consistently aligns the protagonist with the fluidity and freight of the alternate periodic marker *midcentury*.

Roughly the age of the century, Stella Rodney is the perfect protagonist for a novel as intent on assembling and exploring inchoate middles as *The Heat of the Day*. In complement to her characteristic ambivalence and habitual deferral, Stella belongs to several demographic middles: she is upper middle class; she is middle-aged, which in any number of other novels would disqualify her from being caught in the middle between two men; she is a national "hybrid" with citizenship not otherwise or further specified; and, the point Bowen came to emphasize in the novel, her age synchronizes with the twentieth century approaching its middle. Bowen's periodic characterization of her protagonist makes a significant and, her manuscript drafts reveal, deliberate departure from the conventionally national underpinnings of novel characters. A key component in the novel's fraught composition history, Bowen's gradual arrival at Stella's characterization by her generational membership and contemporaneity with the century attests to the midcentury perspective that finally unlocked the writing of the novel for Bowen and turned *The Heat of the Day* into a story of suspension in the middle of the war.

In a promotional blurb she wrote for the novel in late 1948, Bowen noted that Stella, Kelway, and Harrison "have one thing in common: the noon of their lives coincides with the glare of the noon of their century."[29] As it happens, though, the novel emphasizes only Stella's "coincidence" with the twentieth century—and right from the start. The published version of *The Heat of the Day* sketches in Stella's vague backstory by positioning her life in relation to the epoch: "Younger by a year or two than the century, she had grown up just after the first world war with the generation which, *as a generation*, was to come to be made to feel it had muffed the catch" (*HOD* 24). The pileup of verb tenses stitches this flashback into the narrative's retrospect, even as the image of botching "the catch" briskly ironizes the war-as-sport metaphors that reigned in Britain at the start of the First World War.[30] In a similar vein, the emphasis on "the generation, *as a generation*" subtly records the emergence, in England, of the generation as a meaningful unit of cultural expression and protest out of the trenches of the First World War, as well as a certain exhaustion with generational rhetoric in the aftermath of the Second. To the former point, one might think of Wilfred Owen's refusal to address his elegies to "this generation" (his), to which they could be "in no sense consolatory."[31] To the latter, certainly owing in part to nationalist cooptation of the generational protest poetics of the Great War and to rage at the ruling gerontocracy in Britain during the Second World War, British writing of the late 1940s and early 1950s records fatigue with generational rhetoric.[32] (Barbed humor often courses through this fatigue, as in Henry

Green's making funny hay of generation-speak in *Nothing* [1950]. The novel makes a running joke of middle-aged parents who are far less responsible than their adult children.)[33] Stella's itinerant, unmarried, of-the-"now" attitude versus her son Roderick's earnest traditionalism: this opposition participates in a period trope of intergenerational inversion and reinforces Stella's generational-epochal status as a coordinate of her character.

But Stella's contemporaneity with the twentieth century was no given. Bowen's drafts of *The Heat of the Day* reveal that the challenge of working out how to characterize Stella Rodney was second in difficulty only to the related problem of when and how to set the narrative in relation to the Second World War. Studying these drafts entails watching Bowen begin to tie her demographic depiction of the would-be heroine of a would-be suspense novel—a novel predicated on treachery against England—not to Stella's nationality, but rather to her lived age and synchrony with the course of the twentieth century. Most striking about Bowen's gradual arrival at Stella's age, generation, and epochal portent is that these take over in the drafts largely at the expense of clear indications of Stella's nationality. As Bowen wrote and rewrote and then reworked *The Heat of the Day* in the late 1940s, references to the century came to outweigh references to English nationality or, more pointedly still, to Bowen's own settler-colonial caste, the Anglo-Irish, as a mark of the protagonist's character.

The most telling removal comes from a passage that also addresses a dissolving sense of nationality as a site of certainty, posterity, and heritable superiority. An early, much-fussed-over draft of Stella's visit to the suburban home of Robert's family, and to that Englishness Stella sees "suspended in the middle of nothing," has the narrator remarking of Stella: "Her extraction was from the class that for generations has made quite a lively business of nominally dying out: sold lands, what was left of their value in capital, a house she could not care or bear to revisit now in other hands, some tablets in a seldom visited church and some lines in Burke and the smaller print of Dobrett provided her starting point, you could not say for where."[34] "Burke" refers to John Burke, an Irish genealogical writer whose *Burke's Peerage* (first edition, 1826) stood as an authoritative guide to the British aristocracy. (*Burke's* rivaled *Debrett's Peerage*, first published in 1796).[35] The references to "some lines in Burke and the smaller print of Dobrett [sic]" and to "the class" slowly dying out depict Stella, in this early draft of *The Heat of the Day*, as definitively Anglo-Irish. From the final draft, however,

Bowen struck both the *Peerages*, blurred the house, and removed the definite article once used to refer to Stella's class. Stella became not a member of "the" class that had long been "nominally dying out" but rather of "*a* class that has taken an unexpected number of generations to die out" (*HOD* 125, my emphasis).

The small change makes a big difference: it is no doubt possible that Stella, like Bowen, is Anglo-Irish; to many of Bowen's critics, it might seem perverse to suggest that Stella is anything but. Yet the fact remains that in drafting *The Heat of the Day*, Bowen arrived at a protagonist who, having "for intervals lived abroad" and "knowing two or three languages, two or three countries," hails from no definite place (*HOD* 25). Like much else in this novel and the time in which it suspends itself, Stella's nationality remains uncertain. Throughout *The Heat of the Day*, Bowen stresses Stella's age and her membership in a generation, her citizenship not so much of a nation as of the century approaching its middle. By crediting Stella's epochal characterization, however, I do not mean to imply that Bowen was blithe about the condition of statelessness, especially after the war. To the contrary, Bowen's hashing out of her characterization of Stella records an attempt to imagine a life not necessarily bound to a state or to national narratives, a character not defined first by reference to nationality or the corrosive violence of nationalism. An Anglo-Irish writer, Bowen was a stranger to neither; and it is, after all, patriotic work in service of the nation that affords and launders Harrison's ability to harass Stella.

A MIDCENTURY ANGLE OF VISION

Like her protagonist, Bowen was the twentieth century's daughter. Born on June 7, 1899, Bowen was keenly aware, throughout her writing life, of being roughly the same age as the century. Much of her fiction testifies to the appeal that grand and minor synchronicities of this kind held for her imagination. (Recall in this vein how Stella's "very decision that there could not be anyone synchronized with the evidence that there *was*.") The most public phase of Bowen's career spanned the midcentury, when she was working on and later promoting *The Heat of the Day* and gaining renown as a lecturer and broadcaster. Much of Bowen's nonfiction of this period mines twinned and timely interests: first, in how her own life tracked with the progress, such as it was, of the twentieth century; second, in the midcentury present—the *now*—and in the qualities of the art that would best evoke that present. Both of these interests resonate with broader patterns of midcentury reflexivity and with the narrative design of *The Heat of the Day*. Both also stand in refreshing opposition to habitual denigration of midcentury writing and in contrast, too, to ageist assumption. Bowen's many reflections on midcentury contemporaneity attest to the fact that her writing grew more experimental, and stranger, as she aged in step with the century. And her expressly *midcentury* writings find Bowen drawing on her lived age, epochal experience, and aesthetic sensibilities to replace the modernist criterion of the "new"—never quite a fit for her work in any case—with a midcentury feeling of "now," or a feeling, as in *The Heat of The Day*, of a suspended moment cognizant of earlier "nows" but also keenly attuned to its own distinct historicity.

The radio play *A Year I Remember—1918* (1949) offers Bowen's fullest exploration of the first major interest of her nonfiction at the half-century mark: her lived synchronicity with the epoch. First broadcast by the BBC within weeks of the publication of *The Heat of the Day*, the play dramatizes its author's coming of age in step with the twentieth century and with the end of the First World War.[36] When the narrator remarks, "In 1918 I was 18," the citation of the calendar year crystallizes the play's treatment of the maturation narrative as a matter less of sexual or psychological development than of history and historical self-awareness.[37]

The play opens in century-mindedness: "One may live to be a hundred—more than a hundred: it can be done."[38] As evidence, the narrator recalls knowing, during her childhood, centenarian "old ladies" who remembered Waterloo. "'Extraordinary,' I thought, 'to remember history.' For, *I* was a child before 1914. History, to me, was a book closed—only to be taken out in the schoolroom. The *finale* of violence was, Waterloo."[39] The opening quickly if quietly remakes "history" into unending "violence," or violence as it is remembered, experienced, and anticipated across generations and without the lapsed promise of "*finale*." The opening voiceover also heralds the play's understanding of women's and children's experiences as constitutive of "history" rather than irrelevant to it, even and especially as their experiences and recollections might frustrate dominant expectations of historical memory. Bowen thus empathizes early on with one of the "old ladies" who does not recall hearing the news of Waterloo on June 18, 1815. The older woman does, however, remember that "a rabbit bolted across our garden path [with our] dog hot after it" on that day.[40] "How baffling, the memory of another person! But, above all, how baffling one's own!" the narrator exclaims. She goes on, initially in a rhythm reminiscent of Kelway's after Stella confronts him, to note that memory can be

crazy, out of proportion, personal. Storing up nonsense, throwing fact away. If it were not so, the pattern of history would be clearer—but also, perhaps, less coloured? Now, *why*, for instance, should I remember 1918 so much more forcibly than I remember 1914? True, 1918 is four years nearer to me in time; but so many years are behind me, that ought not to matter. All *reason* argues, that as a child brought up inside the illusion of security, I should have been dinted by the outbreak of war.[41]

Yet it is the year of the Great War's end that Bowen, writing not long after the end of the Second World War, remembers "most deeply."[42]

The depth of memory offered in *1918—A Year I Remember* involves not a relay of war events or headline news plotted on a timeline, but rather feelings and impressions. The war calendar of 1918 scans as consistently opaque in the play; the year Bowen remembers is "made up of large shadows, uncertain visions, and small things."[43] Of fall 1918, for example, the narrator records: "October, the French entered St. Quentin, the British, Cambrai. The enemy pulled out of Ostende; we took Lille. . . . But I don't remember; I don't remember. All I remember is the possible Victory coming at us like headlights over dips and hills. To be a young person who didn't know what to make of the world yet, anyhow, under any conditions, was to feel like a rabbit in the middle of the road."[44] Where this image reaches back to those "old ladies" whose youths coincided with Waterloo, just at the end of *A Year I Remember—1918*, Bowen's empathetic gaze reaches forward as well, to midcentury youth. "To be young *now*, after the Second World War—I am always wondering what that must be like. Perhaps though, there is not so much to learn?" the narrator half asks, half states.[45] Extending a pattern of marked parallels between the recollected feeling of 1918 and the early aftermath of the Second World War, Bowen's almost-question suggests that the gruesome repetition and escalation of violence on a global scale means she can indeed imagine something of what it must be like to be young in the late 1940s. Bowen can relate, too, to the mediation of the Second World War and its aftermath. At one point, the play recalls a male announcer in 1918 encouraging his audience to think of "the works or the offices in which you do your bit; the shop or kitchen" as battlegrounds. "That was *1918*—does it sound familiar?" the narrator interjects, roughly equating the official narratives of national resilience promulgated during and after both wars.[46]

Bowen's emphatic "to be young *now*" speaks to the second line of thinking that runs across her nonfiction of around 1950. In a cluster of essays and lectures including "The Poetic Element in Fiction" (1950), "The Cult of Nostalgia" (1951), "English Fiction at Mid-Century" (1953), and "Subject and the Time" (1954), Bowen meditates on the "character" of the contemporary moment and on the project and purpose of arts of the present at the middle of the twentieth century.[47] Published in the *New Republic* in 1953, the review essay "English Fiction at Mid-Century," for example, far exceeds the default promise of its title. The essay enlivens the commonplace *at midcentury* formula by applying a novelist's vocabulary to the public impulse to view the half-century as a meaningful unit. It approaches the twentieth century at its middle in terms of epochal "character," and more specifically as a character living out a lifespan with distinct phases of "development" and "maturity." Rather than argue with the expectation of midcentury assessment, Bowen accepts that

in general, something is expected of, or at, the turn of a century. A term of time by being demarcated acquires character, which, as such, makes itself evident as it matures. So a century halfway along its course may be considered due to declare maturity, to have reached culmination-point, to make seen the fruition of its inherent ideas. The twentieth century's development, however, has been in some directions so violently forced, in others so notably arrested as to seem hardly to be a development at all, or at least to be difficult to recognise if it is one. In European countries, certainly, life and art are still seeking their footing in their actual time— both have the stigmata of an over-long drawn-out adolescence.[48]

Though it accepts the premise that "a century halfway along its course" might well account for itself, the passage turns into a demonstration of the impossibility, by midcentury, of any tidy evaluation of the century's progress toward "maturity" or "fruition." The narrative of epochal "development" promised at "the turn of the century" has stalled at midcentury. Bowen instead elaborates a sense of "our time" as suspended that echoes across her own midcentury writings and chimes with *midcentury* discourse. "English Fiction at Mid-Century" specifically maintains that if there is a problem with recent fiction, the problem is not that fiction's failure to answer the midcentury's constant "call" for a curated display of its collective "significance and expressiveness." The problem is rather that too much of recent fiction seemed to Bowen to lapse into nostalgia "during this phase of apparent self-regard." If rose-colored self-regard was to be understood as English fiction's chief "value" "as an export" at midcentury, then Bowen's characterization of Stella Rodney as the century's contemporary refused to peddle it.[49]

Bowen's critical meditations on the midcentury "now" argue the necessity of contemporary artists' effort to evoke the feeling of suspension in their own present, rather than to lock down on some governing meaning of or outcome for it. As if heeding her own call, Bowen often employs rhetorical questions to structure these writings on the elusive "nature of the contemporary." Interrogative syntax facilitates Bowen's negotiation between what she understands as the midcentury's distinct "now" and all those past "nows" held present somehow in the art of earlier periods.[50] Consider, to this point, the rhetorical questions with which Bowen concludes the BBC lecture "The Cult of Nostalgia," which aims to embolden young writers in their works about their "now": "What of the present, the 'now,' the moment—so disconcerting, so fleeting, so fascinating in its quivering inability to be pinned down? What has great art done but enclose that eternal 'now'?"[51] Or consider the question that opens Bowen's most probing exploration of the aesthetics of the midcentury present, "Subject and the Time": "How do we judge contemporary art?" The lecture offers no answer.[52] Rather than establish criteria or take refuge in the "sublimated familiarity" of received aesthetic values to "judge" the art of the present, Bowen turns her remarks to the "sense" or feeling of the midcentury itself: "Our sense of our time *is*, in fact, a sense. As such, it is ever-open, susceptible, and at its least articulate when it is most honest. Today is to be felt rather than known."[53] Later, Bowen elaborates: "At no time can man have been more aware of time—of his own time, its climate, character and potential meaning. Our art plays intensely, endlessly on our time-consciousness. To an extent, *our time is our art's subject*," no matter its "ostensible, concrete subject."[54]

For Bowen, the vitality of contemporary art around 1950 inheres in "our time-consciousness" not in spite but because of "our" awareness of the irresolution of that consciousness. At its best, the art of the present addresses "our own nagging modern disorder—our frustrated, our haunted, taunted uneasiness with regard to what is our own time," rather than proffering an antidote to it.[55] "Subject and the Time" holds that the author's midcentury "angle of vision may, by its choice, be no less eloquent" than the ostensible subject of her work.[56] For "one aim of art," Bowen writes, "is at once to concentrate and to deepen our sense of the 'now.'"[57]

"IT IS NOT A WAR NOVEL"

Bowen's embrace of the midcentury angle of vision and her thinking about the midcentury *now* shaped her epochal characterization of Stella and, the point to which I now turn, her treatment of both historical setting and history itself—violence—in *The Heat of the Day*. Even thus to posit the import of Bowen's distinctly midcentury *now* chimes with important readings of the temporal dexterity of Bowen's fiction of and about the Second World War. Some of Bowen's most astute critics describe her short stories of the war, *The Heat of the Day*, and her broader postwar fiction as palimpsestic works in which multiple historical vantages configure narrative presents. The adverb *now* became ubiquitous in Bowen's fiction and prose of the late 1940s and early 1950s, which effect Emily C. Bloom ties to the technological and "temporal imperatives" of Bowen's radio work of the period and sees play out in her later novels. In Bloom's account, Bowen's "turn to the 'now,'" which developed alongside her broadcasting career, allowed [her] to resist nostalgic reading and writing in the wake of the twentieth-century wars."[58] And also during them: whereas Bowen's war stories (written during the war) were once customarily read in the tradition of Anglo-Irish Gothic or the "immediate context" of the war, Thomas S. Davis argues that the stories fuse these frames, making a narrative "constellation where the past is legible in terms of the present moment" and the wartime present "understood, and indeed narrated, as another iteration . . . of an eclipsed era's fraught hopes."[59] Finally, in his indispensable reading of *The Heat of the Day* in the context of the postwar adjudication of culpability and criminality, Allan Hepburn finds the novel working "out the effects of history on characters during the war and, in an enlarged perspective, during the postwar as well."[60] "*The Heat of the Day*," he continues, "exists in a double time-frame: 1942 to 1944, the span of the plot, overlaps with 1945 to 1949, when Bowen, thinking about the implications of European history, drafted the novel."[61] What I mean to lay out is something related to and different from such readings of the historical layering of Bowen's fictions of the war and its aftermath, namely, that Bowen's subtle attention to the suspended feeling of the midcentury engendered her novel's suspension in the "lightless middle" of the war.

Suspense is not the only genre *The Heat of the Day* holds in suspension. There are also the war novel and the Blitz romance the book never quite agrees to be. Within *The Heat of the Day* and after its publication, Bowen was at pains to distinguish her work from both. The novel's two flashbacks to the Blitz, for example, occur in a lucid past perfect that registers the emergence of a kind of immediate nostalgia for its atmosphere and inoculates against continued romanticizing of it. "The autumn of 1940 was to appear, by two autumns later, apocryphal, more far away than peace," the narrator reflects, before putting the novel firmly back in the autumn of 1942: "War moved from the horizon to the map. And it was now, when you no longer saw, heard, smelled war, that a deadening acclimitisation to it began to set in." Again: suspension, not suspense. This sensory distance and emotional numbness characterize what the narrator figures, in the same paragraph, as "the lightless middle of the tunnel" (*HOD* 100).[62] Recall that at least three historical vantages inform the Blitz excursuses: the recollected experience of 1940; the narrative setting in 1942; and, comparatively neglected in the criticism, the later, midcentury moment from which the narrator tells the story of *The Heat of the Day* and from which Bowen writes it. This later historical middle seems to have impressed upon Bowen the importance of imaginatively recording the hazy, uncertain middle of the war, a protracted wartime quickly written over by both the "myth of the Blitz" and postwar public victory narratives laced, as Bowen might put it, with "self-regard."[63]

The Heat of the Day also suspends broader war novel plot trajectories and expectations of drama or violence, especially as these had played out in the Great War books to which it was fashionable in the 1940s to compare—and find wanting—Second World War writing. Hence it emerges that Stella, far from being a femme fatale, granted her First World War veteran husband a divorce so that he might return to the nurse who had cared for him during that war. The revelation revises the soldier-nurse plot trajectory enshrined in, for example, Ernest Hemingway's *Farewell to Arms* (1929), a novel otherwise famously ironic about the linguistic and formal conventions of war stories.

At other points, the narrator more directly records how *The Heat of the Day* and its characters diverge from accustomed tropes of war novels. When Roderick visits his mother's rented flat in September 1942, they are alike aware that his "homecoming should have been one more chapter added to an august book, a book on a subject greater than themselves." Instead, "wariness had driven away poetry: from hesitating to feel came the moment when you no longer could. Was this war's doing? By every day, every night, existence was being further drained—you, yourself, made conscious of what was happening only by some moment, some meeting such as tonight's" (*HOD* 58). Figured as a daily sedimentation of unshakeable numbness, wartime, as *feeling*, checks the characters' ability to live up to "the moment" of homecoming. Mother and son both already understand their failure as "a sign, in them, of an impoverishment of the world" (*HOD* 58). The narrative excursus on wartime feeling goes on to describe Stella's blacked-out flat in terms that also describe the prose of *The Heat of the Day*:

The day had gone from the moment Stella had drawn down the fitted blinds and drawn across them the deadening curtains: now nothing took its place. Every crack was stopped; not a mote of darkness could enter—the room, sealed up in its artificial light, remained exaggerated and cerebral.

In spite of this, something happened—petals detached themselves from a rose in the bowl on the escritoire, to fall, one by one, on to Stella's letters on the pulled-out flap.

(*HOD* 59)

I have already suggested that *The Heat of the Day* is itself something of a tightly sealed narrative chamber (every blind fitted, every crack stopped) in which every detail and turn of phrase comes to feel weighted with moment, even as the characters dwell in prolonged suspension. The rose petals falling onto a writing table strewn with letters only reiterates this point: at least metaphorically, the falling petals have an agency (they "detached themselves") that the human beings caught in the "grander" historical situation lack. Stella and Roderick simply are detached. They are characters not in an "august" book—or, by way of a quick pun, in an August 1914 book—but in a September book, a novel of the Second World War, which conflict's start was already dated in Anglo-American literary history by Auden's "September 1, 1939," and more broadly in the works for which Leo Mellor proposes a "prolonged 1939" analysis.[64]

Upon publication of *The Heat of the Day*, Bowen pressed the point that "it is not a war novel," sometimes drawing on a conveniently limited definition of war novels to do so. She herself confronted the awkward task of summarizing the novel in late 1948, when her publisher requested a promotional teaser. The blurb Bowen wrote was never, to my knowledge, used for marketing. It would make for strange dust jacket bait, since it provides little detail about the plot of *The Heat of the Day* and instead makes a series of distinctions between Bowen's novel and war novels as she understands them. While the blurb notes, for two examples, that the novel depicts "no violent act" and ranges beyond the war zone of London, the chief line Bowen draws between her book and a war novel is neither topical nor geographical but temporal. The copy begins: "This is a story set, outwardly, in a particular phase of the Second World War, but it is not a war novel, being perennial in subject. The scene is embattled London, though the experiences, memories and desires of the characters open, also, on other places and times—the past, the future, Ireland, the coast of Kent." It concludes: "All through *The Heat of the Day*, what might be drama runs into little pockets: this is a domestic novel. Within view of the reader there is no violent act. Persons hesitate or calculate; and at the same time are inseparable from history."[65] Expressly so in the novel, since the narrator, authoritative and reflective, routinely interjects to meditate on characters' experience of time, their time, and history. In Hepburn's gloss, and in keeping with most feminist readings of *The Heat of the Day*, Bowen's blurb suggests that her "domestic novel registers the impact of the war on a human, not epochal, scale."[66] Yet among the war's human-scale "impacts" are precisely the characters' felt "acclimatisation" to the feeling of wartime and their experience of a mid-war duration they all seem to understand—and the narrator certainly understands—*as* epochal, even exhausting, in its historical significance. To evince this precise feeling of time, Bowen revised her novel to dwell almost entirely in "a particular phase" of the war.

Until its abrupt concluding chapter, *The Heat of the Day* disdains to date or measure its own fictional progress—or rather, its fictional suspension—by recourse to the war's timeline. Breaking war news intrudes on the plot of *The Heat of the Day* at only one point before its conclusion. Even in this lone instance, the breaking news is murky, at best. At the middle of the novel, chapter 9 of seventeen, Stella travels to Ireland to attend to matters at the estate her son has inherited from his late father's family. The chapter ends with Stella and Donovan, the estate's caretaker, learning of Allied progress in North Africa in the fall of 1942—sort of. Stella is out walking the grounds when

she heard or imagined she heard a call from the house behind her, and turned to walk back towards it. Ahead of her and above she at once saw Donovan standing on the parapet up there, making gestures, unhearably shouting into the air between him and her. She sent back a gesture of not hearing, feeling her heart beat as she quickened her step: he steadied himself again on the parapet before shaping both hands into a megaphone. Vowels rolled down the valley . . .

". . . Egypt!"

"Wait, I—"

"Montgomery's through!"

"Montgomery?"

"A terrible victory!"

Sun blinded her from above the roof of the house as she stumbled up the slope, pulling at grass tufts, stopping to shade her eyes. She panted: "A victory in a day?"

"It's the war turning."

"How did you hear?"

"It's all through the country."

(*HOD* 197–98)

Stella can neither quite hear (Donovan has to make his "hands into a megaphone") nor consistently see Donovan (she is "blinded" by the sun), a sensory bewilderment that perhaps reflects the poor quality of broadcast news service in neutral Ireland during the war. (In a section on "War News in the Country" in her controversial *Notes on Eire*, written for the British secretary of state for foreign affairs between 1940 and 1942, Bowen gives a factual account of the difficulty of getting war news in Ireland and of the further delay in news reaching the countryside.)[67] Stella's sensory bewilderment down the slope from Donovan's "vowels" asserts the haziness of this war news *as* news in the novel. In this instance, Donovan's exclamatory headline report exists in gerundive suspension in the present of the novel—*standing, making, shouting, hearing, feeling, shaping, pulling, turning*—and itself remains suspended: the news is a "shouting in air."

In *The Heat of the Day*, then, the trope of breaking news creates only a vague sense of the historical event and its significance. As a headline, "Egypt! . . . Montgomery's through!" begs for a what, where, when. Donovan is shouting news of the multiphase Second Battle of El Alamein. (No "victory in day.") But trying to use this moment to clarify the imprecise timing of Stella's trip to Ireland, which occurs sometime around late October 1942, does not help much. Instead, recourse to external chronology only points up the feeling of the middle of the war as Bowen's novel recreates that temporal-affective state. Stella and Donovan hear of what Bowen's readers in the late 1940s and early 1950s might well recognize as not only the war's historical middle but also as its *rhetorical* middle. It was the Allied victory at El Alamein that prompted Winston Churchill, at the Lord Mayor's Luncheon on November 10, 1942, to remark in fullest Eliotic mode: "Now this is not the end. It is not even the beginning of the end, but it is, perhaps, the end of the beginning."[68] I have suggested that it is not sufficient to describe *The Heat of the Day* as Second World War novel. It is a novel of the middle of the war, a novel whose depiction of wartime feeling is enabled by Bowen's midcentury "angle of vision." If the midcentury vantage made the middle of the war imaginatively recoverable in *The Heat of the Day*, then it also seems to have made that recovery more urgent. Otherwise, it's difficult to fathom why, as the composition of the novel grew increasingly troublesome, Bowen didn't simply hitch her would-be suspense novel-war novel to the war's timeline and map out a story running with retrospective clarity from dreadful beginning through "lightless middle" to victorious end of the war.

DRAFTING THE MIDDLE

A prolific writer, Bowen was an established presence in British, Irish, and U.S. literary culture well before midcentury. In the 1930s alone, she published four novels, each more commercially and critically successful than the last: *Friends and Relations* (1931), *To the North* (1932), *The House in Paris* (1935), and *The Death of the Heart* (1938). Though Bowen made her name before the war and wrote beguiling short stories during it—"wartime, none of them *war*, stories," she wrote—she did not publish *The Heat of the Day* until four years after the war ended.[69] She began work on the novel in 1944, in London, and had the first five chapters drafted by that summer. She wisely sent copies of these outside the city for safekeeping. Bowen lived at 2 Clarence Terrace, Regent's Park, an area that was bombed in 1941–42 and again in 1944. Bowen's home was damaged in both attacks, and so severely by a V-1 rocket in 1944 as to leave it "hollow inside."[70] In addition to her other literary work during the war—her stories of civilians in war were compiled in *The Demon Lover,* now a canonical collection, in 1945—Bowen contributed to the war effort in two official capacities. She served as an air raid precautions warden and, between 1940 and 1942, she wrote those intelligence briefings from Ireland for the British Ministry of Information, chronicling the neutral Free State's attitude to what it officially called "the emergency."[71]

The exigencies of the war and the demands of her war work necessarily slowed Bowen's pace on *The Heat of the Day.* But beginning as early as the spring of 1944, Bowen's eagerness to finish her new novel became a refrain in her literary correspondence; occasionally the need to finish the book gave her an unassailable excuse for declining requests for contributions to magazines or other invitations.[72] In a pattern with which any number of writers can sympathize, Bowen serially projected completion dates for her novel, only to miss them. After the war, Bowen made significant revisions to the first five chapters of *The Heat of the Day,* finished the rest of the book by 1948, and saw it published early the next year in London and New York—fully a decade after *The Death of the Heart.* Readers were by that point hungry for a new Bowen novel, and the years around the publication of *The Heat of the Day* ushered the author into a "rather more public life" than she had known before the war.[73] (Her first lecture tour in the U.S., in 1951, shows her riding that same wave of literary and cultural Anglophilia that helped bring the Sitwells and Cyril Connolly on their high-profile stateside visits.)

It does not minimize the material and psychological effects of the war on the writer to observe that the writing of *The Heat of the Day* itself proved especially difficult for Bowen. Close examination of the manuscript drafts reveals that in the composition of the novel, no riddle proved trickier than when and how to set the story in relation to the history of the Second World War. When Bowen began *The Heat of the Day,* and for a good while into its drafting, she tied internal narrative events loosely to events in the war. Surely this straightforward strategy would have become only easier to see to completion after 1945 than it was when she started the novel in 1944: by the later 1940s, the timeline of the war was complete and readily available, marked out with the boldface names and spans of battles, land-ings, sites, "strategic bombing" campaigns, and conferences. Bowen could have capitalized on hindsight to finish the arc of her story, narrate cleanly forward through the completed war, and get the book done more promptly. She did the opposite. As Bowen worked and reworked *The Heat of the Day*—experimenting with various narrative chronologies and dating devices over many drafts, resets, typescripts, and scribbled changes—she came to jettison almost entirely the retrospective linear march of the Second World War and to concentrate more and more intently on the feeling of the war's protracted, uncertain "lightless middle."

The process by which Bowen removed references to the historical pro-gression of the war was messy; it played out both across the emerging shape of *The Heat of the Day* as a whole and within discrete scenes. Examples of a narrative timeline in flux proliferate across the manuscript drafts. Meet-ings, letters, and conversations move forward and backward in historical time in various versions, sometimes receiving precise dates, sometimes los-ing them. In one early draft, Bowen dated a letter from Roderick to Stella "November 8, 1943," which put it within weeks of the Tehran Conference; in the finished novel, Roderick writes the same letter to his mother, now undated, sometime in early November 1942. For another example of the draft novel's timeline gradually moving toward the middle of the war rather than forward across it, chapter 4 of the final version rewinds from Septem-ber 1942 to narrate an awkward family funeral in May 1942. This timing, too, took a while to sort out. When revising the first typescript, Bowen added a dating sentence at the end of the chapter in her own hand: "That had all happened in May 1941: it was now late September of that year."[74] Bowen's tacked-on sentence records her working out when to place narra-tive events and not succeeding quite yet. Gradually, she landed many once projective or causal plot trajectories in the novel's abiding middle. Nearly all blunt dating gestures fell out of the novel once Bowen hit on the "lightless middle" of the autumn of 1942 and decided to keep her story within it, dwelling in a narrative and historical phase of incompletion—at least until the novel's end. Before its final chapter, the story of *The Heat of the Day* unfolds over only about nine weeks.

One excision from the drafts names the historical pressure under which Bowen labored to write a fiction set during the war but somehow without hooking fictional plot to retrospective military or geopolitical historiography. Robert Kelway's ex-fiancée appears only parenthetically in the published version of *The Heat of the Day*: "(It was to Decima that he had for a short time been engaged.)" (*HOD* 128). No date, no year. But the specter of Decima—her name so close to "decimate"—gave Bowen more trouble in the writing of the novel than this aside suggests. Bowen first dated Robert's engagement "from June 1938 to November 1939." Later she tried an even more portentous description of the timing of the engagement: Robert and Decima were "engaged in 1939. She was history."[75] Colloquially, Decima "was history" in that she is no longer in Robert's life by the time Stella meets him; in a public sense, she "was history" in that she is marked with the fateful year 1939. At some point in Bowen's writing of *The Heat of the Day*, a minor fictional character stood as a figure for the geopolitical history that presses on the novel. In the final version of *The Heat of the Day*, by contrast, Decima barely features in the plot, and not at all as a character synonymous with "history" or "1939." Historical portent has been reduced to a passing gesture.

In opting finally to date almost no event or character except Stella, the century's child, in *The Heat of the Day*, Bowen refuses to weight aspects of the novel with the putative clarity supplied by postwar retrospective. Stella is a figure not of a victorious nation or of a won war but of a vague middle, and *The Heat of the Day* resides almost entirely in middles, too—in hesitancies and indeterminacies. The narrative temporality of *The Heat of the Day* relies on, and enacts, Bowen's midcentury historical and conceptual vantage. Most obviously, it was only after the war that one could say for certain when its middle was. Less obviously, and reminding us that *midcentury* and *postwar* are not precise synonyms, Bowen's critical interest in the midcentury motivated her novelistic suspension of the very progressive histories, timelines, and reckonings of the Second World War that were proliferating across public culture as she worked on the novel—and that came to intrude on its ending. By the late 1940s, those histories and timelines consolidated into a distinctly partial yet thoroughly postwar hindsight, their meanings increasingly constructed to justify the conduct of the war—as was the case with the United States Strategic Bombing Survey's report—or conscripted to serve in the early cold war. As against that, Bowen's midcentury angle of vision enabled her narrative suspension not simply of Stella's story but also of the quick remaking of wartime feeling into the official history on which early conceptions of the postwar relied. If precisely the kinds of official history (military, political, national, continental) and public narratives that fostered postwar certainty about the temporal duration, political justifications, and ethical dimensions of the war are very much under historiographical scrutiny now, Bowen's novel was already on this scent in the late 1940s.

One need not claim that the novel's fixation on experiences of the middle preponderates over its depiction of wartime London. The two are one and the same, as the novel brings a midcentury curiosity about being in the middle to bear on its narrative restoration of, to borrow from Bowen's blurb, "a particular phase" of a war ongoing. The opening passage of *The Heat of the Day* establishes both the novel's wartime setting and its resolute middleness. The novel begins with "a Viennese orchestra" playing a concert in an "open-air theatre" in Regent's Park, London, a biographically significant site for Bowen (*HOD* 3). The performance provides a way to pass some time, such that the novel opens in a communal version of the habitual waiting that will define it. For most of the otherwise pointedly unoccupied audience, "the concert was the solution of where to be: one felt eased by this place where something was going on" (*HOD* 5). Still, the gathering "Londoners" and "exiled foreigners" hesitate in gateways before entering, for

all they had left behind was in sunshine, while this hollow which was the source of music was found to be also the source of dusk. War had made them idolise day and summer; night and autumn were enemies. And, at the start of the concert, this tarnished bosky theatre, in which no plays had been acted for some time, held a feeling of sequestration, of emptiness the music had not had time to fill. (*HOD* 3–4)

This is a passage about suspension, with "war" as both a thematic and a grammatical subject. Its syntax and diction testify to how the war has infected a civilian population's perceptions of both daily and yearly events (indicated by the sunset and seasonal change). Two years previously, London was the site of action, now it is a "theatre, in which no plays had been acted for some time" (*HOD* 4). As the opening set piece literalizes and domesticates the public metaphor of the theater of war—and specifically, with its "open-air theatre," of air warfare—it adopts the lexicon of armed conflict. In revising the opening passage, Bowen only emphasized this martial vocabulary. She made "war" the primary subject of a sentence that read, in an earlier version, "These people idolized day and summer; war had made night and autumn their enemies."[76] Once "war" came to name the historical setting of the narrative and to replace "these people" as the primary subject of a sentence about a crowd of civilians exposed in the "open-air," violence and militarism infiltrated the vocabulary: dark and fall became *"enemies"*; *"blades* of sunset" cut across the hollow, *"firing* branches through which they traveled, and lay along *ranks* of chairs and faces and hands" (*HOD* 4, my emphases).

Bowen made war inescapable in the opening passage of *The Heat of the Day.* But where in the war are these concert-going people? And when? The atmospheric overture to the novel concludes with listeners gathered "in the middle of Regent's Park. This Sunday on which the sun set was the first Sunday of September 1942" (*HOD* 4). Otherwise out of keeping with the rest of the novel, this opening provision of exact geographical and calendrical coordinates announces that *The Heat of the Day* will unfold in a wholly middle zone. For the novel begins in a park in the middle of London and, moreover, in a "worn glade in the middle of" that park (*HOD* 4); at dusk, the middle time between day and night; and in 1942, at the historical middle of the Second World War. Bowen drew on her midcentury vantage to place her novel at the point of utter suspension between the beginning and the end, at the moment of greatest uncertainty about when or whether the ongoing war would end.

THE END OF SUSPENSION?

On June 2, 1948, Bowen wrote to Daniel George, an editor at her London publisher, with acerbic thanks for his comments on her manuscript. George had made a number of suggestions aimed at sharpening Bowen's sentence structures. (Good luck to him.) Bowen's letter in response focused on the novel's opening passage, where she saw but would not concede his point. Though "I hate 'poetic' prose," she wrote, she also maintained that in many passages in her novel, including its opening evocation of the middle, "prose has to do the work of poetry—do more, in fact, than words can achieve through reason." She felt herself justified in cultivating various "jars, 'jingles' and awkwardnesses" in the "rhythm" of the writing—where "rhythm" means, roughly, "syntax." Bowen's basic point is plain enough: she aims for tension and resonance over clarity.[77]

But her examples in support of her point prove doubly telling: they articulate at the level of style, as matters of syntax and grammar, what this chapter has been describing as this novel's hard-fought suspension of the war's timeline and in a thoroughly middle time:

What I am, in the main, sticking to my guns about are various word orders which you query. I cannot, myself, bear <u>fanciful</u> arrangement of words in sentences. But in this novel, many sentences in which the order is queer are deliberate, because the sentences won't (as I see it) carry the exact meaning, or—still more important— make the exact psychological impact that I desire in any other way. E.g., "This tarnished open-air theatre in which no plays had been acted for some time . . ." You suggest "in which for some time no plays had been acted . . ." But <u>I</u> want the psychological stress to fall on "time," not on "acted"; so therefore I like to give "time" the more <u>sounding</u> position of the two. . . . The same applies to "Nothing more now than suffering the music he sat on tensely . . ." If I reversed this to, "He sat on tensely, nothing more now than suffering the music," something I wish from the effect (impact) of the sentence would be lost.[78]

Bowen's explanation of her syntax in the first example might be a capsule summary of *The Heat of the Day*: the novel means to emphasize an experience of "time" rather than to narrate action ("acted"). Her second example maintains the grammatical and situational aura of suspended activity. Bowen chooses not to front the character ("he") as the subject of the sentence, as George suggested. Instead, she keeps "Nothing more now" in place, thereby delaying the appearance of "he" just a bit longer. If Bowen is right, and "something"—some "effect (impact)"—"would be lost" if her "queer" word orders were copyedited into comparative clarity, then much of what would be lost is the novel's atmosphere of suspension. In defending her style, Bowen articulates a central aim of *The Heat of the Day*: to create a fiction out of the suspension that characterized a range of experience in the middle of the war as it did experience in and of the midcentury "now," self-consciously pitched between manifestly historical past and opaque future. Her novel reimagines a thoroughly middle moment in which people go on and "nothing" can be known or narrated for certain.

But how does one end a novel of such willed suspension, sustained at the levels of genre, motif of waiting, characterization, setting, and style? A novel spent waiting in the middle? What is the end, in the fullest sense, of the suspension of *The Heat of the Day*? The conclusion of the novel walks a delicate line between pronounced "subsidence" and jarring, uncharacteristic rush forward—first to the Little Blitz, then to a nontriumphal narration of the end of the war—and ties up loose plot ends as it winds down. First, on the side of narrative rush: the penultimate chapter begins, "That day whose start in darkness covered Robert's fall or leap from the roof had not yet fully broken when news broke: the Allied landings in North Africa. Talk was of nothing else" (*HOD* 327). The zeugma anticipates the final chapter, which makes two abrupt shifts: tonally, away from the characteristic stylistic suspensions of the narrator and toward the assertive "we" and "our" of nationalist propaganda, and procedurally, away from dwelling in the middle and toward a linear ordering of the war's events, rendered in the trope of a newsreel punctuated by calendar pages turning. Suddenly, in the final chapter, the narrator of *The Heat of the Day* can sound like this:

1942, still with no Second Front, ran out: nothing more than a sort of grinding change of gear for the upgrade was to be felt till the next war year steadied into its course. Cryptic were new 1943 block calendars. February, the Germans capitulated at Stalingrad; March, the Eighth Army broke through the Mareth Line. North African spring teemed with pursuits and astronomic surrenders, with a victoriousness hard, still, not to associate with the enemy. July, the Sicilian landings; the Russian opening of their great leafy Orel summer drive. Mussolini out. September, Italians out, but leaving Italy to it. Landings, beach-heads, Russian tanks lurching across the screens in London; November, Italian rivers, however, being crossed by us in strength. Winter known to have come by the Germans having their winter line shattered. Mussolini back. Pictures, less to be relished than had been hoped, of Berlin learning how it had been for London. The Big Three photographed smiling at Teheran.

(*HOD* 347)

And so forth. It's easy to read the convenience of the newsreel-calendar trope as a failure of the novel's nerve, or to read it as an instance wherein the need for narrative conclusion meant capitulation to the kinds of historical reference Bowen had held in suspension to this point in *The Heat of the Day*. Is it, after all, as impossible to end a novel of suspension in narrative "mid air" as it is inevitable to end a conventional suspense fiction with revelation, confirmation, clarity, and the restoration of the national order and social norms (*HOD* 339)?

I don't think so. Consider what happens in the marked "subsidence" that runs alongside and through even the fast-forward conclusion of *The Heat of the Day*. The final chapter opens with an announcement of a fallow period in the lives of the novel's principal and secondary characters: "There can occur in lives a subsidence of the under soil—so that, without the surface having been visibly broken, gradients alter, uprights cant a little out of the straight. A group of persons, of souls—perhaps not conscious, till now, of so much as being in the same neighborhood—may thus be affected by one happening" (*HOD* 339). The "happening" is "Robert's end," which suspended Stella and Harrison's "extraordinary relationship" in "mid air."

In the final chapter, set a couple years later, Harrison and Stella meet again. Stella gets some answers about Harrison's maneuverings before and after Robert's death; we learn that she is to be married again. Other narrative threads are wrapped up too: Louie reads in the papers of Robert's death, and we watch through her eyes as press coverage turns the "scandalous likeliness" of Stella and Robert's affair into the official story. Robert's treachery is nowhere reported, the would-be culpability of his "woman friend in the luxury flat" in Mayfair falling more in line with misogynist tropes and the national interest. The coroner rules Robert's death a "misadventure," and "the country was spared a demoralising story" (*HOD* 340). Having met Stella once by chance and romanticized her, Louie is both disappointed and liberated by her reported promiscuity.[79] At the end of the novel, Louie perpetrates her own gendered fiction. She launders the scandal of having a child out of wedlock by naming and narrating the child, too, in service of the national social order. Heading "into abeyance in a Midland county"—a thoroughly middle ending, it must be said—Louie names her baby "Thomas Victor," after her late husband, who is not the baby's father, and in celebration of a war won.

The fact of the narrator's pronounced "subsidence" from the narrative is almost overrun by the final chapter's brief, startling insertions of the forward rush of calendar pages, boldface dates, headline newsreels, and propaganda images—the rush, that is, of patriotic histories and military chronologies taking their official, immediate, and already mediated shapes. Yet this coincidence of narrative subsidence and sudden rush effects one last, crucial suspension. What we watch happen, especially in Louie's outcome, is conventional, canonical, and plain untrue narratives of the war taking root in character's lives and public culture. At odds with the story of the middle we have just read, these too clear and, in some cases, salacious stories—Stella becomes something of femme fatale after all—are not simply untrue. They are scripted by normative gendered assumption, their untruth required and certified in the final chapter by precisely the kinds of mainline accounts of the war that *The Heat of the Day* has held in suspension all along. In this reading, the novel's final chapter cements by contradiction the crucial achievement of the book, which is to rescue something—uncounted experience and feeling of the middle—that, if told from the readily available vantages of victorious retrospect or cold war mobilization, "would be lost" to false certainty. The more dexterous *midcentury* helped Bowen find the wartime middle in danger of being written over in and by the postwar, and to write the middle down.

Chapter Four

THE SONIC SUSPENSIONS OF FRANK O'HARA

Watching the botching of Military Governments, the crippling of the U.N., the ineffectual expediency of our national policies, and the mishandling of the Atomic Bomb, has been a bitter experience for all of us, and almost to a man we all waited for discharge.... The months of waiting for discharge in a state of near-inertia served to clarify issues, consolidate standards. It is often necessary to experience to realize fully: my disillusionment with militarism is no longer instinctual, or a matter of principle only, and is a strong spur to achievement in civilian life.

—FRANK O'HARA, FROM AN ESSAY ON HIS MILITARY SERVICE REQUIRED IN HIS COLLEGE APPLICATION (1946)

On May 22, 1950, U.S. President Harry S. Truman issued Proclamation 2889, "Prayer for Peace, Memorial Day," pursuant to a joint resolution with Congress. The proclamation begins: "Since war is the world's most terrible scourge, we should do all in our power to prevent its recurrence." To that end, Truman does not propose, say, nuclear disarmament, but rather rededicates Memorial Day, "which has long been set aside for paying tribute to those who lost their lives in war" as also "henceforth . . . a day for Nationwide prayer for permanent peace."[1] The emptiness of this proclamation—made fewer than five years after Truman issued the orders to drop atomic bombs on two Japanese cities and a month before the start of the Korean War—could hardly be plainer: it is a politician's "thoughts and prayers" on a national-commemorative scale.

Still, many poets and preachers heeded Truman's call, and poems and prayers for Memorial Day appeared in newspapers around the U.S. In Boston, for example, the *Daily Globe* printed the chief chaplain of the U.S. Army's "Prayer for Memorial Day" on its front page on May 29, 1950. The next day, the *Globe's* Woman's Page wedged the newspaper poet Anne Campbell's sonnet "Memorial Day" into the space left over from a diet advice column. Braiding conventional seasonal recompense with national mourning, the poem offers mothers of the war dead weak comfort. Since their "boy[s]" were "caught up in Spring time," they were spared "the Winter of old age." "They died; a grateful nation turned a page, / And moved an inch toward peace. They are content"—and you should be too, the poem admonishes its women readers through its anesthetizing haze of euphemism.[2]

Just across the Charles River that same spring, Frank O'Hara graduated from Harvard University, at twenty-four. His service in the Second World War had delayed his matriculation to college; the G.I. Bill sponsored it. O'Hara, too, wrote a poem for Memorial Day. His has no truck with official paeans, grateful nation platitudes, or executive gloss of the early postwar as a period of aspirational peace. "Memorial Day 1950": read synchronically, the title of O'Hara's poem scans as deliberately and critically generic; the titular citation of the holiday stands at odds with the antimilitarism the poem evinces. Within O'Hara's career, however, the title of this important early poem is unique. For all the poet's signature time-stamping of poems with dateline notations, nods to transport schedules and appointments, odes on Catholic and (to O'Hara) artist saint's days, including seven poems "On Rachmaninoff's Birthday" alone, "Memorial Day 1950" marks the only occasion on which O'Hara titled a poem with a calendar-complete citation of *national holiday + year*. Trenchant in its very generic quality, singular in O'Hara's work, the title of "Memorial Day 1950" has merited almost no comment from O'Hara's critics.[3] This disinterest certainly owes something to accumulated impressions of O'Hara. But it also squares with what we have seen are two historiographically convenient and mutually reinforcing underestimations: on the one hand, of English-language writing around 1950; on the other, of the terms by which the midcentury was marked and conceived of in public culture, including and especially in such unprepossessing chronological registers of the period's fraught historical contemporaneity as *1950* and *midcentury*.

O'Hara's "Memorial Day 1950" takes the midcentury national occasion as artistic provocation. The poem pitches a *1950* survey of two twentieth-century-thus-far phenomena—the self-proclaimed rupture of modernist aesthetics and the continuity of state-sanctioned violence—against the official pieties of the midcentury holiday. No elegy for young men killed in their "Spring time" or salve for their mothers, "Memorial Day 1950" reveals itself in its final lines as a disconsolate paternal elegy: "Now / my father is dead," the penultimate sentence begins.[4] Or, it may be more accurate to write that the poem confirms itself as a defiant paternal elegy. For through-out, "Memorial Day 1950" clocks the damage that parents and authorities inflict on the young, and on young artists especially—"I / wasn't surprised when the older people entered / my cheap hotel room and broke my guitar and my can / of paint"—and apostrophically proclaims the young poet's alternate, chosen parentage ("Fathers of Dada!"). The poem begins:

> Picasso made me tough and quick, and the world;
> just as in a minute plane trees are knocked down
> outside my window by a crew of creators.
> Once he got his axe going everyone was upset
> enough to fight for the last ditch and heap
> of rubbish.
>   Through all that surgery I thought
> I had a lot to say, and named several last things
> Gertrude Stein hadn't had time for; but then
> the war was over, those things had survived
> and even when you're scared art is no dictionary.
> Max Ernst told us that.
>   How many trees and frying pans
> I loved and lost! Guernica hollered look out!
> (CP 17)

As its opening arc alone demonstrates, "Memorial Day 1950" makes a stunning fugue of disparate projects and forms. Along with elegy and micro-*künstlerroman*, the poem splices childhood memoir with "artistic manifesto," nearly impenetrable autobiographical reference with epigrammatic pith, collage assemblage with filmic cut, surreal vision with plain statement, and occasional poem on the U.S. holiday in honor of war dead with the poet's memory of the Second World War and its end.[5] So far as ready critical impressions of O'Hara go these last—Memorial Day 1950 and the war—would seem to be the least important notes sounded in "Memorial Day 1950."

How exactly is the war present in "Memorial Day 1950?" In addition to the titular occasion, consider the phrase that stops and breaks the first verse paragraph in its lineated tracks: "Through all that surgery." Encountered in the fast-paced collage of the poem, the phrase seems first to extend the invocation of Picasso as surreal axman. But "through all that surgery" quickly turns out not, or not only, to elaborate on the poem's initial artist-muse, but also to turn the poem toward "the war" that quickly follows on it. No interpretive "surgery" can responsibly cut away the most plain-spoken remark of the opening of the poem—"but then / the war was over"—from the emerging but recognizably O'Hara gestures that surround it, among them the lightning-quick naming of artists, the seamless shift from first- to second-person address, the ebullience of voice and pace, the surreal imagery in colloquial pitch, and the urgent-giddy exclamation points.[6] At the very least, "but then / the war was over" makes a deflated, antitriumphal recollection of the war's being not won but "over," in perhaps pointed contrast to Truman's call for an aspirational, prayerful "peace."

Yet the war is precisely what falls away in the most thoroughgoing reading of "Memorial Day 1950," which can stand as a metonym for the general erasure of the war in the study of O'Hara. In her foundational book *Frank O'Hara: Poet Among Painters* (1977), Marjorie Perloff neutralizes as emblems of an emerging aesthetic theory and practice the poem's many registers of violence—and of guilt about violence that "I" and "we" inflicted on others. Later lines read: "At that time all of us began to think / with our bare hands and even with blood all over / them, we knew vertical from horizontal, we never / smeared anything except to find out how it lived" (*CP* 17). Perloff reads these as "reference to the doctrine of Action painting . . . the belief that materials used by the artist exist in their own right," which interpretation holds as far as it goes.[7] But both "blood" and the reanimated cliché of blood on one's hands exceed what the aesthetic analogy can explain—indeed exceed that analogy precisely as *blood* names a "material" irreducible to paint; similarly, knowing "vertical from horizontal" rewrites knowing right from wrong.

More than a poem on the general theme of "what it means to make oneself an artist in a world that distrusts art," "Memorial Day 1950" marks itself as a timely depiction of what it meant to come of age as a poet—as *this* poet—during and after "the war" in which he served and amid the public pieties, presidential proclamations, and discursive strategies that made that war into the postwar.[8] It is a distinctly *midcentury* poem about being an artist who distrusts "the world" the postwar was making. To disregard the war and war memory in "Memorial Day 1950" is to rate the poem's understated marks of epochal momentousness as incidental to it—and, it would seem, to the broader work of the poet who wrote it.

A year later, O'Hara compiled his first book-length poetry manuscript for the prestigious Hopwood Award competition at the University of Michigan, where he completed a master's degree in creative writing. He titled the collection "A Byzantine Place: 50 Poems and a Noh Play"; on its title page, he gave his full formal name: "Francis O'Hara." On the competition entry form, he would print his name boldly as "Frank," which small change, read suggestively, turns manuscript and competition into the site at which veteran and student "Francis" turns into poet "Frank O'Hara." That "A Byzantine Place" does not include "Memorial Day 1950" is the stuff of O'Hara lore. The poem's near-miss publication history has preceded it since the 1970s. In his introduction to *The Collected Poems of Frank O'Hara* (1971), John Ashbery contrasts the surprising bulk of that volume to his late friend's famously laissez-faire attitude to collecting and publishing his work. As a case in point, Ashbery explains that "one of his most beautiful early poems, 'Memorial Day 1950,' exists only because I once copied it out in a letter to Kenneth Koch and Kenneth kept the letter."[9] (Koch was also a veteran.)

Like "Memorial Day 1950" and a novel O'Hara worked on in 1950–51—to which he gave another parodic-patriotic title, "The 4th of July"—O'Hara's manuscript for a first book of poems draws on his military service during the Second World War. O'Hara enlisted in the U.S. Navy when he turned eighteen in 1944. Trained as a sonar operator, he served until 1946. In the final summer of the war in the Pacific, from April 22, 1945, through the U.S.'s detonation of atomic bombs over Hiroshima and Nagasaki in early August—actions which horrified O'Hara—he was stationed aboard the USS *Nicholas*. The Seventh Fleet Destroyer helped prepare for the expected combat invasion of Japan and engaged in bombardments, support operations, and the evacuation of Allied prisoners of war at various points across maritime Southeast and East Asia.[10] By the time "the war was over," O'Hara had earned four ribbons and medals, with an operation and engagement star.[11]

In the unfinished novel "The 4th of July," one veteran character's experiences of the Navy and the war roughly correspond to O'Hara's.[12] In the neglected manuscript of "A Byzantine Place," however, the war takes more oblique, surprising, and subversive shapes—and, more to the point of this chapter, *sounds*. The war inheres most powerfully in O'Hara's unpublished book manuscript not in accustomed deposits of topicality or straightforward autobiography, but rather in a pattern of sensory, and most often of auditory, suspension. Put another way, the war remains present—still audible—in the poems of "A Byzantine Place" through an array of sonic suspensions, through listening and sound. Neither entirely extricable from nor reducible to the poet's sonar training and Navy service, the war inflects the soundscape of "A Byzantine Place," whispering through the silences, suspended quiets, sudden hushes, and muted "nows" that alternately punctuate and occasion the poems, and, this chapter argues, that resound across O'Hara's quintessentially postwar career.

For "A Byzantine Place: 50 Poems and a Noh Play," O'Hara won the University of Michigan's prestigious Avery Hopwood Major Award for Poetry in 1951. In at least one key sense, winning the award meant losing the prize. Unlike, for example, the Yale Younger Poets Prize, which would help launch Ashbery's career when he won it in 1956, the Hopwood Award came with $800 but without book publication. This contingency had consequences for the subsequent work and reception of the poet who became Frank O'Hara. He seems to have anticipated this much. In an oft-quoted letter to the painter Jane Freilicher, dated June 6, 1951, O'Hara riffed on the limitation of the Hopwood Award in terms that square with several now fixed impressions of his work:

No publication goes with the Hopwood award, alas, and both Alfred Knopf and Herbert Weinstock of the same "firm" told me it was next to impossible to publish poetry in our time. I think of this with absolute delight when I think how embarrassing my letters will be for my relatives when they have to dig my poems out of them if I ever do get published. Anyway you could fit the people I write for into your john, all at the same time without raising an eyebrow.[13]

Herein lie, already in 1951 and following from the publication that the poetry prize does not entail, inklings of O'Hara as a coterie poet, a poet cavalier about keeping and collecting his poems, a poet of intimate address and of a charming, expressive style as influential as it is inimitable.

It is no reach to posit that "No publication go[ing] with the Hopwood award, alas" proved a decisive nonevent for much of what we know of O'Hara. Irresistible *what-ifs* follow on it: what if "A Byzantine Place: 50

Poems and a Noh Play" had been published in the early 1950s? What would O'Hara's career have looked like? What notes in his poetics might his first book manuscript have primed us to hear? What reverberations from this first collection might sound in his later work? If we imagine "A Byzantine Place" as O'Hara's debut, which of those fixed impressions of his work might be sharpened or shifted? What tones still detected?

It is well to ask, not least because Frank O'Hara is now so very well known. O'Hara is a touchstone poet of the postwar—even *the* touchstone U.S. poet of the postwar period in some of its many generational, aesthetic, historical, and political configurations. So we know O'Hara as a quintessential New York School and New American poet, his work having occupied more space in Donald Allen's field-making anthology *The New American Poetry, 1945–1960* (1960), to which this chapter will return, than any poet saving its rough guide, Charles Olson. We know O'Hara as a postmodern "poet among painters," per Perloff, as well as a poet among filmmakers, sculptors, writers, and jazz, classical, and avant-garde musicians. We know O'Hara, too, as a poet of non- or antinormative kinship, as a poet of friendship and coterie, and of queer experience and community before Stonewall. And we know O'Hara as a cold war poet, some critics suggest too well.[14] Many readers, myself among them, plain love O'Hara too: his work is smart and funny, serious and allergic to self-seriousness. "Memorial Day 1950" and the poems of "A Byzantine Place" lend themselves to reading by many of these lights. Yet, taken separately or together, these important accounts of and contexts for O'Hara's work have not prompted inquiry into his war or its modes of endurance in his poetics.

This chapter introduces an O'Hara whom readers do not yet know and love, whom the unfamiliar moniker of Francis and the unusual unit of a discrete collection of poems (at least for study of this poet) mean to help bring forward. It introduces an O'Hara whose work, I contend, we cannot fully hear, or value, without the heuristic of midcentury suspension as this book has been developing it. Concentrating on the critically neglected manuscript of "A Byzantine Place," this chapter discovers an O'Hara who was from the start a midcentury poet of suspension and the war. Attending to the sonic suspensions of that manuscript, the chapter tunes into how the young Francis O'Hara reimagined what war poetry sounds like—and why. For O'Hara did not simply resist replication of earlier models of antiwar soldier poetry, along with many other poets of and around the Second World War, nor did he refuse, in silent protest, to write of the war at all. Instead, and in keeping with the ethos of "Memorial Day 1950," O'Hara's "Byzantine Place" poems often make a point of silencing, muting, or holding in suspension the attribution of militarist-nationalist "meaning" to state-sanctioned violence. In fact, as it did in Elizabeth Bishop's midcentury exploration of historical suspension, *meaning* recurs across O'Hara's Hopwood manuscript, usually to mark the absence or vagueness of it.

This chapter does not propose to remake Frank O'Hara into a "war poet" in any rote sense. The more instructive query now, in the continuous violence of the long postwar, is how we've left the very question of his status as a war poet largely unasked. For though O'Hara would never have accepted the mantle of "war poet," he meets even the most unreconstructed standards of what makes one: he served as a combatant and wrote poems about his service. As this chapter teases out how the war sounds in "A Byzantine Place," it takes up some of the questions that have run through *Midcentury Suspension*: where did the war go in writing of the immediate postwar period? What did it mean to write of the war, and who was expected or entitled to do it in the years just after 1945? How did and do some of the established period and topical models according to which we make sense of the century's middle elide the more oblique historicity of so much midcentury literature and culture?

If O'Hara's work in many ways epitomizes postwar or cold war poetics as these fields are broadly and variously conceived, then it is also emblematic of how strangely muted, and thus apparently immutable, the war—to which *postwar* always audibly refers, from which *cold war* differentiates itself—remains even amid ongoing debate about how to periodize and think about literary and cultural production of the years after 1945. The broadly historical postwar, the disciplinary Post45, the narrowly aesthetic American postmodernism against which Post45 first defined itself, late modernism in its geographical and temporal extension and self-analysis, cold war studies before or after the containment thesis: none of these period heuristics or historical-aesthetic frames invites one to listen to how deeply infused O'Hara's midcentury collection of poems and his later poetics were not simply with the war on which their chronologies all tacitly or expressly rely but also with the war as it was fast being made into the postwar.

THE HOPWOOD MANUSCRIPT

First, the unpublished manuscript. Forty-seven of the fifty poems included in "A Byzantine Place: 50 Poems and a Noh Play" appear somewhere in Donald Allen's three invaluable volumes of O'Hara's work, *The Collected Poems* (1971), *Early Writing* (1977), and *Poems Retrieved* (rev. ed., 1996). But readers cannot glean a sense, from these or subsequent collections, of how O'Hara put "A Byzantine Place" together. Even a list of the titles of the poems as sequenced in O'Hara's Hopwood manuscript has yet to be published. This is little wonder, perhaps, given how unaccustomed it is to think of O'Hara caring about or conceiving of volumes of his own poems at all. "A Byzantine Place" would warrant critical attention even if for no other reason than to gain a sense of the early work of a major postwar poet. Thus, while my reading ultimately quarries the sound of the war—or how the war sounds—in the emphatic present of the "Byzantine Place" poems, I want to offer first, and for the record, a fuller view of the shape and substance of the manuscript.

"A Byzantine Place: 50 Poems and a Noh Play" collects early work, not in the sense that the manuscript gathers juvenilia or apprentice poems, but insofar as its most insistent quality is the youth of its poet. Resonant with the child-poet poignancy of "Memorial Day 1950," the poems frequently avow youthfulness as an aesthetic value, take youth and childhood as their occasions, sympathize with children, perform insouciant, childlike word-play and sound games, and insist on the poet's own youth, fleeting though he fears it is. While some of O'Hara's stylistic hallmarks are in early evidence—that very youthful energy, an exclamatory joy, a delight in surprising juxtapositions—others are just beginning to emerge. For one example, O'Hara does not directly address a specific, proper-named friend or lover until the very last poem of the manuscript, its titular poem. As positioned in the collection, the poem "A Byzantine Place" reads like a revelatory discovery of this mode of interpersonal address within a community of friends and lovers—in this case a bygone lover, one "Ted" (*PR* 16). For another, "Night Thoughts in Greenwich Village" is the only poem in "A Byzantine Place: 50 Poems and a Noh Play" set in New York, and one of only two poems that even mention the city with which O'Hara is now virtually synonymous. Along with "Night Thoughts," the collection includes "Song (I'm going to New York!)," whose singer cannot wait to get there. Yet

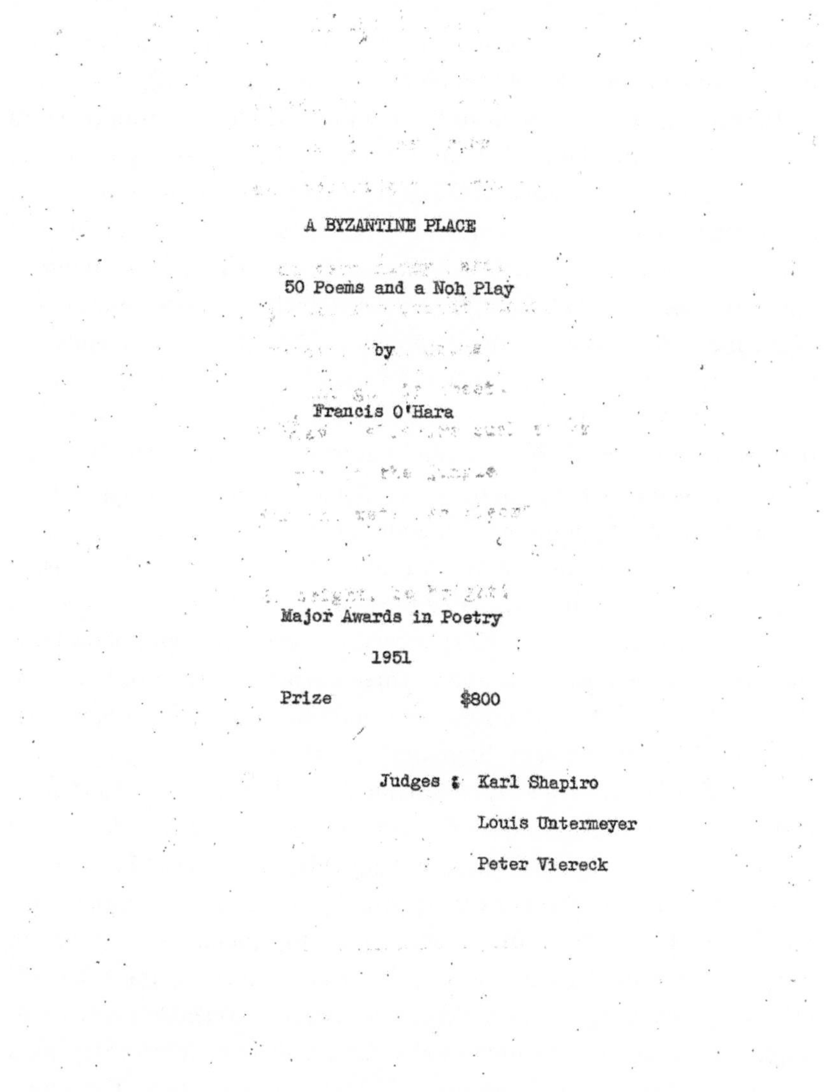

A BYZANTINE PLACE

50 Poems and a Noh Play

by

Francis O'Hara

Major Awards in Poetry

1951

Prize $800

Judges : Karl Shapiro

Louis Untermeyer

Peter Viereck

FIGURE 4.1 Copy of the title page of O'Hara's winning submission for the Hopwood Award, 1951. University of Michigan Special Collections Library. Reproduced by permission of Maureen O'Hara.

at the center of the poem the singer takes audible delight in two Michigan place names: he might be taking himself "far from Ypsilanti and Flint!" but their sounds are too delectable to omit from the poem (*PR* 11).

The geography of "A Byzantine Place" ranges still farther from O'Hara's eventual Manhattan home. In blunt contrast to general neglect of the Second World War in the study of O'Hara's work, these poems recall several of the places and scenes O'Hara saw in his Navy service both stateside and as a sonarman onboard the USS *Nicholas*. "Poem (The stars are tighter)" refers to places where O'Hara was stationed, including New Guinea, Key West, and "when I was in / the Philippines" (*CP* 44). The poem entwines places in the U.S. and abroad without creating hierarchical comparisons of American *heres* to "other" *theres*. In its final turn, "Poem" announces first that "Now you see how the / sky can be everywhere" and finally "all bearings are possible" (*CP* 44). In the navigational lexicon ("bearings") of the poem's final line, no point of orientation assumes preference (*CP* 43–44).[15] And the sky *is* everywhere in "A Byzantine Place": several poems envision sea, sky, and horizon line, such that the poems serially reiterate the visual constants onboard a ship. O'Hara plays with the concept rhyme of the horizon line with the poetic line and in three poems uses the word *horizon*. "Yet Another Fan" (*CP* 50) unfolds as "Gently white planes / rove the horizon"; the eerily quiet poem "Smoking" (*CP* 58) ends with "a grey heart's horizon of / silence, a shadowy cancan line," which surreal visual and aural metaphor also turns down the volume of the clattering cancan dance; and "Noir Cacadou, or The Fatal Music of War," O'Hara's crucial V-J Day poem, elaborates his desire for his lover with sound play: "it will be love and lovely / and level as the horizon from / our exotic and dancing deck" (*PR* 2). In the manuscript of "A Byzantine Place," O'Hara's "horizon" fuses the sailor's fixed visual image of the middle line between two elements with a colloquial expression for the unknowable future. Throughout the Hopwood manuscript, however, it is "the open sea" (*CP* 42), not idiom for the future, that holds open the most possibility and excitement for O'Hara, especially the possibility of open desire.

Other aspects of "A Byzantine Place: 50 Poems and a Noh Play" contradict truisms about O'Hara. In the title poem, for example, O'Hara, whose later walking around New York and composing poems on the observational and conversational fly has if anything been overstated, confronts instead the "white silences" of pieces of paper awaiting his efforts (*PR* 16). In line with avant-garde musicians' and visual artists' investigations of silence, blankness, and suspension at midcentury—think, for example, of the modular panels of Robert Rauschenberg's *White Paintings* (1951), of which he wrote "Today is their creater [sic]"—this synesthetic gesture to the ambience and material conditions of O'Hara's own writing also harmonizes entirely with the sound-world of the collection.[16] At an earlier time, the poem recalls, "these white silences / hadn't pinned me down // It's for ever I write / because the struggle may / knock the breath out of me / I want someone to know" (*PR* 16). By the time one arrives at this reflection on what it is to write—and to imagine a temporal rather than a personal audience for that writing ("for ever" as opposed to, say, "for you")—one is accustomed to the silences and held-breath hushes that often foster such meditations in "A Byzantine Place: 50 Poems and a Noh Play."

Or consider even the competition-ready tidiness of the manuscript as artifact: seventy-six pages, typed cleanly for the most part, with inked-in corrections for typos; neatly double-spaced but for the play; each poem beginning on a new page. This careful, good-student-ish document preparation runs counter to O'Hara's later self-packaging, enshrined in the indelible jacket copy he wrote for *Lunch Poems* (1964): "Often this poet, strolling through the noisy splintered glare of a Manhattan noon, has paused at a sample Olivetti to type up thirty or forty lines of ruminations."[17] But the point is not that subsequent critical attachment to O'Hara's performatively carefree attitude to writing, editing, sequencing, saving, and publishing his poems is wrong. It is rather that the truism is datelined: Ann Arbor, 1951. For if the vision of O'Hara's indifference to posterity was to some degree facilitated by the parameters of the Hopwood Award, the manuscript for which O'Hara won the award has a different story to tell. Beyond mere competition document preparation, Francis O'Hara conceived of "A Byzantine Place: 50 Poems and a Noh Play" as a book: he chose and took care to sequence the fifty poems from among many more finished poems he had available or, like "Memorial Day 1950," might have retrieved from friends.

Perhaps the strongest mark of how much O'Hara cared about the coherence of "A Byzantine Place" as a book manuscript is that he had fun with the sequencing of it. There is a situational humor, for instance, to "Night Thoughts in Greenwich Village" that depends partly on its position as the twenty-fourth poem in "A Byzantine Place." With a light touch, this carpe diem poem does not plead with a beloved but rather rues the immediate obsolescence of the poet's youth and work—a great theme of this collection, as it would prove to be of O'Hara's entire poetry. Writing at the moment when the historical avant-gardes gained the adjective *historical*, O'Hara is incredulous to discover that "I, / at twenty four, already / find the harrowing laugh / of children at my heels— / directed at me! the Dada / baby!" (*CP* 38).[18] Encountering "Night Thoughts in Greenwich Village" in *The Collected Poems of Frank O'Hara* precludes any delight in finding that "twenty four, already" tallies both the poet's woefully (!) old age and the poem's place in the sequence of "A Byzantine Place." "Night Thoughts" winks at its own spot in O'Hara's first collection, as both poet and book manuscript self-consciously push twenty-five.[19]

In the same wink, and putting a finer point on the emphatic youth that runs through "A Byzantine Place," "Night Thoughts" laughingly repudiates the conspicuously aged personae that Anglo-American high modernists once adopted to "make it new." The second poem in the Hopwood manuscript, "Poem (Let's take a walk)," takes the first of what would become a career's worth of poetic strolls by dialing down the haunting opening of T. S. Eliot's "The Love Song of J. Alfred Prufrock" (1915). "Let us go then, you and I, / When the evening is spread out against the sky / Like a patient etherized upon a table" becomes, in the young O'Hara's casual, unpunctuated, ready-for-rain invitation to a lover:

> Let's take a walk you
> and I in spite of the
> weather if it rains hard
>   on our toes[20]
>
> (*CP* 41)

"A Byzantine Place" delights in its youthfulness, and seems thrilled to get in just under the age wire Eliot set for the serious poet in "Tradition and the Individual Talent" (1919). Eliot's dictum has it that an arduous and "great labour" is required to develop "the historical sense, which we may call nearly indispensable to anyone who would continue to be a poet beyond his twenty-fifth year."[21] O'Hara, at twenty-five, had done this labor in every sense, and proclaims his disinterest in wearing it or the "historical sense" heavily.

Youth is not wasted on "A Byzantine Place: 50 Poems and a Noh Play." The collection makes youthfulness and childlike curiosity and delight into the province of the artist, who must remain alive to sensation and "surprise!" ("Today," *CP* 15). The opening poem, "At the Source," invokes "Hebe!," the Greek goddess of youth, as the volume's muse.[22] Several poems mine childhood tropes, adopt childlike tones, or sympathize with children— especially, as in "Memorial Day 1950," with children having the joy of art and life drilled out of them. When "Variations on a Theme by Shelley" asserts, "I don't want my poems / lisped on the numbered / tongues of children. May / they be part of the world," "they" refers equally to "my poems" and "children" whose aesthetic senses and pleasures are only numbed ("*number*ed") by rote poetry lessons (*EW* 84). And "The Clown," one of a handful of poems about growing up and being made to cease "knowing treasures" of the imagination, begins:

> As a child, fleeing, trying his body
> among trees, feeling the wind, even
> then knowing treasures that surprised
>
> him, he cried "I am glorious! it is a
> secret that must not be kept from them!"
> and saw his voice in the sky's clamors.
> (*CP* 26)

Representative of many of the "Byzantine Place" poems, the easy soundplay in the first two lines ("fleeing" turning into "feeling") preserves some of the bliss of the child "trying his body." But the child should have kept his "secret" to himself. Once he shares it with "them," they make demands on him that make him "uneasily older by their seriousness." "They" compel him to be more "like us" (*CP* 27).

Cumulatively, "A Byzantine Place: 50 Poems and a Noh Play" announces Francis O'Hara as young, exuberant, defiant of age and authority, and determined to stay that way. In fact, the manuscript protests the poet's youth a bit too much. The poems are at once motivated and haunted by the poet's fear that his youth is "fleeing" too quickly, if not already fled—that he is already, somehow, too old. The pressure on youth in this manuscript bears connecting to the historical timing of O'Hara's own young adulthood. By accident of his birth, he was among the youngest combatants in the Second World War. After it, O'Hara was on the older side, just barely, of that sudden generational divide that, in the introduction to *Keywords*, Raymond Williams recalls feeling upon his return to Cambridge after four years in an antitank regiment. The war may well have aged O'Hara; it certainly seems to have sharpened his sense of his youth as foreshortened. For as one reads the whole of "A Byzantine Place: 50 Poems and a Noh Play," one comes to realize that while youth speaks loudest across it, youth is never far from the war that whispers through the manuscript, interrupting poems with hushes, bringing them to sudden pauses, and compelling them to listen rather than to chat breezily away.

The poem "Today" offers a pithy example of an eager, playfully alliterative youthful persona running into the war and the vocabulary of war. "Today" tries to be a poem about a series of incongruous and historically unpoetic objects that charm its young speaker (*CP* 15). The poem begins with exclamatory if short-lived relief that these objects "really are beautiful!" Yet war lies just beneath the surface of—and on the page, below—the "sequins" and "sodas" and "stuff" of the two-quatrain poem:

> Oh! kangaroos, sequins, chocolate sodas!
> You really are beautiful! Pearls,
> harmonicas, jujubes, aspirins! all
> the stuff they've always talked about
>
> still makes a poem a surprise!
> These things are with us every day
> even on beachheads and biers. They
> do have meaning. They're strong as rocks.[23]
> (*CP* 15)

The list of the first quatrain is equal parts camp and kid. What makes "Today" a "surprise!" and turns it from jubilant exclamation points to somber periods is the alliterative pair of "beachheads and biers." The word *beachhead* itself dates from the Second World War, and for most readers at the middle of the twentieth century the image of "a fortified position of troops landed on a beach" would likely call up Normandy.[24] The word *biers,* indicating stretchers on which corpses are brought to their graves, follows both alliteratively and associatively on the *beachheads.* Nor can the poem return from this somber alliterative pair to its initial exuberance about candy and sodas and "stuff." It can only proclaim that "these things . . . do have meaning" and are "strong as rocks." Whatever "meaning" "they" have remains unspoken. A poem about willed joy in the present and built on the war of the recent past, "Today" might be taken as an early instance of what Marianna Torgovnick terms the "war complex," a broad cultural phenomenon by which Americans build their self-image on strategic suppressions and deflections of memory of the Second World War.[24] Except that it is not the poem that suppresses the war in the titular present of "Today," but rather a learned critical practice, licensed in no small part by O'Hara's association with other wartimes, of reading through or past the war that O'Hara's poems "still" make audible in their postwar, cold war present. The war itself is right there in "Today," not so much haunting this 1950 poem as sitting right there in it and modulating its tone. The war would remain present in O'Hara's work across "A Byzantine Place: 50 Poems and a Noh Play" and beyond, if not in "expected" ways.

THE EXPECTED LYRICISM

If the war is hidden in plain sight in the geography, scenic view, and even brazen youthfulness of "A Byzantine Place: 50 Poems and a Noh Play," then why do we need the heuristic of midcentury suspension to help us think about O'Hara's war poetics? For one thing, because a search only for plainly referential gestures to the war would seem to ascribe to the category of "war poetry" a predictable topicality; for another, because O'Hara's first book manuscript makes a point of suspending conventions of war poetry—the mold of elegy, the moral authority of the witnessing war poet-hero, tropes of disillusionment—that were already dated by 1951. The Noh-inspired play *Try! Try!* offers the collection's most extensive meditation on, and deflation of, literary and cultural associations with war poetry precisely by turning those associations into cliché, hyperbole, and melodrama. Set "after any war," the play borrows the Japanese dramatic form to depict a soldier's return home to his wife, clearly after the Second World War. Deliberately overwrought, stage-directed to be "extremely stylized throughout," and bracingly funny for being so, the play turns the trope of romantic reunion into barbed riposte to the question of how war writing was expected to sound around 1950.[25]

The emotional climax of the play occurs when the returning soldier Jack comes home to find his wife Violet in the arms of another man, John. John, whom Ashbery played in the original production at the then newly formed Poets Theater in Cambridge, is also the stage manager of the play, which in this case means principally that he manages and modulates the play's sound. At the start of the play, John is "standing in a listening attitude"; throughout it, John tends to an onstage gramophone, stopping its music "for his own speeches, but sometimes play[ing] appropriate music during the others'."[26] At the very moment of Jack's homecoming, everything "freeze[s.]" John steps into the pause, with a speech beginning:

> In this moment of silence, the expected
> lyricism begins. As when the subway stops
> just before reaching a station, they breathe heavily
> for a minute, all of a minute . . . [27]

Announcing a noncommemorative "moment of silence" that lasts "for a minute, all of a minute," this stage-managed suspension of the play's moment of highest tension also offers a figure for the suspension it enacts: the subway car paused before arrival. The line break at "expected" emphasizes the sense of expectancy enjambment creates even as it undermines whatever might be "expected" of "lyricism" about the war. What follows are duly and deliberately clichéd speeches about the wife's and the soldier's experiences of the war: Violet pleads "Oh Jack! my Jackson! / why did you leave me?"; Jack speaks at length and about his war experiences, trying and failing to remake them in the narrative molds of the Norse explorer and the war hero.[28] "Why, I thought of myself as / Eric's son, Lief, going towards / the moon with a world behind me / and a lot of blood to get off my / chest," Jack soliloquizes.[29] But John's onstage framing locates the interest of this melodrama not in its familiar, gendered laments and recitations, but rather in the "moment of silence" itself. In that quiet "minute, all of a minute" spent breathing, not speaking, actors and audience alike recognize that they expect a certain "lyricism" to begin—and thus begin to mistrust that lyricism before Violet and Jack can even begin to speak it.

Put in more humorous terms, the play primes the audience to laugh at the conventionality of its war romance. O'Hara wrote of Noh that the "audience is supposed to know all the plays by heart."[30] As Philip Auslander observes, there was a sense in which "O'Hara's audience did indeed know [*Try! Try!*] by heart—in 1951, the romantic problems of the returning veteran hero were familiar to most Americans [as] the subject of countless movies, novels, and soap operas," which almost invariably resolve with the reinstatement of the normative social order.[31] At the premiere, the audience at Harvard laughed so raucously at the play's arch take on the returning soldier/patient wife plot that Thornton Wilder, who was in the audience, was aghast. He evidently took the play at face value.[32] It merits noting, too, that while the audience at the Poets Theater might be assumed to have at least passing familiarity with Noh, American audiences steeped in *Best Years of Our Lives*–style rehabilitative returns of the soldier were not lining up for Japanese forms at midcentury.

O'Hara's play turns not on providing "the expected / lyricism," but on what he regarded as misplaced, ill-conceived ferment about what Second World War poetry was supposed to sound like—and where it was. The idea that the war's poetry and broader writing were lacking sparked seemingly endless literary, popular, and political comment during the Second World War, as is well known; hence the title of Cecil Day Lewis's metawar poem, "Where Are the War Poets?" (1942), which parrots a common journalistic question.[33] This discourse also prepared the ground for chronic underestimation of midcentury literature. As the preceding chapters of this book all variously attest, the search for and evaluation of the war's literature would both provoke continued pronouncement and punditry as the war became "the recent war" and provide a proxy site for debates about the public worth or work of literature in its wake. Recall, in this vein, Elizabeth Bowen's refusal of victorious postwar hindsight in *The Heat of the Day*; Ellison's resignification of "the war;" or how, in the reception of *The Age of Anxiety*, Auden's treatment of the war became either irrelevant to the long poem or, for a vocal minority on both sides of the Atlantic, its main offense. Recall, too, that this ferment—and some poets' ensuing sense that they were expected to write of the war, and damned if they did or didn't—prompted a wary Elizabeth Bishop to append that equivocal note to her first book of poems, *North & South* (1946): "Most of these poems were written, or partly written, before 1942."[34] Her *Cold Spring* would figure the discursive and atmosphere pressure of "history" at midcentury without settling for or into plain topicality.

Meanwhile, poets who could most easily have been called "war poets"— members of the armed forces who wrote poems about their military or combat experience—increasingly rejected the title, in some cases implying that the term imposed reductive or odiously nationalist readings on their work. Karl Shapiro, for example, won the Pulitzer Prize for Poetry in 1945 for *V-Letter* (1944), a collection he wrote while stationed in Australia and New Guinea and amid what he describes in his introduction to the book as "the peculiarly enlivening circumstances of soldiering." "Since the war began," Shapiro continues, "I have tried to be on guard against becoming a 'war poet.'" He was "on guard" not only because he regards the term *war poet* as deeply and broadly misunderstood but also because "our contemporary man should feel divested of the stock attitudes of the last generation."[35] Not coincidentally, Shapiro was one of the judges of the Hopwood Award competition in 1951 and the only one to rank O'Hara's manuscript first.

For writers working through or out of the Second World War, the poetry of the First World War was, like modernism, at once a formidable legacy and formally and ethically exhausted. Marina MacKay writes of the British situation: "The literature of the Second World War was always going to be different: that it does not take as its raison d'être the position that war is stupid, wasteful and ugly is certainly not because writers mistook state-sanctioned violence on the grand scale for anything other than what it is, but exactly because, after the Great War, they took this as given"—and, indeed, as a view already achieved by the most accomplished of the trench poets, whose repackaging along nationalist lines continued in the early 1940s.[36] The U.S. context may be less familiar, but it offers ample contemporaneous evidence of much the same point—even despite the many important differences between the two nations' involvement in the First and Second World Wars. Already in September 1940, *Poetry: A Magazine of Verse* published Kenneth Fearing's essay "U.S. Writers in War," which diagnoses a condition of "ideological derangement" in which "there is no government or political party anywhere in the world today whose acts square, fully, with its publicly announced purposes."[37] Given this derangement, "It will be enough if the writer refuses to lend himself to the more prodigious lies that mushroom in times like these."[38] In *Poetry*, David Daiches's canon-making essay "Poetry in the First World War" followed immediately on Fearing's contribution. Daiches makes a perceptive ranking of the "best of all the poetry produced as a result of the [previous global] war" as distinct from the patriotic pablum that greeted its start in 1914 and persisted in masking, to borrow from MacKay, its stupid, wasteful ugliness. Daiches celebrates Wilfred Owen for already having done something like what Fearing proposes: refusing to tell "The old Lie."[39]

It was already clear in the 1940s that technologically updated replication of the models of Great War poetry—substituting aerial bombing for trench warfare, for example—would not suffice, even simply to reflect the greater diversity of combatants and combat conditions in the Second World War.[40] It was nonetheless commonplace for critics, reviewers, columnists, and pundits to lament the absence of "a new Wilfred Owen . . . among the armed forces to describe their experiences," as W. H. Auden put it in his review of Marianne Moore's *Nevertheless* (1944).[41] Auden cited this common lament not to participate in the search for a new Owen but to check the search for reiterations of the very precedents he and his cohort had set. Auden bracketed the "where's our Owen?" default in order to nominate Moore's "In Distrust of Merits" as the best poem of the war. In a longer view, Auden's vote for Moore—who was neither a man nor a combatant nor tragically young and who could claim none of the authority to "speak of war" conventionally taken to be conferred only by combat experience—points to the vital work that scholars including Philip Metres, Susan Schweik, and Rachel Galvin have done to challenge the persistent sense that the Second World War failed to produce a distinguished body of poetry and to expand the category of *war poet* to include conscientious objectors, women, and noncombatants, among others.[42] Much of this work attests to poets,' writers,' and critics' crucial refusal to cede the moral right or responsibility to write of war exclusively to military actors or, in Roy Scranton's incisive account, to "war trauma heroes."[43]

Still, what can get lost amid this essential expansion is precisely those poets who qualify, by virtue of military service and combat experience, for inclusion in what I've described as the unreconstructed category of *war poet* and whose work refuses to recite "the expected / lyricism" of the war. I have noted that O'Hara could have claimed the status of "war poet" in its lapsed sense. That he never would have should compel our attention. His antimilitarism was profound and expressed with deepening and self-aware commitment as he watched the war in which he volunteered to serve become the postwar in which he came of age as a poet. Hence this chapter's epigraph, excerpted from the essay on his military service required as part of O'Hara's application to Harvard. It does not follow, however, that O'Hara never wrote anything of significance about the war. His service as a Navy sonarman in the Second World War inflects his would-be first book, but its poems neither sound like prevailing precedents for war poetry in 1951 nor fall in line with the contestation of *war poetry* that accumulated during and after the war. Nor do these early poems replicate the gendered and nationalist projects that the "expected / lyricism" of the Second World War was made to sponsor, as the exaggeration-to-absurdity of these in *Try! Try!* makes plain. O'Hara's poetics of war sounds un-"expected" and has remained largely unsought. In both the poems of "A Byzantine Place" and a memoir of the war O'Hara wrote in late 1948, that poetics is tuned to sound and suspension.

A MUSICAL EAR TURNED MILITARY

Pause, stillness, listening, quiet: the lexicon I've adopted for O'Hara's sonic suspensions hardly aligns with standard accounts of his chatty, relentlessly mobile, energetic poetics. It does chime, however, with the robust body of scholarship, especially in the humanistic social sciences, on war and the silencing effects of both war and everyday violence.[44] In suggesting that the pattern of sonic suspension across "A Byzantine Place" makes the war quietly present in O'Hara's early poems—or, that the volume holds the war in suspension in its lyric present—I want to be clear that I am not asserting a singular antecedent of all pauses and silences in O'Hara's work.[45] Nor do I mean to impose a totalizing narrative of ineluctable trauma on the silences and gaps O'Hara's "Byzantine Place" poems *achieve*. I mean to observe that the silences, pauses, quiets, and blips in these poems sound proximate to O'Hara's service in the U.S. Navy in the Second World War. Listening defined it.

O'Hara received extensive musical instruction in his youth. By the time he turned eighteen, on March 27, 1944, he was an accomplished pianist. Had it not been for the war, O'Hara might well have attended conservatory after high school. Instead, certain he would be drafted and, despite his anti-militarism, he enlisted in the Navy. Once in the service, O'Hara's musical

training and talent fitted him for the job of Sound Navigation and Ranging (sonar) operator. Sonar is the study, monitoring, and measuring of
underwater sounds to navigate or detect submerged seagoing vessels, sub-
marines, weapons, and other threatening manned or unmanned objects.
Its technique and technology predate the Second World War, but it was only
during the war that the U.S. military coined the acronym SONAR to correspond, sonically, to its aerial and visual cousin: radar. The sonar operator
listens, rather than looks, for the "blip." Sonar work turns the outwardly
passive stance of listening into an aggressive, purposeful action. One listens so as to detect targets and threats.[46] The job requires rigorous training
and skilled listening, as the "radioman" learns to detect and place sonic
patterns, pitches, and deviations from standard tones and frequencies in
the loud ocean. In a letter home to his family dated July 7, 1944, O'Hara
gave a helpfully low-tech explanation of how sonar worked and why he'd
been deemed suited to it: "with my years of musical training I would have a
good pitch and be able to operate a machine which sends out sound waves
and can determine what objects are around it by the pitch of the returning
sound."[47]

To offer an illustration that O'Hara, a great moviegoer, might appreci-
ate: Charles Frend's film *The Cruel Sea* (1953) turns sonar's requisite posture of attention into cinematic suspense. In a climactic scene, the crew of
a small British ship uses sonar to detect a German U-boat moving to attack.
For four tense minutes, the crew keeps still and hushed, their eyes trained
on a blank horizon, their ears alert to sonar instruments. The sound track
of the film goes silent except for reverb tones and short beeps as the sonarman outsmarts the enemy. The suspenseful sonar scene has become a set
piece of submarine pictures including Robert Wise's *Run Silent, Run Deep*
(1958) and Wolfgang Petersen's *Das Boot* (1981). But like Elizabeth Bowen's
systematic deflation of such narrative mechanisms of suspense in *The Heat
of the Day*, O'Hara's early meditations on his war experience refuse to dramatize sonar work as a demonstration of heroic male backbone that enables
a gallant sonarman to endure suspense in service of certain and justified
victory. His early poems, in fact, decline to depict sonar in any direct sense
at all, but rather concentrate on its sensory demands and effects.

Sonar training tuned O'Hara's musical ear to war, retooling his special
auditory capacity, perhaps even irrevocably. The irony of artistic proficiency
lending itself to specialized technological warfare was not lost on O'Hara.

He centers this incongruity in "Lament and Chastisement: A Travelogue of War and Personality," the prose memoir of his Navy service he wrote during his junior year of college (1948–49), and which bears on the sound world of "A Byzantine Place." Insofar as O'Hara's memoir dwells more in the monotony of sonar work than in the depiction of cinema-ready drama, it corrects for the gratification of the sonar suspense set piece. Indeed, the memoir as a whole simulates the chaos of war rather than offering catharsis for its violence. In seventeen numbered sections, "Lament and Chastisement" proceeds from O'Hara's first arrival at a naval base to his domestic postings in Key West and San Francisco and finally to a battle-ship in the South Pacific. Any resemblance to straightforward "travelogue" ends with this chronological spine. O'Hara was unwilling to make linear-narrative sense of a war whose prosecution he thought insane and immoral, or, as the memoir's title suggests, to justify rather than to lament his participation in it.

The memoir opens with an internal monologue that hovers between the first-person singular and plural. Its first, sprawling sentence splices the violence done to servicemen *by* the service and the self-canceling habits of mind new recruits develop to cope. Spreading to the length of a paragraph, the sentence refuses to release "you" from its graphic record of sexualized military hazing—"for they had stripped and raped us all and given us cards so we could practice our new trades newly forced in a legal way now that we were broken in and we all looked the same"—or from its recall of compensatory detachment—"shit I'm no dope I knew this was going to happen and I slipped away before you got here I slipped away the real me" (*EW* 112). From this opening follows a range of rhetorical and narrative modes, including stream-of-consciousness, prose poem, prayer, pastiche, montage, incantation, verdict, allusion, dialogue, free indirect discourse, dramatic monologue, seascape, rhetorical question, apostrophe, and even a running joke about Wallace Stevens's Key West philosophizing (e.g., "its only excuse for being there is that Wallace Stevens wrote a poem about it" [*EW* 116]). O'Hara's tone similarly ranges from the funny and jubilant to the outraged and terrified, his syntax from grammatically correct to unpunctuated sprawl. Cumulatively, this array of narrative and stylistic modes at once enlivens "Lament and Chastisement" and refuses to apply any tidy narrative logic either to O'Hara's war experience or to the war itself.

A predominant theme of "Lament and Chastisement" is the perverse contiguity of music and war, or of listening to music and listening for the blip. Section 4, a dramatic monologue spoken by O'Hara's sonar instructor, exemplifies this dynamic, as the instructor peppers his weapons technology training with expressions of horrifically happy certainty about the slaughter of enemies, a certain annoyance with operational bureaucracy, and, at the "center" of the monologue, his candid affection for classical music:

> When you see the button you press it. You must determine the target by sighting along this line and squeezing like on an orange. There are several million Germans in the world and more Japanese who are utter horrors: we shall plant them, not like dragon's teeth but like Parma violets. You get right about center by listening for the mean tone, that's right sweep back and forth across the target and determine its center by your hearing, you've had musical training haven't you? I just love the Symphonie Espagnole. Milstein, of course. That's right fire. Not quite try again. And lead it just a little. That's right a little more. Now when you get an attack plan set up on this sheet you notify the officer of the deck and the communications officer but I don't know how to set it up.
>
> (*EW* 114)

The monologue form trades on listening twice over: O'Hara recalls listening to his sonar instructor in order to learn how to listen for a "target"; to write the dramatic monologue, O'Hara listens internally to his memory of that instructor, transcribing and playing back his rushed, rote directions.

It would be difficult to call this memoir playback of the training comfortably mocking, for the instructor's sudden, apparently incongruous statement of his musical enthusiasm—his "love" for violinist Nathan Milstein's recording of Édouard Lalo's *Symphonie Espagnole*, indicative of another life—is an eerily O'Hara-ish and almost empathetic interjection, albeit one made in a context not typically associated with the poet. When the sonar instructor interrupts his lesson to state his taste, the aside is gratuitous. It neither asks nor pauses for a response from O'Hara the pupil, who is not supposed to be chatting about music. He is supposed to be "listening for the mean tone." At the same time, O'Hara the poet clearly plays in this monologue on the various reverbs of "mean," including "cruel," "average," and "meaningful." The instructor's aside, at once star-tling in its unexpected interruption of instruction and also woven seam-lessly into it, articulates the central incongruity of O'Hara's war memoir and, indeed, of his war experience. Throughout "Lament and Chastise-ment," O'Hara interlaces music and war as, in this instance, he entwines "target" and *Symphonie Espagnole*.

War and music collide again and again in "Lament and Chastisement" as O'Hara recalls a series of occasions on which he listened to, discussed, or remembered music during his naval training and active sonar service. As he does in much of his later work, O'Hara frequently mentions singers, composers, musicians, pieces of music, recordings, performances, and con-cert venues: this is the poet's preferred sonic world. In this college antiwar war memoir, however, references to music repeatedly fold into the destruc-tion of the war. They can't help but do so. Any lifeline that art might offer gives way to chaotic horror or guilt. At one point, O'Hara recalls that sail-ors would gather on shore on their free Sunday afternoons in the Philip-pines, sunning themselves and playing games while "symphonic transcrip-tions" played over the loudspeaker at a makeshift "shell." The word *shell* in this usage abridges the "band shell," from the realm of music, to the term *shell*, from that of mechanized warfare (*EW* 124). At another, starker moment, when O'Hara asks if "even the greatest symphony [could] drown out the screams of Jews?," he frames the rhetorical-philosophical question about art and war as a terrifying competition between kinds of sound (*EW* 125).

O'Hara describes these blaring musical recordings as solutions to the problem of wartime suspension, the combatant's version of the civilian open-air concert with which Bowen opens *The Heat of the Day*. These events, O'Hara writes, provided servicemen with "outlets," means of killing time when the day-to-day work of war paused. In his account, temporary lassi-tude affords the mind space to take in the unrelenting "confusion" of war (*EW* 124). Symphonic recordings provide a "something anything" that one can grasp

amidst this stagger of recognition on every side that sanity lay only barely possi-ble in outlets of this artificial inducement of the self to engage in something any-thing the Fourth *Brandenburg* Concerto established a meaning and a synthesis akin to the Elizabethan chain of being; a finger touched a button and lit up the world there all aglare with death suffering struggle defeat in motion and in blinding

coherence. Not just for that moment, but vividly then, there was everything in a
relationship all alive with indefinability. . . . There was for that moment again the
pitch so high the light so keen
(*EW* 124)

At root, O'Hara remembers in this passage how a piece of music afforded
him temporary relief, how hearing Bach induced in him a brief and "blinding" vision of something like the epiphanic "coherence" of "everything."
Bach's baroque concerto provides a hint of a musical order that the war has
perhaps not entirely co-opted, and O'Hara recalls that he could hear "again
the pitch so high." Yet with the briefest of punctuated beats—at the semi-
colon after the lapsed "chain of being"—this passage concedes that war has
already overtaken its auditory glimpse of transcendent, restorative musical beauty: "a finger touched a button and lit up the world there all aglare."
The phrasing refers locally to the person who puts the record on the sound
system at the "shell." But the contexts of the memoir and of contemporary
idiomatic association alike overwhelm that implication: by the late 1940s,
"the finger on the button" is poised to start nuclear war, to drop bombs and
light up the world not in a metaphorical sense, with music, but with explosion, destruction, and fire. In the musical-martial and moral economy of
"Lament and Chastisement," the finger on the button is now O'Hara's, too.
For as his sonar instructor taught him, "When you see the button you press
it," and his ear is implicated in this war. In his college war memoir, the
cumulative effect of repeated juxtapositions of violence and music proves
elegiac, though not consolatory, in at least one sense: the titular "lament"
rues how a military ear came to displace a musical one. After the war,
O'Hara never did take up playing music seriously again. He became at midcentury a poet.

SONAR POETICS

As musician-turned-sonarman, Francis O'Hara was attuned to sound at its
most beautiful and its most threatening. It would not be unreasonable to
expect that, given O'Hara's sonar training and experience, silences or gaps
in the sound world of "A Byzantine Place: 50 Poems and a Noh Play" would
signal specific threats or vague ominousness. Contra that expectation, one
of the remarkable achievements of O'Hara's first, unpublished book is that

threats and "targets" do not necessarily lurk in its many poems predicated on or evocative of quiets, brief silences, or held pauses. As distinct from the governing horror of playing music turning into waging war in "Lament and Chastisement," the listening poems of "A Byzantine Place" variously modulate the soundscapes of music and war. The quiet, emphatically auditory poems turn, or try to turn, the poet's ear from war back to music and farther back outward to a broader world of sound. Not at all coincidentally, given O'Hara's aesthetic commitments, music was undergoing a similar remaking around 1950, most famously in the works of John Cage that made sound itself into composition. (Cage's *Amores I–II* was the "rather dissonant record" that stage-sound manager John Ashbery put on the gramophone during Jack's big war story speech in *Try! Try!*)[48]

"A Byzantine Place: 50 Poems and a Noh Play" is shot through with sounds musical, natural, mechanical, and spontaneous—with noises in suspension, sudden hushes, and brief silences. The collection contains several surprisingly (for O'Hara) quiet poems and poems that hinge on deliberate acts of listening. At some points, the poet pauses to try to hear something more clearly or to register an unexpected sound or the absence of an expected one. As befits a manuscript written in part over winters in Cambridge and Ann Arbor, "noiseless snow" occasionally mutes sound and the poems' ability to hear it, making them "deaf" (*CP* 31, *PR* 9). Like the fleeting youth that runs through the book, these sonic suspensions are never far from the war as "A Byzantine Place" quietly sounds it. Where military training taught O'Hara to anticipate violence by ear, and where sonar set-pieces maximize the suspense of anticipated attacks and the heroism of thwarting them, O'Hara's war poems more often suspend suspense and deflate the tropes of military and nationalist victory narratives. They are quiet on purpose and in protest, and they reimagine what war poetry sounds like.

Central to this work is a stealthy sonar suspension poem called "A Quiet Poem." Predicated not on the conceit of lyric speech, but rather on twinned tropes of listening and silence, "A Quiet Poem" holds still, as if expecting a sound to intrude on it. None does. All stilled sea, calm sky, and distant horizon, "A Quiet Poem" occupies the same scenic world as O'Hara's Navy memoir and many of the "sea"-toned poems of "A Byzantine Place." Nothing happens, outwardly, in the seven unrhymed couplets of "A Quiet Poem." The first half of the poem watches an airplane in the distant sky, expecting to hear its engine noise. But since the plane makes no sound that reaches the poem's internal listener, the poem in its second half inhabits the absence of anticipated sound. In a surrealistic sequence of thoughts and images, the missing noise of the plane becomes a "thought" echoing in the mind, flipping over and over as a "coin" does when it falls. In the final lines, that figurative "coin" becomes material, at least provisionally. What happens in "A Quiet Poem," then, is that the act or stance of listening prompts figurative thinking. Which is to say that listening makes the poem:

When music is far enough away
the eyelid does not often move

and objects are still as lavender
without breath or distant rejoinder.

The cloud is then so subtly dragged
away by the silver flying machine

that the thought of it alone echoes
unbelievably; the sound of the motor falls

like a coin toward the ocean's floor
and the eye does not flicker

as it does when in the loud sun a coin
rises and nicks the near air. Now,

slowly, the heart breathes to music
while the coins lie in wet yellow sand.
(CP 20)

The cumulative effect of "A Quiet Poem" is of a silence that should be eerie, but somehow isn't. The poem's listener trains his senses on any hint of noise. Yet for all the still quiet announced in the title and achieved in the poem, "A Quiet Poem" does create gentle movement: within its stilled scene, the poem's adjectives and temporal markers chart a course from distance ("far enough away," "distant") to proximity ("near"), and from a general

"When" to a specific "Now," the present in which O'Hara's poems would increasingly live. As "A Quiet Poem" gradually shifts from observing "the silver flying machine"—a markedly naive way of evoking an airplane—to imagining what's underwater, it moves form the territory of radar to the submerged realm of sonar. It holds itself in suspension, to listen.

O'Hara would write dozens of poems titled "Poem." In this case, the sonic modifier "Quiet" points to how hard O'Hara works to keep "A Quiet Poem" still and silent. Noise occurs only in the mind; the "sound of the motor" echoes only in "thought." The poem is set on a visibly calm sea, and its diction and syntax hold the poem "still": it "does not often move." "A Quiet Poem" is muted, too, by its punctuation, which notably lacks O'Hara's exuberant exclamation points, already a typographic signature of his work in "A Byzantine Place." For the first twelve lines, the poem allows its sentences calmly to spill over line breaks and couplets, and to move, by association, from one image to the next. As the sentences spread down the page and move the poem down underwater, O'Hara adopts a policy of synesthesia, producing "quiet" in sight and smell as well as in hearing and sound. O'Hara's muted surrealism confuses sensory effects throughout the poem, so that the "eyelid" follows on distant music and the "sun" looks "loud." As "lavender" becomes an emblem not of potent scent or color, but of environmental stillness, O'Hara's slant rhyme for "lavender," "distant rejoinder," also describes the auditory effect of slant rhyme itself, a near-rhyme whose completion you can just about hear in its very suspension.

Music, which since 1944 had been bound to the war for O'Hara, frames "A Quiet Poem," barely audible on either side of it. Too "far . . . away" to be heard in the first line, music becomes embodied as respiration as in the penultimate line, when "the heart breathes to music." The breath of "A Quiet Poem" thus moves, too, from being held early in the poem ("without breath") to a continuous inhale-exhale at its end ("the heart breathes" in the present). This inscription of breath consolidates the poem's teetering on the edge between potential suspense or anxiety and sustained suspension, and its opting for the latter. It might seem as if a danger has passed at some point in "A Quiet Poem" and that breath held in tension at the beginning is released in relief at the end. But note that there never is any register, or sound, of threat, only the poem in its quiet performance of itself. As it goes from up in the sky to down under water, the poem declines to play out as a sonar suspense scene, or even to name the war. It suspends itself in a quiet that is not quite silence and not quite stasis. Rewriting the overlay of musical training with military training that organizes "Lament and Chastisement," "A Quiet Poem" gradually opens a space in which the ear and "heart" might reopen "to music" and breathe—at least for a moment.

"A REMARK AFTER ANOTHER WAR"

On his entry form for the Hopwood contest, O'Hara dutifully supplied basic information about himself: date of birth, present occupation, permanent address. Next, he printed his answers to two questions: "Married? When? To whom" and "Service record, if any." These two questions were predictable ones to ask of any young adult entering an institutional context or professional space in the years following the Second World War. Yet even bracketing the question of what bearing marital status and military service have on a creative writing competition, note that the phrasing of the form suggests that marriage—"Married? When? To whom"—is less optional than voluntary service ("Service record, if any"). On this point, O'Hara's biographer quotes from a letter the young poet received from a former shipmate in 1950. O'Hara's "buddy" writes that it has been some time since the two men have communicated, so "Now comes the big question. 'Are you married yet?' Sure hope so for it is a wonderful life. If you haven't you don't know what you're missing."[49]

Nearly seventy years after O'Hara filled out the Hopwood competition entry form, his reply to the first question—"No."—reads like a deadpan joke. (So does his "?" in response to "Writing plans." Only an exclamation point could possibly seem more characteristically O'Hara.) Entirely normative in 1951, the compulsory questions about marriage and military service point, respectively, to a thick rope and a fragile string in the O'Hara scholarship. The deservedly thick rope is O'Hara's queer poetics; the unduly fragile string is his poetics of war. Obscure in the study of O'Hara and of postwar poetry, indispensable to an understanding of the poet's period-defining work, "Noir Cacadou, or the Fatal Music of War" braids these threads. This V-J Day poem stands as both the most explicit war poem in "A Byzantine Place" and the volume's most forthright love poem. "Noir Cacadou" disproves any presumed exclusivity between war poetry and queer poetry—an obviously false and yet oddly durable assumption, and one played out, if unwittingly, in the O'Hara scholarship. In answer to an implied generational

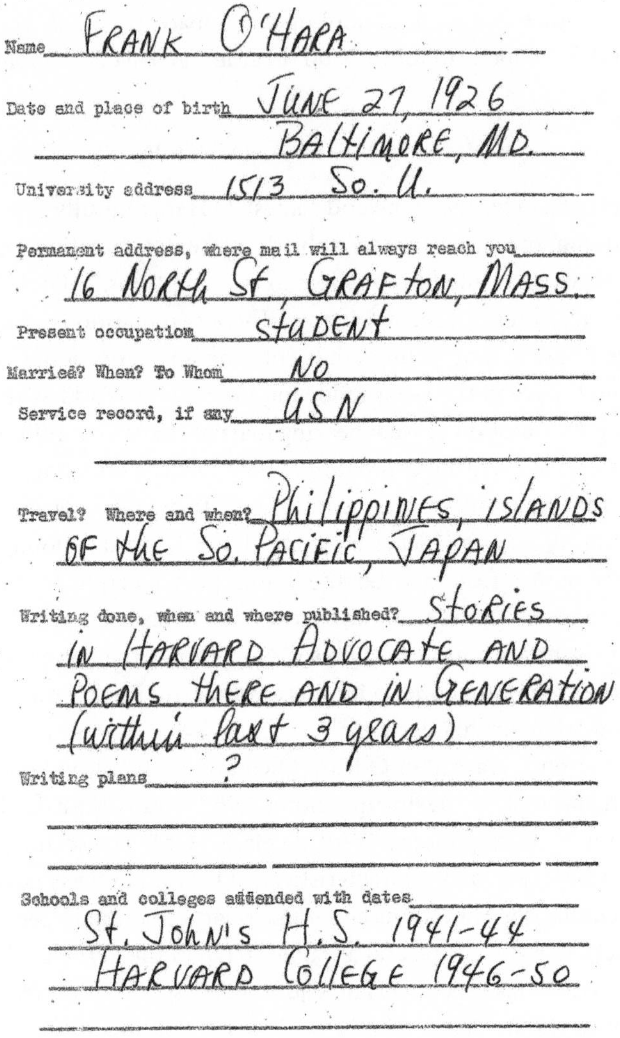

Name FRANK O'HARA

Date and place of birth JUNE 27, 1926
BALTIMORE, MD.

University address 1513 So. U.

Permanent address, where mail will always reach you
16 North St, GRAFTON, MASS.

Present occupation STUDENT

Married? When? To Whom NO

Service record, if any USN

Travel? Where and when? Philippines, ISLANDS
OF the So. PACIFIC, JAPAN

Writing done, when and where published? STORIES
IN HARVARD ADVOCATE AND
POEMS THERE AND IN GENERATION
(within last 3 years)

Writing plans ?

Schools and colleges attended with dates
St. John's H.S. 1941-44
HARVARD COLLEGE 1946-50

FIGURE 4.2 Copy of O'Hara's Hopwood Prize competition entry form, 1951. University of Michigan Special Collections Library. Reproduced by permission of Maureen O'Hara.

question—*where were you when the war ended?*—"Noir Cacadou" offers a muted victory celebration and a forthright elegy for a love affair that must end with the war. In other words, while military victory is quiet, so flat as to be suspect in "Noir Cacadou," the love affair is, at least for the duration of the poem, as "open" as the sea in "A Byzantine Place." The poem subverts in tandem the dominant cultural significations of two silences: first, the silence historically imposed on queer desire; second, since stoic reticence ranks among the distinguishing characteristics of the group known in the U.S. as the "Greatest Generation," the silence popularly venerated in veterans of the Second World War.[50] But where popular historians cast these veterans' silence about the war as exemplary of a bygone, dignified, masculine self-possession and commitment to the nation, O'Hara's V-J Day poem remakes quietness into a register of dissent from both military violence and national mythologization of it.[51]

With a humorous wink and a wistful sigh, the narrative arc of "Noir Cacadou, or the Fatal Music of War" (*PR* 1–2) counters the iconic image and dominant narrative of V-J day in the United States as both are distilled in Albert Eisenstaedt's photograph *V-J Day in Times Square*, published in *Life* on August 27, 1945. In the celebrated photo, the sailor kissing the nurse becomes the clichéd image of spontaneous, sexualized jubilation—and, it goes almost without saying, of a straight sexual fantasy tinged with the violence of the soldier's sudden force. A sexual victory narrative affirms the military one.

O'Hara's V-J Day poem, by pointed contrast, is about two sailors whose love affair must end with the war. The poem's main title refers outwardly to a set of gymnastic exercises often included in Dada soirées in the early twentieth century. It points internally to the costumed, impromptu V-J Day celebration a group of sailors stages onboard a Navy ship, possibly the USS *Nicholas*. But the poem's heart is not in the party, for two reasons. First, the poet is disillusioned with the war. He and his shipmates only go through the motions of celebration, dancing "the measure of being / pleased with ourselves" (*PR* 1). Second, and more immediately pressing to the poet, the end of the war is "fatal" to his love affair with a fellow sailor. The poem's whole effect—lodged in allusions, tone, and narrative, as well as in subtle and bald humor—is to deflate, as in "Memorial Day 1950," the victory narrative that commenced "when the war ended" and to suspend the "meanings" that the war would take on and be made to serve. Variants of the word *meaning* echo across the poem, as they do across "A Byzantine Place: 50 Poems and a Noh Play." In "Noir Cacadou," recollection of the war's end opens not onto immediate, unqualified celebration but onto a series of unanswered questions about what "it"—the war as well as the affair the war enabled—"had meant" or "will mean." Not for the first time in *Midcentury Suspension*, then, we witness a work of literature deferring any assertion of the war's "meaning" while hovering in the historical moment during which the war became the postwar.

O'Hara arranges "Noir Cacadou" into seventeen tercets and what I read as three movements. The first movement (stanzas 1 to 7) describes what a group of sailors were doing when they heard the news of Japan's surrender. They go from "dull" indolence—"We were standing around / with guitars and mandolins / when the war ended"—to rote celebration. "Noir Cacadou" pivots at its middle (stanzas 8 and 9), when the opening depiction of stunned festivity becomes the reason "why" the speaker urgently desires his lover. At the center of the poem, the poet realizes that the end of the war confirms the impossibility of a future with his beloved. In the final part of "Noir Cacadou" (stanzas 10 to 17), the speaker indulges in a last dream vision of sated queer desire—in this case, a sexual connection of men that sits indeterminately, in the poem, between tryst and abiding "love." Standard romantic narratives—whether of overwhelming passion or loving commitment—cannot accommodate these lovers now that "the war [has] ended." As this précis alone perhaps irresistibly suggests, "Noir Cacadou" is Foucault before Foucault: the poem tracks how, in a moment, the cessation of state-sanctioned violence entails the cancellation of a sexual liberty temporarily afforded to these men by virtue of their conscription to that violence.

"Noir Cacadou" gets a bit cheeky on this point, as witness how thoroughly its diction collocates sex and war, camp and combat. The soldiers' costumes include "stovepipes." The word *stovepipes* refers sartorially to tall, cylindrical hats: these are comic, carnival garments—Abraham Lincoln in caricature. In the lexicon of the U.S. military after 1920, however, *stovepipe* also referred to "a portable trench mortar."[52] More bluntly in this vein, the first movement ends with a summary of the sailors' purported general happiness: "We were gay, we had won" (*PR* 1). Later, "Noir Cacadou" collapses the vocabularies of war and sex entirely. Weaponry and navigational devices become bald double entendres: "you will / not know what instrument // you are patting"; we will "wallow lasciviously in arms"; "the sextant shakes and positions / get difficult." One can hear such conflation even in the summary lines, "afterwards / we'll help each other dress" (PR 2, my emphasis).

Beginning with its title, "Noir Cacadou, or the Fatal Music of War" also ties war and the deadly sound of war to music; placed almost at the end of "A Byzantine Place," the poem synthesizes the sonic suspension that suffuses the volume. This is a V-J Day poem that begins in stillness ("We were standing around," "The sea was calm and pale") and ends in quiet, with "flowers at the dummy's feet." It is a war poem in which music, musical instruments, and musical vocabulary predominate. The "fatal music" of the poem registers in its diction, in "guitars and mandolins," "twangings," "measure," "musical / string," "instrument," "vibrating," and a "gong" (PR 1–2). But the energy of "Noir Cacadou" finally inheres less in the musical accompaniment to a doomed romance than in its quiet contraction from a collective "we" and "us" to a specific "you" and "me." First-person plural pronouns pile up in the first part. In the first seven stanzas, the speaker refers to a communal "we," "us," or "ourselves" seven times and to a specific "you" and "me" or "I" only twice. According to the pronouns at the beginning of the poem, the speaker could be any sailor onboard the warship. By the end, "you" and "I" have emerged as a specific "we," lovers in an embodied romance relegated to fantasy by the war's end.

Rather than triumph upon receiving the news of the end of the war, the speaker of "Noir Cacadou, or the Fatal Music of War" wonders: "Whatever / had it meant to us, what // will you mean to me, does nothing end?" Nor can a senior officer do much better at making meaning out of war: "The Admiral said 'Men / you were admirable.'" The playful sonic slippage of the admiral's congratulations casts the comment itself as meaningless and anticlimactic even before the speaker interpolates that "it meant nothing, simply / a remark after another war" (PR 1). To make "it" mean something more would be to afford a "meaning" to the war, possibly at the expense of the men's love for the admiral and one another: "We / loved him as I love you." But there is also a clear-eyed refusal to endorse the logic that the admiral's "Men" are *made* honorable men by their service in the war. For the poem has already made "the war" into "another war," which emendation recasts the Second World War as one in a sequence of wars without "end" (PR 1). Finding that it, too, could only make one more empty remark about ceaseless violence, "Noir Cacadou" chooses not to. The most conspicuous war poem in "A Byzantine Place: 50 Poems and a Noh Play" ends with flowers lain "at the dummy's feet," an image of silence and mourning (*PR* 2). "Noir Cacadou" does not simply end; it turns itself into a quiet poem at its end. This is what Francis O'Hara's unexpected, unsought "lyricism" of war sounds like: it sounds like suspension, with "meaning" expressly deferred.

GENERATION-MAKING IN THE EARLY POSTWAR

With a view to both loosening and deepening our critical grasp on O'Hara's work, this chapter has concentrated on his "Byzantine Place" manuscript and on other relatively obscure documents from early in his career. I'll conclude by panning out from the sound of the war in O'Hara's midcentury book manuscript and toward echoes of those sonic suspensions across his postwar- and cold war–identified work. More specifically, I'll turn in closing to echoes of O'Hara's early poetics in two banner moments of his later career: his inclusion in Donald Allen's *The New American Poetry, 1945–1960* and his best-known poem, "The Day Lady Died" (1959). The anthology marks an early instance of the abrupt erasure of the war in the long reception of O'Hara and thus addresses the lingering question of how it is that O'Hara's war poetics has remained obscure over decades. The anthology piece, an elegy of sorts for Billie Holiday, speaks to the endurance of that war poetics, attuned as they are to sound, hush, pause, rest—to suspension—in O'Hara's more mature work. Put more evocatively, this chapter concludes by moving, one last time, from the strange absence of the midcentury to the import of its unsought presence, or to what midcentury suspension helps us hear in works and writers perhaps deeply valued, like O'Hara, but only partially known.

O'Hara's storied unconcern with or ambivalence about publishing his work notwithstanding, he had released several chapbooks and collaborative projects as well as two volumes of poems before his death in 1966, at forty. If he was "a coterie figure . . . regarded (when regarded at all) as a charming minor poet" when he died, the book that did the most to put him even that much on the map was *The New American Poetry, 1945–1960.*[53] In his preface, Allen explains that he "adopted the unusual device of dividing the poets into five large groups" gathered loosely around geographic locations and their associated oppositional aesthetics: Black Mountain, San Francisco Renaissance, the Beats in their move west from New York to San

Francisco, the New York Poets, and "a fifth group with no geographic definition."[54] The influence of Allen's anthology and his approach to organizing it cannot be overstated and need not be recounted here. Alan Golding
sums both up well: "In terms of its defining 'anti-academic' role in the 1960s
anthology wars, its impact on later collections and editors, its importance
for later poets, and its central place in most readings or structurings of
postwar literary history, Donald Allen's *The New American Poetry* ... is
generally considered the single most influential poetry anthology of the
post-World War II period."[55]

But I want to highlight this antiestablishment collection's most establishment move—namely, the presentation of these younger poets as a
"generation." Recognition of this "strong third generation" of American
poets rested on the far broader emergence of the "generation" as a category of cultural-historical identity and differentiation.[56] In *Keywords*,
Williams notes that the "important development" of *generation* away
from biological and toward "social and historical uses" began "fully" to
happen in the nineteenth century and that the word's cultural uses had
only "multiplied since" the early twentieth.[57] (In this vein, think of the
differences between Gertrude Stein naming the Lost Generation versus
the Beat Generation naming itself; or recall Bowen's generational characterization of Stella Rodney or O'Hara's antinormative answer, in "Noir
Cacadou," to the implicit generational question of where he was when
the war ended.)

In U.S. poetry specifically, the notion of a third generation of new, electric poets relied on some distinctly midcentury math. Let me back up a bit
to explain. It was John Ciardi, one of O'Hara's professors at Harvard, who
suggested he go to the University of Michigan and compete in the Hopwood Prize contest.[58] During O'Hara's senior year, in 1950, it was also
Ciardi who brought out *Mid-Century American Poets*, the now mostly forgotten anthology of contemporary poetry for which Elizabeth Bishop
wrote "It All Depends." Ciardi's title was inevitable but not ineffective.
In his admittedly "didactic" foreword, Ciardi asserts that American poetry
by 1950 had at last shaken off what he regards as the indulgences of
modernism: those "manifestoes and petty dictatorships" for which Ciardi
blames Pound chiefly and which "may easily appear a bit precious and a bit
insane to the contemporary reader."[59] As against such "Bohemian extrava-
gance," the new poets Ciardi selects prove by their very "self-conscious

sanity in an urbane and cultivated poetry" that the United States had, at midcentury, achieved a mature and "self-indebted" poetic tradition. As Ciardi's vocabulary of sanity alone indicates, he means his anthology's roster of consensus to correct for the Pound of the late 1940s as much as for the Pound of the nineteen teens and twenties. In James E. B. Breslin's memorable gloss, Ciardi "took particular care to show how his calm and self-assured generation had freed themselves from the unruly excesses of modernism—as if the decorums of his literary anthology were those of an academic dinner party."[60]

To argue that American poetry reached its genteel maturity at midcentury, Ciardi started his timeline conveniently late, with the poets "of the [nineteen-] twenties."[61] This tardy start facilitated his tracing of three white and patrilineal "generations" of U.S. poets across the twentieth century to 1950: modernists, mid-century American poets—"the spokesmen" of their generation—and a still "newer generation" just getting started and including, one would think, Ciardi's most promising students, among them O'Hara and Ashbery.[62] By this sleight of calculation, the apparently default chronological units—century and generation—of Ciardi's anthology reinforce one another: modernist youth aligns with the twentieth century's youth; well-behaved "mid-century American poets" synchronize as if naturally with the century's middle age. Ciardi braids the organizing logics of the midcentury and the generation together so insistently that their interlacing is almost imperceptible—except that his frequent, often scare-quoted use of the word *generation* testifies to its relative newness, in 1950, as organizing category for twentieth-century U.S. poetry. Ciardi was far from alone in beginning to delineate contemporary poetry along generational lines, but his book marks an especially eager instance in the emergence of the model.[63] By yoking the currency of *midcentury* to an orderly procession of twentieth-century American poetic "generations," Ciardi all but applied the modifier from under whose bland connotations critics long had to dig out the reputations of many poets included in his collection: *middle*.[64] In 1950, one did not need to differentiate between *midcentury* and *middle*. Six years later, George P. Elliott finally cemented the bland term *middle generation*.[65] By then, *midcentury* was no longer in vogue, but the middle generation designation it had recently subtended was here to stay. So was the convenience of *generation* as a sorting mechanism for postwar U.S. poetry.

That convenience was deeply compromised from the start. Where the biological derivation of *generation* could signal broad democratic inclusiveness, in that everyone born around the same time would seem at least to qualify for membership, the term in critical practice often licenses any number of unstated and thus necessarily unjustified exclusions. Most obviously to this point, and without falling into the kind of "glib anachronism" against which Golding cautions with respect to Allen's pathbreaking anthology, two women, Bishop and Muriel Rukeyser, and no people of color rank among the *Mid-Century American Poets* as Ciardi selected them.[66] Nonetheless, the same generational rubric structures *The New American Poetry, 1945–1960*, and to many of the same effects. Allen's brief preface begins, "In the years since the war American poetry has entered upon a singularly rich period. It is a period that has seen published many of the finest achievements of the older generation [as well as of a] wide variety of poets of the second generation, who emerged in the thirties and forties. . . . And we can now see that a strong third generation, long awaited but only slowly recognized, has at last emerged."[67] (The now familiar sense of the midcentury as prolonged hiatus comes through in the phrases "long awaited," "only slowly," and "at last.")

Allen's lineage model matches Ciardi's; the salient difference lies in the constituencies assembled into their stepped generations. In *The New American Poetry*, Pound and William Carlos Williams displace Ciardi's Eliot. Allen replaces mainstream *Mid-Century* picks like Richard Wilbur with experimental "second"-generation poets like Louis Zukofsky. (Bishop and Robert Lowell alone appear favorably in both Allen's "second" and Ciardi's "mid-century" generation.) But the generational math gets a bit muddy when Allen turns to the new, third generation of still younger poets, which by his account begins with Charles Olson. Olson was born a year before Bishop and in the same city, no less (Worcester, Massachusetts). Ciardi's is really a 1940s anthology, Allen's a 1950s one. In fact, Allen's selection barely glimpses the early part of its titular time span: after two poems by Olson, the anthology includes no more poems dated to the 1940s.

It should be difficult not to hear the specialists' adumbration of poetic generations picking up on contemporaneous and lasting popular understanding of the war as a generational event. But the anthologies—and the modes of reading and study they initiated—diverge from that common understanding in one key way: by making the war all but absent from their accounts of the first two "generations" of American poets to come of age during or just after it. "In the years since the war . . ." is as much as Allen has to say about it; Ciardi has nothing. This is not to fault the editors, or to demand that they speak of war. I mean rather to observe that the war around which we still periodize twentieth-century literature, especially in the Anglo-American frame, had already all but dropped out as an explicit reference point from the 1960 anthology that gave enduring shape to study of postwar U.S. poetry and from one of the mainstream *midcentury* anthologies against which Allen pitched his new poets.

In other words, and recalling those many important approaches to O'Hara's work adduced at the opening of this chapter, we come by our general unfamiliarity with O'Hara's war and war memory, and the sound of both, honestly. Yet if something really brings the new American poets together as members of a generation, then that something must include the simple, consequential fact that many of them were born either just in time for or a bit too late to serve in the Second World War. Though not made explicitly pertinent to the influential editorial framing of *The New American Poetry, 1945–1960*, the war recurs at several points across the anthology, as the biographies supplied by the poets most efficiently attest. O'Hara, who lists "Navy 1944–46" in his brief bio, is one of eleven poets who note their service in the Second World War. Apropos the widening scope and diversity of war poets—and war poetry projects—as both a fact and a critical imperative, those who list their service include two women and a conscientious objector.[68] And whereas "Noir Cacadou" stands as the most conspicuous poem about the war in "A Byzantine Place," the poem in which O'Hara made his most conspicuous poetic use of his military service, full stop, "Ode on Michael Goldberg ('s Birth and Other Births)" (1958), was published in *The New American Poetry, 1945–1960*.

"Conspicuous" as in topical, but as distinct from conventional. One of a suite of odes O'Hara wrote in 1957–58, "Michael Goldberg" loosely follows a line through O'Hara's life from his birth in 1926, the first "other birth" than Goldberg's, to its present. Out from the poem's basic biographical arc, a dazzling array of line and stanza shapes radiate. Lines variously run to extended free verse paragraphs and break into tetrameter stanzas, create and leap over gaps in their middles and spread out and down the page like a staircase, lean toward left or right margin and hover toward center, group into temporary pattern and break out into sprawl.[69] The visual and spatial momentum of the poem complements its geographic mobility. The poem travels from the Baltimore and New England of O'Hara's early years to, in its later sections, his New York, including the "back alcove / of the Five Spot" (*CP* 296). Midway through, the poem courses around Southeast and East Asia as these regions were militarized in the war in which O'Hara served and transformed in its wake to marketplaces under global capitalism. Thus as "Michael Goldberg" sails from New Guinea to Manila to Sendai and to Ulithi, among other sites, it also shuttles from O'Hara's war memory to his 1950s grasp of the "interests" of the oil industry: "as the sailors pee into funnels, ambassadors of / green-beer-interests bigger than Standard Oil in the South / Pacific" (*CP* 295).

The war circuit of "Ode on Michael Goldberg ('s Birth and Other Births)" begins and ends in New Guinea, where O'Hara recalls first a stereotypically "native" execution of a predatory man ("he has had his balls sewed into his mouth") and later "the Australians . . . taking over" the campaign and territory (*CP* 294, 296). The images of war experience stitched into the middle of the ode sustain a kind of urgent simultaneity over some seventy lines. Cumulatively, these details undermine the idea of safe return—"to 'return' safe who will never feel safe"—that the ode glimpses as it moves away from its war zone (*CP* 296). (The line borrows both empathy and rhythm from Allen Ginsberg in *Howl* [1956]: "ah, Carl, while you are not safe I am not safe.")[70] Many of the details of O'Hara's war experience also recall and build on patterns and tropes from O'Hara's earlier work. Reminiscent of the romantic charge of "Noir Cacadou," there is "a dark sinking in the wind on the forecastle / when someone you love hits your head and says, 'I'd sail with you any / where, war or no war'" (*CP* 294). Once again, the war gives both opportunity and cover to this love; this time, it is the violence rather than the end of the war that abruptly kills it. He of the intimate wish becomes he

> who was about
> > to die a tough blond death
> > > > like a slender blighted palm
> > in the hurricane's curious hail
> > > > and the maelstrom of bulldozers
> > > and metal sinkings,
> > > > > churning the earth
> > even under the fathomless deaths
> (*CP* 295)

The phrase "fathomless deaths" imports a frankness about violence to the proverbial fathomless depths that O'Hara's sonar training taught him to probe militarily and that "A Quiet Poem" refuses to heroize. For one more example of an echo of O'Hara's earlier work in "Michael Goldberg," the ode replays the overlay of military "killing" onto servicemen's options for killing time, as in these lines: "a basketball game and a concert / later if you live to write, it's not all advancing / towards you, he had a killing desire for their women // but more killing still the absence of desire" (*CP* 294). Among its effects, the repetition of "killing" levels the explanation for why "the natives" killed the predatory man with a self-reflective candor about why—"more killing"—O'Hara and his shipmates are there to behold his corpse.

But isn't it risky to turn to a poem obviously "about" the war toward the end of a chapter arguing that an exclusively topical search for the war in O'Hara's poetics cannot tune in to how his poems effect auditory suspensions in and of it? Maybe. But it's worth the risk. Recall how we got here: my intention has not been to resort to the topicality of "Ode on Michael Goldberg ('s Birth and Other Births)," but rather to convey how manifest the war was in the selection of poems O'Hara gave to Donald Allen for inclusion in *New American Poetry, 1945–1960*. As included in this crucial document in O'Hara's long reception, the Goldberg ode could easily have prompted the kind of topical search this chapter has largely avoided and this book has cautioned against. For the presumption of topicality not only tends to circumscribe the range of responses a "topic" might motivate; it also, as the heuristic of midcentury suspension helps us to see, complies with a temporal schema in which wars are imagined to start and stop punctually, be contained as exceptional wartimes, and cleanly delineate periods of study. In the case of O'Hara, one clear demonstration of why we need the heuristic of midcentury suspension to hear his lingering war is that, despite even poems so plainly "about" the war as "Ode on Michael Goldberg ('s Birth and Other Births)," we have not yet heard it.[71]

V-J DAY TO LADY DAY

O'Hara's best-known poem, "The Day Lady Died" (1959), followed "Ode on Michael Goldberg ('s Birth and Other Births)" in *The New American*

Poetry, 1945–1960. It offers a case in point for how his war-inflected poetics, oriented at midcentury to sound, went on to resonate throughout
his career. Even as this postwar lyric chestnut pivots on the poet's reaction to the news of Billie Holiday's death—his immediate recollection of
a suspended moment constituted by collective, rapt, and breathless listening to her quiet singing—it resounds with O'Hara's early poetry of
sonic suspension. To read "The Day Lady Died" in light of the poems
O'Hara had gathered into "A Byzantine Place: 50 Poems and a Noh
Play" less than a decade earlier is to perceive another set of memories of
sound and collectivity seeping into the auditory experience depicted in
the Holiday elegy—and most especially in the sudden hush with which
the poem ends. A new account of O'Hara becomes possible. The exemplary postwar poet of movement, conversation, and action can be
understood more fully as still a midcentury poet of listening, sound,
and suspension, a poet keenly attuned to the war lurking in the postwar. "The Day Lady Died" indexes the extent to which the chattiness of
the cold war poet Frank O'Hara is founded on the work of the deeply
quiet Francis O'Hara.

"The Day Lady Died" (*LP* 25–26) is classic O'Hara as we've come to
know him, one of his "I do this, I do that" poems. Like "Noir Cacadou,"
the poem answers an unasked "Where were you when *x*?"-style question.
The poem's title frames it as an oblique elegy for Holiday, and the poem in
turn approaches the singer indirectly, by taking an entertaining walk
around New York on the day news of her death broke. The poet gets "a
shoeshine," has "a hamburger and a malted," withdraws cash from the
bank, browses books and magazines, deliberates about gifts for his weekend hosts in the Hamptons, and buys cigarettes and a newspaper. "The
Day Lady Died" is informal in tone and rich in cultural references; it drops
the names of close friends and famous artists; it lists train times and street
names. Until the last stanza, the poem occurs entirely in the present tense.
So far, so good: the immediacy, casual tone, allusive texture, calendrical
play, and urban milieu of "The Day Lady Died" are what's expected from
Frank O'Hara.

Then, at the end of the second stanza, O'Hara sees "a NEW YORK POST
with her face on it." The iconic image of Holiday's face immediately alters
the mood and pace of this lyric memory dated July 17, 1959. The news of the

singer's death shocks the poem into its final stanza break and transports the poet back to the time he heard Holiday sing in a jazz club:

and I am sweating a lot by now and thinking of
leaning on the john door in the 5 SPOT
while she whispered a song along the keyboard
to Mal Waldron and everyone and I stopped breathing
(*LP* 26)

The last stanza of "The Day Lady Died" both depicts and effects suspension in and through sound, and thus fuses key features of O'Hara's midcentury poetry with signatures of his mature persona. In its closing moment, the elegy arrives at a continuous "now" that the poet, embodied, inhabits in the present of the poem and in its recollected past: "I am sweating," it seems, in both. "Sweating" is the first of four gerunds clustered in the final stanza—"thinking," "leaning," and "breathing" follow—and evocative of a held-still, fascinated suspension. Indeed, the recollection of "leaning on the john door" marks the first time the poet stands still in the poem. The singularity of the physical pause of the last stanza is easy to overlook, since O'Hara implies stops along the route of his walk and the ramble of the poem. But before its close, "The Day Lady Died" uses no verb that denotes or holds a full stop. Instead, until the last stanza, the poem rides on its own "going": "I go," "I will . . . go straight to dinner," "I walk," "I go on," "I get," "I just stroll," and "I go back." It concludes, however, in a recollected stillness inspired by listening to live music.

With the sound of war poetry in "A Byzantine Place" in mind, we can read this closing stanza as reaching back much further than to "the day Lady died" or even to the evening when the poet listened to her sing. The closing stanza carries an echo of the poetics O'Hara began to develop just after serving in the Second World War. That poetics relied on, even as it lamented, the imbrication of music and war, harmonious sound and murderous violence. It was predicated on the posture of listening and on the trained practice of assessing sonic effects and experiences.

O'Hara's rapt posture at the end of "The Day Lady Died" facilitates intense listening to a song so quietly "whispered" as to seem directed only at the pianist Mal Waldron, regardless of the audience. But the syntactical and grammatical ambiguity of the last line replicates how hard it is to hear Lady Day's song—does she whisper it to "Mal Waldron" or to "Mal Waldron and everyone"?—and how keenly the poet wanted, and wants, to hear it. Held suspended in the reexperienced intimacy of the performance, the poem ceases with the final amazed, even startled, reaction of the indrawn breath: "and everyone and I stopped breathing." The unpunctuated line leaves "I" or "everyone" or "everyone and I" in suspension. The poem ceases abruptly in music gone quiet but echoing in memory—in a recollected hush that, in O'Hara's poetics, is often a legacy trope of war and violence, of "stopped" breath. Indeed, the only grammatical certainty to be found in the closing pronouns is that "I stopped breathing."

In the same breath, "The Day Lady Died" puts music back into this charged posture of listening, reclaiming the poet's musical ear and remaking lyric around a listener hearing rather than a speaker speaking or, for that matter, a singer singing. At its close, "The Day Lady Died" moves in a flash from the visual impact of a picture—"a NEW YORK POST with her face on it"—to the immediate and lasting impact of a voice, a quiet sound, on its auditor. "The Day Lady Died" dramatizes a sudden, rapt listening that erupts from memory to pause the poet's city walk in the present. As this poem reveals itself to be about listening, it collapses wartime and postwar, world war and cold war, memory and present. It suggests how O'Hara's whole work can be reimagined as pursuing an aesthetic in which listening—to nothingness and casual noises, to whispers and blips, to music and conversations, to silences and street life—becomes the condition of the poet and the base note of the poems. War remains audible, suspended in this postwar work; we have only to listen.

AFTERWORD

At the start of this book, I emphasized the midcentury provenance of Raymond Williams's keywords and structures of feeling. I suggested that the emergence of the first inklings of these concepts in the late 1940s and early 1950s was neither moot nor reducible, by any rigid historicism, to a time we assume we already understand. Williams himself offers a hint in this direction. His introduction to *Keywords: A Vocabulary of Culture and Society* roots the book's influential inquiry and method in his feeling of dislocation upon his return to Cambridge from the Army in late 1945, and it figures that feeling of dislocation in largely temporal terms. My further contention was that Williams's first snags on the line of his inquiry into a vocabulary—into those often unassuming words that range over time, among people, and across disciplines, organizing thinking and feeling, accruing and varying meanings and shadings as they circulate—had something real if not yet entirely perceptible to do with the midcentury in its fullest dimensionality. Williams's initial hunches about keywords, that is, had to do with the very kinds of felt and atmospheric elements of the midcentury that he was, at midcentury, beginning to understand *as*, not as separate from or secondary to, "historical and contemporary substance."[1]

It's that substance and feeling of the midcentury—the period's internal reckonings with its historicity and contemporaneity, its distinctness and diffuseness, its middleness and temporariness—that *Midcentury Suspension* has sought out primarily through still neglected discourses, archival traces, and literary imaginaries of the period itself. My own initial hunch was that much of the inchoate texture and historical feeling of the midcentury had escaped the view of cultural analyses that work within conventional historiographies of the twentieth century and thus take 1945 or 1950 as pivot or break; it seemed as if contours and energies of midcentury literature, in particular, slipped the grasp of the established literary- and cultural-historical periods built out on either side of the epochal midpoint. In the Anglophone North Atlantic context, those period frames typically rely on modernisms or "the war" or both. Either way, the midcentury is left unpictured on its own inchoate terms.[2]

That was an early metacritical observation about where the midcentury falls and how it falls through. Yet it was clear to me early on in researching this book that metacritical argument could only do so much. If *Midcentury Suspension* was to allow felt, elusive senses of the midcentury to emerge, I'd have to find and value less definitive terms and heuristics than those derived from modernism and war. I'd have to try to find them in the vocabulary of the period itself. One day it occurred to me to start looking up that seemingly bland word *midcentury* in the academic and public library catalogs to which I had access. Then in more catalogs. (I have not yet managed to break this habit.) And there it was: a midcentury archive. Its titles were often tucked away in storage or off-site or only available from the far reaches of interlibrary loan or, in at least one case, from deep in the dusty shelves of a colleague's office. (I once spotted a *midcentury* book I hadn't found in any library shelved on a display bookcase in a used furniture store—proof, perhaps, that true and sometimes inconspicuous cultural keywords will always qualitatively exceed the scope of database keywords and search algorithms.) This dispersal of the midcentury print record came to seem to me fitting—a spatial analogue for the period's ungathered possibilities for criticism.

I didn't see that right away. I couldn't have. It was only after I'd read surely too much of that midcentury bibliography that I started to perceive both *midcentury* and *suspension* as keywords of the period around 1950. When I began, I was just curious about the discursive life and substance of the period as it took shape in and beyond the usual prestige source suspects (chief among them, in the U.S., *Partisan Review*). It had not occurred to me that *midcentury*, which sounded like nothing more than a semantic convenience, itself bore weight; nor could I have guessed that in its currency and widespread contemporaneous usage, the term indicated a historical *feeling* as well as a historical present. It only gradually became clear that two of *midcentury*'s once vital, twinned effects were to hold open a whole host of proximities to "history" and "the recent war" and also to indicate or allow for varying degrees of anticipation, experience, and recollection of violence, often without explicitly naming the war.

I didn't go looking for *suspension* either. It snuck up on me across the literature of the midcentury—in the work of the writers on whom this book focuses and in work after work by countless others. Without this literary research, I wouldn't have thought to seek out whether suspension and related concepts spread into broader print culture. They did, as we saw in the introduction. As we also saw there, the allure of suspension as concept reaches across historical epochs. Specifically at midcentury, however, suspension served imaginative, aesthetic, and intellectual efforts—especially literary efforts—to inhabit and articulate something of the present while also, if only briefly, forestalling the co-optation of that present by dominant accounts of the century, its wars, or its then-institutionalizing modernism.

Midcentury Suspension has in turn endeavored to develop a suppler and more robust sense of the historicity of the midcentury than accustomed and expanding period-interpretive models for twentieth-century literature and culture as yet provide. As heuristic, midcentury suspension enables recovery of how midcentury discourse sponsored hypotheses that were quickly written over as baseline certainties of other, longer, dominant period heuristics. Effects as broadly consequential as the promotion of anxiety as the felt condition of postwar democratic citizenship and as field-specific as the generational study of twentieth-century American poetry: these narratives coalesced in no small part around the *midcentury* occasion. More locally, we've seen writers whose works are usually read under brighter lights turn suspension to critically perceptive effect in their midcentury works: Elizabeth Bishop's midcentury trope of suspension remakes lyric into historical subjectivity; W. H. Auden's and Ralph Ellison's affective suspensions frustrate the midcentury anxiety consensus by which *The Age of Anxiety* was co-opted and whose whiteness and putative efficacy

Invisible Man critiques; Elizabeth Bowen's motifs of waiting and the middle resist the clarifying retrospect of postwar historiographies, while Beckett's absurdist waiting undoes them with midcentury humor; and Frank O'Hara's auditory suspensions stand as atypical and nontopical means by which the war sounds, in defiance of any coherent "meaning," in his poetics of the cold war and postwar.

From the vantage of this afterword, it should be clear that as *Midcentury Suspension* moved from Bishop's tropological, to Auden's and Ellison's affective, to Bowen's and Beckett's behavioral, and finally to O'Hara's auditory suspensions around 1950, it also moved closer and closer to the war that is always present in the *postwar* and its functional synonyms. Which brings us back around once more to the critical context for *Midcentury Suspension*. As I researched this book, I took heart from the essential effort underway in and beyond modernist and contemporary literary studies to trouble the pernicious ease with which our fields' period models have tended to reify histories of violence—even in our expansions, interrogations, and updates of our own period-heuristic terms. The discourse of modified modernisms, the substitution of chronological abbreviation ('45) or like gestures for the postwar: such serial adjustments can risk occluding the extent to which the logics—or illogics—of modernist triumph and state-sanctioned violence rely on and reinforce one another and delimit our view of pasts. And, for that matter, of our own endangered presents and futures.[3] The midcentury is crucial to the effort to challenge the standard practice of periodizing—which is also to say thinking—in accordance with a chronology of discrete wars and wartimes or along a long modernist line. It is crucial not simply because *midcentury* ranks as a prime instance of modernist and postwar erasure but because it once offered—and can still afford—substantive alternatives to their imperatives.

In her recent study of Ian Watt—like Williams, a veteran of the Second World War who did field-shaping work in the latter half of the twentieth century—Marina MacKay notes that more and more critics "share [an] interest in the mid-century as unfinished business."[4] Clearly, I welcome and share the interest, but I think of *midcentury* as more of an unopened file. Still, given rigorous recent analyses of long and late modernisms and of palimpsestic wartimes and interwars, can I really maintain that the *midcentury* remains "neglected" or "unpictured?" On and through its own

terms, unquestionably. But contemporary fiction has of late been pointing
a way. A cluster of recent English-language novels depict the late 1940s and
early 1950s in and as a kind of atmospheric haze of uncertainty, though
not necessarily or consistently of suspense and anxiety. Michael Ondaatje
coins an apt term for this effect with the title of his most recent novel:
Warlight (2018). The book depicts the continuation by other means of the
Second World War after the official peace. Much of its slow-burn drama
concerns the early postwar manufacture of comforting official narratives
of the war in public culture, popular imagination, and by British civic and
intelligence services alike in the late 1940s. Centered at Hiroshima in the
summer of 1947, Shirley Hazzard's *The Great Fire* (2003) narrates something akin to a pattern of doctoring or destroying evidence seen in *Warlight*.
Its retrograde colonialist politics notwithstanding, Hazzard's novel stands
in opposition to an American USSBS-style study designed both to suppress evidence of horrific devastation and to produce evidence of the efficacy of the bombing and of American military-scientific prowess. This
novel, too, is uncannily perceptive of the period's felt suspension—even
bibliographically so. The book meditates explicitly throughout on suspensions of various kinds and also indicates that it got the idea of suspension
from midcentury writing. At one point, a character reads Henry Green's
novel *Back* (1946), about a prisoner of war returning, but unable really to
return, to England from the Second World War.

This list could go on. But if such recent fictions share with an increasing
number of literary scholars the sense that the midcentury remains "unfinished business," then these novels also start to get at some things about the
midcentury that we've neglected in critical studies of its literature and culture. Those include, first, the self-conscious middleness that, distinct from
the many beginnings and endings understood to mark the late 1940s and
early 1950s, suffused *midcentury* discourse and habits of mind; and second,
the concomitant sense of suspension, in all its multivalence, as a period
experience, a model of historical apprehension and imaginative depiction,
a structure of feeling around 1950.

Finally, in *Keywords* Williams stresses that his goal is not to purify anyone's usage or vocabulary. Nor is he optimistic about suppler understand-
ings of words helping to solve the problems in which those words are
caught up. It should be clear that my own focus on midcentury suspension

does not equate to a vote for policing our scholarly uses of the term *mid-century*. Nor would I imagine strict attachment to a singular usage of any term as a sign of progress or a cause for optimism in the fields with which this book engages. What *Midcentury Suspension* aims to offer in this line is, to borrow one last time from Williams, "that extra edge of conscious-ness" about our own critical and conceptual vocabularies, the work we do with them, and the work to be done.

NOTES

INTRODUCTION

1. "The Sitwells: *Life* Reports Visit to U.S. by Celebrated Literary Team of Edith and Brother Osbert," *Life,* December 6, 1948, 164–72.
2. The Poetry Foundation website, www.poetryfoundation.org, offers reliable biographical sketches of many of the poets in the Gotham Book Mart photograph. On Villa's popularity among high modernists at midcentury, see Timothy Yu, "'The Hand of a Chinese Master': José Garcia Villa and Modernist Orientalism," *MELUS* 29, no. 1 (Spring 2004): 41–59. Yu also begins at the Gotham reception.
3. Robert Phillips, "Visiting the Gregorys," *New Criterion* 9, no. 1 (September 1990): 24–34.
4. Assessments of the Bollingen Prize controversy include Karen Leick, "Ezra Pound v. *The Saturday Review of Literature*," *Journal of Modern Literature* 25, no. 2 (Winter 2001–2): 19–37; Lem Coley, "'A Conspiracy of Friendliness': T. S. Eliot, Ezra Pound, and the Bollingen Controversy," *Southern Review* 38, no. 4 (Autumn 2002): 809–26; Wai Chee Dimock, "Aesthetics at the Limit of the Nation," *American Literature* 76, no. 3 (Spring 2004): 525–47; and Greg Barnhisel, *James Laughlin, New Directions Press, and the Remaking of Ezra Pound* (Amherst: University of Massachusetts Press, 2005), chapter 3.
5. Stephen Burt, *Randall Jarrell and His Age* (New York: Columbia University Press, 2002), 10.
6. On Moore's long work on La Fontaine, see Linda Leavell, *Holding On Upside Down: The Life and Work of Marianne Moore* (New York: Farrar, Straus and Giroux, 2013), 325–40. For an important revaluation of Moore's project, see Emily Setina, "Marianne Moore's Postwar Fables and the Politics of Indirection," *PMLA* 131, no. 5 (October 2016): 1256–73.

7. On the political malleability of the midcentury design aesthetic, see Greg Castillo, *Cold War on the Home Front: The Soft Power of Midcentury Design* (Minneapolis: University of Minnesota Press, 2010).

8. For a helpful reflection on the expanding body of scholarship that revalues midcentury British literature and on scholarly usage of *midcentury*, to which the introduction will return, see Allan Hepburn, *A Grain of Faith: Religion in Mid-Century British Literature* (Oxford: Oxford University Press, 2018), especially 15–16. Hepburn's book is part of the Oxford Mid-Century Studies series, which itself testifies to increased literary-critical interest in the middle of the twentieth century.

9. Malcolm Bradbury, "'Closing Time in the Gardens': Or, what happened to writing in the 1940s?," in *No, Not Bloomsbury* (New York: Columbia University Press, 1988), 69. Scholarly citations of this essay include Patrick Deer, *Culture in Camouflage: War, Empire, and Modern British Literature* (Oxford: Oxford University Press, 2009), 2; Gill Plain, *Literature of the 1940s: War, Postwar and "Peace"* (Edinburgh: Edinburgh University Press, 2013), 2; Guy Woodward, *Culture, Northern Ireland, and the Second World War* (Oxford: Oxford University Press, 2015), 7. On a related note, James Clements points out that the connotation of "middling" also attaches to the "mid-century [British] novelist lost somewhere in the no-man's-land between modernism and postmodernism." James Clements, *Mysticism and the Mid-Century Novel* (New York: Palgrave Macmillan, 2012), 1.

10. Elizbeth Bishop to Robert Lowell, August 22, 1948, in *Words in Air: The Complete Correspondence Between Elizabeth Bishop and Robert Lowell*, ed. Thomas Travisano with Saskia Hamilton (New York: Farrar, Straus and Giroux, 2008), 49–50.

11. Amy Hungerford, "On the Period Formerly Known as the Contemporary," *American Literary History* 20, nos. 1–2 (Spring-Summer 2008): 410.

12. Alain Badiou, *The Century*, trans. Alberto Toscano (Cambridge: Polity, 2007), 5.

13. Badiou, *The Century*, 5, 1, 3.

14. Badiou, *The Century*, 6, 3.

15. Badiou, *The Century*, 5.

16. Badiou, *The Century*, 5.

17. Badiou, *The Century*, 6. Bertolt Brecht, Paul Celan, Fernando Pessoa, and Jean-Paul Sartre loom large in Badiou's canon.

18. Badiou, *The Century*, 3.

19. George Orwell, "Politics and the English Language," *Why I Write* (New York: Penguin, 2005), 102–20. For an insightful reading of the figures—including Empson, Williams, Orwell, and Ian Watt—and ethics that created this period scrutiny and, more specifically, drove the critical recommitment to "plain style" in midcentury Britain, see Marina MacKay, *Ian Watt: The Novel and the Wartime Critic* (Oxford: Oxford University Press, 2018), chapter 3.

20. John Haffenden, *William Empson*, vol. 1: *Among the Mandarins* (Oxford: Oxford University Press, 2008), 2.

21. Raymond Williams, *Keywords: A Vocabulary of Culture and Society*, new. ed. (New York: Oxford University Press, 2015), xxvii. Examples of the adaptability of *Keywords* include New York University Press's Keywords series and Wiley-Blackwell's Keywords in Literature and Culture series. New Left critique of Williams also likely contributed to a general downplaying of the origin of *Keywords*. See Colin

MaCcabe foreword to *Keywords,* xvi–xviii; and Terry Eagleton, "Criticism and Politics: The Work of Raymond Williams," *New Left Review,* no. 95 (January-February 1976): 3–23.

22. Sianne Ngai observes that when, in *Marxism and Literature* (1977), Williams "states his methodological reasons for introducing [structures of feeling,] it becomes clear that his primary aim is to mobilize an entire affective register, *in* its entirety, and *as* a register, in order to enlarge the scope and definition of materialist analysis." Sianne Ngai, *Ugly Feelings* (Cambridge, MA: Harvard University Press, 2005), 360, n. 28.

23. Williams, *Keywords,* xxiii.

24. Williams, *Keywords,* xxvii.

25. Williams, *Keywords,* xxiii.

26. Williams, *Keywords,* xxiii–xxiv.

27. Williams, *Keywords,* xxxiii.

28. Williams, *Keywords,* xxiv.

29. Williams, *Keywords,* xxiv.

30. Williams, *Keywords,* xxiv.

31. For a sensitive analysis of Williams's engagement with and revision of T. S. Eliot's *Notes Towards the Definition of Culture* in and subsequent to his own *Culture and Society* (1956), see Jason M. Baskin, *Modernism Beyond the Avant-Garde: Embodying Experience* (Cambridge: Cambridge University Press, 2019), chapter 4, especially 153–65.

32. Williams, *Keywords,* xxv.

33. Williams, *Keywords,* xxv.

34. Williams, *Keywords,* xxvii.

35. I do not mean to imply that no thinkers before the twentieth century recognized the portent of a midcentury mark, but rather to flag the quantitative and qualitative distinction of the mid-twentieth century's self-recognition. Jean le Rond d'Alembert opened his *Elements of Philosophy* (1759) with, in Ernst Cassirer's paraphrase, "the observation that in the intellectual life of the last three hundred years the mid-century mark has consistently been an important turning point." Cassirer takes D'Alembert's cue to champion the substance of thought by declaring that "Cartesian philosophy triumphantly alters the world picture" in the mid-seventeenth century. In contrast, the unit of the "half-century" itself incited an extraordinary volume and variety of epochal stocktaking in the middle of the twentieth century. Ernst Cassirer, *The Philosophy of the Enlightenment,* trans. Fritz C. A. Koelln and James P. Pettegrove (Princeton: Princeton University Press, 2009), 3.

36. Charles Olson, "Projective Verse, 1950," *Poetry New York* 3 (October 1950): 13–22: 13.

37. "Dickens Chronology," University of California Santa Cruz Dickens Project, http://dickens.ucsc.edu/resources/chronology.html.

38. L. P. Hartley, *The Go-Between* (New York: New York Review Books Classics, 2002), 17.

39. Hartley, *The Go-Between,* 308.

40. Hartley, *The Go-Between,* 31.

41. Hartley, *The Go-Between,* 32.

42. *The Antarctic Today: A Mid-Century Survey by the New Zealand Antarctic Society* (Wellington: A. H. and A. W. Reed, 1952); Jacob Blaustein, *The Mid-Century Challenge to American Life* (New York: American Jewish Committee, 1950).

43. Gertrude P. Schroeder, *The Growth of Major Steel Companies, 1900–1950* (Baltimore: Johns Hopkins University Press, 1953); Mabel Newcomer, *The Big Business Executive: The Factors That Made Him, 1900–1950* (New York: Columbia University Press, 1955); Archibald Macbride Hunter, *Interpreting the New Testament, 1900–1950* (Norwich: SCM, 1951).

44. Jerome Clarke Hunsaker's *Aeronautics at the Mid-Century* (New Haven: Yale University Press, 1952) was based on his Terry Lectures at Yale in 1951; Charles Philip Issawi, *Egypt at Mid-Century* (Oxford: Oxford University Press, 1954); T. C. Bannister, ed., *The Architect at Mid-Century: Evolution and Achievement* and F. R. Bellamy, ed., *The Architect at Mid-Century: Conversations Across the Nation* (New York: Reinhold, 1954); Robert Richman, ed., *The Arts at Mid-Century* (New York: Horizon, 1954); André Siegfried, *America at Mid-Century* (New York: Harcourt, Brace, 1955).

45. Rolfe Arnold Scott-James, *Fifty Years of English Literature, 1900–1950* (London: Longmans, 1951); Leon Edel, *The Psychological Novel, 1900–1950* (New York: Lippincott, 1955).

46. The Regnery series also included Alan S. Downer, *Fifty Years of American Drama*; Frederick J. Hoffman's *Modern Novel in America, 1900–1950*; Mary Brodbeck, James Grey, and Walter P. Metzger, *American Non-Fiction, 1900–1950*; and Ray Benedict West, *The Short Story in America, 1900–1950*.

47. Wallace Fowlie, ed. and trans., *Mid-Century French Poets: Selections, Translations, and Critical Notices* (New York: Twayne, 1955); Phyllis Maud Jones, ed., *Modern Verse, 1900–1950* (Oxford: Oxford University Press, 1955); Louis Untermeyer, ed., *Modern British Poets* and *Modern American Poets*, midcentury ed. (New York: Harcourt, 1950); John Ciardi, ed., *Mid-Century American Poets* (New York: Twayne, 1950).

48. John Ciardi foreword to *Mid-Century American Poets*, ix–xxx: ix.

49. Edward Brunner, *Cold War Poetry: The Social Text in the Fifties Poem* (Urbana: University of Illinois Press, 2001), 39–40.

50. Edward M. Cifelli, *John Ciardi: A Biography* (Fayetteville: University of Arkansas Press, 1997), 138.

51. Frances Frost, *Mid-Century* (New York: Creative Age, 1946), 3.

52. Theodore H. White, *Fire in the Ashes: Europe in Mid-Century* (New York: Sloane, 1953); Eric Sevareid, *In One Ear: 107 Snapshots of Men and Events Which Make a Far-Reaching Panorama of the American Situation at Mid-Century* (New York: Knopf, 1952); William L. Shirer, *Midcentury Journey* (New York: Farrar, Straus, and Young, 1952); Erwin D. Canham, *Awakening: The World at Mid-Century* (New York: Longmans, Green, 1951); Frederick Lewis Allen, *The Big Change: America Transforms Itself, 1900–1950* (New York: Harper and Row, 1952).

53. Foreword to *History Today* 1, no. 1 (January 1951): 9.

54. The published proceedings are Pierce Butler, ed., *Librarians, Scholars, and Booksellers at Mid-Century* (Chicago: University of Chicago Press, 1953); Robert D. Miller, ed., *General Education at Mid-Century* (Tallahassee: Florida State University, 1950); A. Curtis Wilgus, ed., *The Caribbean at Mid-Century* (Gainesville: University

of Florida Press, 1951); University of Minnesota Graduate School Social Sciences Research Center, *The Social Sciences at Mid-Century: Papers Delivered at the Dedication of Ford Hall, April 19–21, 1951* (Minneapolis: University of Minnesota Press, 1952).

55. Winston Spencer Churchill, "The Twentieth Century—Its Promise and Its Realization," in *The Social Implications of Scientific Progress*, ed. John Ely Buchard (Cambridge, MA: Technology Press of the Massachusetts Institute of Technology and New York: Wiley, 1950), 34–76. Buchard annotates the speech with copious references to its coverage, including in the *Cincinnati Times-Star* (Ohio), the *Eastern Daily Press* (Norwich, England), the *South Wales Evening Post* (Swansea), the *Boston Sunday Times*, and the *Enterprise* (Lisbon Falls, Maine), as well as the major New York and London papers.

56. *Time* 55, no. 1 (January 2, 1950).

57. "The Mid-Century Youth Conference: Our Opinions," *Chicago Defender*, December 16, 1950, 6.

58. "Local Women Supporting Mid-Century Register," *Philadelphia Tribune*, November 7, 1950, 5.

59. Mary L. Dudziak, *Cold War Civil Rights: Race and the Image of American Democracy* (Princeton: Princeton University Press, 2000).

60. "Year of Consecration," *Philadelphia Tribune*, December 31, 1949.

61. "Slate Mid-Century Conference of Peace in Chicago on May 29," *New York Amsterdam News*, May 27, 1950.

62 W. E. B. Du Bois, *Writings: The Suppression of the African Slave Trade, The Souls of Black Folk, Dusk of Dawn, Essays* (New York: Literary Classics of the United States, 1986), 359.

63. The quoted phrase comes from Winston Churchill, "The Sinews of Peace," March 4, 1956. Churchill also instructed his listeners in Fulton, Missouri thus: "Do not suppose that we shall not come through these dark years of privation as we have come through the glorious years of agony, or that half a century from now, you will not see 70 or 80 millions of Britons spread about the world and united in defense of our traditions, our way of life, and of the world causes which you and we espouse." For reliable full text, see the International Churchill Society, https://winstonchurchill.org/resources/speeches/1946-1963-elder-statesman/the-sinews-of-peace/. On January 20, 1949, Truman called on the half-century mark early in his "Four Points" speech: "The first half of this century has been marked by unprecedented and brutal attacks on the rights of man, and by the two most frightful wars in history. The supreme need of our time is for men to learn to live together in peace and harmony." The website of the Harry S. Truman Library and Museum provides reliable full text at http://www.trumanlibrary.org/calendar/viewpapers.php?pid=1030.

64. George F. Kennan, *American Diplomacy, 1900–1950*, expanded ed. (Chicago: University of Chicago Press, 1984), 3.

65. Virginia A. Smith, "Television at Mid-Century," *Los Angeles Times*, April 23, 1950, H20.

66. Among many examples, see "1950 Mid-Century Fashions Faces Ideas," *Vogue*, January 1950; "Mid-Century Review," *Boston Globe*, January 1, 1950; *Washington Post*, January 1, 1950; *Time*, January 2, 1950.

67. "Mid-Century Issue," *Life,* January 2, 1950, 3.

68. United Press, "Time Experts in a Battle on Just What Time It Is," *New York Times,* December 29, 1949.

69. A reader in Scarsdale, New York, complained to the *Times* that its December 25, 1949, issue "contained several references to the current year and month as ending the first half of the twentieth century." The newspaper was no better than those "many over-eager persons [who] likewise jumped the gun fifty years ago, trying to get into the twentieth century a year ahead of the rest." Charles H. Seaver, "Mid-Century Mark," letter to the editor, *New York Times,* January 1, 1950. A week later, Godfrey M. Lebhar wrote to counter Seaver; see his letter to the editor, *New York Times,* January 8, 1950.

70. "Mid-Century," *Times* (London), January 1, 1951.

71. Michael North, *Reading 1922: A Return to the Scene of the Modern* (Oxford: Oxford University Press, 1999), 9.

72. Raymond Williams and Michael Orrom, *Preface to Film* (London: Film Drama Limited, 1954), 21. In *Preface to Film,* Williams is the sole author of "The Dramatic Tradition," whence this and all subsequent quotations from the book.

73. Williams, "The Dramatic Tradition," *Preface to Film,* 21–22.

74. Williams, "The Dramatic Tradition," *Preface to Film,* 22.

75. Williams, "The Dramatic Tradition," *Preface to Film,* 21.

76. Raymond Williams, "The Analysis of Culture," *The Long Revolution* (London: Chatto & Windus, 1961), 57–70; Raymond Williams, "Structures of Feeling," *Marxism and Literature* (New York: Oxford University Press, 1977), 128–35.

77. Marjorie McKenzie, "Pursuit of Democracy," *Pittsburgh Courier,* January 14, 1950.

78. McKenzie, "Pursuit of Democracy."

79. Eric F. Goldman, *The Crucial Decade and After: America, 1945–1960* (New York: Random House, 1960), 173.

80. Wallace Stevens, "Motive for Metaphor," in *Transport to Summer* (New York: Knopf, 1947), 7.

81. Jonathan Crary, *Suspensions of Perception: Attention, Spectacle, and Modern Culture* (Cambridge, MA: MIT Press, 1999), 10. Chapter 2 returns to Paul Saint-Amour's related discussion of the "large semantic range" covered by *suspension* and associated terms. Paul K. Saint-Amour, *Tense Future: Modernism, Total War, and Encyclopedic Form* (New York: Oxford University Press, 2015), 99.

82. Crary, *Suspensions of Perception,* 1.

83. Crary, *Suspensions of Perception,* 4.

84. Crary, *Suspensions of Perception,* 5. Note that being "open to control" does not necessarily equate to being controlled *by* "external agencies" or, as studies of attention and subject formation in "long" eighteenth- and nineteenth-century English literature variously argue, by ideologies encoded in genres. See Elisha Cohn, *Still Life: Suspended Development in the Victorian Novel* (Oxford: Oxford University Press, 2016); Nicholas Dames, *The Physiology of the Novel: Reading, Neural Science, and the Form of Victorian Fiction* (Oxford: Oxford University Press, 2007); Anne-Lise François, *Open Secrets: The Literature of Uncounted Experience* (Stanford, CA: Stanford University Press, 2008); and Natalie M. Phillips, *Distraction: Problems of Attention in Eighteenth-Century Literature* (Baltimore: Johns Hopkins University Press, 2016).

85. Crary, *Suspensions of Perception*, 1, 10.

86. The early epistolary form and subsequent serial marketing of the English novel required readers internal and external to plots to await next installments; the very idea of "plot" requires dilation so as to induce attention. For a classic example on the latter point, see Peter Brooks, *Reading for the Plot: Design and Intention in Narrative* (New York: Knopf, 1984). The contested category of lyric—whether understood as ancient genre, transhistorical mode, or "post-Enlightenment idea, developed steadily over the course of the nineteenth and twentieth centuries"—is characterized by a temporality that is both compressed and expansive, momentary and dilatory. For the quoted phrase, see Virginia Jackson and Yopie Prins general introduction to *The Lyric Theory Reader: A Critical Anthology* (Baltimore: Johns Hopkins University Press, 2014), 1–2. Accounts of poetics not bound to questions of lyric also rely on various kinds of suspension. Giorgio Agamben, for example, proceeds from Paul Valery's definition of the poem as "a prolonged hesitation between sound and sense" to argue that enjambment, specifically, sustains that "hesitation." Giorgio Agamben, *The End of the Poem: Studies in Poetics*, trans. Daniel Heller-Roazen (Stanford, CA: Stanford University Press, 1999), 109. Paul Alpers selects *suspension* as "the word that best conveys how the oppositions and disparities of Virgilian pastoral are related to each other and held in the mind: "As opposed to words like 'resolve,' 'reconcile,' or 'transcend,' 'suspend' implies no permanently achieved new relation, while at the same time it conveys absorption in the moment." Paul Alpers, *What Is Pastoral?* (Chicago: University of Chicago Press, 1996), 68.

87. Edmund Burke, *A Philosophical Enquiry Into the Origin of Our Ideas of the Sublime and Beautiful*, ed. Paul Guyer (Oxford: Oxford University Press, 2015), 47.

88. Consider, in this vein, Kant's description of the "free play of the imagination and the understanding" in judgments of taste. Immanuel Kant, *Critique of the Power of Judgment*, ed. Paul Guyer, trans. Paul Guyer and Eric Matthews (Cambridge: Cambridge University Press, 2000), 103.

89. John Keats, *Letters of John Keats to His Family and Friends*, ed. Sidney Colvin (Cambridge: Cambridge University Press, 2011), 48.

90. Samuel Taylor Coleridge, *Biographia Literaria*, ed. Adam Roberts (Edinburgh: Edinburgh University Press, 2014), 208.

91. Aristotle, *Poetics* 24.

92. T. S. Eliot, "Tradition and the Individual Talent," in *The Sacred Wood: Essays on Poetry and Criticism* (London: Faber, 1997), 39–40.

93. I borrow "apparition" from Ezra Pound, "In a Station of the Metro" (1913); https://www.poetryfoundation.org/poetrymagazine/poems/12675/in-a-station-of-the-metro.

94. Steve Ellis, *British Writers and the Approach of World War II* (Cambridge: Cambridge University Press, 2014), 1; Leo Mellor, *Reading the Ruins: Modernism, Bombsites, and British Culture* (Cambridge: Cambridge University Press, 2011), 31.

95. For the quoted phrase, see Mellor, *Reading the Ruins*, 31.

96. For illuminating readings of *Four Quartets* in late modernist contexts of the Second World War, the diminution of the British Empire, and transatlanticism, respectively, see Marina MacKay, *Modernism and World War II* (Cambridge: Cambridge University Press, 2007), chapter 3; Jed Esty, *A Shrinking Island: Modernism*

and National Culture in England (Princeton: Princeton University Press, 2004), chapter 3; and Genevieve Abravanel, *Americanizing Britain: The Rise of Modernism in the Age of the Entertainment Empire* (Oxford: Oxford University Press, 2012), chapter 5.

97. T. S. Eliot, *Four Quartets* (New York: Harcourt, 1943), 49.
98. Eric Hayot, *On Literary Worlds* (Oxford: Oxford University Press, 2012), 152.
99. Hayot, *On Literary Worlds*, 157.
100. Hayot, *On Literary Worlds*, 154.
101. The phrase "crucial decade" comes from Goldman's popular history, and refers to 1945–55. Several critics have recently argued the consequences of periodizing the twentieth century by conceptualizing or simply assuming a break at 1945. Especially apropos in the present context are Gill Plain and George Hutchinson, whose studies embrace the arbitrary quality of the decade to revalue the literature of the whole 1940s in the U.S. and UK, respectively. Gill Plain, *Literature of the 1940s*; George Hutchinson, *Facing the Abyss: American Literature and Culture in the 1940s* (New York: Columbia University Press, 2018).
102. Already in 2002, Marjorie Perloff's discussion of the "tired dichotomy that has governed our discussion of twentieth-century poetics for much too long: that between *modernism* and *postmodernism*" was more accustomed than provocative. Marjorie Perloff, *21st-Century Modernism: The "New" Poetics* (Malden, MA: Blackwell, 2002), 1–2. Consensus binary fatigue has not resulted in a full field effort to develop suppler historical categories for twentieth-century literature and culture. But studies of modernist and contemporary literature have challenged the narrow picture of modernism advanced by postmodernism in its heyday. Among scholars who pay particular attention to how post-postmodernist novelists reanimate the political, ethical, aesthetic, and formal concerns of modernist novels, and in ways that exceed explanation by way of recidivism or blunt anxiety of influence, see Hungerford, "On the Period Formerly Known as the Contemporary"; David James, *Modernist Futures: Innovation and Inheritance in the Contemporary Novel* (Cambridge: Cambridge University Press, 2012); Rebecca L. Walkowitz, *Cosmopolitan Style: Modernism beyond the Nation* (New York: Columbia University Press, 2006).
103. Marks of the renovation of modernist studies at the turn of the present century include the founding of the Modernist Studies Association in 1998 and the publications of, to cite one early and key example in each of the "what," "when," and "how" modes, respectively: North, *Reading 1922*; Tyrus Miller, *Late Modernism: Politics, Fiction, and the Arts Between the World Wars* (Berkeley: University of California Press, 1999); and Lawrence Rainey, *Institutions of Modernism: Literary Elites and Public Culture* (New Haven: Yale University Press, 1998).
104. Essential projects in the geographical and geopolitical expansion of modernism include Jessica Berman, *Modernist Commitments: Ethics, Politics, and Transnational Modernism* (New York: Columbia University Press, 2011); Matthew Hart, *Nations of Nothing but Poetry: Modernism, Transnationalism, and Synthetic Vernacular Writing* (Oxford: Oxford University Press, 2010); Eric Hayot and Rebecca Walkowitz, eds., *A New Vocabulary of Global Modernism* (New York: Columbia University Press, 2016); Peter Kalliney, *Commonwealth of Letters: British Literary Culture and the Emergence of Postcolonial Aesthetics* (Oxford: Oxford

University Press, 2013); Aarthi Vadde, *Chimeras of Form: Modernist Internationalism Beyond Europe, 1914–2016* (New York: Columbia University Press, 2016); Walkowitz, *Cosmopolitan Style*; Mark Wollaeger, ed., with Matt Eatough, *The Oxford Handbook of Global Modernisms* (Oxford: Oxford University Press, 2012). See also the essay cluster "Scale and Form; or, What Was Global Modernism?," ed. Thomas S. Davis and Nathan K. Hensley, *Modernism/modernity* PrintPlus 2, cycle 4 (January 2018).

105. For early accounts of the emergence of such strands, see Douglas Mao and Rebecca Walkowitz, "Introduction: Modernisms Bad and New," in *Bad Modernisms* (Durham: Duke University Press, 2005); and "The New Modernist Studies," *PMLA* 123, no. 3 (May 2008): 737–48. Several works on later modernisms are especially apropos to the present book and helped hone its focus on the particularities of the midcentury. Tyrus Miller theorizes modernism from "the perspective of its end," which counters modernists' own emphasis on the new or originary. Miller, *Late Modernism*, 5. Marina MacKay argues that modernist tropes, preoccupations, and innovations "scripted" the Second World War and the end of modernism alike in English culture. MacKay, *Modernism and World War II*, 2. Thomas Davis shows how British "late modernism figures everyday life as the scene where structural changes in the world-system attain legibility." Thomas S. Davis, *The Extinct Scene: Late Modernism and Everyday Life* (New York: Columbia University Press, 2015), 4. On "intermodernism," see Kristin Bluemel, "Introduction: What Is Intermodernism?," in *Intermodernism: Literary Culture in Mid-Twentieth-Century Britain* (Edinburgh: Edinburgh University Press, 2009). On specific cold war–era commodifications, institutionalized programs, and state co-optations of modernist aesthetics and practices, see Greg Barnhisel, *Cold War Modernists: Art, Literature, and American Cultural Diplomacy* (New York: Columbia University Press, 2015); Robert Genter, *Late Modernism: Art, Culture, and Politics in Cold War America* (Philadelphia: University of Pennsylvania Press, 2010); and Fredric Jameson, *A Singular Modernity: Essay on the Ontology of the Present* (London: Verso, 2002). Susan Stanford Friedman's influential account of a long historical "planetary" modernism rightly asserts the inseparability of the spatial from the temporal rethinking of modernist studies. On its own, she writes, "the planetary turn in a modernist studies confined within conventional periodization reinstates modernisms of the West as the powerful center to the rest's weak periphery, as the origin point with which all others must engage and through which they must be understood." Susan Stanford Friedman, *Planetary Modernisms: Provocations on Modernity Across Time* (New York: Columbia University Press, 2015), 7.

106. Hayot catalogs strategies scholars employ in good faith "to break open the house of modernism," but finds that these strategies still create "literary value by placing authors and artists into an already existing theory of modernism whose center remains European. . . . The furniture changes; the foundation is unmoved." Hayot, *On Literary Worlds*, 4–5.

107. For the "intense self-scrutiny" of contemporary modernist studies, see David James and Urmila Seshagiri, "Metamodernism: Narratives of Continuity and Revolution," *PMLA* 129, no. 1 (January 2014): 88. On weak theorizing of modernism, see especially Saint-Amour, *Tense Future*, 37–43; Paul K. Saint-Amour, ed., "Weak Theory," special issue, *Modernism/modernity* 25, no. 3 (September 2018).

108. Elizabeth Bishop, "At the Fishhouses," in *Poems, Prose, and Letters* (New York: Literary Classics of the United States, 2008), 52.
109. Bishop, "Arrival at Santos," in *Poems, Prose, and Letters*, 65.
110. Samuel Beckett, *Waiting for Godot: A Tragicomedy in Two Acts*, trans. Samuel Beckett (New York: Grove, 1982), passim.

1. THE TIMELY SUSPENSIONS OF ELIZABETH BISHOP'S *A COLD SPRING*

Epigraph: Elizabeth Bishop, *Poems, Prose, and Letters*, ed. Robert Giroux and Lloyd Schwartz (New York: Literary Classics of the United States, 2008), 686. Page references to *Poems, Prose, and Letters* (*PPL*) are hereafter provided in text.

1. Six reviews of *North & South*, including those cited in the main text, are collected in Lloyd Schwartz and Sybil P. Estess, eds., *Elizabeth Bishop and Her Art* (Ann Arbor: University of Michigan Press, 1983), 177–93.
2. Given that "It All Depends" marks the only time Bishop ever wrote for publication about her own poetics, it occupies strangely little space in the relevant scholarship. The statement's brevity and ostensible air of dismissiveness of Ciardi's project have perhaps been mistaken as grounds for critical dismissal. Nor do gendered descriptions of "It All Depends" as "decidedly sullen" or "marked by a special testiness" help. Edward Brunner, *Cold War Poetry: The Social Text in the Fifties Poem* (Urbana: University of Illinois Press, 2001), 58. "It All Depends" was not reprinted in either of the first two posthumous editions of Bishop's prose. It is included in *PPL*, 686–87.
3. Elizabeth Bishop, "Efforts of Affection: A Memoir of Marianne Moore" (c. 1969) and "A Brief Reminiscence and a Brief Tribute" (1974), in *PPL*, 471–99, 728–31.
4. Bishop to Katharine S. White, June 21, 1951, in *Elizabeth Bishop and "The New Yorker": The Complete Correspondence*, ed. Joelle Biele (New York: Farrar, Straus and Giroux, 2011), 67.
5. Bishop to Robert Lowell, July 11, 1951, in *Words in Air: The Complete Correspondence Between Elizabeth Bishop and Robert Lowell*, ed. Thomas Travisano with Saskia Hamilton (New York: Farrar, Straus and Giroux, 2008), 122. Mia L. McIver notes that "pectin" is a figure of suspension, a substance "jelling somewhere between liquid and solid." Mia McIver, "Elizabeth Bishop's Lyric Vision," *Journal of Modern Literature* 34, no. 4 (Summer 2011): 192.
6. Brett C. Millier dates Bishop's completion of "A Cold Spring" to her second stay at Yaddo, in the winter of 1950. Brett Millier, *Elizabeth Bishop: Life and the Memory of It* (Berkeley: University of California Press, 1993), 223. But Bishop typically sent her completed poems to the *New Yorker* right away, and the magazine accepted "A Cold Spring" on July 18, 1951. Biele, *Elizabeth Bishop and "The New Yorker,"* 67–68.
7. Dates in parentheses note the year of each poem's first publication.
8. Notable exceptions include Thomas Travisano, *Elizabeth Bishop: Her Artistic Development* (Charlottesville: University Press of Virginia, 1988), chapter 4; Peggy Samuels, *Deep Skin: Elizabeth Bishop and Visual Art* (Ithaca, NY: Cornell University Press, 2010).

9. Usages of *suspension* are unique to the midcentury in Bishop's career. She used a form of the word in only one other poem published in her lifetime, "Squatter's Children" (1956), wherein "The sun's suspended eye / blinks casually" over a *favela* (*PPL* 76).

10. Most apropos in the present context are Siobhan Phillips, *The Poetics of the Everyday: Creative Repetition in Modern American Verse* (New York: Columbia University Press, 2009), chapter 3; Victoria Harrison, *Elizabeth Bishop's Poetics of Intimacy* (Cambridge: Cambridge University Press, 1993). See also Thomas S. Davis, *The Extinct Scene: Late Modernism and Everyday Life* (New York: Columbia University Press, 2015); Liesl Olson, *Modernism and the Ordinary* (Oxford: Oxford University Press, 2009).

11. Gillian White, *Lyric Shame: The "Lyric" Subject of Contemporary American Poetry* (Cambridge, MA: Harvard University Press, 2014), 45. For earlier assessments of the biographical imperatives of Bishop criticism, see Langdon Hammer, "The New Elizabeth Bishop," *Yale Review* 82, no. 1 (January 1994): 135–49; and Bonnie Costello, "Elizabeth Bishop's Impersonal Personal," *American Literary History* 15, no. 2 (Summer 2003): 334–66. Recent additions to Bishop's archive reinvigorate the biographical paratext, as witness the first scholarly treatments of Bishop's "letters" to her psychotherapist, Dr. Ruth Foster, in 1947: Lorrie Goldensohn, "Approaching Elizabeth Bishop's Letters to Ruth Foster," *Yale Review* 103, no. 1 (January 2015): 1–19; Heather Treseler, "One Long Poem," *Boston Review*, August 17, 2016. http:// bostonreview.net/poetry/heather-treseler-elizabeth-bishop-foster-letters.

12. For a useful synthesis of Bishop scholarship premised on geography and a refreshing recalibration of the sociality of Bishop's geographic imaginary, see Susannah L. Hollister, "Elizabeth Bishop's Geographic Feeling," *Twentieth-Century Literature* 58, no. 3 (Fall 2012): 399–400, 428n3.

13. Elizabeth Bishop Papers, Archives and Special Collections Library, Vassar College Libraries, box 77, folder 4.

14. Elizabeth Bishop Papers, Archives and Special Collections Library, Vassar College Libraries, box 57, folder 3. My best guess is that the canceled words are *task* and *say*.

15. Wallace Stevens, "The Motive for Metaphor," in *Collected Poems* (New York: Vintage, 1990), 288; Philip Larkin, "Coming," in *Collected Poems*, ed. Anthony Thwaite (New York: Farrar, Straus and Giroux, 2004), 47; Gerard Manley Hopkins, "Spring," in *Poems and Prose*, ed. W. H. Gardner (New York: Penguin, 1953), 28.

16. In the *New Yorker*, Bishop's approximation of sonnet form was still more pronounced. In the magazine, "A Cold Spring" breaks into three stanzas, with the first and second running to fourteen and fifteen lines, respectively. The poem looks on the page like a double sonnet followed by a longer third stanza. See Elizabeth Bishop, "A Cold Spring," *New Yorker*, May 31, 1952, 31. Since Bishop's *Complete Poems* (1969), the only stanza break has occurred at line 14, which makes a single thirty-five-line stanza follow a would-be sonnet. In both versions, the sonnet form is in the air of the poem but held in suspension.

17. Self-inscription might be considered a variation of, for example, the "triangulated address" that Jonathan Culler describes as "the root-form of presentation for lyric," that is, lyric's "address to the reader by means of address to someone or something

else." See Jonathan Culler, *Theory of the Lyric* (Cambridge, MA: Harvard University Press, 2015), 186.

18. Siobhan Phillips reads these "effortless phrases" as moving the poem from past to present to future even as its "serenity imagines the peace of living by natural temporality." Phillips, *The Poetics of the Everyday*, 134–35.

19. Bonnie Costello finds a related qualification of seasonal advance in "A Cold Spring:" "The poem makes a successful transition from spring to summer. . . . Yet the present and future are imagined in the evening and the pastures are shadowy, thus countering the sense of seasonal beginnings with the brief passing of a single day." Bonnie Costello, *Elizabeth Bishop: Questions of Mastery* (Cambridge, MA: Harvard University Press, 1991), 69.

20. Stephen Best and Sharon Marcus's influential work on "surface reading," for example, resists symptomatic critical practices engendered broadly by academic "acceptance of psychoanalysis and Marxism and metalanguages" in the 1970s and 1980s, and more specifically by Fredric Jameson's *The Political Unconscious: Narrative as a Socially Symbolic Act* (Ithaca, NY: Cornell University Press, 1981). Stephen Best and Sharon Marcus, "Surface Reading: An Introduction," in "The Way We Read Now," ed. Sharon Marcus and Stephen Best, special issue, *Representations* 108, no. 1 (Fall 2009): 1.

21. See, for example, Rita Felski, *The Limits of Critique* (Chicago: University of Chicago Press, 2015); Wai Chee Dimock, "Weak Theory: Henry James, Colm Tóibín, and W. B. Yeats," *Critical Inquiry* 39, no. 4 (Summer 2013): 732–53.

22. See Mutlu Konuk Blasing, *Politics and Form in Postmodern Poetry: O'Hara, Bishop, Ashbery, Merrill* (Cambridge: Cambridge University Press, 1995); James Longenbach, *Modern Poetry After Modernism* (Oxford: Oxford University Press, 1997); Thomas Travisano, *Midcentury Quartet: Bishop, Lowell, Jarrell, Berryman and the Making of a Postmodern Aesthetic* (Charlottesville: University Press of Virginia, 1999).

23. *Infiltrate* became a military verb during the Second World War. As the lexicon of the cold war developed in the late 1940s and early 1950s, the verb acquired its implication of covert behind-enemy-lines movement "for the purpose of political subversion" (*Oxford English Dictionary*, s.v. "infiltrate," accessed May 20, 2019). A *cold war referential index* reading could enlist the composition history of "A Cold Spring." Bishop worked on the poem during weekend visits, in 1950, to Jane Dewey's farm in Havre de Grace, Maryland. Dewey was director of terminal ballistics research at the U.S. Army Proving Ground at nearby Aberdeen, Maryland. On August 23, 1950, Bishop wrote with a studied naivete to Lowell of Dewey's work, noting that "the rural scene shakes slightly once in a while as Jane practices her art about 15 miles away, & then there is a faint 'boom.'" *Words in Air*, 108.

24. Scholars of cold war poetry have corrected once received impressions of Bishop as an apolitical poet. See Steven Gould Axelrod, "Elizabeth Bishop and Containment Policy," *American Literature* 75, no. 4 (December 2003): 843–67; Camille Roman, *Elizabeth Bishop's World War II–Cold War View* (New York: Palgrave, 2001). For broader contestations of the gendered critical constructions of Bishop's politics and probing readings of her views on postwar and cold war institutions and politics, albeit without reference to *A Cold Spring*, see Betsy Erkkila, "Elizabeth Bishop, Modernism, and the Left," *American Literary History* 8, no. 2 (Summer

1996): 284–310; Gillian White, "*Words in Air* and 'Space' in Art: Bishop's Midcentury Critique of the United States," in *Elizabeth Bishop in the Twenty-First Century: Reading the New Editions*, ed. Angus Cleghorn, Bethany Hicok, and Thomas Travisano (Charlottesville: University Press of Virginia, 2012), 255–73; Kamran Javadizadeh, "The Institutionalization of the Postwar Poet," *Modernism/modernity* 23, no. 1 (January 2016): 113–39, especially 130–35; and Harris Feinsod, *The Poetry of the Americas: From Good Neighbors to Countercultures* (Oxford: Oxford University Press, 2017), chapters 1 and 5.

25. Samuels, *Deep Skin*, 19. Samuels is the only critic to concentrate on a kind of suspension specifically as an intrinsic principle of Bishop's poetics. Semantic and conceptual synonyms for suspension do, however, figure in the extrinsic vocabulary critics use to characterize Bishop's work. Bonnie Costello's readings are unfailingly attentive to Bishop's experiments with perspective, spatiality, and temporality, such that Bishop's poetics "amount to a critique of the single vantage point of integrated, timeless subjectivity." Costello, *Elizabeth Bishop*, 9. Langdon Hammer sees "Bishop's letterlike writing in her poems [as] the generic equivalent of the recurrent images of conflux and equivocation in Bishop's poetry—images that do not resolve into binary oppositions but evoke instead a state of in-betweenness." The letters and poems seek "a suspended condition," a generic form of suspension that resonates, as Hammer notes, with Jeredith Merrin's description of Bishop's trope of gendered "thirdness." Langdon Hammer, "Useless Concentration: Life and Work in Elizabeth Bishop's Letters and Poems," *American Literary History* 9, no. 1 (Spring 1997): 162–80, 164. Jeredith Merrin, "Elizabeth Bishop: Gaiety, Gayness, and Change," in *Elizabeth Bishop: The Geography of Gender*, ed. Marilyn May Lombardi (Charlottesville: University of Virginia Press, 1993), 167.

26. Samuels, *Deep Skin*, 181.

27. Samuels, *Deep Skin*, 187.

28. Samuels, *Deep Skin*, 2.

29. The North Atlantic poems lack the comparatively obvious topicality of Bishop's most canonical cold war poem, "View of the Capitol from the Library of Congress" (1951). Notably, "View of the Capitol" has a humor about its own explicit topicality that is lost in most critical readings of it but was not lost on the editors of the *New Yorker*, who formatted the poem to recall the shape of a postcard when it appeared in the magazine on July 1, 1957. Bishop wrote "Cape Breton" between the summer of 1947 and early 1949 and published it in the *New Yorker* on June 18, 1949, two months after the signing of the North Atlantic Treaty Organization agreement on April 4, 1949. The freighted political geography necessarily invoked by the poem's title is borne out by, among other details: the poem's register of the diminution of the British Empire in a flagless and sparsely populated Canadian seascape and the scenic recurrence of edges, cliffs, and a "brink" that puncture the general mist, creating a landscape of dangerous edges. The cliffs themselves are, in one iteration, "nervous" (*PPL* 49). Before 1956, the *OED* cites only one usage, in 1840, of *brink* as a term related to precipitate militarism; the word *brinkmanship* was not coined until 1956 (*Oxford English Dictionary*, s.v. "brink," accessed May 22, 2019).

30. Elizabeth Bishop Papers, Archives and Special Collections Library, Vassar College Libraries, box 75, folder 3b. Millier, *Elizabeth Bishop*, 180.

31. Lowell praised "your *New Yorker* fish poem," the first of Bishop's poems about which he ever wrote to her: "Perhaps, it's your best. . . . The description has great splendor, and the human part, tone, etc., is just right. I question a little the word *breast* in the last four or five lines—a little too much in its context perhaps; but I'm probably wrong." Lowell to Bishop, August 21, 1947, *Words in Air*, 7.

32. On the echo of Wordsworth, see Guy Rotella, *Reading and Writing Nature: The Poetry of Robert Frost, Wallace Stevens, Marianne Moore, and Elizabeth Bishop* (Boston: Northeastern University Press, 1991), 221; Costello, *Elizabeth Bishop*, 111–12.

33. Vicki Graham was the first to analyze the line of iambic pentameter at the end of the opening stanza. Graham, "Bishop's 'At the Fishhouses,'" *Explicator* 53, no. 2 (Winter 1995): 114–17. For the most thorough reading of the poem's meter, see Vidyan Ravinthiran, *Elizabeth Bishop's Prosaic* (Lewisburg, PA: Bucknell University Press, 2015), 67–77.

34. In the *New Yorker*, the first forty lines of the poem comprised two stanzas. The first stanza break was struck with a pun at line 32: "The old man accepts a Lucky Strike" (*PPL* 51). In *Poems: North & South—A Cold Spring*, Bishop collapsed the whole section of the poem connected to the "old man" at harborside into one stanza.

35. In Costello's memorable gloss, the middle sestet is "a kind of physical and meditational ladder." Costello, *Elizabeth Bishop*, 112. Per Susan Stewart, the last line of the middle stanza also makes a "self-referential pun" on the poem's baseline meter to this point, its "intervals of four or five feet." Susan Stewart, "Lyric Possession," *Critical Inquiry* 22, no. 1 (Autumn 1995): 60.

36. Elizabeth Bishop Papers, Archives and Special Collections Library, Vassar College Libraries, box 75, folder 3 (notebook), box 56, folder 7 (drafts).

37. Randall Jarrell, "The Poet and His Public," *Partisan Review* 13, no. 4 (September-October 1946): 498–99; excerpted in Schwartz and Estess, *Elizabeth Bishop and Her Art*, 180–81.

38. Bishop to Austin Olney, October 31, 1954, Elizabeth Bishop Papers, Archives and Special Collections Library, Vassar College Libraries, box 41, folder 2. For a thoroughgoing reading of what Jarrell meant by "I have seen it," see Zachariah Pickard, "The Morality of Aesthetic Action: Elizabeth Bishop, Randall Jarrell, and the Politics of Poetry," *American Literature* 79, no. 2 (June 2007): 393–411.

39. It took Bishop some time to weave the famous claim into the poem. It entered "At the Fishhouses" only in what appears to be the third autograph draft. By the penultimate typescript, Bishop had removed the two lines beginning with "I have seen it" only to handwrite them back into the poem at the bottom of the page, with an arrow pointing to their spot. Elizabeth Bishop Papers, Archives and Special Collections Library, Vassar College Libraries, box 56, folder 7.

40. David Kalstone's is among the most sensitive biographical readings of "At the Fishhouses" and of Bishop's broader revisitation, in the 1940s and 50s, of her childhood memories of Nova Scotia. David Kalstone, *Becoming a Poet: Elizabeth Bishop with Marianne Moore and Robert Lowell*, ed. Robert Hemenway (Ann Arbor: University of Michigan Press, 2001), especially 118–22 and "Prodigal Years."

41. James Longenbach, *Modern Poetry After Modernism* (Oxford: Oxford University Press, 1997), 29.

42. In part by supplying a lyric *I* where the poem does not, Steven Gould Axelrod aims to resolve the grammatical slippages at the close of "At the Fishhouses": "As

Bishop's lyric 'I' acknowledges. . . . history"—which, I note, is not quite the same thing as the poem's "our knowledge"—"not only moves like a water current ('flowing'), but also flies off like a bird ('flown')." Steven Gould Axelrod, "Bishop, History, and Politics," in *Cambridge Companion to Elizabeth Bishop*, ed. Angus Cleghorn and Jonathan Ellis (New York: Cambridge University Press, 2014), 37.

43. Travisano, *Elizabeth Bishop*, 127.

44. Elizabeth Bishop Papers, Archives and Special Collections Library, Vassar College Libraries, box 56, folder 7.

45. For the "lability of historical understanding," see Axelrod, "Bishop, History, and Politics," 37; for "the vital role of history in Bishop's work," see Travisano, *Elizabeth Bishop*, 123.

46. Katharine S. White to Bishop, February 25, 1947, in Biele, *Elizabeth Bishop and "The New Yorker,"* 29.

47. Elizabeth Bishop, *North & South* (Boston: Houghton Mifflin, 1946), iv. See also Bishop to Ferris Greenslet, January 22, 1945, in *One Art: Letters*, ed. Robert Giroux (New York: Farrar, Straus and Giroux, 1994), 125–26.

48. For the richest account of Bishop's engagements with the shifting politics and aesthetics of *Partisan Review* in the 1930s and early 1940s, see John Lowney, *History, Memory, and the Literary Left: Modern American Poetry, 1935–68* (Iowa City: University of Iowa Press, 2006), chapter 3.

49. Mary McCarthy, "The Hiroshima 'New Yorker,'" *politics* 3 (November 1946): 367.

50. On *Partisan Review*'s centerward drift in the late 1940s, see Terry A. Cooney, *The Rise of the New York Intellectuals: "Partisan Review" and Its Circle* (Madison: University of Wisconsin Press, 1986), chapter 10 and the epilogue.

51. William Barrett, "The Resistance," *Partisan Review* 13, no. 4 (September-October 1946): 482.

52. Robert Warshow, "Melancholy to the End," *Partisan Review* 14, no. 1 (January-February 1947): 86.

53. Warshow, "Melancholy to the End," 88.

54. Harold Rosenberg, "The Herd of Independent Minds: Has the Avant-Garde Its Own Mass Culture?" *Commentary*, September 1948, https://www.commentary magazine.com/articles/the-herd-of-independent-mindshas-the-avant-garde-its -own-mass-culture/#2.

55. Reinhold Niebuhr, *Faith and History: A Comparison of Christian and Modern Views of History* (New York: Scribner, 1949), 13, 9.

56. John Dewey, "The Crisis in Human History," *Commentary: A Jewish Review*, March 1946. https://www.commentarymagazine.com/articles/the-crisis-in-human -history/

57. Sidney Hook, "On Historical Understanding," *Partisan Review* 15, no. 2 (February 1948): 231–39, 231. Hook was reviewing Karl Popper's *The Open Society and Its Enemies* (1945), a critique of teleological historicisms.

58. On *Partisan Review*'s reputation among literary figures in the late 1940s and its postwar politics, see Evan Kindley, "Big Criticism," *Critical Inquiry* 38, no. 1 (August 2011): 71–95, especially 76–82. The subsequent prominence of *Partisan Review* for literary critics and historians can probably be taken as given. But for one representative example, an authoritative account of poetry and criticism in the

U.S. after the Second World War begins by remarking that in the winter of 1945 "a critic in *Partisan Review* could plausibly claim: 'no one will deny that the discussion of poetry is one of the highest proofs of civilization that a society can give.'" The gambit speaks as much to the cultural prestige of the little magazine—which, unlike the "critic," merits naming—as it does to the bygone cultural centrality of literary criticism that it means to emphasize. Robert von Hallberg, "Poetry, Politics, and Intellectuals," in *The Cambridge History of American Literature*, vol. 8: *Poetry and Criticism, 1940–1995*, ed. Sacvan Bercovitch (Cambridge: Cambridge University Press, 1996), 13. The unmentioned "critic" was writing not of U.S. but of South American poetry; see Ramón J. Sender, "A Rhapsodic Age?" *Partisan Review* 12, no. 1 (Winter 1945): 107–11, 107.

59. Katharine S. White to Bishop, March 29, 1948, in Biele, *Elizabeth Bishop and "The New Yorker,"* 34. Throughout this chapter, I restore the comma that appeared in the title of "Over 2,000 Illustrations and a Complete Concordance" when the poem was first published in *Partisan Review* 15, no. 6 (June 1948): 631–33.

60. Bishop to William Maxwell, April 8, 1948, in Biele, *Elizabeth Bishop and "The New Yorker,"* 35.

61. William Maxwell to Bishop, May 3, 1948, in Biele, *Elizabeth Bishop and "The New Yorker,"* 36.

62. Jean-Paul Sartre, "Literature in Our Time," *Partisan Review* 15, no. 6 (June 1948): 639, 636.

63. For the pithy summary of *Dialectic of Enlightenment* quoted in the main text, see Leela Gandhi and Deborah L. Nelson, editors' introduction to "Around 1948: Interdisciplinary Approaches to Global Transformation," special issue, *Critical Inquiry* 40, no. 4 (Summer 2014): 285.

64. *PPL* preserves only one stanza break in "Over 2,000 Illustrations," before "Everything only connected," which likely owes to the accidental omission of the break between lines 31 and 32 in Bishop's *Complete Poems* (1969). See Candace W. MacMahon, *Elizabeth Bishop: A Bibliography, 1927–79* (Charlottesville: University of Press of Virginia, 1980), 152.

65. On the temporal dimensions of the phrase "infant sight," see Costello, *Elizabeth Bishop*, 137–38; Linda Anderson, *Elizabeth Bishop: Lines of Connection* (Edinburgh: Edinburgh University Press, 2013), 82.

66. Incidentally, Ashbery rated "Over 2,000 Illustrations" the "marvelous" exception to what he saw as the otherwise disappointing rule of *A Cold Spring*. As if to substantiate his estimation of the poem, Ashbery notes that it "first appeared in *Partisan Review* in 1948." *Partisan* is the only magazine Ashbery mentions, which further attests to the reputation of the magazine. John Ashbery, "The Complete Poems," in Schwartz and Estess, *Elizabeth Bishop and Her Art*, 204.

67. Costello, *Elizabeth Bishop*, 135.

68. Alan Golding, *From Outlaw to Classic: Canons in American Poetry* (Madison: University of Wisconsin Press, 1995), 80, 191n10.

69. Elizabeth Bishop Papers, Archives and Special Collections Library, Vassar College Libraries, box 56, folder 9.

70. Elizabeth Bishop Papers, Archives and Special Collections Library, Vassar College Libraries, box 56, folder 9.

71. White, *Lyric Shame*, 76–77.

72. In the original edition of *Poems: North & South—A Cold Spring*, "Cape Breton" preceded "At the Fishhouses," its place-name title locating the otherwise geographically unmarked Nova Scotia harbor poem. Along with the coastal scenery of Nova Scotia, Bishop's best approximation of a childhood home, the two poems both suggest lost parents toward their ends. "At the Fishhouses" sees maternal "rocky breasts" and "Cape Breton" watches as "a man carrying a baby gets off" a bus and walks out of view (*PPL* 50, 52).

73. Bishop's handwritten notes on the last draft typescript show her still puzzling over the final line and moving it toward the gerundive. Elizabeth Bishop Papers, Archives and Special Collections Library, Vassar College Libraries, box 56, folder 12.

74. On the history of Cape Breton, see *The Island: New Perspectives on Cape Breton's History, 1713–1990*, ed. Kenneth Donovan (Fredericton, New Brunswick and Sydney, Nova Scotia: Acadiensis Press and University College of Cape Breton Press, 1990); Stephen J. Hornsby, *Nineteenth-Century Cape Breton: A Historical Geography* (Montreal: McGill-Queen's University Press, 1992).

75. Reinhold Niebuhr, "The Crisis of the Individual: Will Civilization Survive Technics?" *Commentary* December 1945, https://www.commentarymagazine.com/articles/the-crisis-of-the-individual-will-civilization-survive-technics/.

76. Elizabeth Bishop Papers, Archives and Special Collections Library, Vassar College Libraries, box 56, folder 12.

77. Mutlu Konuk Blasing, for example, concludes of "Cape Breton" that "Bishop's descriptive reserve maintains her distance from personal and public history: it is an empowering powerlessness that keeps the historical scriptures undecipherable and voiceless, if at the expense of silencing her own past." Mutlu Konuk Blasing, *Politics and Form in Postmodern Poetry: O'Hara, Bishop, Ashbery, and Merrill* (Cambridge: Cambridge University Press, 1995), 93.

78. John Keats, *Letters of John Keats to His Family and Friends*, ed. Sidney Colvin (Cambridge: Cambridge University Press, 2011), 48.

79. Anderson, *Elizabeth Bishop*, 124.

80. John Hollander, "Elizabeth Bishop's Mappings of Life," in Schwartz and Estess, *Elizabeth Bishop and Her Art*, 245.

81. Bishop to Paul Brooks, July 28, 1953 and September 10, 1953, in Giroux, *One Art*, 268–270; Bishop to Austin Olney, April 25, 1954 and May 9, 1954, in Giroux, *One Art*, 293–95.

82. The most chilling professional document in Bishop's Vassar archive is a chronology, handwritten over legal-pad pages and sent to Bishop by Houghton Mifflin editor Austin Olney in early 1955. The chronology lists every missed deadline, unkept promise, and change of mind or timeline for Bishop's second book over the previous two years. Elizabeth Bishop Papers, Archives and Special Collections Library, Vassar College Libraries, box 41, folder 2.

2. W. H. AUDEN, RALPH ELLISON, AND THE MIDCENTURY ANXIETY CONSENSUS

Epigraphs: Rollo May, *The Meaning of Anxiety* (New York: Ronald, 1950), 3. All subsequent citations of *The Meaning of Anxiety* refer to this edition unless otherwise noted. Ralph Ellison, *Invisible Man* (New York: Vintage, 1995), 16. Page references to this edition (*IM*) are hereafter provided in main text.

1. For a paradigmatic example, see Sigmund Freud, *A General Introduction to Psychoanalysis*, trans. G. Stanley Hall (New York: Boni and Liveright, 1920), chapter 25, "Fear and Anxiety." See also May, *The Meaning of Anxiety*, 189, 190, 207–10. For cultural- and medical-historical framings of the common distinction between fear and anxiety, see, respectively, Joanna Bourke, *Fear: A Cultural History* (Emeryville, CA: Shoemaker & Hoard, 2006 [2005]), 189–92 and passim; and Allan V. Horwitz, *Anxiety: A Short History* (Baltimore: Johns Hopkins University Press, 2013), 4, 17, and passim.

2. See Søren Kierkegaard, *The Concept of Anxiety*, ed. and trans. Reidar Thomte with Albert B. Anderson (Princeton: Princeton University Press, 1980), especially part 1, "Anxiety as the Presupposition of Hereditary Sin and as Explaining Hereditary Sin Retrogressively in Terms of Its Origin"; Freud's revision of his account of separations that cause and repressions that subsequently maintain anxiety in *Inhibitions, Symptoms, and Anxiety*, trans. Alix Strachey, rev. and ed. James Strachey (New York: Norton, 1959); and Martin Heidegger, *Being and Time: A Revised Edition of the Stambaugh Translation*, trans. Joan Stambaugh, rev. Dennis J. Schmidt (Albany: State University of New York Press, 2010), especially 178–89.

3. Sianne Ngai, *Ugly Feelings* (Cambridge, MA: Harvard University Press, 2005), 215.

4. *Diagnostic and Statistical Manual [of] Mental Disorders*, prepared by the Committee on Nomenclature of the American Psychiatric Association (Washington, DC: American Psychiatric Association Mental Hospital Service, 1952), 31.

5. Raymond Williams, *The Long Revolution* (London: Chatto & Windus, 1961), 50. Williams cites novels of the 1950s as the case in point for selective tradition. This evidentiary choice reflects both the time of his writing and his abiding sense, evinced again later, in *Keywords* (1976), that something about the midcentury historical present both pressed upon and eluded its own actors.

6. Andrew S. Finstuen notes that one function of habitual critcal citation of the period's anxiety is to counter "halcyon portrayals of American life after the war[, which] neglect the palpable cultural uncertainty of the period." Andrew Finstuen, *Original Sin and Everyday Protestants: The Theology of Reinhold Niebuhr, Billy Graham, and Paul Tillich in an Age of Anxiety* (Durham, NC: University of North Carolina Press, 2009), 13. Literary and cultural historians of the cold war U.S. have long understood that the political anxieties engendered by containment map onto a set of anxieties about gender, sexuality, and privacy. For a synthesis and invaluable complication of this narrative, see Deborah Nelson, *Pursuing Privacy in Cold War America* (New York: Columbia University Press, 2002), especially chapter 1.

7. Mary L. Dudziak, *Wartime: An Idea, Its History, Its Consequences* (Oxford: Oxford University Press, 2012), 68.

8. Dudziak, *Wartime*, 66. Dudziak's image for the fact of anxiety in the cold war period is the Doomsday Clock, which first appeared in 1947. But the clock's asymptotic relationship to the cataclysm of which it warned also served to acclimate people to being anxious.

9. Paul K. Saint-Amour, *Tense Future: Modernism, Total War, Encyclopedic Form* (Oxford: Oxford University Press, 2015), 17.

10. Saint-Amour's point holds open the possibility that varying degrees of immediacy can further sharpen or differentiate felt experience of each of those "three simultaneous relations." Saint-Amour, *Tense Future*, 307.

11. Saint-Amour, *Tense Future*, 37.

12. For recent reflections on the stature of *Invisible Man*, see Lawrence Buell, *The Dream of the Great American Novel* (Cambridge, MA: Harvard University Press, 2014), 181; Mark Greif, *The Age of the Crisis of Man: Thought and Fiction in America, 1933–1973* (Princeton: Princeton University Press, 2015), 145, 165.

13. On Auden's preeminence in the 1930s, see Samuel Hynes, *The Auden Generation: Literature and Politics in England in the 1930s* (Princeton: Princeton University Press, 1982); on his influence on younger American poets, see Aidan Wasley, *The Age of Auden: Postwar Poetry and the American Scene* (Princeton: Princeton University Press, 2011). For revaluations of Ellison's later career that offer more expansive treatments of his interlocutors, see Timothy Parrish, *Ralph Ellison and the Genius of America* (Amherst: University of Massachusetts Press, 2012); Richard Purcell, *Race, Ralph Ellison, and American Cold War Intellectual Culture* (New York: Palgrave Macmillan, 2013).

14. For a feminist contestation of the convenient phrase "affective turn," see Ann Cvetkovich, *Depression: A Public Feeling* (Durham, NC: Duke University Press, 2012), 3–10. Jonathan Flatley provides a useful taxonomy of the related terms "affect," "emotion," "mood"/"*Stimmung*," and "structure of feeling" in his *Affective Mapping: Melancholia and the Politics of Modernism* (Cambridge, MA: Harvard University Press, 2008), 11–27; Ngai offers a related discussion of how the "subjective-objective problematic" central to aesthetics also plays out broadly in the "philosophy of *emotion*," and specifically in contemporary theorists' efforts to and motives for distinguishing between emotion and affect. Ngai, *Ugly Feelings*, 24–26. Like Ngai, I am not invested in this chapter in making hard distinctions among affect, feeling, emotion, and mood. But my reason is at least as historical as it is informed by affect theory: I mean to get at the popularly anxious discursive surround of the midcentury, rather than to isolate specialized categories of feeling or affect within it.

15. Ralph Ellison, "The Invisible Man" and W. H. Auden, "Music Is International" both appeared in "Art on the American *Horizon*," special issue, *Horizon*, nos. 93–94 (October 1947). Ralph Ellison, "Invisible Man: Prologue to a Novel" and W. H. Auden, "Some Reflections on Music and Opera" both appeared in *Partisan Review* 19, no. 1 (January-February 1952).

16. Ellison and Auden's mutual proximity, in print and otherwise, can be extended backward in time to at least 1939, when Ellison went to hear Auden speak at a League of American Writers event. Arnold Rampersad, *Ralph Ellison: A Biography* (New York: Knopf, 2007), 125. It stretches forward to 1957, by which point Ellison would describe "the Age of Anxiety" as "truly more than a poetic conceit," something he was less likely to grant, in my view, in *Invisible Man*. Ellison, "Society, Morality, and the Novel," *The Collected Essays of Ralph Ellison*, ed. John F. Callahan (New York: Modern Library, 2003), 727. The writers' proximity in print stretches still further forward to 1981, when, in the introduction to the thirtieth-anniversary edition of *Invisible Man*, Ellison cites, so as to counter, a definition of democracy he attributes to Auden. In "the early, more optimistic

days of this republic. . . . democracy was considered not only a collectivity of individuals, as was defined by W. H. Auden, but a collectivity of politically astute citizens who, by virtue of our vaunted system of universal education and freedom of opportunity, would be prepared to govern." Ralph Ellison, introduction to *IM*, xxi.

17. This shorthand may serve the aims of critical economy, but it also maintains the comparative prestige of a midcentury canon defined by works such as C. Wright Mills, *White Collar: The American Middle Classes* (Oxford: Oxford University Press, 1951); David Riesman, with Nathan Glazer and Reuel Denney, *The Lonely Crowd* (New Haven: Yale University Press, 1950); William H. Whyte, *The Organization Man* (New York: Simon & Schuster, 1956); and Sloan Wilson, *The Man in the Gray Flannel Suit* (New York: Simon & Schuster, 1955), as well as the 1956 film adaptation directed by Nunnally Johnson. On the human condition, compare Greif's centering of "crisis of man" discourse in American intellectual life from the 1930s to the 1970s—in particular, his description of the specific contours of a reconstructed and primarily literary (novelistic) humanism in the U.S. in the 1940s—with Lyndsey Stonebridge's attention, in her study of second-generation Freudians and late modernists in Britain, to "a moment that comes after modernism but just before the war and its shocking moral aftermath became the 'human condition.'" Greif, *Age of the Crisis of Man*, especially chapter 4; Lyndsey Stonebridge, *The Writing of Anxiety: Imagining Wartime in Mid-Century British Culture* (New York: Palgrave Macmillan, 2007), 8.

18. Stonebridge, *The Writing of Anxiety*, 136n5.

19. Ngai, *Ugly Feelings*, 213.

20. May, *The Meaning of Anxiety*, 3–4.

21. May delivered a paper on the "historical roots of modern anxiety theories" at the meeting. May, *The Meaning of Anxiety*, 18n2.

22. Foreword to Paul H. Hoch and Joseph Zubin, eds., *Anxiety: The Proceedings of the Thirty-ninth Annual Meeting of the American Psychopathological Association* (New York: Grune & Stratton, 1950). See also May, preface to *The Meaning of Anxiety*, v–vi.

23. Harold Basowitz, Harold Persky, Sheldon J. Korchin, and Roy R. Grinker, *Anxiety and Stress: An Interdisciplinary Study of a Life Situation* (New York: McGraw-Hill, 1955), 10.

24. Horwitz, *Anxiety*, 127.

25. May, too, cites earlier works by these prominent theologians: Niebuhr's *The Nature and Destiny of Man* (1941) and Tillich's *The Protestant Era* (1947).

26. Paul Tillich, *The Courage to Be* (New Haven: Yale University Press, 1952), 57.

27. Alan Watts, *The Wisdom of Insecurity* (New York: Vintage, 1951). Louis Finkelstein, "Modern Man's Anxiety: Its Remedy," *Commentary*, December 1, 1946, https://www.commentarymagazine.com/articles/modern-mans-anxiety-its -remedy/.

28. Wayne E. Oates, *Anxiety in Christian Experience* (Philadelphia: Westminster, 1955), 8.

29. Norman Vincent Peale and Smiley Blanton, *The Art of Real Happiness* (New York: Prentice Hall, 1950); Norman Vincent Peale, *The Power of Positive Thinking: 10 Traits for Maximum Results* (New York: Fireside, 2003), 118.

30. Solid histories of these drugs, their marketing, and their effects include David Herzberg, *Happy Pills in America: From Miltown to Prozac* (Baltimore: Johns Hopkins University Press, 2009), especially chapter 1; Andrea Tone, *The Age of Anxiety: America's History of America's Turbulent Affair with Tranquillizers* (New York: Basic Books, 2008).

31. "Anxiety: Modern Man's Chief Enemy," Dios Chemical Co., Saint Louis, Missouri, 1952, 3.

32. Robert Lowell, *New Selected Poems*, ed. Katie Peterson (New York: Farrar, Straus and Giroux, 2017), 78.

33. Quoted in "It Comes Hard," *Time* 51, no. 3 (January 19, 1948): 64.

34. J. Isaacs, *An Assessment of Twentieth-Century Literature: Six Lectures Delivered in the BBC Third Programme* (London: Secker & Warburg, 1951), 45, 67.

35. "Is a Possum Neurotic?," *Time* 64, no. 16 (October 18, 1954): 75.

36. *Mad* 30 (December 1956): cover.

37. Freud, *Inhibitions*, 100.

38. Greif, *The Age of the Crisis of Man*, 5. Building on Eric Hobsbawm's *The Age of Extremes: A History of the World, 1914–1991* (New York: Vintage, 1994), Greif reconstructs long-midcentury American intellectuals' understanding of the twentieth century as an epoch of continuous crisis, "a single movement, in a way," as opposed to period marked by discrete wartimes. Greif, 4.

39. Hannah Arendt, preface to the first edition, in *Origins of Totalitarianism*, new ed. (New York: Harvest, 1973), vii.

40. Arthur M. Schlesinger Jr., *The Vital Center: The Politics of Freedom* (New Brunswick, NJ: Transaction, 1998), 1.

41. Daniel Cordle distinguishes between narratives of nuclear disaster and narratives of nuclear anxiety. See Daniel Cordle, *States of Suspense: The Nuclear Age, Postmodernism, and United States Fiction and Prose* (Manchester: Manchester University Press, 2008), especially chapter 1. In a review essay, Steven Belletto makes a helpful survey of early twenty-first-century developments in cold war cultural studies, with particular attention to some scholars' resistance "to let[ting] containment stand as the controlling metaphor of cold war life." Steven Belletto, "Curbing Containment: Cold War Studies in the Twenty-first Century," *Contemporary Literature* 48, no. 1 (January 2007), 152.

42. May, preface to *The Meaning of Anxiety*, vi.

43. My attention to May's address to democratic citizenship diverges from George Cotkins's account of *The Meaning of Anxiety* in his authoritative history of existentialism in the U.S. Cotkin concludes that in May's work, "Kierkegaardian anxiety had miraculously become apolitical and non-religious, something that a proper attitude, desire for change and growth, and courage to create or love might overcome." George Cotkin, *Existential America* (Baltimore: Johns Hopkins University Press, 2003), 67.

44. May, *The Meaning of Anxiety*, 11.

45. May, *The Meaning of Anxiety*, 11.

46. May, *The Meaning of Anxiety*, 11–12.

47. Rollo May, *The Meaning of Anxiety*, rev. ed. (New York: Norton, 1977), 3.

48. *Oxford English Dictionary*, s.v. "anxiety," phrase "Age of Anxiety," accessed May 21, 2019.

49. In large part because *The Age of Anxiety* is an "almost intractably difficult poem," scholars have concentrated on elucidating its systems of reference and the rigors of its poetics. The quoted phrase comes from Susannah Young-Ah Gottlieb, *Regions of Sorrow: Anxiety and Messianism in Hannah Arendt and W. H. Auden* (Stanford, CA: Stanford University Press, 2003), 70. For the most thorough readings of the poem, see Gottlieb, chapter 2; and Edward Mendelson, *Early Auden, Later Auden: A Critical Biography* (Princeton: Princeton University Press, 2017), 557–74. On the poem's allusive and allegorical density, see John R. Boly, "Auden and the Romantic Tradition in *The Age of Anxiety*," *Daedalus: Proceedings of the American Academy of Arts & Sciences* 111, no. 2 (Spring 1982): 149–77; Edward Callan, "Allegory in Auden's *The Age of Anxiety*," *Twentieth-Century Literature* 10, no. 4 (January 1965): 155–65. On the poem's meter, see Christine Brooke-Rose, "Notes on the Metre of Auden's 'The Age of Anxiety,'" *Essays in Criticism: A Quarterly Journal of Literary Criticism* 13 (1963): 253–64; Chris Jones, *Strange Likeness: The Use of Old English in Twentieth-Century Poetry* (Oxford: Oxford University Press, 2006), chapter 2, especially 113–21.
50. Alan Jacobs, introduction to *The Age of Anxiety: A Baroque Eclogue*, by W. H. Auden, ed. Alan Jacobs (Princeton: Princeton University Press, 2011), xii. Page references to this edition (*AA*) are hereafter provided in the main text.
51. "The age" can name a present (e.g., the digital age); expand to take in broad spans of geological or historical time (the Stone Age); or elevate a figure or idea to era-defining centrality (e.g., Hugh Kenner's Pound era).
52. Laurence Sears, "Anxiety in the United States of America," in *Educational Freedom in the Age of Anxiety: Yearbook of the John Dewey Society 1953*, ed. H. Gordon Hullfish (New York: Harper, 1953), 4.
53. Among representative examples of tautological validation or acceptance of Auden's title, see Walter Elder, review of *The Age of Anxiety*, *Atlantic Monthly*, September 1947, 127; Nicholas Moore, "The Frozen Heart," *Poetry*, May 1949, 22; C. G. Paulding, review of *The Age of Anxiety*, *Commonweal*, August 29, 1947, 485.
54. Stonebridge observes astutely that "anxiety about the human condition, at least by the 1950s, had begun to displace a possibly more troubled set of anxieties about the psychic and political consequences of the Second World War and its aftermath." Stonebridge reads the inherent anachronism of Auden's title as a case in point: "By the time a culture recognizes itself as anxious, to an extent it has ceased to be so but, rather, has become self-consciously fearful about its anxieties, which is something different." I take Auden's title, however, to *make* much the same point, rather than simply to instance it, and thus revalue the poem's explicit setting during the war and among civilians and members of the armed forces. Stonebridge, *The Writing of Anxiety*, 135–36, n.5.
55. May, *The Meaning of Anxiety*, 5.
56. For the quoted phrase: United States Strategic Bombing Survey, *Summary Report (European War)* (Maxwell Air Force Base, AL: Air University Press, 1987 [1945]), 3. On drafts of *The Age of Anxiety*: the first forty pages of one important notebook have been torn out, and the extant typescripts contain mostly verse in close to its published form. See Jacobs, introduction to *AA*, xlii–xlix. On the USSBS: its defining characteristic was its military-civilian composition. Along with

military personnel, the USSBS included several hundred civilians "with an assimilated rank designated according to their incomes." James Stern, *The Hidden Damage* (New York: Harcourt, 1947), 3.

57. Nicholas Nabokov, "Excerpts from Memories," in *W. H. Auden: A Tribute*, ed. Stephen Spender (New York: Macmillan, 1975), 136.

58. Nabokov, "Excerpts from Memories," 145. While in Germany, Auden wrote a handful of letters to friends, all of which move quickly from noting the "interest" of the work to lamenting the devastating sadness of it. "Some Letters from Auden to James and Tania Stern," in W. H. Auden, *"In Solitude, for Company": W. H. Auden After 1940*, ed. Katherine Bucknell and Nicholas Jenkins (Oxford: Clarendon, 1995), 93–94; and James Stern, "The Indispensable Presence," in Spender, *W. H. Auden: A Tribute*, 126.

59. Gottlieb, *Regions of Sorrow*, 4. Mendelson notes that memories of the USSBS did not enter the poet's work until 1949, in the opening of "Memorial for the City." Mendelson, *Early Auden, Later Auden*, 596. For a reading of "Memorial" in relation to Auden's experience in Germany, see Rachel Galvin, *News of War: Civilian Poetry, 1936–1945* (Oxford: Oxford University Press, 2018), 155–59. For an account of Auden's service in the USSBS Morale Division, see Claire Seiler, "Auden and the Work of *The Age of Anxiety*," in *Auden at Work*, ed. Bonnie Costello and Rachel Galvin (New York: Palgrave Macmillan, 2015), 250–74.

60. United States Strategic Bombing Survey Morale Division, *The Effects of Strategic Bombing on German Morale*, vol. 1 (Washington, DC: U.S. Government Printing Office, May 1947), iv.

61. USSBS Morale Division, *The Effects of Strategic Bombing*, 109.

62. The results of the interview study did not always line up with Morale Division expectations. For example, table 54 of the report "illustrates the absence of a relationship between degree of fear and willingness to surrender." The accompanying analysis finds that "the apprehensive people, who felt the war would seriously affect their lives, had poorer morale than their stolid countrymen who had not anticipated the trials of war and air attacks. Anticipation, instead of helping to cushion the shock, proved to be a symptom, like worry, related to morale." USSBS Morale Division, *The Effects of Strategic Bombing*, 36.

63. USSBS Morale Division, *The Effects of Strategic Bombing*, 109 (emphasis in original).

64. USSBS Morale Division, *The Effects of Strategic Bombing*, 110.

65. W. G. Sebald, *On the Natural History of Destruction*, trans. Anthea Bell (New York: Random House, 2004), 12. On the sophistication of the Morale Division study, see Jean M. Converse, *Survey Research in the United States: Roots and Emergence, 1890–1960*, new ed. (New Brunswick, NJ: Transaction, 2010), 212–13.

66. W. H. Auden, "September 1, 1939," in *Selected Poems of W. H. Auden*, ed. Edward Mendelson (New York: Vintage, 2007), 96.

67. Auden, *Selected Poems*, 43.

68. Mendelson, *Early Auden, Later Auden*, 557.

69. I cull this representative list from John Fuller's indispensable *W. H. Auden: A Commentary* (Princeton: Princeton University Press, 1998), 369–87.

70. For the quoted phrase, see Gottlieb, *Regions of Sorrow*, 72.

71. On pastoral "convenings," see Paul Alpers, *What Is Pastoral?* (Chicago: University of Chicago Press, 1996), 81.

72. W. H. Auden, "In Memory of W. B. Yeats," in *Collected Poems*, ed. Edward Mendelson (New York: Modern Library, 2007), 246.

73. Randall Jarrell, Verse Chronicle, *Nation* 165, no. 16 (October 18, 1947): 424.

74. Gottlieb, *Regions of Sorrow*, 121. Gottlieb describes four endings to *The Age of Anxiety*: Rosetta's and Malin's final speeches, the final paragraphs of the epilogue, and a short prayer Auden omitted from the end of the poem. A version of the prayer was printed in a pamphlet in 1946 and later published, in *Epistle to a Godson* (1969), as "Anthem." In Gottlieb's reading, the prayer would have imposed a compromised conclusion on the poem; instead, *The Age of Anxiety* is "effectively left without a definitive ending—suspended between the conclusions of Malin and Rosetta" or, in my view, suspended between the war and the postwar. Gottlieb, *Regions of Sorrow*, 128–30.

75. Patric Dickinson, review of *The Age of Anxiety*, *Horizon*, May 1949, 377. Favorable reviews include Louise Bogan, *New Yorker*, July 26, 1947, 64–65; Jacques Barzun, "Workers in Monumental Brass," *Harper's*, September 1947, back matter, i–ii.

76. "Eclogue, 1947," *Time* 50, no. 3 (July 21, 1947), 100.

77. Dickinson, review of *The Age of Anxiety*. See also Delmore Schwartz, "Auden and Stevens," *Partisan Review* 14, no. 5 (September–October 1947): 530.

78. "Third Avenue Eclogue," *Times Literary Supplement*, October 23, 1948, 376.

79. Wrey Gardiner, review of *The Age of Anxiety*, *Poetry Quarterly*, 107.

80. Dickinson, review of *The Age of Anxiety*, 377.

81. For a full account, see Michael Shelden, *Friends of Promise: Cyril Connolly and the World of "Horizon"* (New York: Harper and Row, 1989).

82. William Phillips, "Portrait of the Artist as an American," "Art on the American *Horizon*," special issue, *Horizon*, nos. 93–94 (October 1947): 19.

83. Saul Bellow, "Man Underground," *Commentary*, June 1952: 608.

84. Cyril Connolly, introduction to "Art on the American *Horizon*," special issue, *Horizon*, nos. 93–94 (October 1947): 2.

85. Connolly, introduction, 2.

86. A bowdlerized version of the story was published in the U.S., in advance of the novel, in John Hersey's short-lived *Magazine of the Year*. See Ralph Ellison, "Battle Royal," *'48: Magazine of the Year* 2, no. 1 (January 1948): 14–32.

87. Lawrence Jackson describes the appearance of "The Invisible Man" in *Horizon* as "pivotal." It made "American critics . . . take notice of Ellison's work in a way that its publication in any U.S. journal—arguably even *Partisan Review*—never would have aroused." Lawrence Jackson, *Ralph Ellison: Emergence of Genius* (Athens: University of Georgia Press, 2007), 349.

88. Jackson, *Ralph Ellison*, 363.

89. Parrish, *Ralph Ellison and the Genius of America*, 113.

90. Jacques Barzun, "The Higher Learning in America," "Art on the American *Horizon*," special issue, *Horizon*, nos. 93–94 (October 1947): 99–100.

91. Donald Gibson observes that the grandfather "advocates . . . a war so private and subjective that the enemy does not even recognize that he is at war." Donald Gibson, *The Politics of Literary Expression: A Study of Major Black Writers* (Westport, CT: Greenwood, 1981), 66.

92. Kenneth W. Warren, *So Black and Blue: Ralph Ellison and the Occasion of Criticism* (Chicago: University of Chicago Press, 2003), 3.

93. Warren offers a concise historical overview of competing political readings of *Invisible Man* through the years just after the author's death in 1994. Warren, *So Black and Blue*, 13–20. Recent defenses of Ellison's democratic vision include Danielle S. Allen, *Talking to Strangers: Anxieties of Citizenship Since "Brown v. Board of Education"* (Chicago: University of Chicago Press, 2004), chapter 8; Parrish, *Ralph Ellison*; Ross Posnock, "Mourning and Melancholy: Explaining the Ellison Animus," in *The New Territory: Ralph Ellison and the Twenty-First Century*, ed. Marc C. Conner and Lucas E. Morel (Jackson: University Press of Mississippi, 2016), 285–93. Parish and Posnock explicitly respond to critiques of Ellison's abandonment of leftist politics and longer capitulation to mainstream American liberalism by Barbara Foley, *Wrestling with the Left: The Making of Ralph Ellison's "Invisible Man"* (Durham, NC: Duke University Press, 2010) and by biographer Rampersad, in *Ralph Ellison*.

94. African Americans feature in May's *The Meaning of Anxiety* only in one case study of two pregnant "Negro girls.'" One has a "special sensitivity to racial discrimination and resulting defiance [that] may be termed a 'normal' rather than a 'neurotic' reaction." Later, "for both Negro girls, the fact of illegitimate pregnancy did not present as much of an anxiety-creating situation as for the white girls." May, *The Meaning of Anxiety*, 321, 326.

95. Critics have long debated the meaning of the grandfather's deathbed speech. For readings of it in relation to respectability politics, the necessity of citizens' sacrifice, and aspirational American principle, respectively, see David M. Ball, *False Starts: The Rhetoric of Failure and the Making of American Modernism* (Evanston, IL: Northwestern University Press, 2014), 150–66, especially 151–52; Allen, *Talking to Strangers*, 103–4; and James E. Seaton, "Affirming the Principle," in *Ralph Ellison and the Raft of Hope: A Political Companion to "Invisible Man,"* ed. Lucas E. Morel (Lexington: University Press of Kentucky, 2004), especially 22–26.

96. See Badia Sahar Ahad's related account of Ellison's and Richard Wright's doubts about whether the psychoanalytic paradigm that "emerged as a dominant social force" in the 1940s–50s could have "curative effects on African Americans who were the unfortunate victims of an uneven US democracy." Badia Sahar Ahad, *Freud Upside Down: African American Literature and Psychoanalytic Culture* (Urbana: University of Illinois Press, 2010), 84, 83; see especially chapter 4.

97. Foley writes that the novel "continues to discourage pinpointing the historical moment, although the narrator's reference to 'the chamber with the deadly gas that ends in the oven so hygienically clean' [*IM*, 575] suggests that, even if the protagonist has not been shown going through the war, he has endured that historical *agon*." Foley, *Wrestling with the Left*, 326.

98. On Ellison in the Merchant Marine, see Jackson, *Ralph Ellison*, 282–83.

99. Ellison also wrote a short story, "In a Strange Country" (1944), on this theme.

100. The Double-V campaign is one obvious precedent. On this context, see Jansen B. Werner, "Black America's Double War: Ralph Ellison and 'Critical Participation During World War II," *Rhetoric & Public Affairs* 18, no. 3 (Fall 2015): 441–70.

101. Saint-Amour, *Tense Future*, 37.

102. Mark Greif reads the Paint Factory hospital scene as the novel's key turning point, or what he conceives as its turn from the episodic exposés in the first half of the novel, which dominate the criticism of it, to the less fully analyzed "over theorizing" that characterizes its second half. Greif, *The Age of the Crisis of Man*, 168.

103. On Rinehart's cool, see Lee Konstantinou, *Cool Characters: Irony and American Fiction* (Cambridge: Harvard University Press, 2016), 59–76.

104. Two of the strongest and, in the present context, most apropos recent readings on either side of the line are Amanda Anderson's recuperative account of the novel's liberalism and Barbara Foley's forensic analysis of Ellison's revisions of *Invisible Man*, which she reads as a systematic abandonment of what could have been a leftist, forcefully antiracist novel in order to align the book with the demands of a market primed for cold war anticommunism. Anderson premises her reading of the epilogue on *negation*; Foley centers on *excision*. Anderson concludes: "at [the] core [of *Invisible Man*] lies a profound orientation toward liberal principles, one that subtends the broader invocation of democratic aspiration and vital diversity. That we see these principles primarily through their negation does not undermine their force or the power of Ellison's liberalism." Amanda Anderson, *Bleak Liberalism* (Chicago: University of Chicago Press, 2016), 128. Foley adduces earlier drafts of the epilogue's key passages, including one that would have counterpointed political leaders' "ambivalence" to "the dubious quest for 'integrated personality.'" Foley notes as a liability something Anderson would probably hail as strength, namely, that the draft's "valorizing" of ambivalence "is suggestively akin to [Arthur] Schlesinger [Jr.]'s privileging of 'anxiety' over 'certitude.'" To Foley, this privileging of ambivalence "hardly offers a probing analysis of the psychology of leadership." It does, however, offer a spot-on account of democratic *citizenship* as it was affectively constructed and circulated at midcentury. Foley's further point here is to note that the draft passage does not "deny to a Communist the same complexity of self that it attributes to rulers of bourgeois regimes." Foley, *Wrestling with the Left*, 340.

105. *Responsibility* is an Ellison keyword, one whose communal, individual, and literary implications he wrestled with throughout his career. Within months of his beginning to draft *Invisible Man*, however, Ellison wrote to Kenneth Burke of anxiety and responsibility as imperatives of African American life and possible counters to American militarism. Fully to understand "all the 'felt experience' which being a Negro American entails . . . reveals . . . a sense of responsibility that makes Kierkegaard seem like a phlegmatic sleepwalker. . . . How well I understand the possibility of civil war you mention! But don't you see the war exists already and its effects are in many ways more serious than any mere shedding of blood? It has warped our culture, truncated our ability to think deeply and broadly and schooled us to drop atom bombs on a defenseless city. . . . And I sometimes wonder why Negroes haven't a larger responsibility in this matter than we suspect. Perhaps by not fighting, by not producing widespread civil conflict, we have done America and the world more harm than 'progress.'" Ralph Ellison to Kenneth Burke, November 25, 1945, in *The Selected Letters of Ralph Ellison*, ed. John F. Callahan and Marc C. Conner (New York: Random House, 2019), 202–3.

106. May, *The Meaning of Anxiety*, 234.

3. ELIZABETH BOWEN AND SAMUEL BECKETT WAITING IN THE MIDDLE

Epigraphs: Elizabeth Bowen, "English Fiction at Mid-Century," in *People, Places, Things: Essays by Elizabeth Bowen*, ed. Allan Hepburn (Edinburgh: Edinburgh University Press, 2008), 321. Samuel Beckett, *Waiting for Godot: A Tragicomedy in Two Acts*, trans. Samuel Beckett (New York: Grove, 1982), 73.

1. Raymond Williams, *Keywords: A Vocabulary of Culture and Society*, new ed. (Oxford: Oxford University Press, 2015), xxvii.

2. In "her scathing portrait of the Kelway ménage, Bowen lets forth all her Yeatsian abhorrence of the middle class, laced with a strong dose of misogyny." Maud Ellmann, *Elizabeth Bowen: The Shadow Across the Page* (Edinburgh: Edinburgh University Press, 2003), 158–59.

3. Elizabeth Bowen, *The Heat of the Day* (New York: Random House, 2002), 125. Page references to this edition *(HOD)* are hereafter provided in the main text.

4. For "the very nature of the contemporary," "our sense of the 'now,'" and "angle of vision," see Elizabeth Bowen, "Subject and the Time," in *Listening In: Broadcasts, Speeches, and Interviews*, ed. Allan Hepburn (Edinburgh: Edinburgh University Press, 2010), 147, 149, 151.

5. Victoria Glendinning, *Elizabeth Bowen: A Biography* (New York: Knopf, 1978), 188. James Knowlson stresses that "the ground had been well prepared" for Beckett's "siege in the room" after 1945. James Knowlson, *Damned to Fame: The Life of Samuel Beckett* (London: Bloomsbury, 1996), 353.

6. For an assessment of and intervention in this pattern, see Sinéad Mooney, "Unstable Compounds: Bowen's Beckettian Affinities," *Modern Fiction Studies* 53, no. 2 (Summer 2007): 238–56.

7. Beckett, *Waiting for Godot*, 5. Page references to the Grove edition (Godot) are hereafter provided in the main text.

8. Vivian Mercier's famous synopsis appeared in his review of *Waiting for Godot* for the *Irish Times* on February 18, 1956.

9. Seán Kennedy, "'Humanity in Ruins': Beckett and History," in *The New Cambridge Companion to Samuel Beckett*, ed. Dirk Van Hulle (Cambridge: Cambridge University Press, 2015), 185.

10. Emilie Morin, *Beckett's Political Imagination* (Cambridge: Cambridge University Press, 2017), 130. The historicist and archival turn in Beckett scholarship followed in large part on the publication of Knowlson, *Damned to Fame*. For a useful compendium of scholarship in this line, see Anthony Uhlmann, ed., *Samuel Beckett in Context* (Cambridge: Cambridge University Press, 2013). Julian Murphet's contribution to that volume wisely cautions: "No interpretive strategy is more tempting, or more futile, than to suppose a direct correspondence between a Beckett work and its historical situation—equally, however, not to hazard the connections is to betray the formal promise of each work's rigorous self-enclosure: that it safeguards the unvoiced, nameless suffering written out of official histories." Julian Murphet, "France, Europe, the World: 1945–1989," in Uhlmann, *Samuel Beckett in Context*, 126. The view of ahistorical Beckett has itself been historicized. Marjorie Perloff observes that "for the first wave of Beckett critics in postwar France— critics for whom war memories were not only painful but embarrassing, given

the collaboration of the Vichy government—it was preferable to read Beckett as addressing man's alienation and the human condition rather than anything as specific as everyday life in the years of Resistance." Marjorie Perloff, " 'In Love with Hiding': Samuel Beckett's War," *Iowa Review* 35, no. 1 (Spring 2005): 77.

11. "*Waiting for Godot* not only stages the latent conditions of the period after the Second World War—it positively condenses an entire sea of latency into a single *Stimmung*." Hans Ulrich Gumbrecht, *After 1945: Latency as Origin of the Present* (Stanford, CA: Stanford University Press, 2013), 25.

12. Perloff, " 'In Love with Hiding,' " 77.

13. Samuel Beckett, *En attendant Godot* (Paris: Minuit, 2002), 93.

14. Kennedy, "Humanity in Ruins," 188.

15. The United States Department of Defense was broadly known to be calculating various first and second nuclear strike probabilities, which included weighing the likely numbers of civilian casualties. NATO's website provides reliable full text of the North Atlantic Treaty at https://www.nato.int/cps/en/natolive/official_texts _17120.htm, accessed May 29, 2019.

16. Mooney, "Unstable Compounds," 241.

17. Marina MacKay, " 'Is Your Journey Really Necessary?': Going Nowhere in Late Modernist London," *PMLA* 124, no. 5 (October 2009): 1611.

18. Bowen, "How I Write: A Conversation with Glyn Jones," in *Listening In*, 272.

19. Ellmann, *Elizabeth Bowen*, 154.

20. Allan Hepburn, *Intrigue: Espionage and Culture* (New Haven: Yale University Press, 2005), 136. Hepburn offers the definitive reading of *The Heat of the Day* within the spy novel tradition, arguing that Bowen's hybrid spy story/love story domesticates the key intrigue novel tropes of betrayal, disloyalty, and treachery. Hepburn, *Intrigue*, chapter 6.

21. *Oxford English Dictionary*, s.v. "suspense," compound "suspense novel, suspense story," accessed May 29, 2019.

22. *Oxford English Dictionary.*, s.v. "wait," accessed May 29, 2019.

23. Neil Corcoran, *Elizabeth Bowen: The Enforced Return* (Oxford: Oxford University Press, 2004), 171.

24. Elizabeth Hardwick, "Elizabeth Bowen's Fiction," *Partisan Review* 16, no. 11 (November 1949): 1118.

25. Orville Prescott, review of *The Heat of the Day*, *New York Times*, February 21, 1949.

26. Diana Trilling, review of *The Heat of the Day*, *Nation* 168, no. 9 (February 1949): 254.

27. Glendinning, *Elizabeth Bowen*, 189–91; Hermione Lee, *Elizabeth Bowen: An Estimation* (London: Vision, 1981), 178–81.

28. Patrick Deer, *Culture in Camouflage: War, Empire, and Modern British Literature* (Oxford: Oxford University Press, 2009), 186.

29. Elizabeth Bowen, promotional blurb for *The Heat of the Day*, Elizabeth Bowen Collection 1923–1975, Harry Ransom Center, University of Texas at Austin, box 5, folder 5. This collection is hereafter cited in these notes as "Bowen Collection."

30. Paul Fussell excavates the "sporting spirit" in his classic *The Great War and Modern Memory* (Oxford: Oxford University Press, 2013), 26–31.

31. Wilfred Owen, preface to his projected book of poems, in *The Collected Poems of Wilfred Owen*, ed. C. Day Lewis (New York: New Directions, 1965), 31.

32. Marina MacKay notes that "the failures of the gerontocracy are a recurrent trope in political discourse during the early years of the Second World War." MacKay, *Modernism and World War II*, 74.

33. Generational rhetoric comes in for comedic deflation in *Waiting for Godot* too. At one point, the play finds Pozzo, as he waxes "*Lyrically*," reducing the phrase "our generation" from conciliatory rhetorical occasion to demographic datum in the space of four short sentences: "Let us not then speak ill of our generation, it is not any unhappier than its predecessors. (*Pause.*) Let us not speak well of it either. (*Pause.*) Let us not speak of it at all. (*Pause. Judiciously.*) It is true the population has increased." Beckett, *Waiting for Godot*, 32.

34. Elizabeth Bowen, drafts of *The Heat of the Day*, Bowen Collection, box 5, folder 3.

35. *Burke's Peerage and Gentry* is available online: http://www.burkespeerage.com. *Debrett's* contemporary iteration can be found at http://www.debretts.com/people /essential-guide-to-the-peerage.aspx, accessed May 29, 2019.

36. The play aired on the BBC Third Programme on March 10 and 11, 1949. Elizabeth Bowen, *Listening In*, 347, unnumbered note.

37. Bowen, "A Year I Remember—1918," in *Listening In*, 66.

38. Bowen, "A Year I Remember—1918," in *Listening In*, 63.

39. Bowen, "A Year I Remember—1918," in *Listening In*, 63.

40. Bowen, "A Year I Remember—1918," in *Listening In*, 64.

41. Bowen, "A Year I Remember—1918," in *Listening In*, 64–65.

42. Bowen, "A Year I Remember—1918," in *Listening In*, 75.

43. Bowen, "A Year I Remember—1918," in *Listening In*, 75.

44. Bowen, "A Year I Remember—1918," in *Listening In*, 72.

45. Bowen, "A Year I Remember—1918," in *Listening In*, 75.

46. Bowen, "A Year I Remember—1918," in *Listening In*, 66.

47. Bowen, "English Fiction at Mid-Century," in *People, Places, Things*, 321.

48. Bowen, "English Fiction at Mid-Century," in *People, Places, Things*, 321.

49. Bowen, "English Fiction at Mid-Century," in *People, Places, Things*, 321, 324.

50. Bowen, "Subject and the Time," in *Listening In*, 147.

51. Bowen, "The Cult of Nostalgia," in *Listening In*, 102.

52. Bowen, "Subject and the Time," in *Listening In*, 147.

53. Bowen, "Subject and the Time," in *Listening In*, 148, 147.

54. Bowen, "Subject and the Time," in *Listening In*, 150 (my emphasis).

55. Bowen, "Subject and the Time," in *Listening In*, 148.

56. Bowen, "Subject and the Time," in *Listening In*, 151.

57. Bowen, "Subject and the Time," in *Listening In*, 149

58. Emily C. Bloom, *The Wireless Past: Anglo-Irish Writers and the BBC, 1931–1968* (Oxford: Oxford University Press, 2016), 97.

59. Thomas S. Davis, *The Extinct Scene: Late Modernism and Everyday Life* (New York: Columbia University Press, 2016), 179.

60. Allan Hepburn, "Trials and Errors: *The Heat of the Day* and Postwar Culpability," in *Intermodernism: Literary Culture in Mid-Twentieth-Century Britain*, ed. Kristin Bluemel (Edinburgh: Edinburgh University Press, 2009), 134.

61. Hepburn, "Trials and Errors," 134. Like *The Heat of the Day*, Bowen's late 1940s journalism about the Paris Peace Conference, Prague, and Hungary dwells in impression and atmosphere rather than clear delineation of the implications of

recent history. Hepburn collects these writings in Bowen, *People, Places, Things*, 66–92.

62. Analysts of the narrative effects of the Blitz passages include Beryl Pong, who argues that the flashbacks to the Blitz are structural manifestations of the novel's wartime theme of spatial and temporal displacement. Petra Rau goes further, arguing that Bowen's Blitz passages "in fact *predict* the myth of the Blitz." Beryl Pong, "Space and Time in the Bombed City: Graham Greene's *The Ministry of Fear* and Elizabeth Bowen's *The Heat of the Day*," *Literary London* 7, no. 1 (March 2009), http://www.literarylondon.org/london-journal/march2009/pong.html. Petra Rau, "The Common Frontier: Fictions of Alterity in Elizabeth Bowen's *The Heat of the Day* and Graham Greene's *The Ministry of Fear*," *Literature and History* 14, no. 1 (May 2005): 32.

63. I borrow the phrase "myth of the Blitz" from Rau, "The Common Frontier," 32.

64. Leo Mellor, *Reading the Ruins: Modernism, Bombsites and British Culture* (Cambridge: Cambridge University Press, 2011), 31.

65. Elizabeth Bowen Papers, blurb, 1948, box 5, folder 5.

66. Hepburn, "Trials and Errors," 134.

67. "The break in the habit of listening in is energetically regretted by the country people." Elizabeth Bowen, *Notes on Eire: Espionage Reports to Winston Churchill, 1940–2* (Cork, Ireland: Aubane Historical Society, 1999), 33.

68. Martin Gilbert chronicles the battle and Allied victory at El Alamein during the summer and fall of 1942. Martin Gilbert, *The Second World War: A Complete History*, rev ed. (New York: Holt, 1991), 350–80. He quotes Churchill's famed remark on p. 376.

69. Elizabeth Bowen, "Postscript by the Author," in *The Demon Lover and Other Stories* (London: Jonathan Cape, 1945), 217.

70. On the bombing of Bowen's London home, see Glendinning, *Elizabeth Bowen*, chapter 8; Lee, *Elizabeth Bowen*, 164–65. For the quoted phrase see Glendinning, *Elizabeth Bowen*, 159.

71. On the language of "emergency" in Éire, see Anna Teekell, *Emergency Writing: Irish Literature, Neutrality, and the Second World War* (Evanston, IL: Northwestern University Press, 2018), chapter 1.

72. Among representative examples from Bowen's unpublished correspondence: on April 25, 1944, "I am very anxious to finish my novel"; on February 19, 1945, Bowen did not foresee writing any new short stories for "eight or nine months . . . as it is essential that I should finish my novel"; on September 30, 1946, she was "putting on a great spurt to finish my novel before the end of the year." Bowen Collection, box 10, folder 5.

73. Glendinning, *Elizabeth Bishop*, 214.

74. Bowen, *The Heat of the Day* composite manuscript, Bowen Collection, box 5, folder 3.

75. Bowen, *The Heat of the Day* composite manuscript, Bowen Collection, box 5, folder 3.

76. Bowen, *The Heat of the Day* composite manuscript, Bowen Collection, box 5, folder 2.

77. "Bowen's insistence on a prose style as twisted and indirect as the motives of her characters" has been a point of, alternately, critical disappointment or defense since

the very first reviews of the novel. For the quoted phrase, see Michael North, *What Is the Present?* (Princeton: Princeton University Press, 2018), 109.

78. Bowen Collection, box 10, folder 4.

79. On this point, see Ellmann, *Elizabeth Bowen*, 165–66.

4. THE SONIC SUSPENSIONS OF FRANK O'HARA

Epigraph: quoted in Brad Gooch, *City Poet: The Life and Times of Frank O'Hara* (New York: Harper Perennial, 1993), 95.

1. Proclamation No. 2889, 3 C.F.R. 37 (May 22, 1950).

2. Roy H. Parker, "A Prayer for Memorial Day, *Boston Daily Globe*, May 29, 1950. Anne Campbell, "Memorial Day," *Boston Daily Globe*, May 30, 1950. The *Globe* published eight of Campbell's Memorial Day poems between 1932 and 1953, with a near unbroken run between 1948 and 1953.

3. John Lowney reads "Memorial Day 1950" as consistent with Fredric Jameson's association of "the postwar crisis of historical memory" with postmodernism. He acknowledges in passing that the poem's title indicates "a moment of reflection at the midpoint of the twentieth century." John Lowney, "The 'Post-Anti-Esthetic' Poetics of Frank O'Hara," *Contemporary Literature* 32, no. 2 (1991): 248.

4. Frank O'Hara, *The Collected Poems of Frank O'Hara*, ed. Donald Allen (Berkeley: University of California Press, 1995 [1971]), 18. Page references to this edition (*CP*) are hereafter provided in the main text. For the quoted phrase, see Marjorie Perloff, *Frank O'Hara: Poet Among Painters* (Chicago: University of Chicago Press, 1997), 48.

5. For the quoted phrase, see Perloff, *Frank O'Hara*, 48.

6. Lytle Shaw offers the subtlest account of O'Hara's development as a coterie poet. Shaw notes that "compared to the poems of the mid-1950s and after, the use of proper names [in "Memorial Day 1950"] is flatter, more an inventory than an inventive strategy." Lytle Shaw, *Frank O'Hara: The Poetics of Coterie* (Iowa City: University of Iowa Press, 2006), 50.

7. Perloff, *Frank O'Hara*, 50.

8. Perloff, *Frank O'Hara*, 51.

9. John Ashbery, introduction to *CP*, vii.

10. Gooch, *City Poet*, 85.

11. Gooch, *City Poet*, 89.

12. On O'Hara's work on "The 4th of July," see Gooch, *City Poet*, 163–66. In the chapters "Birth" and "Navy," Gooch also quotes liberally from the unfinished novel to animate his narrative of O'Hara's childhood and service in the war.

13. Quoted in Donald Allen, editor's note, in Frank O'Hara, *Poems Retrieved*, rev. ed., edited by Donald Allen (San Francisco: Grey Fox, 1996), xv. Page references to this edition (*PR*) are hereafter provided in the main text.

14. Already in 1997, Perloff surveyed the O'Hara scholarship and cautioned against "turn[ing] this mercurial and highly individual poet into a mere representative of fifties' queer sensibility or Cold War politics." Perloff, *Frank O'Hara*, xiv.

15. In a related reading, Paul Giles argues that the last line could indicate "infinite possibility [but] its larger resonance also alludes to a scene of geographical

orientation and disorientation where, under the omnipresent sky, all mappings become 'possible' and it is correspondingly easy to lose one's 'bearings.'" Paul Giles, *Antipodean America: Australasia and the Constitution of U.S. Literature* (Oxford: Oxford University Press, 2013), 396–97.

16. Robert Rauschenberg to Betty Parsons, October 18, 1951, SFMOMA. The "white paintings" were first exhibited in 1953. https://s3-us-west-1.amazonaws.com/sfmoma -media-dev/www-media/2018/10/27183144/WHIT_98.308_034.pdf, accessed June 14, 2019.

17. Frank O'Hara, *Lunch Poems* (San Francisco: City Lights, 1964). Page references to this edition (*LP*) are hereafter provided in the main text.

18. On the historical avant-gardes: among many helpful analyses of how Paul Goodman's important essay "Advance Guard Art 1900–1950" (1951) influenced O'Hara, see Andrew Epstein, *Beautiful Enemies: Friendship and Postwar American Poetry* (Oxford: Oxford University Press, 2006), 29–32; Michael Magee, *Emancipating Pragmatism: Emerson, Jazz, and Experimental Writing* (Tuscaloosa: University of Alabama Press, 2004), 134–42.

19. Less than halfway through his fifty poems, O'Hara was already worrying about what "fifty" will look like. The poem immediately preceding "Night Thoughts," "Poem (All the mirrors in the world)," wishes to be spared the horrors of aging as young people imagine them: "When I am fifty shall my / face drift into those elongations // of innocence and confront me? / Oh rain, melt me! mirror, kill!" *CP*, 39.

20. In the "Byzantine Place" manuscript, there is no comma after "walk" in the first line of this poem, though one appears there in *CP*. The main text restores the lack of punctuation.

21. T. S. Eliot, "Love Song of J. Alfred Prufrock," in *T. S. Eliot: Collected Poems, 1909–1962* (London: Faber, 2002), 3; "Tradition and the Individual Talent," in *The Sacred Wood: Essays on Poetry and Criticism* (London: Faber, 1997), 39–40.

22. Frank O'Hara, *Early Writing*, ed. Donald Allen (Bolinas, CA: Grey Fox, 1977), 80. Page references to this edition (*EW*) are hereafter provided in the main text.

23. This poem has one of the handful of typos in the original manuscript of "A Byzantine Place": "aspiring" is corrected by hand to "aspirins."

24. Marianna Torgovnick, *The War Complex: World War II in Our Time* (Chicago: University of Chicago Press, 2005). *Oxford English Dictionary*, s.v. "beachhead," accessed May 29, 2019.

25. Frank O'Hara, *Try! Try!*, in *Amorous Nightmares of Delay: Selected Plays* (Baltimore: Johns Hopkins University Press, 1997), 18. There are two versions of *Try! Try!* I refer exclusively to the first, which was included in "A Byzantine Place." For O'Hara's later, compressed reworking of the play, see O'Hara, *Selected Poems of Frank O'Hara*, ed. Mark Ford (New York: Knopf, 2008), 35–54.

26. O'Hara, *Amorous Nightmares of Delay*, 18.

27. O'Hara, *Amorous Nightmares of Delay*, 22. There is no comma after "In this moment of silence" in the Hopwood manuscript.

28. O'Hara, *Amorous Nightmares of Delay*, 22.

29. O'Hara, *Amorous Nightmares of Delay*, 23.

30. O'Hara, *Amorous Nightmares of Delay*, 17.

31. Philip Auslander, *The New York School Poets as Playwrights: O'Hara, Ashbery, Koch, Schuyler, and the Visual Arts* (New York: Peter Lang, 1989), 56–57.

32. Gooch, *City Poet*, 181.
33. Cecil Day Lewis, "Where Are the War Poets?," in *Collected Poems of C. Day Lewis* (London: Jonathan Cape, 1954), 228.
34. Elizabeth Bishop, *North & South* (Boston: Houghton Mifflin, 1946), iv.
35. Karl Shapiro, introduction to *V-Letter and Other Poems* (Cornwall, NY: Cornwall, 1944), vi.
36. Marina MacKay, *Modernism and World War II* (Cambridge: Cambridge University Press, 2007), 5.
37. Kenneth Fearing, "U.S. Writers in War," *Poetry: A Magazine of Verse* 56, no. 6 (September 1940): 320.
38. Fearing, "U.S. Writers in War," 322.
39. David Daiches, "Poetry in the First World War," *Poetry: A Magazine of Verse* 56, no. 6 (September 1940): 327. Wilfred Owen, "Dulce et Decorum Est," in *The Collected Poems of Wilfred Owen*, ed. Cecil Day Lewis (New York: New Directions, 1964), 55.
40. For a sensitive recovery of the work of three British bomber-poets, see Daniel Swift, *Bomber County: The Poetry of a Lost Pilot's War* (New York: Farrar, Straus and Giroux, 2010), chapter 7.
41. W. H. Auden, "Beauty Is Everlasting," in *The Complete Works of W. H. Auden, Prose*, vol 2: 1938–1949, ed. Edward Mendelson (Princeton: Princeton University Press, 2002), 235. Lorrie Goldensohn addresses the British and American dimensions of this habit of looking back over the shoulder of the Second World War to the Great War's poetry. See Lorrie Goldensohn, *Dismantling Glory: Twentieth-Century Soldier Poetry* (New York: Columbia University Press, 2006), chapter 3.
42. Susan Schweik, *A Gulf So Deeply Cut: American Women Poets and the Second World War* (Madison: University of Wisconsin Press, 1992); Philip Metres, *Behind the Lines: War Resistance Poetry on the American Homefront Since 1941* (Iowa City: University of Iowa Press, 2007). Rachel Galvin's study of noncombatant poets of the Spanish Civil War and Second World War probes the authority historically afforded to "flesh witnessing." Rachel Galvin, *News of War: Civilian Poetry 1936-45* (New York: Oxford University Press, 2017), 13–16 and passim.
43. Roy Scranton, "The Trauma Hero: From Wilfred Owen to *Redeployment* and *American Sniper*," *Los Angeles Review of Books*, January 25, 2015, https://lareview ofbooks.org/article/trauma-hero-wilfred-owen-redeployment-american-sniper/.
44. For anthropological, ethnographic, and historical studies of how silence variously enables and follows on violence as it has defined experience for particular groups and communities, see Nancy Scheper-Hughes, *Death Without Weeping: The Violence of Everyday Life in Brazil* (Berkeley: University of California Press, 1992); Allen Feldman, *Formations of Violence: The Narrative of the Body and Political Terror in Northern Ireland* (Chicago: University of Chicago Press, 1991); Carolyn Nordstrom, *Global Outlaws: Crime, Money, and Power in the Contemporary World* (Berkeley: University of California Press, 2007) and *Shadows of War: Violence, Power, and International Profiteering in the Twenty-First Century* (Berkeley: University of California Press, 2004); Gyanendra Pandey, *Routine Violence: Nations, Fragments, Histories* (Stanford, CA: Stanford University Press, 2006).
45. As "A Midcentury 'Spring'" already addresses, with respect to Bishop's suspensions, multivalence attends on any literary gap or silence, pause or breath-catch;

the historical rise of literary theory has left us with nothing if not the insight that gaps and elisions within texts are sites of cultural, historical, or ideological meaning.

46. On the history and technology of sonar, see Tony Devereux *Messenger Gods of Battle: Radio, Radar, Sonar: The Story of Electronics in War* (London: Brassey's, 1991); Willem Dirk Hackmann, *Seek and Strike: Sonar, Anti-Submarine Warfare, and the Royal Navy, 1914–54* (London: Her Majesty's Stationery Office, 1984).

47. Quoted in Gooch, *City Poet*, 66.

48. Gooch, *City Poet*, 181.

49. Quoted in Gooch, *City Poet*, 86.

50. On the reticence said to define the Greatest Generation: "It is a generation that, by and large, made no demands of homage from those who followed and prospered . . . because of its sacrifices. It is a generation of towering achievement and modest demeanor." Tom Brokaw, *The Greatest Generation* (New York: Random House, 1998), 11.

51. In his definitive history of gay men's and women's service in World War II, Allan Bérubé addresses how silence about homosexuality in the military ramified from the level of individual experience (in that silence helped men "to deny—even to themselves—that they had had sex with a man") up to the level of the total bureaucratic system. Bérubé concludes that Selective Service and other elements of mobilization for the war paradoxically "helped to loosen the constraints that [had] locked so many gay people in silence, isolation, and self-contempt." Allan Bérubé, *Coming Out Under Fire: The History of Gay Men and Women in World War II* (New York: Free Press, 1990), 40–41, 256.

52. *Oxford English Dictionary*, s.v. "stovepipe," accessed August 23, 2018.

53. Perloff, *Frank O'Hara*, xi.

54. Donald Allen, preface to *The New American Poetry, 1945–1960*, ed. Donald Allen (Berkeley: University of California Press, 1999), xii.

55. Alan Golding, "*The New American Poetry* Revisited, Again," *Contemporary Literature* 39, no. 2 (Summer 1998): 180. Elsewhere, Golding cites Allen's as the "definitive post-World War II model" of the "aesthetically revisionist anthology," as distinct from the "identity-based" revisionist anthology. Alan Golding, *From Outlaw to Classic: Canons in American Poetry* (Madison: University of Wisconsin Press, 1995), 30.

56. Allen, preface to *The New American Poetry*, xi.

57. Williams, *Keywords*, 96–97.

58. Gooch, *City Poet*, 160.

59. Ciardi, foreword to *Mid-Century American Poets* (New York: Twayne, 1950), xiii.

60. James E. B. Breslin, *From Modern to Contemporary: American Poetry, 1945–1965* (Chicago: University of Chicago Press, 1983), 24.

61. Ciardi, foreword, xxvi.

62. Ciardi, foreword, xxvi.

63. For a roughly contemporaneous example, see John Berryman, "Waiting for the End, Boys," *Partisan Review* 15, no. 2 (February 1948): 254–67.

64. See Suzanne Ferguson, ed., *Jarrell, Bishop, Lowell, and Co.: Middle Generation Poets in Context* (Knoxville: University of Tennessee Press, 2003); Eric Haralson,

ed., *Reading the Middle Generation Anew: Culture, Community, and Form in Twentieth-Century American Poetry* (Iowa City: University of Iowa Press, 2006).

65. Elliott gave the poets "the formal title that Ciardi had refused to produce: 'the middle generation.'" Edward Brunner, *Cold War Poetry: The Social Text in the Fifties Poem* (Urbana: University of Illinois Press, 2001), 57.

66. Golding, "*The New American Poetry* Revisited, Again," 197.

67. Allen, preface to *The New American Poetry*, xi.

68. Frank O'Hara, biographical note, in Allen, *The New American Poetry*, 442. Per their biographical notes, during the war Helen Adam "worked summers in the land army," Brother Antoninus "served as a conscientious objector," and Denise Levertov "received partial training and lots of experience as a (civilian) nurse." Allen, *The New American Poetry*, 427, 440.

69. George F. Butterick and Robert J. Bertholf tie the formal energy of the poem to O'Hara's collaboration with Michael Goldberg on the art book *Odes* (New York: Tiber, 1960), https://www.poetryfoundation.org/poets/frank-ohara.

70. Allen Ginsberg, *Howl and Other Poems* (San Francisco: City Lights, 1956), 16.

71. Some friends did apply the silent veteran narrative to O'Hara, though not necessarily in accordance with the traumatic or stoic paradigms. Jo LeSueur recalled, "Frank never in the nine and a half years I lived with him talked about what he did in the war. . . . Not surprisingly, this response to the past was carried over into his writing. But in *Try! Try!* we have something of an exception. Offhand, I can think of only two other works of his that touch on World War II: *Lament and Chastisement* . . . and his 'Ode to Michael Goldberg('s Birth and Other Births),' which evokes his childhood as well." Joe LeSueur, introduction to O'Hara, *Amorous Nightmares of Delay*, xvi–xvii.

AFTERWORD

1. Raymond Williams, *Keywords: A Vocabulary of Culture and Society* (Oxford: Oxford University Press, 2015), xxxv. The language in the main text of "elements" and suspension point back to Williams's first formulation of structures of feeling. Raymond Williams and Michael Orrom, *Preface to Film* (London: Film Drama Limited, 1954), 21–22.

2. Williams's introduction to *Keywords* helps on this point, too, in so far as he pluralizes and thereby defamiliarizes the war from which he returned to Cambridge. "In 1945, after the ending of the wars with Germany and Japan," he begins. *Keywords*, xxiii.

3. Michael North writes that "if the reasons for the persistence of modernism"—visible especially in the urgency of efforts to conceptualize the present—"are neither aesthetic nor historical, then it may be that they are structural in nature. Modernism persists in the present because it still dictates the way in which we can discuss the present, because it owns the terms by which we mark off as distinct the time we happen to live in." Michael North, "The Afterlife of Modernism," *New Literary History* 50, no. 1 (Winter 2019): 93.

4. Marina MacKay, *Ian Watt: The Novel and the Wartime Critic* (Oxford: Oxford University Press, 2019), 3.

SELECT BIBLIOGRAPHY

Chapter endnotes provide complete citation for every work quoted or drawn from in *Midcentury Suspension*. This select bibliography lists key sources of various kinds, but does not duplicate all citations.

Abravanel, Genevieve. *Americanizing Britain: The Rise of Modernism in the Age of the Entertainment Empire*. Oxford: Oxford University Press, 2012.

Agamben, Giorgio. *The End of the Poem: Studies in Poetics*. Translated by Daniel Heller-Roazen. Stanford, CA: Stanford University Press, 1999.

Ahad, Badia Sahar. *Freud Upside Down: African American Literature and Psychoanalytic Culture*. Urbana: University of Illinois Press, 2010.

Allen, Danielle S. *Talking to Strangers: Anxieties of Citizenship Since Brown v. Board of Education*. Chicago: University of Chicago Press, 2004.

Allen, Donald, ed. *The New American Poetry, 1945–1960*. Berkeley: University of California Press, 1999.

Alpers, Paul. *What Is Pastoral?* Chicago: University of Chicago Press, 1996.

Anderson, Amanda. *Bleak Liberalism*. Chicago: University of Chicago Press, 2016.

Anderson, Linda. *Elizabeth Bishop: Lines of Connection*. Edinburgh: Edinburgh University Press, 2013.

"Anxiety: Modern Man's Chief Enemy." Saint Louis, MO: Dios Chemical, 1952.

Arendt, Hannah. *The Origins of Totalitarianism*. New ed. New York: Harvest, 1973.

Auden, W. H. *The Age of Anxiety: A Baroque Eclogue*. Edited by Alan Jacobs. Princeton: Princeton University Press, 2011.

——. *Collected Poems*. Edited by Edward Mendelson. New York: Modern Library, 2007.

——. *"In Solitude, for Company": W. H. Auden After 1940*. Edited by Katherine Bucknell and Nicholas Jenkins. Oxford: Clarendon, 1995.

——. *Prose*, vol 2: 1939–1948. *The Complete Works of W. H. Auden*. Edited by Edward Mendelson. Princeton: Princeton University Press, 2002.

——. *Selected Poems*. Edited by Edward Mendelson. New York: Vintage, 2007.

Axelrod, Steven Gould. "Bishop, History, and Politics." In *The Cambridge Companion to Elizabeth Bishop*, edited by Angus Cleghorn and Jonathan Ellis, 35–48. Cambridge: Cambridge University Press, 2014.

——. "Elizabeth Bishop and Containment Policy." *American Literature* 75, no. 4 (2003): 843–67.

Badiou, Alain. *The Century*. Translated by Alberto Toscano. Cambridge: Polity, 2007.

Barnhisel, Greg. *Cold War Modernists: Art, Literature, and American Cultural Diplomacy*. New York: Columbia University Press, 2015.

Barrett, William. "The Resistance." *Partisan Review* 13, no. 4 (October 1946): 479–88.

Barzun, Jacques. "The Higher Learning in America." "Art on the American *Horizon*." Special issue, *Horizon*, nos. 93–94 (October 1947): 99–104.

Baskin, Jason M. *Modernism Beyond the Avant-Garde: Embodying Experience*. Cambridge: Cambridge University Press, 2019.

Basowitz, Harold, Harold Persky, Sheldon J. Korchin, and Roy R. Grinker. *Anxiety and Stress: An Interdisciplinary Study of a Life Situation*. New York: McGraw-Hill, 1955.

Beckett, Samuel. *Waiting for Godot: A Tragicomedy in Two Acts*. Translated by Samuel Beckett. New York: Grove, 1982.

Belletto, Steven. "Curbing Containment: Cold War Studies in the Twenty-first Century." *Contemporary Literature* 48, no. 1 (January 2007): 150–64.

Bellow, Saul. "Man Underground." *Commentary*, June 1952: 608–10.

Berman, Jessica. *Modernist Commitments: Ethics, Politics, and Transnational Modernism*. New York: Columbia University Press, 2011.

Bérubé, Allan. *Coming Out Under Fire: The History of Gay Men and Women in World War II*. New York: Free Press, 1990.

Best, Stephen, and Sharon Marcus. "Surface Reading: An Introduction." *Representations* 108, no. 1 (Fall 2009): 1–21.

Biele, Joelle, ed. *Elizabeth Bishop and "The New Yorker": The Complete Correspondence*. New York: Farrar, Straus and Giroux, 2011.

Bishop, Elizabeth. *Complete Poems*. New York: Farrar, Straus and Giroux, 1969.

——. *North & South*. Boston: Houghton Mifflin, 1946.

——. *One Art: Letters*. Edited by Robert Giroux. New York: Farrar, Straus and Giroux, 1994.

——. *Poems: North & South—A Cold Spring*. Boston: Houghton Mifflin, 1955.

——. *Poems, Prose, and Letters*. New York: Literary Classics of the United States, 2008.

Bishop, Elizabeth, and Robert Lowell. *Words in Air: The Complete Correspondence Between Elizabeth Bishop and Robert Lowell*. Edited by Thomas Travisano with Saskia Hamilton. New York: Farrar, Straus and Giroux, 2008.

Blasing, Mutlu Konuk. *Politics and Form in Postmodern Poetry: O'Hara, Bishop, Ashbery, and Merrill*. Cambridge: Cambridge University Press, 1995.

Bloom, Emily C. *The Wireless Past: Anglo-Irish Writers and the BBC, 1931–1968*. Oxford: Oxford University Press, 2016.

Bluemel, Kristin. *Intermodernism: Literary Culture in Mid-Twentieth-Century Britain*. Edinburgh: Edinburgh University Press, 2009.

Bourke, Joanna. *Fear: A Cultural History*. Emeryville, CA: Shoemaker & Hoard, 2006.

Bowen, Elizabeth. *The Demon Lover and Other Stories*. London: Jonathan Cape, 1945.
——. *The Heat of the Day*. New York: Random House, 2002.
——. *Listening In: Broadcasts, Speeches, and Interviews*. Edited by Allan Hepburn. Edinburgh: Edinburgh University Press, 2010.
——. *The Mulberry Tree*. Edited by Hermione Lee. New York: Harcourt, 1986.
——. *Notes on Eire: Espionage Reports to Winston Churchill, 1940–42*. Cork: Aubane Historical Society, 1999.
——. *People, Places, Things: Essays by Elizabeth Bowen*. Edited by Allan Hepburn. Edinburgh: Edinburgh University Press, 2008.
Bradbury, Malcolm. "'Closing Time in the Gardens': Or, What Happened to Writing in the 1940s." In *No, Not Bloomsbury*, 67–86. New York: Columbia University Press, 1988.
Breslin, James E. B. *From Modern to Contemporary: American Poetry, 1945–65*. Chicago: University of Chicago Press, 1985.
Brooks, Peter. *Reading for the Plot: Design and Intention in Narrative*. New York: Knopf, 1984.
Brunner, Edward. *Cold War Poetry: The Social Text in the Fifties Poem*. Urbana: University of Illinois Press, 2001.
Buell, Lawrence. *The Dream of the Great American Novel*. Cambridge, MA: Harvard University Press, 2014.
Burke, Edmund. *A Philosophical Enquiry into the Origin of Our Ideas of the Sublime and the Beautiful*. Edited by Paul Guyer. Oxford: Oxford University Press, 2015.
Burt, Stephen. *Randall Jarrell and His Age*. New York: Columbia University Press, 2002.
Campbell, Anne. "Memorial Day." *Boston Daily Globe*, May 30, 1950.
Cassirer, Ernst. *The Philosophy of the Enlightenment*. Translated by Fritz C. A. Koelln and James P. Pettegrove. Princeton: Princeton University Press, 2009.
Castillo, Greg. *Cold War on the Home Front: The Soft Power of Midcentury Design*. Minneapolis: University of Minnesota Press, 2010.
Churchill, Winston Spencer. "The Twentieth-Century—Its Promise and Its Realization." In *The Social Implications of Scientific Progress*, edited by John Ely Buchard, 34–76. New York: Wiley, 1950.
Ciardi, John, ed. *Mid-Century American Poets*. New York: Twayne, 1950.
Cifelli, Edward M. *John Ciardi: A Biography*. Fayetteville: University of Arkansas Press, 1997.
Clements, James. *Mysticism and the Mid-Century Novel*. New York: Palgrave Macmillan, 2012.
Coleridge, Samuel Taylor. *Biographia Literaria*. Edited by Adam Roberts. Edinburgh: Edinburgh University Press, 2014.
Committee on Nomenclature, American Psychiatric Association. *Diagnostic and Statistical Manual [of] Mental Disorders*. Washington, DC: APA Mental Hospital Service, 1952.
Conner, Marc C., and Lucas E. Morel, eds. *The New Territory: Ralph Ellison and the Twenty-First Century*. Jackson: University of Mississippi Press, 2016.
Connolly, Cyril. "Introduction to "Art on the American *Horizon*." Special issue, *Horizon*, nos. 93–94 (October 1947): 1–11.
Converse, Jean M. *Survey Research in the United States: Roots and Emergence*. New Brunswick, NJ: Transaction, 2010.

Cooney, Terry A. *The Rise of the New York Intellectuals: "Partisan Review" and Its Circle*. Madison: University of Wisconsin Press, 1986.

Corcoran, Neil. *Elizabeth Bowen: The Enforced Return*. Oxford: Oxford University Press, 2004.

Cordle, Daniel. *States of Suspense: The Nuclear Age, Postmodernism, and United States Fiction and Prose*. Manchester: Manchester University Press, 2008.

Costello, Bonnie. *Elizabeth Bishop: Questions of Mastery*. Cambridge, MA: Harvard University Press, 1991.

——. "Elizabeth Bishop's Impersonal Personal." *American Literary History* 15, no. 2 (Summer 2003): 334–66.

Cotkin, George. *Existential America*. Baltimore: Johns Hopkins University Press, 2003.

Crary, Jonathan. *Suspensions of Perception: Attention, Spectacle, and Modern Culture*. Cambridge, MA: MIT Press, 1999.

Culler, Jonathan. *Theory of the Lyric*. Cambridge, MA: Harvard University Press, 2015.

Cvetkovich, Ann. *Depression: A Public Feeling*. Durham, NC: Duke University Press, 2012.

Davis, Thomas S. *The Extinct Scene: Late Modernism and Everyday Life*. New York: Columbia University Press, 2016.

Day Lewis, Cecil. *The Collected Poems of C. Day Lewis*. London: Jonathan Cape, 1954.

Deer, Patrick. *Culture in Camouflage: War, Empire, and Modern British Literature*. Oxford: Oxford University Press, 2009.

Dewey, John. "The Crisis in Human History." *Commentary: A Jewish Review*, March 1946. https://www.commentarymagazine.com/articles/the-crisis-in-human -history/.

Dimock, Wai Chee. "Weak Theory: Henry James, Colm Tóibín, and W. B. Yeats." *Critical Inquiry* 39, no. 4 (Summer 2013): 732–53.

Du Bois. W. E. B. *Writings: The Suppression of the African Slave Trade, The Souls of Black Folk, Dusk of Dawn, Essays*. New York: Literary Classics of the United States, 1986.

Dudziak, Mary L. *Cold War Civil Rights: Race and the Image of American Democracy*. Princeton: Princeton University Press, 2000.

——. *Wartime: An Idea, Its History, Its Consequences*. Oxford: Oxford University Press, 2012.

Eagleton, Terry. "Criticism and Politics: The Work of Raymond Williams." *New Left Review I*, no. 95 (February 1976): 3–23.

Eliot, T. S. *Four Quartets*. New York: Harcourt, 1943.

Elizabeth Bishop Papers. Archives and Special Collections Library, Vassar College Libraries.

Elizabeth Bowen Collection 1923–1975. Harry Ransom Center, University of Texas at Austin.

Ellis, Steve. *British Writers and the Approach of World War II*. Cambridge: Cambridge University Press, 2014.

Ellison, Ralph. *The Collected Essays of Ralph Ellison*. Edited by John F. Callahan. New York: Modern Library, 2003.

——. *Invisible Man*. New York: Vintage, 1995.

——. "The Invisible Man." "Art on the American *Horizon*." Special issue, *Horizon*, nos. 93–94 (October 1947): 104–18.

——. *The Selected Letters of Ralph Ellison*. Edited by John F. Callahan and Marc C. Conner. New York: Random House, 2019.

Ellmann, Maud. *Elizabeth Bowen: The Shadow Across the Page*. Edinburgh: Edinburgh University Press, 2003.

Erkkila, Betsy. "Elizabeth Bishop, Modernism, and the Left." *American Literary History* 8, no. 2 (Summer 1996): 284–310.

Esty, Jed. *A Shrinking Island: Modernism and National Culture in England*. Princeton: Princeton University Press, 2004.

Fearing, Kenneth. "U.S. Writers in War." *Poetry: A Magazine of Verse* 56, no. 6 (September 1940): 318–23.

Feinsod, Harris. *The Poetry of the Americas: From Good Neighbors to Countercultures*. Oxford: Oxford University Press, 2017.

Felski, Rita. *The Limits of Critique*. Chicago: University of Chicago Press, 2015.

Finkelstein, Louis. "Modern Man's Anxiety: Its Remedy." *Commentary: A Jewish Review*, December 1946. commentarymagazine.com/articles/modern-mans-anxiety -its-remedy.

Finstuen, Andrew S. *Original Sin and Everyday Protestants: The Theology of Reinhold Niebuhr, Billy Graham, and Paul Tillich in an Age of Anxiety*. Durham, NC: University of North Carolina Press, 2009.

Flatley, Jonathan. *Affective Mapping: Melancholia and the Politics of Modernism*. Cambridge, MA: Harvard University Press, 2008.

Foley, Barbara. *Wrestling with the Left: The Making of Ralph Ellison's Invisible Man*. Durham, NC: Duke University Press, 2010.

Foreword. *History Today*, January 1951.

Freud, Sigmund. *A General Introduction to Psychoanalysis*. Translated by G. Stanley Hall. New York. Boni and Liveright, 1920.

——. *Inhibitions, Symptoms, and Anxiety*. Edited by James Strachey. Translated by Alix Strachey. Rev. ed. New York: Norton, 1959.

Friedman, Susan Stanford. *Planetary Modernisms: Provocations on Modernity Across Time*. New York: Columbia University Press, 2015.

Frost, Frances. *Mid-Century*. New York: Creative Age, 1950.

Fuller, John. *W. H. Auden: A Commentary*. Princeton: Princeton University Press, 1998.

Fussell, Paul. *The Great War and Modern Memory*. 25th anniversary ed. Oxford: Oxford University Press, 2013.

Galvin, Rachel. *News of War: Civilian Poetry 1936–1945*. Oxford: Oxford University Press, 2017.

Gandhi, Leela, and Deborah L. Nelson. Editors' introduction to "Around 1948: Interdisciplinary Approaches to Global Transformation." Special issue, *Critical Inquiry* 40, no. 4 (2014): 285–97.

Genter, Robert. *Late Modernism: Art, Culture, and Politics in Cold War America*. Philadelphia: University of Pennsylvania Press, 2010.

Giles, Paul. *Antipodean America: Australasia and the Constitution of U.S. Literature*. Oxford: Oxford University Press, 2013.

Ginsberg, Allen. *Howl and Other Poems*. San Francisco: City Lights, 1956.

Glendinning, Victoria. *Elizabeth Bowen*. New York: Knopf, 1978.

Goldensohn, Lorrie. "Approaching Elizabeth Bishop's Letters to Ruth Foster." *Yale Review* 103, no. 1 (January 2015): 1–19.

Golding, Alan C. *From Outlaw to Classic: Canons in American Poetry*. Madison: University of Wisconsin Press, 1995.

Goldman, Eric F. *The Crucial Decade and After: America, 1945–1960*. New York: Random House, 1960.

Gooch, Brad. *City Poet: The Life and Times of Frank O'Hara*. Reprint ed. New York: Harper Perennial, 2014.

Gottlieb, Susannah Young-Ah. *Regions of Sorrow: Anxiety and Messianism in Hannah Arendt and W. H. Auden*. Stanford, CA: Stanford University Press, 2003.

Graham, Vicki. "Bishop's 'At the Fishhouses.'" *Explicator* 52, no. 2 (Winter 1995): 114–17.

Green, Henry. *Back*. London: Chatto & Windus, 1946.

Greif, Mark. *The Age of the Crisis of Man: Thought and Fiction in America, 1933–1973*. Princeton: Princeton University Press, 2015.

Gumbrecht, Hans Ulrich. *After 1945: Latency as Origin of the Present*. Stanford, CA: Stanford University Press, 2013.

Haffenden, John. *William Empson*, vol. 1, *Among the Mandarins*. Oxford: Oxford University Press, 2008.

Hallberg, Robert van. "Poetry, Politics, and Intellectuals." In *The Cambridge History of American Literature*, vol. 8, *Poetry and Criticism, 1940–1995*, 9–259. Edited by Sacvan Bercovitch. Cambridge: Cambridge University Press, 1996.

Hammer, Langdon. "The New Elizabeth Bishop." *Yale Review* 82, no. 1 (January 1994): 135–49.

——. "Useless Concentration: Life and Work in Elizabeth Bishop's Letters and Poems." *American Literary History* 9, no. 1 (Spring 1997): 162–80.

Haralson, Eric, ed. *Reading the Middle Generation Anew: Culture, Community, and Form in Twentieth-Century American Poetry*. Iowa City: University of Iowa Press, 2006.

Hardwick, Elizabeth. "Elizabeth Bowen's Fiction." *Partisan Review* 16, no. 11 (November 1949): 1114–21.

Hart, Matthew. *Nations of Nothing but Poetry: Modernism, Transnationalism, and Synthetic Vernacular Writing*. Oxford: Oxford University Press, 2010.

Hartley, L. P. *The Go-Between*. New York: New York Review Books Classics, 2002.

Hayot, Eric. *On Literary Worlds*. Oxford: Oxford University Press, 2012.

Hazzard, Shirley. *The Great Fire*. New York: Picador, 2003.

Heidegger, Martin. *Being and Time: A Revised Edition of the Stambaugh Translation*. Translated by Joan Stambaugh. Revised by Dennis J. Schmidt. Albany: State University of New York Press, 2010.

Hepburn, Allan. *A Grain of Faith: Religion in Mid-Century British Literature*. Oxford: Oxford University Press, 2018.

——. *Intrigue: Espionage and Culture*. New Haven: Yale University Press, 2005.

——. "Trials and Errors: The Heat of the Day and Postwar Culpability." In *Intermodernism: Literary Culture in Mid-Twentieth-Century Britain*, 131–49.

Herzberg, David. *Happy Pills in America; From Miltown to Prozac*. Baltimore: Johns Hopkins University Press, 2009.

Hobsbawm, Eric. *The Age of Extremes: A History of the World, 1914–1991*. New York: Vintage, 1994.

Hoch, Paul H., and Joseph Zubin, eds. *Anxiety: The Proceedings of the Thirty-Ninth Annual Meeting of the American Psychopathological Association*. New York: Grune & Stratton, 1950.

Hollister, Susannah L. "Elizabeth Bishop's Geographic Feeling." *Twentieth-Century Literature* 58, no. 3 (Fall 2012): 399–438.

Hook, Sidney. "On Historical Understanding." *Partisan Review* 15, no. 2 (February 1948): 231–39.

Hopkins, Gerard Manley. *Poems and Prose.* Edited by W. H. Gardner. New York: Penguin, 1953.

Hopwood Archive no. 405: Frank O'Hara, "A Byzantine Place: 50 Poems and a Noh Play," 1951. Special Collections Library, University of Michigan.

Horwitz, Allan V. *Anxiety: A Short History.* Baltimore: Johns Hopkins University Press, 2013.

Hullfish, H. Gordon. *Educational Freedom in an Age of Anxiety.* New York: Harper, 1953.

Hungerford, Amy. "On the Period Formerly Known as the Contemporary." *American Literary History* 20, no. 1–2 (Spring-Summer 2008): 410–19.

Hutchinson, George. *Facing the Abyss: American Literature and Culture in the 1940s.* New York: Columbia University Press, 2018.

Isaacs, J. *An Assessment of Twentieth-Century Literature: Six Lectures Delivered in the BBC Third Programme.* London: Secker & Warburg, 1951.

"Is a Possum Neurotic?" *Time* 64, no. 16 (October 18, 1954): 75.

"It Comes Hard." *Time* 51, no. 3 (January 19, 1948): 64.

Jackson, Lawrence. *Ralph Ellison: Emergence of Genius.* Athens: University of Georgia Press, 2007.

Jackson, Virginia, and Yopie Prins, eds. *The Lyric Theory Reader: A Critical Anthology.* Baltimore: Johns Hopkins University Press, 2014.

James, David. *Modernist Futures: Innovation and Inheritance in the Contemporary Novel.* Cambridge: Cambridge University Press, 2012.

James, David, and Urmila Seshagiri. "Metamodernism: Narratives of Continuity and Revolution." *PMLA* 129, no. 1 (2014): 87–100.

Jameson, Fredric. *The Political Unconscious: Narrative as a Socially Symbolic Act.* Ithaca, NY: Cornell University Press, 1981.

——. *A Singular Modernity: Essay on the Ontology of the Present.* London: Verso, 2002.

Jarrell, Randall. "The Poet and His Public." *Partisan Review* 13, no. 4 (September–October 1946): 488–500.

Javadizadeh, Kamran. "The Institutionalization of the Postwar Poet." *Modernism/modernity* 23, no. 1 (2016): 113–39.

Kalliney, Peter. *Commonwealth of Letters: British Literary Culture and the Emergence of Postcolonial Aesthetics.* Oxford: Oxford University Press, 2013.

Kalstone, David. *Becoming a Poet: Elizabeth Bishop with Marianne Moore and Robert Lowell.* Edited by Robert Hemenway. Ann Arbor: University of Michigan Press, 2001.

Kant, Immanuel. *Critique of the Power of Judgment.* Edited by Paul Guyer. Translated by Paul Guyer and Eric Matthews. Rev. ed. Cambridge: Cambridge University Press, 2000.

Keats, John. *Letters of John Keats to His Family and Friends.* Edited by Sidney Colvin. Cambridge: Cambridge University Press, 2011.

Kennan, George. *American Diplomacy, 1900–1950.* Expanded ed. Chicago: University of Chicago Press, 1984.

Kennedy, Seán. "Humanity in Ruins." In *The Cambridge Companion to Samuel Beckett*, edited by Dirk Van Hulle, 184–99. Cambridge: Cambridge University Press, 2015.

Kindley, Evan. "Big Criticism." *Critical Inquiry* 38, no. 1 (August 2011): 71–95.

Knowlson, James. *Damned to Fame: The Life of Samuel Beckett*. London: Bloomsbury, 1996.

Konstantinou, Lee. *Cool Characters: Irony and American Fiction*. Cambridge, MA: Harvard University Press, 2016.

Larkin, Philip. *Collected Poems*. Edited by Anthony Thwaite. New York: Farrar, Straus and Giroux, 2004.

Leavell, Linda. *Holding On Upside Down: The Life and Work of Marianne Moore*. New York: Farrar, Straus and Giroux, 2013.

Lee, Hermione. *Elizabeth Bowen: An Estimation*. London: Vision, 1981.

"Local Women Supporting Mid-Century Register." *Philadelphia Tribune*, November 7, 1950.

Longenbach, James. *Modern Poetry After Modernism*. Oxford: Oxford University Press, 1997.

Lowell, Robert. *Lord Weary's Castle*. Boston: Harcourt Brace, 1946.

——. *New Selected Poems*. Edited by Katie Peterson. New York: Farrar, Straus and Giroux, 2017.

Lowney, John. *History, Memory, and the Literary Left: Modern American Poetry, 1935–68*. Iowa City: University of Iowa Press, 2006.

MacKay, Marina. "'Is Your Journey Really Necessary?': Going Nowhere in Late Modernist London." *PMLA* 124, no. 5 (October 2009): 1600–13.

——. *Ian Watt: The Novel and the Wartime Critic*. Oxford: Oxford University Press, 2018.

——. *Modernism and World War II*. Cambridge: Cambridge University Press, 2007.

——. *Modernism, War, and Violence*. London: Bloomsbury, 2017.

MacMahon, Candace. *Elizabeth Bishop: A Bibliography*. Charlottesville: University of Virginia Press, 1980.

Mao, Douglas, and Rebecca Walkowitz. "The New Modernist Studies." *PMA* 123, no. 3 (May 2008): 737–48.

May, Rollo. *The Meaning of Anxiety*. New York: Ronald, 1950.

——. *The Meaning of Anxiety*. Rev. ed. New York: Norton, 2015.

McCarthy, Mary. "The Hiroshima 'New Yorker.'" *Politics* 3 (November 1946): 367.

McIver, Mia L. "Elizabeth Bishop's Lyric Vision." *Journal of Modern Literature* 34, no. 4 (Summer 2011): 192–96.

McKenzie, Marjorie. "Pursuit of Democracy: Views Journalists Squeezing Last Vestige of Historicity from Passing of Mid-Century." *Courier*, January 14, 1950, sec. 19.

Mellor, Leo. *Reading the Ruins: Modernism, Bombsites and British Culture*. Cambridge: Cambridge University Press, 2011.

Mendelson, Edward. *Early Auden, Later Auden: A Critical Biography*. Princeton: Princeton University Press, 2017.

Merrin, Jeredith. "Elizabeth Bishop: Gaiety, Gayness, and Change." In *Elizabeth Bishop: The Geography of Gender*, edited by Marilyn May Lombardi. Charlottesville: University of Virginia Press, 1993.

Metres, Philip. *Behind the Lines: War Resistance Poetry on the American Homefront Since 1941*. Iowa City: University of Iowa Press, 2007.

"Mid-Century." *Times*, January 1, 1951.

"Mid-Century Issue." *Life*, January 2, 1950.

Miller, Tyrus. *Late Modernism: Politics, Fiction, and the Arts Between the World Wars*. Berkeley: University of California Press, 1999.

Millier, Brett C. *Elizabeth Bishop: Life and the Memory of It*. Berkeley: University of California Press, 1993.

Morin, Emilie. *Beckett's Political Imagination*. Cambridge: Cambridge University Press, 2017.

Mooney, Sinéad. "Unstable Compounds: Bowen's Beckettian Affinities." *MFS: Modern Fiction Studies* 53, no. 2 (Summer 2007): 238–56.

Morel, Lucas E., ed. *Ralph Ellison and the Raft of Hope: A Political Companion to Invisible Man*. Lexington: University Press of Kentucky, 2004.

Murphet, Julian. "France, Europe, and the World: 1945-1989." In *Samuel Beckett in Context*, edited by Anthony Uhlmann, 126–38. Cambridge: Cambridge University Press, 2013.

Nelson, Deborah. *Pursing Privacy in Cold War America*. New York: Columbia University Press, 2002.

Ngai, Sianne. *Ugly Feelings*. Cambridge, MA: Harvard University Press, 2005.

Niebuhr, Reinhold. "The Crisis of the Individual: Will Civilization Survive Technics?" *Commentary: A Jewish Review*, December 1945. https://www.commentarymagazine.com/articles/the-crisis-of-the-individual-will-civilization-survive-technics/.

——. *Faith and History: A Comparison of Christian and Modern Views of History*. New York: Scribner, 1949.

North, Michael. "The Afterlife of Modernism." *New Literary History* 50, no. 1 (Winter 2019): 91–112.

——. *Reading 1922: A Return to the Scene of the Modern*. Oxford: Oxford University Press, 1999.

——. *What Is the Present?* Princeton: Princeton University Press, 2018.

Oates, Wayne E. *Anxiety in Christian Experience*. Philadelphia: Westminster, 1955.

O'Hara, Frank. *Amorous Nightmares of Delay: Selected Plays*. Baltimore: Johns Hopkins University Press, 1997.

——. *The Collected Poems of Frank O'Hara*. Edited by Donald Allen. Berkeley: University of California Press, 1995.

——. *Early Writing*. Bolinas, CA: Grey Fox, 1977.

——. *Lunch Poems*. San Francisco: City Lights, 1964.

——. *Poems Retrieved*. Edited by Donald Allen. San Francisco: Grey Fox, 1996.

Olson, Charles. "Projective Verse 1950." *Poetry New York* 1, no. 3 (October 1950): 13–22.

Ondaatje, Michael. *Warlight*. New York: Knopf, 2018.

Orwell, George. *Why I Write*. New York: Penguin, 2005.

Owen, Wilfred. *The Collected Poems of Wilfred Owen*. Edited by C. Day Day Lewis. New York: New Directions, 1965.

Parrish, Timothy. *Ralph Ellison and the Genius of America*. Amherst: University of Massachusetts Press, 2012.

Peale, Norman Vincent. *The Power of Positive Thinking: 10 Traits for Maximum Results*. New York: Fireside, 2003.

Peale, Norman Vincent, and Smiley Blanton. *The Art of Real Happiness*. New York: Prentice Hall, 1950.

Perloff, Marjorie. *Frank O'Hara: Poet Among Painters*. Chicago: University of Chicago Press, 1997.

———. "'In Love with Hiding': Samuel Beckett's War." *Iowa Review* 35, no. 1 (2005): 76–103.

———. *21st-Century Modernism: The "New" Poetics*. Malden, MA: Blackwell, 2002.

Phillips, Siobhan. *The Poetics of the Everyday: Creative Repetition in Modern American Verse*. New York: Columbia University Press, 2010.

Phillips, William. "Portrait of the Artist as an American." "Art on the American *Horizon*." Special issue, *Horizon*, nos. 93–94 (October 1947): 12–19.

Pickard, Zachariah. "The Morality of Aesthetic Action: Elizabeth Bishop, Randall Jarrell, and the Politics of Poetry." *American Literature* 79, no. 2 (2007): 393–411.

Plain, Gill. *Literature of the 1940s: War, Postwar and "Peace."* Edinburgh: Edinburgh University Press, 2013.

Pong, Beryl. "Space and Time in the Bombed City: Graham Greene's *The Ministry of Fear* and Elizabeth Bowen's *The Heat of the Day*." *Literary London: Interdisciplinary Studies in the Representation of London* 7, no. 1 (2009): n.p.

Pound, Ezra. *The Pisan Cantos*. Edited by Richard Sieburth. New York: New Directions, 2003.

Purcell, Richard. *Race, Ralph Ellison and American Cold War Intellectual Culture*. New York: Palgrave Macmillan, 2013.

Rainey, Lawrence. *Institutions of Modernism: Literary Elites and Public Culture*. New Haven: Yale University Press, 1999.

Rampersad, Arnold. *Ralph Ellison: A Biography*. New York: Knopf, 2007.

Rau, Petra. "The Common Frontier: Fictions of Alterity in Elizabeth Bowen's *The Heat of the Day* and Graham Green's *The Ministry of Fear*." *Literature and History* 14, no. 1 (May 2005): 31–55.

Ravinthiran, Vidyan. *Elizabeth Bishop's Prosaic*. Lewisburg, PA: Bucknell University Press, 2015.

Roman, Camille. *Elizabeth Bishop's World War II–Cold War View*. New York: Palgrave, 2001.

Rosenberg, Harold. "The Herd of Independent Minds: Has the Avant-Garde Its Own Mass Culture?" *Commentary*, September 1948. https://www.commentarymagazine .com/articles/the-herd-of-independent-mindshas-the-avant-garde-its-own-mass -culture/.

Rotella, Guy. *Reading and Writing Nature: The Poetry of Robert Frost, Wallace Stevens, Marianne Moore, and Elizabeth Bishop*. Boston: Northeastern University Press, 1991.

Saint-Amour, Paul K. *Tense Future: Modernism, Total War, Encyclopedic Form*. Oxford: Oxford University Press, 2015.

Samuels, Peggy. *Deep Skin: Elizabeth Bishop and Visual Art*. Ithaca, NY: Cornell University Press, 2010.

Sartre, Jean-Paul. "Literature in Our Time." Translated by Bernard Frechtman. *Partisan Review* 15, no. 6 (June 1948): 634–53.

Schlesinger, Jr., Arthur. *The Vital Center: The Politics of Freedom*. New Brunswick, NJ: Transaction, 1998.

Schwartz, Lloyd, and Sybil P. Estess, eds. *Elizabeth Bishop and Her Art*. Ann Arbor: University of Michigan Press, 1983.

Schweik, Susan. *A Gulf So Deeply Cut: American Women Poets and the Second World War*. Madison: University of Wisconsin Press, 1992.

Scranton, Roy. "The Trauma Hero: From Wilfred Owen to Redeployment and American Sniper." *Los Angeles Review of Books*, January 25, 2015. https://lareviewofbooks .org/article/trauma-hero-wilfred-owen-redeployment-american-sniper/

Sebald, W. G. *On the Natural History of Destruction*. Translated by Anthea Bell. New York: Random House, 2004.

Shapiro, Karl. *V-Letter and Other Poems*. Cornwall, NY: Cornwall, 1944.

Shaw, Lytle. *Frank O'Hara: The Poetics of Coterie*. Iowa City: Iowa University Press, 2006.

Shelden, Michael. *Friends of Promise: Cyril Connolly and the World of Horizon*. New York: Harper & Row, 1989.

"Slate Mid-Century Conference of Peace in Chicago on May 29." *New York Amsterdam News*, May 27, 1950.

Smith, Virginia A. "Television at Mid-Century." *Los Angeles Times*, April 23, 1950.

Søren Kierkegaard. *The Concept of Anxiety*. Edited by Reidar Thomte and with Albert B. Anderson. Translated by Reidar Thomte. Princeton: Princeton University Press, 1980.

Spender, Stephen, ed. *W. H. Auden: A Tribute*. New York: Macmillan, 1975.

Stern, James. *The Hidden Damage*. New York: Harcourt, 1947.

Stevens, Wallace. *Collected Poems of Wallace Stevens*. New York: Vintage, 1990.

——. *Transport to Summer*. New York: Knopf, 1947.

Stewart, Susan. "Lyric Possession." *Critical Inquiry* 22, no. 1 (Autumn 1995): 34–63.

Stonebridge, Lyndsey. *The Writing of Anxiety: Imagining Wartime in Mid-Century British Culture*. New York: Palgrave Macmillan, 2007.

Swift, Daniel. *Bomber County: The Poetry of a Lost Pilot's War*. New York: Farrar, Straus and Giroux, 2010.

Teekell, Anna. *Emergency Writing: Irish Literature, Neutrality, and the Second World War*. Evanston, IL: Northwestern University Pres, 2018.

"The Sitwells: Life Reports Visit to U.S. by Celebrated Literary Team of Edith and Brother Osbert." *Life*, December 6, 1948, 164–72.

"Third Avenue Eclogue." *Times Literary Supplement*, October 23, 1948.

Tillich, Paul. *The Courage to Be*. New Haven: Yale University Press, 1952.

Tone, Andrea. *The Age of Anxiety: America's History of America's Turbulent Affair with Tranquillizers*. New York: Basic Books, 2008.

Torgovnick, Marianna. *The War Complex: World War II in Our Time*. Chicago: University of Chicago Press, 2005.

Travisano, Thomas. *Elizabeth Bishop: Her Artistic Development*. Charlottesville: University of Virginia Press, 1988.

——. *Midcentury Quartet: Bishop, Lowell, Jarrell, Berryman and the Making of a Postmodern Aesthetic*. Charlottesville: University of Virginia Press, 1999.

Uhlmann, Anthony, ed. *Samuel Beckett in Context*. Cambridge: Cambridge University Press, 2013.

United Press. "Time Experts in a Battle on Just What Time It Is." *New York Times*, December 29, 1949.

United States Strategic Bombing Survey. *The Effects of Strategic Bombing on German Morale*. 2 vols. Washington, DC: US Government Printing Office, 1947.

——. *Summary Report for the European War.* Maxwell Air Force Base, AL: Air University Press, 1987.

Van Hulle, Dirk, ed. *New Cambridge Companion to Samuel Beckett.* Cambridge: Cambridge University Press, 2015.

Walkowitz, Rebecca. *Cosmopolitan Style: Modernism Beyond the Nation.* New York: Columbia University Press, 2007.

Warren, Kenneth W. *So Black and Blue: Ralph Ellison and the Occasion of Criticism.* Chicago: University of Chicago Press, 2003.

Warshow, Robert. "Melancholy to the End." *Partisan Review* 14, no. 1 (Winter 1947): 86–88.

Wasley, Aidan. *The Age of Auden: Postwar Poetry and the American Scene.* Princeton: Princeton University Press, 2011.

Watts, Alan. *The Wisdom of Insecurity.* New York: Vintage, 1951.

White, Gillian. *Lyric Shame: The "Lyric" Subject of Contemporary American Poetry.* Cambridge, MA: Harvard University Press, 2014.

——. "Words in Air and 'Space' in Art: Elizabeth Bishop's Midcentury Critique of the United States." In *Elizabeth Bishop in the Twenty-First Century: Reading the New Editions,* edited by Angus Cleghorn, Bethany Hicok, and Thomas Travisano, 255–73. Charlottesville: University of Virginia Press, 2012.

Williams, Raymond. *Keywords: A Vocabulary of Culture and Society.* New ed. Oxford: Oxford University Press, 2015.

——. *The Long Revolution.* London: Chatto & Windus, 1961.

——. *Marxism and Literature.* Oxford: Oxford University Press, 1977.

Williams, Raymond, and Michael Orrom. *Preface to Film.* London: Film Drama Limited, 1954.

Woodward, Guy. *Culture, Northern Ireland, and the Second World War.* Oxford: Oxford University Press, 2015.

"Year of Consecration." *Philadelphia Tribune,* December 31, 1949.

Yu, Timothy. "'The Hand of a Chinese Master': José Garcia Villa and Modernist Orientalism." *MELUS* 29, no. 1 (Spring 2004): 41–59.

INDEX